Holub on Patterns: Learning Design Patterns by Looking at Code

ALLEN HOLUB

Apress®

Holub on Patterns: Learning Design Patterns by Looking at Code

Copyright © 2004 by Allen Holub

Lead Editor: Gary Cornell
Technical Reviewer: Ken Arnold
Editorial Board: Steve Anglin, Dan Appleman, Ewan Buckingham, Gary Cornell, Tony Davis,
    Jason Gilmore, Chris Mills, Steve Rycroft, Dominic Shakeshaft, Jim Sumser
Project Manager: Tracy Brown Collins
Copy Edit Manager: Nicole LeClerc
Copy Editor: Kim Wimpsett
Production Manager: Kari Brooks
Production Editor: Janet Vail
Proofreader: Nancy Sixsmith
Compositor and Artist: Diana Van Winkle, Van Winkle Design Group
Indexer: Ann Rogers
Artist: Diana Van Winkle, Van Winkle Design Group
Interior Designer: Diana Van Winkle, Van Winkle Design Group
Cover Designer: Kurt Krames
Manufacturing Manager: Tom Debolski

Library of Congress Cataloging-in-Publication Data:
Holub, Allen I.
    Holub on patterns : learning design patterns by looking at code /
    Allen Holub.
      p. cm.
    Includes index.
    ISBN 1-59059-388-X (alk. paper)
    1. Software patterns. 2. Object-oriented programming (Computer science) I. Title.
QA76.76.P37H65 2004
005.1—dc22

2004019635

Printed and bound in the United States of America 9 8 7 6 5 4 3 2 1

Distributed to the book trade in the United States by Springer-Verlag New York, Inc. 233 Spring Street, 6th Floor, New York, New York 10013 and outside the United States by Springer-Verlag GmbH & Co. KG, Tiergartenstr. 17, 69112 Heidelberg, Germany.

In the United States: phone 1-800-SPRINGER (1-800-777-4643), fax 201-348-4505, e-mail orders@springer-ny.com, or visit http://www.springer-ny.com. Outside the United States: fax +49 6221 345229, e-mail orders@springer.de, or visit http://www.springer.de.

For information on translations, please contact Apress directly at 2560 Ninth Street, Suite 219, Berkeley, CA 94710. Phone 510-549-5930, fax 510-549-5939, e-mail info@apress.com, or visit http://www.apress.com.

The source code for this book is available to readers at http://www.holub.com/goodies/patterns.

For Deirdre, Philip, and Amanda

Contents

About the Author xi
About the Technical Reviewer xiii
Acknowledgments xv
Preface xvii

■CHAPTER 1   **Preliminaries: OO and Design Patterns 101** 1

Patterns vs. Idioms 1
So What Is a Design Pattern, Anyway? 2
So, What's It All Good For? 5
The Role of Patterns in Design 6
        The Tension Between Patterns and Simplicity 6
Classifying Patterns. 7
        On Design, Generally 9
        Programming FORTRAN in Java 10
        Programming with Your Eyes Open. 12
What Is an Object? 12
        Balderdash! 13
        An Object Is a Bundle of Capabilities 13
        How Do You Do It Wrong? 15
        So How Do You Do It "Right?" 17
Cellular Automata 20
Getters and Setters Are Evil. 24
        Render Thyself 27
        JavaBeans and Struts 28
        Refactoring 29
        Life Without Get/Set. 30
        When Are Accessors and Mutators Okay? 32
        Summing Up the Getter/Setter Issues 34

■CHAPTER 2   **Programming with Interfaces,
and a Few Creational Patterns** 37

Why extends Is Evil 37
Interfaces vs. Classes 38
    Losing Flexibility 39
    Coupling 40
    The Fragile-Base-Class Problem 41
    Multiple Inheritance 47
    Frameworks and the Template-Method and
        Factory-Method Patterns 48
    Summing Up Fragile Base Classes 55
When extends Is Appropriate 56
Getting Rid of extends 58
    Factories and Singletons 59
    Singleton 61
    Threading Issues in Singleton 62
    Double-Checked Locking (Don't Do It) 64
    Killing a Singleton 65
    Abstract Factory 67
    Pattern Stew 70
    Dynamic Creation in a Factory 73
    Command and Strategy 75
Summing Up 80

■CHAPTER 3   **The Game of Life** 81

Get a Life 82
Charting the Structure of Life 83
The Clock Subsystem: Observer 86
    Implementing Observer: The Publisher Class 93
The Clock Subsystem: The Visitor Pattern 104
The Menuing Subsystem: Composite 108
The Menuing Subsystem: Facade and Bridge 116
The MenuSite 117
The Core Classes 139
    The Universe Class 139
    The Cell Interface 145
    The Resident Class 148
    The Neighborhood Class 151

Mediator 161
Composite Revisited 163
    Prototype 166
Composite Redux 168
Flyweight. 172
    Flyweight Pools 176
Memento. 178
Loose Ends 180
Summing Up. 185

■CHAPTER 4   **Implementing Embedded SQL** 187

The Requirements. 187
The Architecture 188
The Data-Storage Layer. 189
    The Table Interface 192
    The Bridge Pattern. 197
    Creating a Table, Abstract Factory. 198
    Creating and Saving a Table: Passive Iterators and Builder 202
    Populating the Table 213
    Examining a Table: The Iterator Pattern 216
    Implementing Transactions (Undo) with the Command Pattern. . . 226
    Modifying a Table: The Strategy Pattern. 231
    Selection and Joins 235
    Miscellany 241
    Variants on the Table: The Decorator Pattern 250
Adding SQL to the Mix 259
    SQL-Engine Structure 260
    Input Tokenization, Flyweight Revisited,
       and Chain of Responsibility 262
    The Scanner: Chain of Responsibility. 269
    The ParseFailure Class 277
The Database Class 279
    Using the Database 280
    The Proxy Pattern. 283
    The Token Set and Other Constants 287
The Interpreter Pattern 295
    Supported SQL 295
    Watching the Interpreter in Action 318
The JDBC Layer 325

The State Pattern and JDBCConnection 332
    Statements 338
    The Adapter Pattern (Result Sets) 339
    Finishing Up the Code 344
    When Bridges Fail 344
Whew! 345

■APPENDIX   **A Design-Pattern Quick Reference** 347

Creational Patterns 349
    Abstract Factory 350
    Builder 352
    Factory Method 354
    Prototype 356
    Singleton 358
Structural Patterns 361
    Adapter 362
    Bridge 364
    Composite 366
    Decorator 368
    Facade 370
    Flyweight 372
    Proxy 374
Behavioral Patterns 377
    Chain of Responsibility 378
    Command 380
    Interpreter 382
    Iterator 384
    Mediator 386
    Memento 388
    Observer (Publish/Subscribe) 390
    State 392
    Strategy 394
    Template Method 396
    Visitor 398

■INDEX 401

About the Author

ALLEN HOLUB has worked in the computer industry since 1979. He now works as a consultant, helping companies not squander money unnecessarily on software. He provides training in OO Design and Java and also provides design-process-mentoring and design-review services, provides technical due diligence, and even writes programs on occasion.

Allen's programming experience covers the gamut from operating systems to compilers and from application programs to web services. He was an early adopter of Java, programming in it since its release in 1995. He worked in C++ for eight years before that and has also worked in C, Perl, Pascal, PL/M, FORTRAN, SQL, and various assembly languages. He learned design the hard way, by beating his head against programs that he'd rather not admit that he'd written, and is now a recognized expert in OO Design, UML, and process. He served as a chief technology officer at NetReliance, Inc., and sits on the board of advisors for Ascenium Corp. and Ontometrics. He is the security-track chair for the Software Development Conference.

Allen wrote for JavaWorld from 1998 to 2004 and is now a contributing editor at *SD Times*. He has authored nine books (including *Holub on Patterns*, *Taming Java Threads*, and *Compiler Design in C*) and 100+ magazine articles (for *Dr. Dobb's Journal*, *Programmers Journal*, *Byte*, *MSJ*, and others). He wrote the popular "OO-Design Process" column for the IBM developerWorks Component Zone, and he was the technical editor of CMP Media's Java Solutions. Allen teaches regularly for the University of California (Berkeley) Extension (OO Design and Java).

Contact Allen at `http://www.holub.com/allen.html`.

Acknowledgments

This book, of course, owes an enormous amount to the Gang of Four: Gamma, Helm, Johnson, and Vlissides. Without them, the book wouldn't exist.

Ken Arnold did a spectacular job of reviewing this book. I've never experienced a tech review as thorough and as thoughtful as Ken's. His detailed comments improved this book immensely, and I'm indebted to him.

A small portion of this book appeared originally in my *Java Toolbox* column on JavaWorld (http://www.javaworld.com).

Preface

This is a book about programming in an object-oriented way and about how to use design patterns to solve commonplace problems in object-oriented systems.

I've based this book on the philosophy that the best way to learn and understand the design patterns is to see them in action, all jumbled up, just as they occur in the real world.

Consequently, this book presents design patterns to you by looking at computer programs. My intent is to both clarify and bring down to earth Gamma, Helm, Johnson, and Vlissides's seminal work *Design Patterns: Elements of Reusable Object-Oriented Software* (Addison-Wesley, 1995). (The four authors are often called the *Gang of Four* [or GoF], and their book is usually called the *Gang-of-Four book*.) The current volume puts the GoF book into context, presenting and teaching design patterns as they occur in the real world. By the time you're done, you'll have seen all of the Gang-of-Four patterns but in the context of real computer programs.

Don't get me wrong—this book does not pretend to supplant the GoF book but rather to complement it. Gamma, Helm, Johnson, and Vlissides made an enormous contribution to the OO-design community with their work, and this book certainly wouldn't exist without it. The GoF approach is abstruse and dense to many programmers, however, thus the need for the current volume.

The current book is atypical—it's "inside out" when compared to other books on design patterns. Rather than catalog the design patterns and present unrealistically simple examples in each section of the catalog, this book describes two computer programs in terms of the design patterns they use. You see how the patterns appear in real programs and how the patterns interact with one another in complex ways.

The splendid isolation of a catalog-of-design-patterns approach (such as the original *Design Patterns*) simply doesn't permit this real-world understanding. The catalog is great if you've already worked on code that demonstrates the pattern. If you don't have prior experience with such code, however, the catalog approach is impenetrable. Also, catalogs can leave you with a good intellectual understanding of the patterns but with almost no understanding of how to actually use the patterns to produce real code.

Prerequisites

I'm assuming that you know Java and have written at least a few programs in it. In particular, I use anonymous inner classes a lot, so you'll have to be solid on that syntax. You also need to be familiar with the "core" Java packages such as *java.io* and the basics of the user-interface subsystems (Swing and AWT). This is all stuff you probably got when you learned the language.

I'm also assuming that you know the basics of object-oriented programming: inheritance, interfaces, polymorphism, and so on. Later in the book I'll talk about things such as the down-side of extends, but to make sense of these discussions, you'll have to know what extends does. I assume that you already know the upside, so I won't bore you with a treatise on what OO-language features such as inheritance are good for. Don't interpret a discussion of the negative side of an idiom or language feature as indicating that there is no positive side to that idiom or feature. I'm just assuming that you don't need to be told something you already know.

Finally, I assume a nodding familiarity with UML, the "Unified" Modeling Language—a graphical design notation useful for showing, among other things, the static (class) structure of a program and how the objects that comprise the program interact at runtime.

Should you need to come up to speed before you continue, I've listed references for all these topics on the web page discussed in the section "Resources and References." You can probably muddle through the UML without much formal understanding of the subject. Without Java, though, you'll be completely lost.

Assumptions

I assume throughout this book that you want to know how to build solid object-oriented solutions, so I don't qualify every statement that I make with that assumption. Often, reasonable procedural alternatives exist to OO strategies, but I don't discuss these alternatives.

What I mean to accomplish by mentioning this obvious, I hope, point is to head off the inevitable critics who will complain that the entire book is invalid simply because it doesn't explicitly discuss every alternative to every problem, including the hard-core procedural alternatives.

Examples of topics that I know will set off the banshees include implementation encapsulation (which implies that the most common use of get/set functions should be assiduously avoided) and the overuse of implementation inheritance (which creates unnecessary coupling relationships).

Warning! Warning! Will Robinson!

Finally, I also want to warn you about me.

If you haven't figured it out by now, I have opinions and intend to express them, and I don't usually qualify my statements with apologies. If you don't like that, buy a different book.

Everyone has opinions, and hiding those opinions under a veneer of impartiality accomplishes nothing but obfuscation. You're welcome to disagree with me, but please disagree because you have a strong argument to support your beliefs. "Nobody does it that way" is not a strong argument. Neither is its converse: "Everybody does it."

I'm sometimes accused of being "dogmatic." If by "dogmatic" you mean that I defend ideas forcefully when I find that those ideas work well in real code (and conversely disparage ideas that fail miserably in practice), then I guess I am dogmatic. I think of my attitude as pragmatic, though, not dogmatic. I'm hard-nosed about following OO principles, because every time I've violated those principles, I've had to rewrite the code. I just don't have time to do things twice.

My practical bias is reflected in the structure of this book, building it around code rather than an academic taxonomy. It may annoy you when, in the interest of making something easy to understand to a programmer, I loosen up the language a bit. This is a book for programmers, though, not for theoreticians. (I find it odd that I'm also sometimes accused of being "academic," as if that's a pejorative. The real academics usually don't like my work because it's not sufficient formal and relies too heavily on code rather than mathematics.)

I also allow myself occasional digressions into relevant design topics rather than staying strictly focused on the patterns. I'm assuming that you need to know why I do things, not just what I'm doing. I'm writing as if we are sitting around a table talking, not as if I'm standing at a podium giving a formal lecture. If you want formality, I refer you to the Gang-of-Four *Design Patterns* book. It's an excellent book that presents this material in a highly structured fashion that will be more to your taste.

Resources and References

Rather than augment this book with a "Resources" section that will be out-of-date before the book hits the streets, I've built a Design-patterns resources web page at `http://www.holub.com/goodies/patterns/`. You'll find links to all the code in this book on that page, and you'll also find things such as reading lists and links to other patterns-related sites on the web.

Further!

So now that you've been warned, it's time to get to work. Design patterns (and thinking in a design-patterns way) are wonderful things. They can help you work more effectively, they can make your code vastly easier to maintain, and they can provide you with a vocabulary that will make communication with other programmers and designers much more effective. This book shows you how design patterns really work and how to use them to write excellent code.

CHAPTER 1

■ ■ ■

Preliminaries: OO and Design Patterns 101

Normally a book of this sort would start with a quote from Christopher Alexander, the architect (of buildings) who came up with the notion of a design pattern. I've found that though Alexander is a brilliant man who writes wonderful books, his prose can be a bit opaque at times, so I'll skip the mandatory quote. His ideas launched the entire design-pattern movement, however.

Similarly, the seminal book on design patterns in software is Gamma, Helm, Johnson, and Vlissides's *Design Patterns: Elements of Reusable Object-Oriented Software* (Addison-Wesley, 1995). (The four authors are jokingly called the *Gang of Four* by most working designers.) My book wouldn't exist if the Gang-of-Four book hadn't been written, and I (and OO programmers in general) owe an enormous debt of gratitude to the authors. Nonetheless, the Gang-of-Four book is a formal academic presentation of patterns, and most beginners find it too dense to penetrate. At the risk of losing some academic precision, I'll take a kinder and gentler approach.

Patterns vs. Idioms

Let's start exploring the notion of a *pattern* by discussing simple programming idioms. Many design patterns are used so commonly that, in many programmers' minds, they cease to be patterns at all but are idioms of the language. That is, you don't think of these patterns as anything special—they're just "how things are done." Some people distinguish between patterns and idioms based on usage (for example, a pattern is represented in a formal way, and an idiom isn't). I don't see a distinction, however. An idiom is just a pattern, the use of which has become commonplace.

Derivation is a great example of the evolution of pattern to idiom. Back in the early 1980s when C was king, derivation was a design pattern. You can find several examples of an "extends" relationship in C. For example, the standard implementation of `malloc()` uses a header (the base class) that's extended to create another struct (the derived class), which effectively inherits the `free()` method from the base class.

Abstract functions were also part of the Derivation pattern. It was commonplace in C to pass around tables of function pointers, initialized differently for different "classes." This is exactly how C++ implements both abstract methods and interface inheritance, but back in the C world, we didn't have a name for it.

Derivation wasn't built into C, and most C programmers weren't programming in an object-oriented way, so Derivation was not a programming idiom—it was a pattern. It was something you saw in many programs that had to solve similar problems, but it wouldn't occur naturally to your average C programmer.

Nowadays, of course, derivation and interfaces are just built into the language; they've become idioms.

So What *Is* a Design Pattern, Anyway?

Design patterns are, first and foremost, discovered, not invented. When Christopher Alexander looked at many successful buildings, concentrating on one aspect of that building (such as what makes a room "pleasant"), certain *patterns started to emerge*. Successful "pleasant" rooms tend to solve certain classes of problems (such as lighting) in similar ways. By the same token, when you look at several programs written by diverse programmers, and when you focus on a particular implementation problem that those programs must solve (isolating subsystems, for example), patterns start to emerge there as well. You find that several programmers independently develop similar techniques to solve similar problems. Once you're sensitive to the technique, you tend to start seeing patterns everywhere you look. It's not a pattern, though, unless you find it in several independently developed programs. It's a sure sign that authors don't know what they're talking about when they say, "We've invented a design pattern that...." They may have come up with a design, but it's not a pattern unless several people invent it independently. (It's possible, of course, for an invented "pattern" to become a real pattern if enough people adopt it.)

A design pattern, then, is a general technique used to solve a class of related problems. It isn't a specific solution to the problem. Probably every architect who came up with an observably pleasant room brought light into that room in a different way, and probably every programmer implemented their solution differently. The pattern is the general structure of the solution—a "metasolution" if you will—not the solution itself.

You can find a good analogy in music. You can think of the notion of "classical music" as a compositional pattern. You can identify music that fits the "classical music" pattern because it sounds like classical music. The individual pieces are quite different, however.

Given the broad nature of a pattern, you can't cut-and-paste a design pattern from one program to another (though you *might* be able to reuse a specific solution if the current context is similar to the original one). This particular issue is an enormous point of confusion amongst people new to patterns. Judging by the comments I've seen on the web, many programmers seem to think that if a book doesn't present the same examples as the Gang-of-Four book, the author doesn't understand patterns. This attitude simply shows that the person who wrote the comment doesn't understand patterns; they've confused the piece of code that demonstrates the pattern with the pattern itself. For that reason, I'll try to give several different examples for each of the patterns I discuss so you can see how the pattern relates to disparate concrete implementations—and I won't use the Gang-of-Four examples unless they're relevant to real programming issues (many aren't).

To make things more complicated, the actual objects and classes that participate in a pattern almost always participate in other patterns at the same time. Focus on it one way, and it looks like one thing; change your focus, and it looks like something else. To make things even more confusing, many pattern implementations share identical static structures. When you look at the UML static-structure diagrams in the Gang-of-Four book, they all look the same: You'll see an interface, a client class, and an implementation class. The difference between patterns lies in the dynamic behavior of the system and in the intent of the programmer, not in the classes and the way they interconnect.

I'll try to illustrate these problems with an example from the architecture of buildings, focusing on two domains: ventilation and lighting.

In the ventilation domain, I don't want a room to feel "stuffy." Looking at several rooms that indeed are comfortable, a pattern, which I'll call *Cross Ventilation*, emerges. The rooms that participate in this pattern have an air source and an air exit directly across from one another at window height. Air enters at the source, flows across the room, and then leaves from the exit. Having identified (and named) the pattern, I create a capsule description—called the *intent* by the Gang of Four—that summarizes the general problem and the solution addressed by the pattern. In the case of Cross Ventilation, my intent is to "eliminate stuffiness and make a room more comfortable by permitting air to move directly across the room horizontally, at midbody height." Any architectural mechanism that satisfies this intent is a legitimate reification (I'll explain that word in a moment) of the pattern. (The Gang of Four's use of the word *intent* in this context is pretty strange. I don't use it much in this book, preferring words such as *purpose*.)

Reification is an obscure word, but I've found it pretty handy. It's not commonly used in the literature, however. Literally, *to reify* means "to make real." A reification of an idea is a concrete realization of that idea, and a given idea may have millions of possible reifications. I use *reify*, rather than some more commonplace word, to emphasize what a pattern isn't. A pattern is not "instantiated," for example. Every instantiation of a class is identical (at least in structure) to every other instantiation. This isn't so with a design pattern. Similarly, a reification is not an "implementation" of a pattern—the reification of a pattern is a design, not code, and a given design has many possible legitimate implementations.

So, what are some of the reifications of Cross Ventilation? You could have a window across from a window, a window across from a door, two doors across from each other, a window across from "negative" ventilator that sucked in air, input and output ventilators on opposite walls, or a huge bellows operated by an orangutan jumping up and down on it across from a gaping hole in the other wall. In fact, you don't even need walls: A room with no walls at all on two opposite sides would fit the pattern. A given pattern has myriad reifications.

Though there's a lot of flexibility in reifying the pattern, you can't pick and choose the attributes you like. For example, simply having air entrances and exits isn't sufficient if the height and directly-across-from requirements aren't met. Putting the entrance and exit in the ceiling, for example, isn't a legitimate reification of the pattern (as any of us who occupy stuffy big-building offices with ceiling ventilators can attest).

To summarize, the intent of Cross Ventilation is to "eliminate stuffiness and make a room more comfortable by permitting air to move directly across the room horizontally, at midbody height." The *participants* in the pattern, be they windows, doors, or orangutans, have the *roles* of air entrance and exit.

Moving to the lighting domain: After looking at many rooms I notice that the most pleasant rooms have windows on two adjacent walls. That's why corner offices are so desirable: The multi-directional natural-light source makes the room seem more pleasant. Dubbing this pattern *Corner Office*, I come up with the following intent: I intend to "make a room more pleasant by locating two sources of natural light on two adjacent walls." Again, there are a myriad reifications: windows on two walls, windows on one wall and French doors on the other, French doors on two walls. You could argue that windows on one wall and mirrors on an adjacent wall would also fit since the reflected natural light does serve as a light source. If I were Bill Gates, I could put a window on one wall and a 600-inch plasma display that showed what you'd see if the wall wasn't there on the other, but that's not a legitimate reification because the plasma display isn't "natural light." You have, of course, millions of ways to implement the Window and French Door patterns as well.

Now let's consider a concrete design—the plans for a building. Figure 1-1 shows reifications of both Cross Ventilation and Corner Office in a single design. I've put both an architectural diagram and the equivalent UML in the figure. Patterns are identified using UML 1.5's *collaboration* symbol. The pattern name is put into an oval, with dashed lines extending to the classes that participate in the patterns. The lines are annotated with the role that that class plays within the pattern.

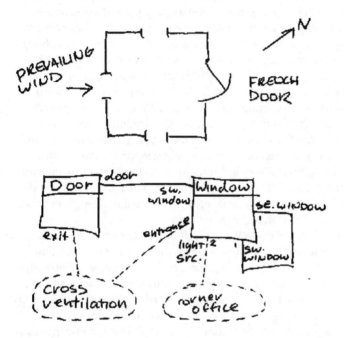

Figure 1-1. *Combined reification of Cross Ventilation and Corner Office*

The southwest window serves as an air entrance in Cross Ventilation, and the door across from it serves as an exit. The other two windows don't participate in Cross Ventilation since the prevailing wind is from the southwest. Refocusing, the southwest and southeast windows participate in Corner Office as the two light sources. Neither the door nor the northwest window is a participant since they aren't significant sources of light. That southwest window is interesting because it participates in two patterns simultaneously. It has the role of "air source" in Cross Ventilation and "light source" in Corner Office. The objects and classes that participate in various patterns often intermesh in this way.

It's critical to note that there's no way to identify the patterns simply from structure. For example, the wind may be blocked by another structure, in which case none of the windows can be an air entrance. By the same token, one of the windows may be two feet away from the blank wall on the building next door or look onto a hallway, so it wouldn't be a significant light source (though it could be an air entrance or exit). As you'll see when you start looking at the actual patterns, you need contextual information—including the intent of the architect—to identify a design pattern in a computer program. You can't just look at a UML diagram and identify all the patterns. You have to know the intended use of the objects or classes. You'll see many examples of this phenomenon in the examples in subsequent chapters.

Reopening the cut-and-paste issue, I'm hoping you can now see how a pattern can be reified into a vast number of designs, each of which could be implemented in myriad ways. To say that you can cut-and-paste a pattern in a design tool is nonsensical. Nonetheless, many object-oriented CASE tools claim to have "pattern libraries," from which you can insert patterns into your designs. In practice, these libraries contain prebuilt UML structure for the single reification of a given pattern that's presented in the Gang-of-Four book. Though pasting one of these structures into your design can be useful at times, don't confuse this "paste" operation with actually using a pattern in a design. A good design almost always must use a custom reification that's appropriate in context. The mindless cut-and-paste approach is no more designing than paint-by-numbers is painting.

So, What's It All Good For?

So, if patterns are so amorphous, what are they good for?

When I first read the Gang-of-Four book, I was unimpressed. It seemed like nothing but a pedagogic presentation of stuff that most competent designers had already discovered, usually by beating their heads against brick walls trying to find elegant solutions to the problems that the patterns addressed. True, had I read the book a few years earlier, my head would have many fewer bumps on it, but the whole thing seemed to be much ado about nothing.

I thought that way until the first time I needed to discuss a project with another designer. He pointed at a piece of the design and said, "These interfaces comprise a bridge between these two subsystems; the bridge itself is implemented with this set of object adapters." I was struck with the economy of what just happened. In two sentences, he had eliminated probably half an hour of elaborate explanation. Maybe there was something to all this pattern stuff after all.

Then I went to a presentation at the first Java One, where all of AWT was described in terms of patterns. The description was both short and lucid—much shorter and clearer, in fact, than could possibly have been the case had the speaker not taken a patterns approach.

I went back and reread the book before starting my next design project and then consciously tried to think of my next design in terms of the patterns. That is, I started asking myself, "What am I trying to accomplish here, and are there any patterns that address this problem?" (using the purpose section of the pattern description to see what was relevant). When the answer was "yes," I used the pattern right off the bat. I found that taking this approach noticeably shortened the design time and that the resulting design was better quality as well. The better I knew the patterns, the faster things went. Moreover, my initial design needed much less refinement than usual to be acceptable.

I was hooked.

The patterns provide an organizational framework that vastly improves communication, which in the long run is what design is all about. Conversations that previously took hours could happen in a few minutes, and everyone could get more real work done in less time. I went back and read everything about patterns that I could lay my hands on and discovered that the Gang-of-Four book just scratched the surface. Hundreds of documented patterns were out there on the web and in the literature, and many of these were applicable to work I was doing. In practice, I've found that a solid familiarity with the patterns that are relevant to my work have made that work go much faster and given me much better results. (By "solid," I mean that you know the stuff cold—you don't have to look things up in a book.)

The Role of Patterns in Design

When do patterns come up in the design process, and what role do they play in design? The answer to this question varies with the methodology you're using—I hope that you *do* use a methodology—but design patterns are of interest primarily at the implementation level, so they start coming up when you start thinking about implementation. The deeper question then is, when does analysis (which concerns itself with the problem domain) stop and design (which concerns itself with implementation) begin?

The best analogy that I know is in the design and construction of buildings. The plans of a building don't show every construction detail. They show where the walls go, but not how to build a wall. They show where the plumbing fixtures go, but not how to route pipes. When the building is constructed, design activities involving wall construction and pipe routing *do* happen, but the artifacts are rarely kept since the implementation speaks for itself. A carpenter, for example, may use a "stud-placement" pattern to build a strong wall. The design shows where the wall goes, but not how to build the wall.

Moving the analogy to software: In most projects, design activities should stop when you get the point that a *good* programmer can implement without difficulty. I would never consider putting the mechanics of creating a window with Swing into a design. That's just something that the programmer should know how to do, and if the code is written up to professional standards (well-chosen names, good formatting, comments where necessary, and so on), the implementation choices should be self-documenting.

Consequently, design patterns are often not spelled out in detail in the design documents but, rather, represent decisions that the implementer makes. Patterns applied by an implementer are rarely documented in depth, though the name of the participants (or other comment) should identify what's going on. (For example, WidgetFactory reifies Factory).

Of course, exceptions exist to this don't-design-patterns rule. The software equivalent of the windows used in the Corner Office pattern may well appear in the design documents (which show you where to place the windows). Similarly, very complex systems, where much more detail is required in the design (in the same way that the architectural plans for a skyscraper are more detailed than those of a small house), often document the patterns in depth.

The Tension Between Patterns and Simplicity

A related issue is the complexity that patterns tend to introduce into a system. If "foolish consistency is the hobgoblin of little minds," unnecessary complexity is the hobgoblin of bad programmers. Just like Emerson's "little statesmen and philosophers and divines" who adore consistency, many "little" programmers and architects think that patterns are good for their own sake and should be used at every possible opportunity. That mindless approach almost guarantees a fragile, unmaintainable mess of a program. Every pattern has a downside that serves as an argument for not using it.

Simple systems are easier to build, easier to maintain, smaller, and faster than complex ones. A simple system "maximizes the work done," by increasing "the amount of work not done." A program must do exactly what's required by the user. Adding unasked-for functionality dramatically increases development time and decreases stability.

Simplicity is often not an easy goal to achieve. Programmers love complexity, so they have a strong tendency to overcomplicate their work. It's often easier to quickly build an overly complex system than it is to spend the time required to make the system simple. Programmers who suspect that requirements will be added (or change) over time tend to add support for requirements that *may* exist in the future. It's a bad idea to complicate the code because you think that something *may* have to change in the future, however. (Whenever I try to predict the future, I'm wrong.) Programmers need to write the code in such a way that it's easy to add new features or modify existing ones, but not add the features now.

The flip side of this problem is oversimplification of an inherently complex problem. You really want to do "exactly" what's needed; removing required functionality is as bad as adding unnecessary functionality. One example of oversimplification is an "undo" feature. Alan Cooper—the inventor of Visual Basic and well-known UI guru—argues that you never want to ask users if they *really* want to do something. Of course they do—why else would they have asked to do it in the first place? How many times have you *not* deleted a file because that stupid confirmation dialog pops up? The best solution to the unwanted deletion or similar problem is to do what the user asks but then provide a way to undo it if the user makes a mistake. That's what your editor does, for example. (Imagine an editor that asked, "Do you *really* want to delete that character?") Undo is hard to implement, however, and a tendency exists to disguise laziness in the garb of simplicity. "A complete undo system adds too much complexity, so let's just throw up a confirmation dialog."

These three requirements—simplicity, completeness, and ease of modification—are sometimes at odds with one another. The patterns described in this book help considerably when it comes time to change or add something, but by the same token, the patterns complicate the code. Unfortunately, no hard-and-fast rule describes when using a pattern is a good idea—it's a seat-of-the-pants judgment call on the part of the programmer. A sensitive seat comes from experience that many designer/programmers simply don't have (and, as Ken Arnold—coauthor of the original book on Java programming—points out, from a sense of aesthetics that many don't cultivate.) Thus, you end up with bad programs that use design patterns heavily. Simply using pattern doesn't guarantee success.

On the other hand, the building blocks of patterns, such as the heavy use of interfaces, are always worth incorporating into the code, even when a full-blown pattern is inappropriate. Interfaces don't add much complexity, and down-the-line refactoring is a lot easier if the interfaces are already in place. The cost of doing it now is low, and the potential payoff is high.

Classifying Patterns

It's sometimes useful to classify patterns in order to make it easier to choose appropriate ones. Table 1-1, taken from the Gang-of-Four book, shows you one way to look at the Gang-of-Four patterns. But you can also create similar tables of your own that categorize the patterns in different ways, however.

The Gang of Four broke the patterns into two scopes: Class patterns require implementation inheritance (extends) to be reified. Object patterns should be implemented using nothing but interface inheritance (implements). It's not an accident that there are many more Object than Class patterns. (You'll find more on this issue in the next chapter.)

Within a scope, the patterns are further divided into three categories. The Creational patterns all concern themselves with object creation. For example, Abstract Factory provides you with a means of bringing objects into existence without knowing the object's actual class name. (I'm simplifying here, but I'll explain this notion in depth later in the book.) The Structural patterns are all static-model patterns, concerned with the structural organization of your program. For example, Bridge describes a way to separate two subsystems from each other so that either subsystem can be modified without affecting the other. The Behavioral patterns are all dynamic-model patterns, addressing the way that various objects will interact at runtime. Chain of Responsibility, for example, describes an interobject message-passing system that allows a message to be fielded by the particular object that knows how to deal with it. You don't have to know which object that will be at compile time—it's a runtime decision.

Table 1-1. *The Gang-of-Four Design Patterns Classified*

Purpose				
		Creational	**Structural**	**Behavioral**
S c o p e	**Class**	Factory Method	Class Adapter	Interpreter Template Method
	O b j e c t	Abstract Factory Builder Prototype Singleton	Bridge Composite Decorator Facade Flyweight Object Adapter Proxy	Chain of Responsibility Command Iterator Mediator Memento Observer State Strategy Visitor

I'll cover all these patterns in depth (though not in order), but bear in mind that there are many other pattern categories than the ones identified by the Gang of Four. Examples include real-time programming patterns, threading patterns, Java Enterprise JavaBean (EJB) patterns, and so forth.

One other issue is the interdependence between patterns. For example, as you'll see later in the book, Command appears in one form or another in most of the other Behavioral patterns. The Gang-of-Four book includes a diagram showing these dependency relationships, but frankly, the diagram looks like a mess of spaghetti and is of little practical use. The main thing to remember is that the various patterns are indeed related to each other, sometimes in significant and intricate ways.

If you have trouble distinguishing one pattern from another, you aren't alone. Most often the confusion is caused precisely because of the natural interdependence of patterns. My advice is to focus on the intent/purpose section of the pattern description—remember, any reification that satisfies the designer's intent is legitimate. Looking solely at the structure—natural for a programmer—often adds confusion instead of clarity. You'll find, for example, that the patterns in the Structural category have almost identical static structures, but these structures are used toward profoundly different ends. The patterns are as much about communication as about software, so don't focus solely on the software issues.

On Design, Generally

The other main preliminary topic I have to discuss before leaping into the patterns themselves is OO design generally.

First, Object-Oriented Design (OOD) and Object-Oriented Programming (OOP) are very different things. The design process starts at requirements gathering, involves an orderly progression through tasks such as use-case analysis, and arrives, eventually, at a design from which you code. The programming process starts with the design or some portion of the design, and using concepts such as derivation, encapsulation, and design patterns results in a computer program—a realization of the design. Many people confuse programming with design. Simply because you've used Java for six years, understand subclassing, and can write 1,000 lines of debugged code a day doesn't mean that you know OOD. In fact, the contrary is more likely: many spectacularly good programmers don't understand the basic principles of OOD.

A good analog is in the building trades. Buildings are *designed* by architects, and they're *built* by contractors. In the same way, OO systems are designed by OO designers and implemented by OO programmers. These two roles can be filled the same people, but often aren't. Architects have to know how to construct a building, or they couldn't come up with a workable design. Contractors, on the other hand, don't have to have much understanding at all of what architects do. (This isn't to say that there aren't architects who will happily design buildings that can't be built or lived in or that there aren't contractors who can easily identify a bad design when they see it.) The best programmers are also good architects, and the best architects are good programmers. This melding of skills is particularly important in the now-fashionable Agile methodologies, where design and coding go on in parallel. No Agile methodology supports the notion of a puppet-master architect who pulls all the strings while the programmers dance.

That being said, many programmers are experienced craftsmen and craftswomen who produce beautiful code but don't understand the design process at all—they're builders, not designers. Please don't think that I'm in any way degenerating the considerable skills of a good builder, but the ad-hoc designs that these programmers come up with are often less than ideal.

A recent Standish Group report, which looked at thousands of programming projects over multiple years, determined that roughly 72 percent of software projects were failures. The lack of up-front design, and everything that entails (requirements gathering, for example), was pegged the primary cause of this failure. That is, even skilled architects can fail when they abandon the architectural process.

This book is about OO programming and architecture, not about process. Design patterns are typically implementation details that are applied by OO programmers when they translate the initial design to code. You can't arrive at a reasonable design, however, without using a reasonable process. (The Agile processes are certainly reasonable.) You can't arrive at reasonable code without the benefit of a reasonable design (which may evolve). Simply applying design patterns to your code in an ad-hoc way will not make your programs significantly better and may make them worse. Unnecessary complexity—and many patterns are complex—never improves anything.

So, please don't confuse the topics discussed elsewhere in this book with the OOD process as a whole. Patterns are just a small part of the puzzle—and in some ways an insignificant part. This isn't a book about OOD—it's a book about moving an OO design toward a concrete implementation. To really apply design patterns effectively, you need to know how to design. You need to know the process. I've listed several books on the subject of design on the web page mentioned in the preface, and I recommend you peruse them.

Programming FORTRAN in Java

Given that this book takes a hard-line attitude toward OO programming, it seems worthwhile to discuss the differences between OO and procedural approaches at the system (as compared to structural) level. Procedural approaches to programming can be characterized as "data-centric." A procedural program is structured around the flow of data between subroutines that manipulate or examine that data. The database is central to the design of the program; in fact, many procedural programs do little beyond exposing database tables via a nice user interface. Procedural systems tend to be heavily hierarchical, centered on the notion of "global control." A global entity (a subroutine toward the top of a hierarchy) performs work on data that it collects from elsewhere—either from subroutines beneath it in the hierarchy or by harvesting global data created earlier. The main disadvantage of procedural systems is in debugging and maintenance. The shared data creates "coupling" relationships (undesirable dependencies) between subroutines. When you change one subroutine, you affect others. In extreme cases, the effects of a seemingly trivial change could take months to become clear and to fix.

Object-oriented systems, on the other hand, are networks of intercooperating agents that communicate by means of some messaging system. The objects are peers—there's no one object that's clearly in charge, issuing directives to the other objects. I'll discuss the characteristics of a well-done object throughout the remainder of this chapter, but a few broad principles are worth introducing now. Looking at an object from the outside, you should have no idea how it's implemented. It should be possible to replace the entire implementation without affecting any of the client objects (objects that use the one you've just changed). Though objects sometimes pass other objects to each other, data doesn't flow through the system in a procedural sense. An object jealously guards its data and performs operations on that data in response to receiving some message. Objects don't give the data to other objects unless absolutely necessary, and then, the data is itself encapsulated in another object. These two concepts (*implementation hiding* and *data abstraction*) are key.

One good way to tell the difference between an object-oriented and procedural system is to note what happens when you change something. In procedural systems, changes tend to "ripple out" into the rest of the program; large changes in behavior typically require wide-spread modification of the code. Object-oriented systems tend to concentrate changes into one place. A single change in the code tends to make large changes in program behavior. For example, if you need to change a data format used for persistent storage, procedural systems often must be changed in several places because each procedure is responsible for parsing the data. In an OO system, you'd change the object that's stored persistently, and that's it.

Of course, OO principles such as data abstraction (hiding the way that a bunch of functions work by hiding the data structures from the users of those functions) have been around for a long time and are the foundation of any quality programming—procedural or otherwise. The C language file-I/O system and Ken Arnold's Curses library are both object oriented, for example. A procedural system can look object oriented in places. A "pure" OO system is characterized primarily by the consistent and meticulous use of concepts such as data abstraction.

OO systems have other key differences from procedural ones. For example, object-oriented systems tend to be models of real-world processes. This train of thought gets you into the entire OOD process, however, and this book is primarily about OO structure, so I won't follow this avenue further.

Unfortunately, many people who grew up in a procedural world think of an OO approach to a problem as wrong, not different. I'm always flabbergasted by the controversy that my articles on OO technique seem to engender. When I published (in the online magazine JavaWorld) early drafts of the sections of this book, I was shocked by the invective that was hurled at me for discussing far-from-earth-shattering concepts—concepts that have been tossed around in the literature for 30 years. I was called "incompetent," "clueless," "a shyster," " a dunderhead," and various other epithets that aren't polite to print. My articles are "badly thought out" and "tosh." One reader actually threatened physical violence, titling an invective-filled epistle (which the site removed) with "THIE [sic] AUTHOR SHOULD BE SMACKED AROUND WITH A PIPE!"

Don't confuse "familiar" with "correct." Many programmers assume that the libraries they use regularly are "right," and if that library does things in a certain way, then that library sets a standard. This disease is particularly prevalent with people who learn programming from how-to books focused on particular tasks. If the only architecture they've ever seen is EJB and Struts, they'll tend to classify everything that doesn't look like EJB and Struts as bad. Just because we've done things historically in a particular way doesn't mean that that's the best way to do things; otherwise, we'd all still be programming in assembly language.

I had an interesting discussion many years ago with the person who led Microsoft's C++ and Foundation Class (MFC) efforts. When I brought up that MFC wasn't particularly object oriented, his response was that he was well aware of that fact, but most of the people who programmed Microsoft systems didn't understand OO concepts. It wasn't Microsoft's job to teach OO, he said. Consequently, Microsoft deliberately created a procedural system in C++, because that system would be "easier to understand." That OO-is-hard-to-understand philosophy is still dominant at Microsoft. The .NET APIs are procedural in structure, for example, and C# has language features that encourage procedural thinking. So, it's not surprising to find Microsoft applications that don't follow some of the basic principles of OO systems. Many Microsoft programmers seem to take violent exception to any OO practice that doesn't jibe with the way .NET does things, however. They're confusing "familiarity" with "correct."

Please don't try to apply procedural thinking to OO systems, and don't criticize an OO technique that I'm describing simply because the approach isn't procedural. Many common OO notions simply aren't embodied in a lot of existing code that you may have seen. Saying that some coding practice isn't viable in an OO system isn't the same as saying that code that uses those practices is never viable. I'm not going to bring this point up every time I discuss an OO approach to a problem, however.

Finally, bear in mind that a "pure" OO solution isn't always required. As is the case with most design issues, there are always trade-offs and risks. For example, a simple web site that's using Servlets to put a thin front end on a database probably doesn't need to be object oriented. The risk is that, as the small program evolves, it turns into a mass of unmaintainable spaghetti code. Similarly, many programmers don't understand OO concepts, so if your system doesn't have a significant long-term maintainability requirement and if business requirements are not likely to change, assigning a programmer to it who quickly implements a procedural solution isn't necessarily a bad decision. The risk, of course, is that the lifetime of that program is longer than you expect, or that significant changes to the business rules indeed occur, and it ends up being less expensive to just toss the original code than it is to try to modify it. Nothing is inherently wrong with choosing a procedural solution; but you should make that choice knowing the risks you're taking.

Programming with Your Eyes Open

So, let's talk about my general philosophy of design.

Design is a series of informed choices, trade-offs, and risk management. If you don't understand both sides of an issue, you can't make an intelligent choice or manage risk effectively; in fact, if you don't understand all the ramifications of what you're doing, you're not designing at all. You're just stumbling in the dark. It's not an accident that every chapter in the Gang-of-Four book includes a "Consequences" section that describes when using a pattern is inappropriate and why.

Moreover, "good" and "bad" aren't absolutes. A "good" decision in one context may be "bad" in another. Every choice has a good and a bad side and is made in the context of overall criteria that are defined by necessity. Decisions aren't binary. You often have shades of goodness—consequences associated with your decisions—that can mean that none of the possibilities you're contemplating is "best." Moreover, a decision that seems good right now may not seem so good six months from now.

Saying that some language feature or common programming idiom has problems isn't the same thing as saying that you should never use that feature or idiom under any circumstances. By the same token, simply because a feature or idiom is in common use doesn't mean you should use it. Lots of programs are written by uninformed programmers, and simply being hired by Sun, Microsoft, or IBM doesn't magically improve someone's programming or design abilities. You'll find a lot of great code in the Java packages. You'll also find a lot of code that, I'm sure, the author is embarrassed to admit to writing.

To further muddy the waters, some design idioms are pushed for marketing or political reasons. Sometimes a programmer makes a bad decision, but the company wants to push what the technology can *do*, so it deemphasizes the way in which you have to do it. It's making the best of a bad situation. In this context, adopting any programming practice simply because "that's the way you're supposed to do things" is acting irresponsibly. Many failed EJB projects give proof to this principle. EJB can be a good technology when used appropriately; it can literally bring down a company when used inappropriately.

The point I'm trying to make is that you shouldn't be programming blindly. By understanding the havoc that a feature or idiom can wreak, you're in a much better position to decide whether using that feature or idiom is appropriate. Your choices should be both informed and pragmatic, made from a position of strength. That's why I'm bothering to write this book, so that you can approach your programming with your eyes open.

What Is an Object?

What does object orientation actually mean?

The patterns discussed in this book are creatures of OO systems. If a system as a whole isn't really object oriented, you don't get much benefit from using an OO pattern in some corner of the code. I've found that many programmers, even programmers who have been working with languages such as C++ or Java for years, don't have a good grasp of what exactly constitutes an OO system, however, so I have to make sure we're all clear on this point.

Balderdash!

Bjarne Stroustrup, the creator of C++, once characterized OO programming as "buzzword-oriented programming," and certainly one of the most abused (or at least misunderstood) buzzwords in the pack is *object* itself. Since the idea of an object is so central, a full discussion of what exactly an object actually is is essential to understanding OO systems and their needs.

First of all, think of an OO system as a bunch of intelligent animals inside your machine (the objects) talking to each other by sending *messages* to one another. Think "object." Classes are irrelevant—they're just a convenience provided for the compiler. The animals that comprise this system can be classified together if they have similar characteristics (if they can handle the same messages as other objects in the class, for example), but what you have at runtime is a bunch of objects, not classes. What programmers call *classes* are really classes of objects. That is, objects that have the same properties comprise a class of objects. This usage is just English, not techno-speak, and is really the correct way to think about things. We're doing object-oriented design, not class-based design.

The most important facet of OO design is *data abstraction*. This is the CIA, need-to-know school of program design. All information is hidden. A given object doesn't have any idea of what the innards of other objects look like, any more than you may know what your spouse's gallbladder looks like. (In the case of both the object and the gallbladder, you really don't want to know either.)

You may have read in a book somewhere that an object is a data structure of some sort combined with a set of functions, called *methods*, that manipulate that data structure. Balderdash! Poppycock!

An Object Is a Bundle of Capabilities

First and foremost, an object is defined by what it can *do*, not by how it does it. In practical terms, this means an object is defined by the messages it can receive and send. The "methods" that handle these messages comprise its sole interface to the outer world. The emphasis must be on what an object can do—what capabilities it has—not on how those capabilities are implemented. The "data" is irrelevant. Most OO designers will spend considerable time in design before they even think about the data component of an object. Of course, most objects will require some data in order to implement their capabilities, but the makeup of that data is—or at least should be—irrelevant.

The *prime directive* of OO systems is as follows:

> *Never ask an object for information that you need to do something; rather, ask the object that has the information to do the work for you.*

Ken Arnold says, "Ask for help, not for information."

I'll explain the whys and wherefores in a moment, but this prime directive engenders a few rules of thumb that you can apply to see if you're really looking at an object-oriented system (I've presented them in a rather pithy way; details follow):

- Objects are defined by "contract." They don't violate their contract.

- All data is private. Period. (This rule applies to all implementation details, not just the data.)

- It must be possible to make any change to the way an object is implemented, no matter how significant that change, by modifying the single class that defines that object.

- "Get" and "set" functions are evil when used blindly (when they're just elaborate ways to make the data public). I've a lot more to say on this issue later in the "Getters and Setters Are Evil" section.

If the system doesn't follow these rules, it's not object oriented. It's that simple. That's not to say non-OO systems are bad—many perfectly good procedural systems exist in the world. Nonetheless, not exposing data is a fundamental principle of OO, and if you violate your principles, then you're nothing. The same goes for OO systems. If they violate OO principles, they're not OO by definition; they're some sort of weird hybrid that you may or may not ever get to work right. When this hybrid system goes down in flames and takes the company with it, don't blame OO. Note, however, that an OO system can be written in a procedural language (and vice versa). It's the principles that matter, not the language you're using.

Don't be fooled, by the way, by marketing hype such as "object based" and "there are lots of ways to define an object." Translate this sort of sales-speak as follows: "Our product isn't really OO—we know that, but you probably don't, and your manager (who's making the purchase decision) almost certainly doesn't, so we'll throw up a smoke screen and hope nobody notices." In the case of Microsoft, it has just redefined OO to mean something that fits with its product line. Historically, VB isn't in the least bit OO, and even now that VB has transmogrified into an OO language, most VB programs aren't object oriented because the Microsoft libraries aren't object oriented. (How many Microsoft programmers does it take to screw in a light bulb? None—let's define darkness as the new industry standard.)

Now for the "whereas" and "heretofores."

First, the notion of a *contract*: An object's contract defines the way in which the object appears to behave from the outside. The users of the objects assume that this behavior won't change over time. The interfaces that an object implements are part of the contract (so you can't lightly change method arguments or return values, for example), but other aspects of the contract can include performance guarantees, size limitations, and so forth. The object's implementation isn't part of the contract. You should be able to change it at will.

The rules in the earlier list are really just ways of enforcing the notion of a contract. Exposed implementation details would effectively make those details part of the object's contract, so the implementation couldn't change (as you discovered bugs or introduced new business requirements).

Similarly, the nuanced interpretation of the everything-is-private rule is this: If it's not private, then it's part of the contract and can't be changed. The decision to make a field public may well be correct in some (rare) situations, but the consequences of making that decision are significant.

The notion of a contract also comes into play with the third rule I mentioned earlier. Ideally, the scope of a change is limited to a single class, but interdependencies are sometimes necessary. For example, the HashMap class expects contained objects to implement hashCode(). This expectation is part of the contained object's contract.

How Do You Do It Wrong?

The main reason for following the rules in the previous section is that the code becomes easier to maintain, because all the changes that typically need to be done to fix a problem or add a feature tend to be concentrated in one place. By the way, don't confuse ease of maintenance with lack of complexity. OO systems are usually more complex than procedural systems but are easier to maintain. The idea is to organize the inevitable complexity inherent in real computer programs, not to eliminate it—a goal that an OO designer considers impossible to meet.

Consider a system that needs to get a name from some user. You may be tempted to use a TextField from which you extract a String, but that just won't work in a robust application. What if the system needs to run in China? (Unicode—Java's character set—comes nowhere near representing all the ideographs that comprise written Chinese.) What if someone wants to enter a name using a pen (or speech recognition) rather than a keyboard? What if the database you're using to store the name can't store Unicode? What if you need to change the program a year from now so that both a name and employee ID are required every place that a name is entered or displayed? In a procedural system, the solutions you may come up with as answers to these questions usually highlight the enormous maintenance problems inherent in these systems. There's just no easy way to solve even the simplest-seeming problem, and a vast effort is often required to make simple changes.

An OO solution tries to encapsulate those things that are likely to change so that a change to one part of the program won't impact the rest of the program at all. For example, one OO solution to the problems I just discussed requires a Name class whose objects know how to both display themselves and to initialize themselves. You'd display the name by saying, "Display your- self over there," passing in a Graphics object or perhaps a Container to which the name could drop in a JPanel that displayed the name. You would create a UI for a name by asking an empty Name object to "initialize yourself using this piece of this window." The Name object may choose to create a TextField for this purpose, but that's its business. You, as a programmer, simply don't care *how* the name goes about initializing itself, as long as it gets initialized. (The implementa- tion may not create a UI at all—it may get the initial value by getting the required information from a database or from across a network.)

Getting back to my Visual Basic critique from a few paragraphs back, consider the way that a UI generated by VB (or VB-like systems, of which there are legions) is typically struc- tured: You create a Frame class whose job is to collect messages coming in from "control" or "widget" objects in response to user actions. The Frame then sends messages into the object system in response to the user action. Typically, the code takes the following form:

1. "Pull" some value out of a widget using a "get" method.

2. "Push" that value into a "Business" object using a "set" method.

This architecture is known as Model/View/Controller (MVC)—the widgets comprise the "view," the Frame is the "controller," and the underlying system is the "model."

MVC is okay for implementing little things such as buttons, but it fails miserably as an application-level architecture because MVC requires the controller to know way too much about how the model-level objects are implemented. Too much data is flowing around in the system for the system to be maintainable.

Rather than take my word for it, let's explore a few of the maintenance problems that arise when you try to develop a significant program using the MVC architecture I just described. Taking the simple problem I mentioned earlier of needing to add an employee ID to every screen that displays an employee, in their VB-style architecture you'll have to modify every one of these screens by hand, modifying or adding widgets to accommodate the new ID field. You'll also have to add facilities to the Employee class to be able to set the ID, and you'll also have to examine *every* class that uses an Employee to make sure that the ID hasn't broken anything. (For example, comparing two Employee objects for equality must now use the ID, so you'll have to modify all this code. If you had encapsulated the identity into a Name class, none of this work would be necessary. The Name objects would simply display themselves in the new way. Two Name objects would now compare themselves using the ID information, but your code that called `fred.compareTo(ginger)` or `fred.equals(ginger)` wouldn't have to change at all.

You can't even automate the update-the-code process, because all that WYSIWYG functionality touted in the advertisements hides the code-generation process. In any event, if you automatically modify machine-generated code, your modifications will be blown away the next time somebody uses the visual tool. Even if you don't use the tool again, modifying machine-generated code is always risky since most of the VB-style tools are picky about what this code looks like, and if you do something unexpected in your modifications, the tool is likely to become so confused that it'll refuse to do anything at all the next time you *do* need to use it. Moreover, this machine-generated code is often miserable stuff, created with little thought given to efficiency, compactness, readability, and other important issues.

The real abomination in MVC architecture is the "data-bound grid control," a table-like widget that effectively encapsulates the SQL needed to fill its cells from a database. What happens when the underlying data dictionary changes? All this embedded SQL breaks. You'll have to search out every screen in the system that has a data-bound control and change that screen using a visual tool. Going to a "three-tier" system, where the UI layer talks to a layer that encapsulates the SQL, which in turn talks to the database, does nothing but make the problem worse since the code you have to modify has been distributed into more places. In any event, if the middle tier is made of machine-generated code (usually the case), then it's very existence is of little use from a maintenance point of view.

All this modifying-every-screen-by-hand business is way too much work for me. Any time savings you may have made in using some tool to produce the initial code is more than lost as soon as the code hits maintenance.

The appeal of these systems often lies in familiarity. They help you program in an unfamiliar OO language using a familiar procedural mind-set. This sort of I-can-program-FORTRAN-in-any-language mindset precludes your leveraging the real maintenance benefits of OO systems, however. I personally think there's absolutely no reason to use Java unless you're indeed implementing an OO design. Java is simple only when compared against C++. You're better off just using some procedural that really is simple if you want to write procedural systems. (I don't agree with many Java proponents who claim that the side benefits of Java such as type safety, dynamic loading, and so forth, justify writing procedural Java.)

On the other hand, if you *are* doing an OO design, a language designed to implement OO systems (such as Java) can make the implementation dramatically easier. Many C programmers try to program in Java as if they were programming in C, however, implementing procedural systems in Java rather than OO systems. This practice is really encouraged by the language, which unfortunately mimics much of C and C++'s syntax, including flaws such as the messed-up precedence of the bitwise operators. Java mitigates the situation a bit because it's more of a "pure" OO language than C++. It's harder, though not impossible, to abuse. A determined individual can write garbage code in any language.

So How Do You Do It "Right?"

Because the OO way of looking at things is both essential and unfamiliar, let's look at a more involved example of both the wrong (and right) way to put together a system from the perspective of an OO designer. I'll use an ATM machine for this example (as do many books), not because any of us will be implementing ATMs but because an ATM is a good analog for both OO and client/server architectures. Look at the central bank computer as a server object and an ATM as a client object.

Most procedural database programmers would see the server as a repository of data and the client as a requester of the data. Such a programmer may approach the problem of an ATM transaction as follows:

1. The user walks up to a machine, inserts the card, and punches in a PIN.

2. The ATM then formulates a query of the form "give me the PIN associated with this card," sends the query to the database, and then verifies that the returned value matches the one provided by the user. The ATM sends the PIN to the server as a string—as part of the SQL query—but the returned number is stored in a 16-bit int to make the comparison easier.

3. The user then requests a withdrawal.

4. The ATM formulates another query; this time it's "give me the account balance." It stores the returned balance, scaled appropriately, in a 32-bit int.

5. If the balance is large enough, the machine dispenses the cash and then posts an "update the balance for this user" to the server.

(By the way, this isn't how real ATM machines work.)

So what's wrong with this picture? Let's start with the returned balance. What happens when Bill Gates walks into the bank wanting to open a non-interest-bearing checking account and put all his money in it? You *really* don't want to send him away, but last time you looked he was worth something like 100 gigabucks. Unfortunately, the 32-bit int you're using for the account balance can represent at most 20 megabucks (4 gigabucks divided by 2 for the sign bit divided by 100 for the cents). Similarly, the 16-bit int used for the PIN can hold at most 4 decimal digits. And what if Bill wants to use "GATES" (five digits) for his PIN? The final issue is that the ATM formulates the SQL queries. If the underlying data dictionary changes (if the name of a field changes, for example), the SQL queries won't work anymore. (Though this example is obviously nonsensical, consider the before-the-euro lira and the pain of transitioning to the euro.)

The procedural solution to all these problems is to change the ROMs in every ATM in the world (since there's no telling which one Bill will use) to use 64-bit doubles instead of 32-bit ints to hold account balances and to 32-bit longs to hold 5-digit PINs. That's an enormous maintenance problem, of course.

Stepping into the real world for a moment, the cost of software deployment is one of the largest line items on an IT department's budget. The client/sever equivalent of "swapping all the ROMs"—deploying new versions of the client-side applications—is a *big* deal. You can find similar maintenance problems inside most procedural programs, even those that don't use databases. Change definitions of a few central data types or global variables (the program's equivalent of the data dictionary), and virtually every subroutine in the program may have to be rewritten. It's exactly this sort of maintenance nightmare that OO solves.

To see how an OO point of view can solve these problems, let's recast the earlier ATM example in an object-oriented way, by looking at the system as a set of cooperating objects that have certain capabilities. The first step in any OO design is to formulate a "problem statement" that presents the problem we're trying to solve entirely in what's called the "problem domain." In the current situation, the problem domain is Banking. A problem statement describes a *problem*, not a computer program. I could describe the current problem as follows:

> *A customer walks into a bank, gets a withdrawal slip from the teller, and fills it out. The customer then returns to the teller, identifies himself, and hands him or her the withdrawal slip. (The teller verifies that the customer is who he says he is by consulting the bank records). The teller then obtains an authorization from a bank officer and dispenses the money to the customer.*

Armed with this simple problem statement, you can identify a few potential "key abstractions" (classes) and their associated operations, as shown in Table 1-2. I'll use Ward Cunningham's CRC-Card format (discussed in more depth shortly).

Table 1-2. *Use-Case Participants Listed in CRC-Card Format*

Class	Responsibility	Collaborates With
Bank Records	Creates withdrawal slips. Verifies that the customers are who they say they are.	Teller: Requests empty deposit slip.
Bank Officer	Authorizes withdrawals.	Teller: Requests authorization
Withdrawal Slip	Records the amount of money requested by the teller.	Bank Records: Creates it. Bank Officer: Authorizes the withdrawal. Teller: Presents it to customer.
Teller	Gets deposit slips from the Bank Records and routes the deposit slip to the Bank Officer for authorization.	Bank Records: Creates deposit slips. Bank Officer: Authorizes transactions.

The server, in this model, is really the Bank-Officer object, whose main role is to authorize transactions. The Bank, which is properly a server-side object as well, creates empty deposit slips when asked. The client side is represented by the Teller object, whose main role is to get a deposit slip from the Bank and pass it on. Interestingly, the customer (Bill) is external to the system so doesn't show up in the model. (Banks certainly have customers, but the customer isn't an attribute of the bank any more than the janitorial service is part of the bank. The customer's accounts could be attributes, certainly, but not the actual customers. You, for example, don't define yourself as a piece of your bank.) An OO ATM system just models the earlier problem statement. Here's the message flow:

1. Bill walks up to an ATM, presents his card and PIN, and requests a withdrawal.

2. The `Teller` object asks the server-side `BankRecords` object, "Is the person with this card and this PIN legitimate?"

3. The `BankRecords` object comes back with "yes" or "no."

4. The `Teller` object asks the `BankRecords` object for an empty `WithdrawalSlip`. This object will be an instance of some class that implements the `WithdrawalSlip` interface and will be passed from the `BankRecords` object to the `Teller` object *by value*, using RMI. That's important. All that the `Teller` knows about the object is the interface it implements—the implementation (the .class file) comes across the wire along with the object itself, so the `Teller` has no way of determining how the object will actually process the messages sent to it. This abstraction is a *good* thing because it lets you change the way that the `WithdrawalSlip` object works without having to change the `Teller` definition.

5. The `Teller` object tells the `WithdrawalSlip` object to display a user interface. (The object complies by rendering a UI on the ATM screen using AWT.)

6. Bill fills in the withdrawal slip.

7. The `Teller` object notices that the initialize-yourself operation is complete (perhaps by monitoring the OK key) and passes the filled-out `WithdrawalSlip` object to the server-side `BankOfficer` object (again by value, using RMI) as an argument to the message, "Am I authorized to dispense this much money?"

8. The server-side `BankOfficer` object comes back with "yes" or "no."

9. If the answer is "yes," the ATM dispenses the money. (For the sake of simplicity, I won't go into how that happens.)

Of course, this isn't the only (or even the ideal) way to do things, but the example gets the idea across—bear with me.

The main thing to notice in this second protocol is that all knowledge of how a balance or PIN is stored, how the server decides whether it's okay to dispense money, and so forth, is hidden inside the various objects. This is possible because the server is now an object that implements the "authorization" capability. Rather than requesting the data that you need to authorize a transaction, the `Teller` asks the (server-side) `BankOfficer` object (which has the data) to do the work for it. No data (account balance or PIN) is shipped to the ATM, so there's no need to change the ATM when the server code changes.

Also note that the `Teller` object isn't even aware of how the money is specified. That is, the requested withdrawal amount is encapsulated entirely within the `WithdrawalSlip` object. Consequently, a server-side change in the way that money is represented is entirely transparent to the client-side `Teller`. The bank's maintenance manager is happily sleeping it off in the back office instead of running around changing ROMs.

If only ATMs had been written this way in Europe, translation to the euro would have been a simple matter of changing the definition of the `WithdrawalSlip` (or `Money`) class on the server side. Subsequent requests for a `WithdrawalSlip` from an ATM would get a euro-enabled version in reply.

Cellular Automata

Let's expand our notions of OO to include things such as interfaces with another example that will pave the way for understanding the Game of Life program used later in the book.

A good case study of a natural OO system is a class of programs called *cellular automata*. These programs solve complex problems in a very object-oriented way: A large problem is solved by a collection of small, identical objects, each of which implements a simple set of rules, and each talks only to its immediate neighbors. The individual cells don't actually know anything about the larger problem, but they communicate with one another in such a way that the larger problem seems to solve itself.

The classic example of a cellular automaton, a solution for which is way beyond the scope of this book, is traffic modeling. The problem of predicting traffic flow is extremely difficult; it's a classic chaos-theory problem. Nonetheless, you can model traffic flow in such a way that watching the simulation in action can help you make predictions based on the model's behavior. Predicting traffic flow and simulating it are different problems, and cellular automata are great at simulating chaotic processes.

I'll spend a few pages discussing the traffic-flow problem, not only because it demonstrates automata, but also because the example illustrates several basic principles of OO design that I want you to understand before you can look at an OO system such as Game of Life.

Most programs work by implementing an algorithm—a single (though often complex) formula that has well-defined behavior when presented with a known set of inputs. Any solution that attempts to model traffic flow in an entire city using a single (complex) algorithm is just too complicated to implement. As is the case with most chaos problems, you don't even know how to write an algorithm to "solve" the traffic-flow problem.

Cellular automata deal with this problem by avoiding it. They don't use algorithms per se, but rather they model the behavior of a tractable part of the system. For example, rather than modeling traffic flow for an entire city, a cellular automaton breaks up the entire street grid into small chunks of roadway and models only this small chunk. The road chunks can talk to adjoining road chunks, but the chunks don't know anything about the entire street grid.

You can model the behavior of a small chunk of Roadway pretty easily. The chunk has a certain capacity based on number of lanes, and so on. There's a maximum speed based on the percentage of capacity and speed limits, and there's a length. That's it. Cars arrive at one end of the road and are pushed out the other end sometime later. We'll need two additional objects to round out the system: a Car, and a Map, both of which also have easy-to-model behavior. (I'll talk about these other objects in a moment.)

The various objects in this system must communicate across well-defined interfaces. (Figure 1-2 shows the entire conversation I'm about to discuss.)

The Road interface has two methods.

1. Can you take *N* cars?

    ```
    boolean canYouAcceptCars(int n, Road fromThisRoad )
    ```

2. Give me *N* cars.

    ```
    Car[] giveMeCars(int n)
    ```

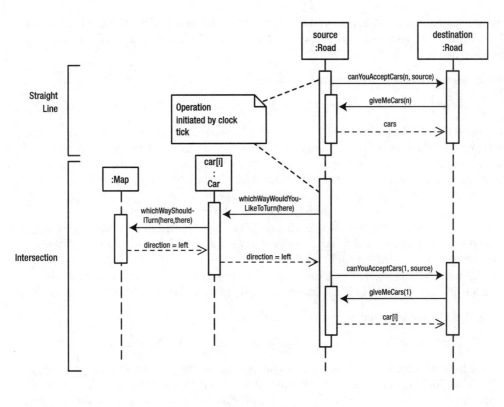

Figure 1-2. *UML sequence diagram for the traffic model*

Road segments communicate using a simple handshake. The current segment decides that it has to get rid of a couple of cars, so it asks an adjacent segment if it can take them (Message 1). The adjacent segment accepts the cars by asking for them (Message 2).

You'll see this two-part handshake again in Chapter 3. The initial request has to carry with it a Road reference that the receiving Road can use to request the cars; otherwise the receiving segment doesn't know which source segment is making the request. A segment in the middle of the block talks to two neighbors (the two adjacent Road segments), an intersection has four neighbors, and so forth. (These connections are set up when the street grid is created and would be implemented as constructor arguments.)

The Road segment has a few rules that it uses internally to decide when to evict cars. For example, the average effective speed of a Car (the difference in time between when the Car enters the Road and when it leaves) may be a function of traffic density—the number of Cars on the segment. Different road types (highway, alley, and so on) may implement these rules differently. These rules are known only by the Road, however. As is the case in any OO system, these sort of rules can be changed radically without impacting the surrounding code, because the interface to a Road segment doesn't change.

The next object you need is a Car. The Road is primarily a caretaker of Cars. Since the speed limit and Road-segment length are attributes of the Road, the Road can easily determine how long to hold onto a particular car without having to interact with the Car at all.

The only difficulty is an intersection. The Road needs to know to which neighbor to route the Car. Solve this problem with a second simple interface. (The Car implements this one, and the Road uses it.)

1. You are *here*; which way would you like to turn?

```
Direction whichWayWouldYouLikeToTurn(Location here)
```

Again, the Road couldn't care less how the Car answers the question, as long as it gets an answer. When the code is in debugging, the method that handles this message may print a query on a console and do whatever you type. The real system would need an automated solution, of course, but you can make the change from manual to automated by changing the Car class alone. None of the rest of the system is affected.

Notice that the Car doesn't know exactly where it is (just like the real world that we're modeling). The Road does know where it is (its Location), however, so the Road passes its Location into the Car. Since the Location changes, the Car doesn't bother to store it internally. The Car needs only a single attribute: a destination.

The Car needs a way to answer the which-way-do-you-want-to-turn question, so you need one more object: a Map. The Map needs another one-message interface.

2. I am *here*, and I need to go *there*; which way should I turn?

```
Direction whichWayShouldITurn(Location here, Location there)
```

Again, the Car has no idea how the map answers the question, as long as it gets an answer. (This routing problem is, by far, the hardest part of the system to write, but the problem has already been solved by every GPS navigator on the market. You may be able to buy the solution.) Note how the Car is passed its location, which it relays to the Map. This process, called *delegation*, is also commonplace in OO systems. A given object solves a problem by delegating to a contained object, passing that contained object any external information it needs. As the message propagates from delegator to delegate, it tends to pick up additional arguments.

The last piece of the puzzle is figuring out how cars get onto the Road to begin with. From the perspective of traffic modeling, a house is really a kind of dead-end Road called a *driveway*. Similarly, an office building is a kind of Road called a *parking lot*. The house and office-building objects implement the Road interface, know the Road segments to which they're connected, and inject cars (or accept them) into the system at certain times of day using the Road interface—all easy code to implement.

Now let's add a user interface. It's a classic requirement of OO systems that an object not expose implementation details. Our goal is maintainability. If all the implementation information is a closely guarded secret of the object, then you can change the implementation of that object without impacting the code that uses the object. That is, the change doesn't "ripple out" into the rest of the system. Since all changes are typically concentrated in a single class definition, OO systems are easy to maintain, but only if they follow this encapsulation rule. (You may have a good reason to violate the encapsulation occasionally, but do so knowing that your system will be harder to maintain as a consequence.)

The encapsulation requirement implies that a well-designed object will have at least some responsibility for creating its own UI. That is, a well-done class won't have getter or setter methods because these methods expose implementation details, introducing down-the-line maintenance problems as a consequence. If the implementation of the object changes in such a way that the type or range of values returned by a getter method needs to change, for example, you'll have to modify not only the object that defines the getter but also all the code that calls the "getter." I'll talk more about this issue and about how to design systems without getter and setter methods in a moment.

In the current system, you can build a UI by adding a single method to the Road interface.

3. Draw a representation of yourself along this *line*:

```
drawYourself(Graphics g, Point begin, Point end);
```

The Road UI could indicate the average speed of the traffic (which will vary with traffic density) by changing the line color. The result would be a map of the city where traffic speed is shown in color. The Map, of course, needs to know about Roads, so the Map builds a rendition of itself, delegating drawing requests to Road objects when necessary. Since the Road objects render themselves, there's no need for a bunch of getter methods that ask for the information that some external UI builder needs to do the rendering: methods such as getAverageSpeed() are unnecessary.

Now that the groundwork is done, you'll set the wheels in motion, so to speak. You hook up Roads, driveways, and parking lots to each other at compile time. Put some cars in the system (also at compile time), and set things going. Every time a clock "ticks," each Road segment is notified, decides how many cars it needs to get rid of, and passes them along. Each Road segment automatically updates its piece of the UI as the average speed changes. Voilà! Traffic flow.

Once you've designed the messaging system, you're in a position to capture what you've learned in a static-model diagram. Associations exist only between classes whose objects communicate with one another, and only those messages that you need are defined. Figure 1-3 shows the UML. Note that it would have been a waste of time to start with the static model. You need to understand the message flow before you can understand the relationships between classes.

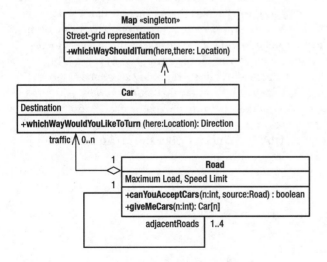

Figure 1-3. *UML static-model diagram for the traffic model*

If you want hands-on experience playing with a traffic simulator of this sort, look at Maxis Software's SimCity. Having not seen the source code, I don't actually know if SimCity *is* implemented as an automaton, but I'd be shocked if it wasn't one. It certainly acts like it on at the user-interface level, so it will do for our purposes. Maxis has a free online version of SimCity Classic on its web site (http://www.maxis.com).

Getters and Setters Are Evil

As I mentioned earlier, it's a fundamental precept of OO systems that an object not expose any of its implementation details. This way, you can change the implementation without needing to change the code that *uses* the object. It follows that you should avoid getter and setter functions, which typically do nothing but provide access to implementation details (fields), in OO systems. Note that neither the ATM nor traffic-flow example used getter or setter methods to do their work.

This isn't to say that your functions shouldn't return values or that "get" or "set" functionality is never appropriate. Objects must sometimes move through the system to get work done. Nonetheless, get/set functions are often used inappropriately as a means of accessing otherwise private fields, and it's that usage that will give you the most trouble. I'll discuss what I consider to be appropriate uses of get/set methods at the end of this section. Getter and setter methods (often called *accessors* and *mutators*, though the word *accessor* is commonly used for both) usually indicate a lack of clear, up-front thinking about the problem you're solving. Programmers often put them into class definitions because they don't want to think about how objects of that class will actually communicate at runtime. The presence of a getter lets you defer that thinking until you're actually coding. This behavior is plain laziness; it isn't "programming for flexibility."

Consider this trivial example of why "getters" should be avoided: There may be 1,000 calls to a getX() method in your program, and every one of those calls assumes that the return value is a particular type. The return value of getX() may be stored in a local variable, for example, and the variable type must match the return-value type. If you need to change the way that the object is implemented in such a way that the type of *X* changes, you're in deep trouble. If *X* used to be an int, but now has to be a long, you'll now get 1,000 compile errors. If you fix the problem incorrectly by casting the return value to int, the code will compile cleanly but won't work. (The return value may be truncated.) You have to modify the code surrounding every one of those 1,000 calls to compensate for the change. I, at least, don't want to do that much work.

Now consider the case of a Money class. Originally written to handle only U.S. dollars, it has a getValue() method that returns a double and a setValue() that sets a new value. The first problem is that you can do nonsensical things with money, illustrated in the following code:

```
Money a, b, c;
//...
a.setValue( b.getValue() * c.getValue() );
```

What does it mean to multiply $2 by $5?

The second problem is more significant: You need to internationalize the application to handle multiple currencies. You go into the class and add a field called currency that's set (internally) to values such as US_DOLLAR, YEN, LEU, and HRYVNA. Small change; big problems.

In any event, what's getValue() going to return? It can't just return a double because that value no longer tells you anything useful. You need to know the currency, too. It can't normalize the return value on U.S. dollars because the exchange rate changes by the minute. What are you going to do with the value in any case? You can't just print it, because you need the currency again. You could augment getValue() with getCurrency(), but now all the code that uses the value must also get the currency and normalize on some standard currency locally. That's a lot of work that may need to be duplicated in 1,000 places in the code. You also have to find every screen in the system where the value of money is displayed and change the display logic to include currency. This "simple" change is rapidly becoming an incredible mess.

Another example: Think of all the problems that were caused by System.in, System.out, and System.err when the Reader and Writer classes were introduced to Java. These three fields were public, which is itself anathema. Simply wrapping them (with a System.getOut() that returned System.out, for example) doesn't improve the actual problem: System.out and System.err need to be a (Unicode-based) Writer objects, not (byte-based) PrintStream objects. Ditto for System.in and Reader. Changing the declared types of the objects that hold System.out isn't, in and of itself, enough. Writers are used differently than Output streams. They have different semantics and different methods. You have to change (or at least examine) all the code surrounding the use of System.out access as a consequence. If your program had been writing Unicode using the old System.out, for example, it needed two write() calls to write a single glyph. It also needed some logic to extract the high and low bytes of the glyph to write them separately. All that code has to be removed with the Writer version.

The problem is compounded by force of habit. When procedural programmers come to Java, they tend to start out by building code that looks familiar. Procedural languages don't have classes, but they do have things such as the C struct (think: a class without methods; everything's public). It seems natural, then, to mimic a struct by building class definitions with virtually no methods and nothing but public fields. These procedural programmers read somewhere that fields should be private, however, so they make the fields private and supply public get/set methods. They haven't achieved much other than complicating the public access, though. They certainly haven't made the system object oriented.

Procedural programmers will argue that a public accessor that wraps a private field is somehow "better" than a public field because it lets you control access. An OO programmer will respond that all access—controlled or otherwise—leads to potential maintenance problems. Controlled access may be better than unfettered access, but that doesn't make the practice good. The accessor-is-better-than-direct-access argument misses the real point entirely: The vast majority of your classes don't need the accessor (or mutator) methods at all. That is, if the messaging system is designed carefully (I'll talk about how in a moment), then you can probably dispense with the get/set methods entirely and make your classes more maintainable as a consequence.

This isn't to say that return values are bad or that you can eliminate all "get" methods from your program—you can't. But minimizing the getter/setter functions will make the code more maintainable.

From a purely practical perspective, heavy use of get/set methods make the code more complicated and less agile. Consider a typical procedural "god" class, which collects the information that it needs to do some piece of work from other objects. The god-class implementation is littered with "get" calls. What if the object that already has the data does the work, though? That is, what if you moved the code that does real work from the god class to the place where the data is stored? The accessor calls disappear, and the code is simplified.

The get/set methods also make the program inflexible (it can't accommodate new business requirements easily) and hard to maintain. Perhaps the most important principle of OO systems is *data abstraction*: The way in which an object goes about implementing a message handler should be completely hidden from other objects. That's one of the reasons that all of your instance variables (the nonconstant fields of a class) should be `private`. If you make an instance variable `public`, then you can't change the field as the class evolves over time, because you'd break the external code that used the field. You really don't want to search out 1,000 uses of some class simply because you make a change to that class.

Naive getter and setter methods are dangerous for the same reason that `public` fields are dangerous: They provide external access to implementation details. What if you need to change the type of the accessed field? You also have to change the return type of the accessor. This return value is used lots of places, though, so you'll have to change all of that code as well. I want the effects of a change to be limited to a single class definition, however. I don't want them to ripple out into the entire program.

This principle of implementation hiding leads to a good acid test of the quality of an OO system: Can you make massive changes to a class definition—even throw out the whole thing and replace it with a completely different implementation—without impacting any of the code that uses objects of that class? This sort of modularization makes maintenance much easier and is central to the notion of object orientation. Without implementation hiding, there's little point in using other OO features.

Since accessors violate the principle of encapsulation, you can argue quite reasonably that a system that makes heavy or inappropriate use of accessors simply isn't object oriented. More to the point, if you go through a design process, as compared to just coding, you'll find that there will be hardly any accessors in your program. The process is important.

You'll notice that there are no getter/setter methods in the traffic-modeling example. There's no getSpeed() method on a Car or getAverageSpeed() method on a Road segment. You don't need getLocation() or setLocation() methods on the Car because you're storing location information in the Road, where it belongs. You don't need a setAverageSpeed() on the Road because it figures its own speed. You don't need a getAverageSpeed() on the Road because no other object in the system needs that information. The lack of getter/setter methods doesn't mean that some data doesn't flow through the system; the Road passes its location to the Car, for example. Nonetheless, it's best to minimize data movement as much as possible. You can go a long way toward getting it "right" by observing the following rule: **Don't ask for the information that you need to do some work; ask the object that has the information to do the work for you.**

For example, you don't say the following:

```
Money a, b, c;
//...
a.setValue( a.getValue() + b.getValue() );
```

Rather, you ask the Money object to do the work, as follows:

```
Money a, b, c;
//...
a.increaseBy( b );
```

You don't say, "Give me this attribute so I can print it." You say, "Give me a printable rendering of this attribute" or "print yourself."

Another way to cast this rule is to think about coarse-grained vs. fine-grained operations. A coarse-grained operation asks an object to do a lot of work. A fine-grained operation asks the object to do only a small amount of work. Generally, I prefer coarse-grained methods because they simplify the code and eliminate the need for most getter and setter methods.

Accessor and mutator methods end up in the model because, without a well-thought-out dynamic model to work with, you're only guessing how the objects of a class will be used. Consequently, you need to provide as much access as possible, because you can't predict whether you'll need it. This sort of design-by-guessing strategy is inefficient at best because you end up wasting time writing methods that aren't used (or adding capabilities to the classes that aren't needed). When you follow the static-model-first approach, the best you can hope for is a lot of unnecessary work developing these unused or too-flexible methods. At worst, the incorrect static model creates so much extra work that the project either fails outright, or if you manage to get it built, the maintenance cost is so high that a complete rewrite is less expensive. Remembering back to the traffic-flow example, I used the static model to capture relationships that I discovered while modeling the messaging system. I didn't design the static model first and then try to make the dynamic model work within the confines of that static model.

By designing carefully, focusing on what you need to do rather than how you'll do it, you'll eliminate the vast majority of getter/setter methods in your program.

Render Thyself

Probably the most shocking thing I've done in the traffic-model example is put a drawYourself(...) method on the Road segment. I've (gasp!) put UI code into the business logic! Consider what happens when the requirements of the UI change, though. For example, I may want to represent the Road as a bifurcated line with each direction having its own color. I may want to actually draw dots on the lines representing the cars, and so on. If the Road draws itself, then these changes are all localized to the Road class. Moreover, different types of Roads (parking lots, for example) can draw themselves differently. The downside, of course, is that I've added a small amount of clutter to the Road class, but that UI clutter is easily concentrated in an inner class to clean up things.

Also, bear in mind that I haven't actually put any UI code into the business logic. I've written the UI layer in terms of AWT or Swing, both of which are abstraction layers. The actual UI code is in the AWT/Swing implementation. That's the whole point of an abstraction layer—to isolate your "business logic" from the mechanics of a subsystem. I can easily port to another graphical environment without changing the code, so the only problem is a little bit of clutter. This clutter is easily eliminated by concentrating it into an inner class (or by using the Facade pattern, which I'll discuss soon).

Note that only the most simple classes can get away with a simplistic drawYourself() method. Usually, you need finer control. Objects sometimes need to draw themselves in various ways (HTML, a Swing JLabel, and so on), or you may need to render only a few of the object's attributes.

Moreover, an object doesn't need to physically draw itself on the screen to isolate its implementation from the rest of the program. All you need is some sort of universal (with respect to the program) representation. An object could pass an XML rendering of itself to a display subsystem, for example. A helper class along the lines of java.text.NumberFormat could transform this representation for specific locals. The Money class that I discussed earlier could return a Unicode String rendering that concatenates the currency symbol and value, represented in a localized fashion. You could even return a .gif image or a JLabel.

My main point is that if these attribute representations are handled properly, then you can still change the internal workings of a class without impacting the code that uses the representation. (A representation of some object or attribute that's presented in such a way that it can be displayed, but not manipulated, is a variant on the Memento pattern, discussed later in the current chapter. Also, you can use several design patterns [notably, Builder] to allow an object to render itself but nonetheless isolate the UI-creation code from the actual object. I'll discuss this pattern further in Chapter 4.)

JavaBeans and Struts

"But," you may object, "what about JavaBeans, Struts, and other libraries that use accessors and mutators?" What about them? You have a perfectly good way to build a JavaBean without getters and setters; the `BeanCustomizer`, `BeanInfo`, and `BeanDescriptor` classes all exist for exactly this purpose. The designers of the JavaBean specification threw the getter/setter idiom into the picture because they thought it'd be an easy way to for a junior programmer to create a bean, something you could do while you were learning how to do it "right." Unfortunately, nobody did that.

People often let the "tail wag the dog" when they talk about JavaBeans (or whatever library they use that has procedural elements). People seem to forget that these libraries started out as some programmer's personal attempt at solving a problem. Sometimes the programmers had a procedural bias; sometimes they had an OO bias. Sometimes the designers deliberately "dumbed down" an interface because they knew a lot of people just wouldn't "get it" otherwise.

The JavaBeans get/set idiom is an example of this last problem. The accessors were meant solely as a way to tag certain properties so that they could be identified by a UI-builder program or equivalent. You weren't supposed to call these methods yourself. They were there so that an automated tool (such as a UI builder) could use the introspection APIs in the `Class` class to infer the existence of certain "properties" by looking at method names. This approach hasn't worked out well in practice. It has introduced a lot of unnecessary methods to the classes, and it has made the code vastly too complicated and too procedural. Programmers who don't understand data abstraction actually call the tagging methods, and the code is less maintainable as a consequence. For this reason, a "metadata" feature will be incorporated into the 1.5 release of Java (due out in mid-2004). Instead of using the following get/set idiom to mark an attribute, like so:

```
private int  property;
public  int  getProperty (          ){ return property;  }
public  void setProperty (int value){ property = value; }
```

you'll be able to say something like this:

```
private @property int property;
```

The UI-construction tool or equivalent will be able to use the introspection APIs to find the properties, rather than having to examine method names and infer the existence of a property from a name. More to the point, no runtime accessor is damaging your code.

Returning to Struts, this library isn't a model of OO architecture and was never intended to be. The MVC architecture embodied in Struts pretty much forces you to use get/set methods. You can reasonably argue, that given the generic nature of Struts, it *can't* be fully OO, but other

UI architectures manage to hide encapsulation better than MVC. (Perhaps the real solution is to avoid an MVC-based UI framework altogether. MVC was developed almost 30 years ago, and we've learned a lot since then.) There's one compelling reason for using Struts: The library contains a lot of code that you don't have to write, and it's "good enough" for many purposes. If "good enough" is good enough, go for it.

To sum up, people have told me that fundamental concepts of object orientation, such as implementation hiding, are "hogwash," simply because the libraries that these people use (JavaBeans, Struts, .NET, and so on) don't embody them. That argument is, I think, hogwash.

Refactoring

The other argument I've heard to justify the use of accessors and mutators is that an integrated development environment such as Eclipse or its cousins make it so easy to refactor a method definition to return a different argument type that there's no point in worrying about this stuff. I still worry, though.

Firstly, Eclipse just refactors within the scope of the existing project. If your class is being reused in many projects, then you have to refactor all of them. A company that properly reuses class will have many groups of programmers all working on separate projects in parallel, and these other programmers won't take kindly to your telling them that they have to refactor all their code because of some specious change you want to make to a shared class.

Secondly, automated refactoring works great for simple things, but not for major changes. The ramifications of the change are typically too far-reaching for an automated tool to handle. You may have to change SQL scripts, for example, and the effects of the change may ripple indirectly into the methods that are called from the place where the refactoring is made.

Finally, think about the changes to Money and System.out discussed earlier. Simply changing a few return-value types isn't sufficient to handle the changes I discussed. You have to change the code that surrounds the getter invocation as well. Though it's hard to argue that refactoring the code isn't a good thing, you can't do this sort of refactoring with an automated tool.

People who use the automated-refactoring argument also tend not to understand the most important issue: Overuse of accessors and mutators at the key-abstraction level is an indication of a poorly designed messaging system. In other words, the code is probably structured so poorly that maintenance is unnecessarily difficult, whether or not you can refactor easily. A redesign is required, not a refactor.

Using the earlier System.out example as a characteristic, imagine that you redesigned Java to print a String on the console as follows:

```
String s = "hello world";

s.print( String.TO_CONSOLE );
```

and loaded a String like this:

```
s.load( String.FROM_CONSOLE );
```

All the byte-vs.-Unicode problems would disappear into the String class implementation. Any changes from byte-based to glyph-based I/O would disappear. Since the whole point of the Reader and Writer interfaces is to load and store strings, you could dispense with them entirely. Overloads of print(...) and load(...) could handle file I/O.

You can argue with me about whether things *should* be done in this way. You can also quibble about whether TO_CONSOLE should be a member of the String or File class. Nonetheless, the redesign eliminated the need for System.out and its accessors. Of course, you can think of a billion things to do with a string and can reasonably argue that *all* of those things shouldn't be part of the String class, but design patterns (Visitor, Strategy, and so on) can address this problem.

Life Without Get/Set

So, how do you end up with a design without getters and setters in it? That is, how do you design a messaging system that minimizes the need for accessors and mutators? The solution is in design, not in coding. There's no simplistic just-replace-this-code-with-that-code solution because the problem has to do with the way you think about the interaction of objects. You can't just refactor the get/set methods out of the code—you have to rebuild the code from scratch with a fundamentally different structure.

The OO-design process is centered on *use cases*: stand-alone tasks performed by an end user that have some useful outcome. "Logging On" isn't a use case because there's no outcome that's useful in the problem domain. "Drawing a Paycheck" is a use case. In the earlier ATM example, I was flushing out the "Depositing Funds" use case.

An OO system, then, implements the activities needed to play out the various "scenarios" that comprise a use case. The runtime objects that have roles in the use case act out their roles by sending messages to one another. Not all messages are equal, however. You haven't accomplished much if you've just built a procedural program that uses objects and classes.

Back in 1989, Kent Beck and Ward Cunningham were teaching classes on OO design, and they were having problems getting programmers to abandon the get/set mentality. They characterized the problem as follows:

> *The most difficult problem in teaching object-oriented programming is getting the learner to give up the global knowledge of control that is possible with procedural programs, and rely on the local knowledge of objects to accomplish their tasks. Novice designs are littered with regressions to global thinking: gratuitous global variables, unnecessary pointers, and inappropriate reliance on the implementation of other objects.*

When they talk about "global knowledge of control," they're describing the "god" class I discussed earlier—a class whose objects collect information from elsewhere and then process that information (rather than allowing the object that has the data to do the processing). That "inappropriate reliance on the implementation of other objects" is an accessor or mutator call.

Cunningham came up with a teaching methodology that nicely demonstrates the design process: the CRC card. The basic idea is to make a set of 4×6 index cards that are laid out in the following three sections:

Class: The name of a class of objects.

Responsibilities: What those objects can do. These responsibilities should be focused on a single area of expertise.

Collaborators: Other classes of objects to which the current class of objects can talk. This set should be as small as possible.

The initial pass at the CRC card is just guesswork—things will change.

In class, Beck and Cunningham picked a use case and made a best guess at determining which objects would be required to "act out" the use case. They typically started with two objects and added others as required as the scenario played out. People from the class were selected to be those objects and were handed a copy of the associated CRC card. If several objects of a given class were needed, several people represented those objects. The students literally acted out the use case. Here are the rules I use when acting out a use case with CRC cards:

- Perform the activities that comprise the use case by talking to one another.

- You can talk only to your collaborators. If you need to talk to someone else, talk to a collaborator who can talk to the other person. If that turns out not to be possible, add a collaborator to your CRC card.

- You may not ask for the information you need to do something. Rather, you must ask the collaborator who has the information to do the work. It's okay to give your collaborators some bit of information that they need to do the work, but keep this sort of passing to a minimum.

- If something needs to be done and nobody can do it, create a new class (and CRC card) or add a responsibility to an existing class (and CRC card).

- If a CRC card gets too full, you must create another class (CRC card) to handle some of the responsibilities. Complexity is limited by what you can fit on a 4×6 index card.

- Stick to the "domain" of the problem (accounting, purchasing, and so on) in both your vocabulary and your processes. That is, model what would happen if real people who were domain experts were solving the problem. Pretend computers don't exist. It's not very often that two people say "getX" to each other in the course of doing some task, so in practice, the get/set methods won't even come up.

Once you've worked out a conversation that solves the problem, turn on a tape recorder or transcribe it. That transcription is the program's "dynamic model." The finished set of CRC cards is the program's "static model." With lots of fits and starts, it's possible to solve just about any problem in this way.

The process I just described *is* the OO-design process, albeit simplified for a classroom environment. Some people design real programs this way, using CRC cards, but the technique tends not to scale to nontrivial programs. More often than not, designers develop the dynamic and static models in UML, using some formal process (for example, RUP, Crystal, and even some flavors of Extreme Programming). The point is that an OO system is a conversation between objects. If you think about it for a moment, get/set methods just don't come up when you're having a conversation. By the same token, get/set methods won't appear in your code if you design in this way before you start coding.

The modeling must stay in the "problem domain" as long as possible, as I mentioned in the last rule. What gets most people in trouble is that they think they're doing domain modeling but are actually modeling at the implementation level. If your messaging system isn't using the vocabulary of the problem domain—if it doesn't make sense to an average end user of your program—then you're doing implementation-level modeling. Things such as computers (or worse, the databases or UI-construction kits) have no place at this level of modeling.

In CRC modeling, for example, you need to keep the conversation in the problem domain by using the vocabulary and processes that real users would use. This way the messaging system reflects the domain directly. The database is just an internal thing that some of the classes use as a persistence mechanism and won't appear in the initial model at all.

If you keep the message structure in the problem domain, then you'll eliminate the vast majority of get/set methods, simply because "get" and "set" isn't something your domain experts do when solving most problems.

When Are Accessors and Mutators Okay?

If you must pass information between objects, encapsulate that information into other objects. A "get" function that returns an object of class Money is vastly preferable to one that returns a double.

It's best if a method returns an object in terms of an interface that the object implements because the interface isolates you from changes to the implementing class. This sort of method (that returns an interface reference) isn't really a getter in the sense of a method that just provides access to a field. If you change the internal implementation of the provider, you must change the definition of the returned object to accommodate the changes, of course. You can even return an object of different class than you used to return as long as the new object implements the expected interface. The external code that uses the object through its interface is protected.

In general, though, I try to restrict even this relatively harmless form of accessor to return only instances of classes that are *key abstractions* in the system. (If the class or interface name appears regularly in the English, domain-level description of the problem, then it's a key abstraction.)

Generally, messages should carry as little data as possible with them as arguments, but it's better to "push" data into an object than to "pull" it out. Put another way, it's better to delegate to another object, passing it some bit of information that it doesn't have, than it is for that object to call one of your methods to get the information. This isn't to say that return values are bad, but insofar as it's possible, you should return either objects that encapsulate their implementation or booleans, which give away nothing about implementation. In an ATM machine, it's better to ask "am I authorized to give Bill $20?" (a Boolean result) than it is to say "give me Bill's account balance" and make the decision locally.

One big exception exists to the no-getter-or-setter rule. I think of all OO systems as having a "procedural boundary layer." The vast majority of OO programs run on procedural operating systems and talk to procedural databases, for example. The interfaces to these external procedural subsystems are by their nature generic. The designer of JDBC hasn't a clue about what you'll be doing with the database, so the class design has to be unfocused and highly flexible. UI-builder classes such as Java's Swing library are another example of a "boundary-layer" library. The designers of Swing can't have any idea about how their classes will be used; they're too generic. Normally, it would be a bad thing to build lots of flexibility that you didn't use because it increases development time. Nonetheless, the extra flexibility is unavoidable in these boundary APIs, so the boundary-layer classes are loaded with accessor and mutator methods. The designers really have no choice.

In fact, this not-knowing-how-it-will-be-used problem infuses all of the Java packages. It's difficult to eliminate all the accessors and mutators if you can't know how objects of the class are actually used. Given this constraint, the designers of Java did a pretty good job of hiding as much implementation as they could. This isn't to say that the design decisions that went into JDBC and its ilk apply to your code. They don't. You *do* know how the classes are going to be used, so you don't have to waste time building unnecessary flexibility.

I should also mention constant values, which are often accessed directly as public members. Here's my advice:

- Don't do it if you don't have to do it. It's better to have a list scale to fit its contents than have a MAX_SIZE, for example.

- Use the new (JDK 1.5) enum facility whenever possible rather than expressly declared and initialized static final int values. Alternatively, use the typesafe-enum pattern described by Joshua Bloch in his book *Effective Java Programming Language Guide* (Addison-Wesley, 2001).

  The basic notion is to define an enum like this:

  ```
  private static class Format{ private Format(); }
  public static final Format SINGLE_LINE  = null;
  public static final Format POPUP_DIALOG = new Format();
  public static final Format PANEL        = new Format();

  public displayYourselfAs( Format how )
  {   // display the current value of calendar in
      // the format specified.
  }
  ```

  Since the argument to displayYourselfAs(...) is a Format object, and since only two instances of (and three references to) format can possibly exist, you can't pass a bad value to displayYourselfAs(...). Had you used the following more common int-enum idiom:

  ```
  public static final int SINGLE_LINE  = 0;
  public static final int POPUP_DIALOG = 1;
  public static final int PANEL        = 2;

  public displayYourselfAs( int how )
  {   //...
  }
  ```

  you could pass an arbitrary nonsense value (say, -1) to the method. Bloch devotes ten pages to this idiom, and I refer you to his book for more information.

- If you do have to expose a constant, make sure that it's really a constant. Java's final keyword guarantees that a reference can't be changed to reference something else, but it doesn't protect the referenced object. If an object is used as a constant, you have to write the class in such a way that the object can't be modified. (Java calls this kind of class *immutable*, but other than declaring all the fields of the class as final, there's no language mechanism to guarantee immutability. You just program the class that way.)

Consider Java's `Color` class. Once the object is created, you can't change the color, simply because the color class doesn't expose any methods that change the color. Consider this code:

```
public static final Color background = Color.RED;
//...
c.darken();
```

The call to `darken()` doesn't modify the object referenced by `background`; rather, it returns a new `Color` object that's a shade darker than the original. The foregoing code doesn't do anything, since the returned `Color` object isn't stored anywhere, and you can't say this:

```
background = c.darken();
```

because background is final.

Finally, it's sometimes the case that an object is a "caretaker" for other objects. For example, a Java `Collection` holds a bunch of objects that were passed into it from outside. Though the words "get" and "set" are often used in the names of the methods that give an object to a caretaker and fetch the object back from the caretaker, these methods don't expose any information about how the caretaker works, so they're also okay. In general, if you pass something into an object, it's reasonable to expect to be able to get that something back out again.

Databases are extreme examples of caretakers of data, though their interfaces are pushed even further in the direction of get/set methods because a database is a fundamentally procedural thing—a big bag of data; a database is part of the "boundary layer" I discussed earlier. Consequently, it's impossible to access a procedural database in an OO way. The get/set methods are unavoidable. Nonetheless, you can (and should) encapsulate the procedural calls to the database layer into higher-level domain objects and then write your code in terms of the interfaces to these encapsulating objects. Inside the encapsulating objects, you'll be doing what amounts to get/set calls on the database. Most of the program won't see this work, however, because they'll be interacting with the higher-level encapsulating object, not the database.

Summing Up the Getter/Setter Issues

So let's sum up: I'm *not* saying that return values are bad, that information can't flow through the system, or that you can eliminate all accessors and mutators from your program. Information has to flow, or the program won't do anything. That information should be properly encapsulated into objects that hide their implementation, however.

The basic issues are as follows:

- The maintainability of a program is inversely proportional to the amount of data that flows between objects.

- Exposing implementation harms maintainability. Make sure that the accessor or mutator really is required before you add it.

- Classes that directly model the system at the domain level, sometimes called *business objects*, hardly ever need accessors or mutators. You can think of the program as partitioned broadly into generic libraries that have to relax the no-getter/no-setter rule and domain-specific classes that should fully encapsulate their implementation. Getters and setters at this level are an indication that you didn't do enough up-front design work. In particular, you probably didn't do enough dynamic modeling.

- By keeping the design process in the problem ("business") domain as long as possible, you tend to design messaging systems that don't use getters and setters because statements such as "Get this" or "Set that" don't come up in the problem domain.

- The closer you get to the procedural boundary of an OO system (the database interface, the UI-construction classes, and so on), the harder it is to hide implementation. The judicious use of accessors and mutators has a place in this boundary layer.

- Completely generic libraries and classes also can't hide implementation completely so will always have accessors and mutators.

- Sometimes it's not worth the trouble to fully encapsulate the implementation. Think of trivial classes such as `Point` and `Dimension`. Similarly, private implementation classes (a `Node` class defined as a `private` inner class of `Tree`, for example) can often used a relaxed encapsulation model. On the other hand, think of all the problems that were caused by `System.in`, `System.out`, and `System.err` when the `Reader` and `Writer` classes were introduced, and what if I want to add units (feet, inches) to a `Dimension`?

At a JavaOne conference (I think in 1991) James Gosling was asked to give some pithy piece of programming advice to the multitude. He chose to answer (I'm paraphrasing) that maintainability was inversely proportional to the amount of data that moves between objects. The implication is that you can't get rid of all data movement, particularly in an environment where several objects have to collaborate to accomplish some task, but you should try to minimize date flow as much as possible.

When I have to pass information around, I use the following two rules of thumb:

- Pass around objects (ideally in terms of the interfaces they implement) rather than raw data.

- Use a "push" model, not a "pull" model. For example, an object may delegate to a collaborator, passing the collaborator some piece of information that the collaborator needs to do its work. The alternative—the collaborator "pulling" the information from the delegator using a getter method—is less desirable. The Flyweight pattern relies on this "push" model.

Converting a pull to a push is often just a matter of routing the message differently.

Maintainability is a continuum, not a binary. Personally, I like to err in the direction of easy maintenance, because maintenance really begins two seconds after you write the code. Code that's build with maintenance in mind tends to come together faster and have fewer bugs.

Nonetheless, you must decide where on that ease-of-maintenance continuum you want to place your program. The Java libraries are, for the most part, examples of how you need to compromise maintainability to get generic functionality. The authors of the Java packages hid as much implementation as they could, given the fact that the libraries were both completely generic and also on the procedural boundary. The price they paid is that it's difficult to make structural changes to libraries such as Swing because too many existing programs depend on implementation specifics.

Not all of the Java libraries expose implementation. Think of the Crypto APIs (in *javax.crypto*) and the URL/URLConnection classes, which expose hardly any information and are extraordinarily flexible as a consequence. The Servlet classes are good example of an encapsulated implementation that nonetheless supports information movement, though they could go even further by providing an abstraction layer that you could use to build HTML.

So, when you see methods starting with the "get" or "set," that's a clue. Ask yourself whether the data movement is really necessary. Can you change the messaging system to use coarser-grained messages that will make the data movement unnecessary? Can you pass the information as a message argument instead of using a separate message? Would an alternative architecture work better at hiding implementation? If you have no alternative, though, go ahead and use it.

CHAPTER 2
■ ■ ■

Programming with Interfaces, and a Few Creational Patterns

Programming in terms of interfaces is a fundamental concept in OO systems in general and the Gang-of-Four design patterns in particular. Nonetheless, many Java programmers make little use of interfaces (and overuse the extends relationship). This chapter explains the problems with extends and how you can solve some of those problems with interfaces. I also introduce a few of the Creational patterns that simplify interface-based programming.

Why *extends* Is Evil

The extends keyword is evil—maybe not at the Charles-Manson/Vlad-the-Impaler level, but bad enough that reputable designers don't want to be seen in public with it. The Gang-of-Four *Design Patterns* book is, in fact, largely about replacing implementation inheritance (extends) with interface inheritance (implements). That's why I've devoted this entire chapter to using interfaces. I'll also introduce a couple of design patterns in this chapter: Template Method, Abstract Factory, and Singleton.

Before launching into the discussion of extends, I want to head off a few misconceptions.

First, the next few sections talk in depth about how extends can get you into trouble. Since I'm focusing on the downside with such intensity, you may come to the conclusion that I think you should never use extends. That's not the case. I'm assuming you already are familiar with the upside of extends and its importance in OO systems, so I don't talk about that upside at all. I don't want to qualify every statement I make with an "on the other hand," so please excuse me if I give the wrong impression at times. Implementation inheritance is certainly a valuable tool when used appropriately.

Second, an important issue is the language itself. Simply because a language provides some mechanism doesn't mean that that mechanism should be used heavily or thoughtlessly. Adele Goldberg—a pioneer of object orientation—once quipped,

> *Many people tell the story of the CEO of a software company who claimed that his product would be object oriented because it was written in C++. Some tell the story without knowing that it is a joke.*

Java programmers sometimes confuse language features, such as extends, with object orientation itself. They will equate a statement such as "extends has problems" with "don't do things in an OO way." Don't make this mistake. Inheritance is certainly central to OO, but you can put inheritance into your program in lots of ways, and extends is just one of these ways.

Language features such as extends certainly make it easier to implement OO systems, but simply using derivation does not make a system object oriented. (*Polymorphism*—the ability to have multiple implementations of the same type—is central to object-oriented thinking. Since the notion of polymorphism is unique to OO, you could reasonably argue that a system that doesn't use polymorphism isn't object oriented. Nonetheless, polymorphism is best achieved through interfaces, not extends relationships.)

To my mind, *data abstraction*—the encapsulation of implementation details within the object—is just as central to OO thinking as polymorphism. Of course, procedural systems can use data abstraction, but they don't have to do so. Hard-core data abstraction is not optional in an OO system, however.

As I discussed in the preface, using a language feature mindlessly, without regard to the negative consequences of using the feature, is a great way to create bad programs. Implementation inheritance (extends) is valuable in certain situations, but it also can cause a lot of grief when used incorrectly. Polymorphism (redefining base-class behavior with a derived-class override) is central to object orientation, and you need some form of inheritance to get polymorphism. Both extends and implements are forms of inheritance, though. The class that implements an interface is just as much a derived class as one that extends another class.[1]

The similarity between extends and implements is quite clear in a language such as C++, simply because C++ doesn't distinguish between the two syntactically. For you C++ programmers, a C++ interface is a virtual base class containing nothing but "pure" virtual functions. The lack of syntactic sugar to support interface-based programming doesn't mean that C++ doesn't support interfaces. It's just that it doesn't have an interface keyword.

Interfaces vs. Classes

I once attended a Java User's Group meeting where James Gosling (Java's inventor) spoke about some eminently forgettable topic. Afterward, in a memorable Q&A session, someone asked him, "If you could do Java over again, what would you change?" His reply was, "I'd leave out classes." After the laughter died down, he explained that the real problem wasn't classes per se but rather implementation inheritance (the extends relationship). Interface inheritance (the implements relationship) is much preferred. Avoid implementation inheritance whenever possible.

---

1. Pedagogically, an interface defines a *type*, not a class, so is not properly called a *base class*. That is, when you say *class*, you really mean a "class of objects that share certain characteristics." Since interfaces can't be instantiated, they aren't really "classes of objects," so some people use the word *type* to distinguish interfaces from classes. I think the argument is pedantic, but feel free to use whatever semantics you want.

Losing Flexibility

So, why? The first problem is that explicit use of a concrete-class name locks you into a specific implementation, making down-the-line changes unnecessarily difficult.

At the core of the contemporary "agile" development methodologies is the concept of parallel design and development. You start programming before you have fully specified the program. This way of working flies in the face of traditional wisdom—that a design should be complete before programming starts—but many successful projects have proven that you can use the technique to develop good-quality code even more rapidly (and cost effectively) than with the traditional pipelined approach. Agile development isn't a good fit for every project, but it works nicely on small projects whose requirements change during development.

At the core of Agile parallel development is the notion of flexibility. You have to write your code in such a way that you can incorporate newly discovered requirements into the existing code as painlessly as possible. Rather than implementing features you *may* need, you implement only the features you *do* need, but in a way that accommodates change. Without flexibility, parallel development simply isn't possible. Programming to interfaces is at the core of flexible structure. To see why, let's look at what happens when you don't use them. Consider the following code:

```
void f()
{   LinkedList list = new LinkedList();
    //...
    modify( list );
}

void modify( LinkedList list )
{
    list.add( ... );
    doSomethingWith( list );
}
```

Suppose that a new requirement for fast lookup has now emerged, so the LinkedList isn't working. You need to replace it with a HashSet. In the existing code, that change is not localized since you'll have to modify not only the initial definition (in f ()), but also the modify() definition (which takes a LinkedList argument). You'll also have to modify the definition of doSomethingWith(), and so on, down the line.

So, let's rewrite the code as follows so that modify() takes a Collection rather than a LinkedList argument:

```
void f()
{   Collection list = new LinkedList();
    //...
    modify( list );
}

void modify( Collection list )
{   list.add( ... );
    doSomethingWith( list );
}
```

Let's also presuppose that you make that change—from LinkedList to Collection every-where else the concrete-class name appears in your code. This change makes it possible to turn the linked list into a hash table simply by replacing the new LinkedList() with a new HashSet() in the original definition (in f()). That's it. No other changes are necessary.

As another example, compare the following code, in which a method just needs to look at all the members of some collection:

```
f()
{
    Collection c = new HashSet();
    //...
    examine( c );
}

void examine( Collection c )
{   for( Iterator i = c.iterator(); i.hasNext() ;)
        //...
}
```

to this more-generalized version:

```
void f()
{
    Collection c = new HashSet();
    //...
    examine( c.iterator() );
}

void examine( Iterator i )
{   for(; i.hasNext() ; i.next() )
        //...
}
```

Since examine() now takes an Iterator argument rather than a Collection, it can traverse not only Collection derivatives but also the key and value lists that you can get from a Map. In fact, you can write iterators that generate data instead of traversing a collection. You can write iterators that feed information from a test scaffold or a file to the program. g2() can accommodate all these changes without modification. It has enormous flexibility.

Coupling

A more important problem with implementation inheritance is *coupling*, the undesirable reliance of one part of a program on another part. Global variables are the classic example of why strong coupling is bad. If you change the type of a global variable, for example, all the code that uses that variable—that is *coupled* to the variable—can be affected, so all this code must be examined, modified, and retested. Moreover, all the methods that use the variable are coupled to each other through the variable. That is, one method may incorrectly affect the behavior of another method simply by changing the variable's value at an awkward time. This problem is particularly hideous in multithreaded programs.

You should strive to minimize coupling relationships. You can't eliminate coupling altogether, because a method call from an object of one class to an object of another is a form of coupling. Without some coupling, you'd have no program. Nonetheless, you can minimize coupling considerably by diligently following OO precepts, the most important being that the implementation of an object should be completely hidden from the objects that use it. For example, any fields that aren't constant should always be `private`. Period. No exceptions. Ever. I mean it. (You can occasionally use `protected` methods to good effect, but `protected` instance variables are an abomination; `protected` is just another way to say `public`.)

As I discussed in depth in Chapter One, you should never use accessors and mutators (get/set functions that just provide access to a field) for the same reason—they're just overly complicated ways to make a field `public`. Methods that return full-blown objects rather than a basic-type value are reasonable in situations where the class of the returned object is a key abstraction in the design. Similarly, a function called `getSomething()` can be reasonable if it's a fundamental activity of the object to be a provider of information. (A `getTemperature()` on a `Thermometer` object makes sense, provided that this method returns a `Temperature`.) If the easiest way to implement some method is simply to return a field, that's fine. It's not fine to look at things the other way around ("I have this field, so I need to provide access").

I'm not being pedantic here. I've found a direct correlation in my own work between the "strictness" of my OO approach, how fast the code comes together, and how easy it is to maintain the code. Whenever I violate a central OO principle such as implementation hiding, I find myself rewriting that code (usually because the code is impossible to debug). I don't have time to write programs twice, so I'm really good about following the rules. I have no interest in purity for the sake of purity—my concern is entirely practical.

The Fragile-Base-Class Problem

Now let's apply the concept of coupling to inheritance. In an implementation-inheritance system (one that uses `extends`), the derived classes are tightly coupled to the base classes, and this close connection is undesirable. Designers have applied the moniker "the fragile-base-class problem" to describe this behavior. Base classes are considered "fragile" because you can modify a base class in a seemingly safe way, but this new behavior, when inherited by the derived classes, may cause the derived classes to malfunction. You just can't tell whether a base-class change is safe simply by examining the methods of the base class in isolation; you have to look at (and test) all derived classes as well. Moreover, you have to check all code that *uses* both base-class *and* derived-class objects, since the new behavior may also break this code. A simple change to a key base class can render an entire program inoperable.

Let's look at the fragile-base-class and base-class-coupling problems together. The following class extends Java's `ArrayList` class to make it behave like a stack (a bad idea, as you'll see in a moment):

```
class Stack extends ArrayList
{   private int topOfStack = 0;

    public void push( Object article )
    {   add( topOfStack++, article );
    }

    public Object pop()
```

```
    {    return remove( --topOfStack );
    }

    public void pushMany( Object[] articles )
    {    for( int i = 0; i < articles.length; ++i )
             push( articles[i] );
    }
}
```

Even a class as simple as this one has problems. Consider what happens when a user leverages inheritance and uses the ArrayList's clear() method to pop everything off the stack, like so:

```
Stack aStack = new Stack();
aStack.push("1");
aStack.push("2");
aStack.clear();
```

The code compiles just fine, but since the base class doesn't know anything about the index of the item at the top of the stack (topOfStack), the Stack object is now in an undefined state. The next call to push() puts the new item at index 2 (the current value of the topOfStack), so the stack effectively has three elements on it, the bottom two of which are garbage.

One (hideously bad) solution to the inheriting-undesirable-methods problem is for Stack to override all the methods of ArrayList that can modify the state of the array to manipulate the stack pointer. This is a lot of work, though, and doesn't handle problems such as adding a method like clear() to the base class after you've written the derived class.

You could try to fix the clear() problem by providing an override that threw an exception, but that's a *really* bad idea from a maintenance perspective. The ArrayList contract says nothing about throwing exceptions if a derived class doesn't want some base-class method to work properly. This behavior will be completely unexpected. Since a Stack is an ArrayList, you can pass a Stack to an existing method that uses clear(), and this client method will certainly not be expecting an exception to be thrown on a clear() call. It's impossible to write code in a polymorphic environment if derived-class objects violate the base-class contract at all, much less this severely.

The throw-an-exception strategy also moves what would be a compile-time error into runtime. If the method simply isn't declared, the compiler kicks out a method-not-found error. If the method is there but throws an exception, you won't find out about the call until the program is actually running. Not good.

You would not be wrong if you said that extending ArrayList to define a Stack is bad design from a conceptual level as well. A Stack simply doesn't need most of the methods that ArrayList provides, and providing access to those methods through inheritance is not a good plan. That is, many ArrayList operations are nonsensical in a Stack.

As an aside, Java's Stack class doesn't have the clear() problem because it uses the base-class size() method in lieu of a top-of-stack index, but you could still argue that java.util.Stack should not extend java.util.Vector. The removeRange() and insertElementAt() methods inherited from Vector have no meaning to a stack, for example. There's nothing to stop someone from calling these methods on a Stack object, however.

A better design of the Stack class uses encapsulation instead of derivation. That way, no inherited methods exist at all. The following new-and-improved version of Stack contains an ArrayList object rather than deriving from ArrayList:

```
class Stack
{   private int        topOfStack = 0;
    private ArrayList theData     = new ArrayList();

    public void push( Object article )
    {   theData.add( topOfStack++, article );
    }

    public Object pop()
    {   return theData.remove( --topOfStack );
    }

    public void pushMany( Object[] articles )
    {   for( int i = 0; i < articles.length; ++i )
            push( articles[i] );
    }

    public int size()    // current stack size.
    {   return theData.size();
    }
}
```

The coupling relationship between Stack and ArrayList is a lot looser than it was in the first version. You don't have to worry about inheriting methods you don't want. If changes are made to ArrayList that break the Stack class, you would have to rewrite Stack to compensate for those changes, but you wouldn't have to rewrite any of the code that used Stack objects. I do have to provide a size() method, since Stack no longer inherits size() from ArrayList.

So far so good, but now let's consider the fragile-base-class issue. Let's say you want to create a variant of Stack that keeps track of the maximum and minimum stack sizes over a period of time. The following implementation maintains resettable "high-water" and "low-water" marks:

```
class MonitorableStack extends Stack
{
    private int highWaterMark = 0;
    private int lowWaterMark  = 0;

    public void push( Object o )
    {   push(o);
        if( size() > highWaterMark )
            highWaterMark = size();
    }

    public Object pop()
```

```
      {   Object poppedItem = pop();
          if( size() < lowWaterMark )
              lowWaterMark = size();
          return poppedItem;
      }

      public int  maximumSize() { return highWaterMark; }
      public int  minimumSize() { return lowWaterMark;  }
      public void resetMarks () { highWaterMark = lowWaterMark = size(); }
  }
```

This new class works fine, at least for a while. Unfortunately, the programmer chose to
inherit the base-class pushMany() method, exploiting the fact that pushMany() does its work by
calling push(). This detail doesn't seem, at first, to be a bad choice. The whole point of using
extends is to be able to leverage base-class methods.

One fine day, however, somebody runs a profiler and notices the Stack is a significant
bottleneck in the actual execution time of the code. Our intrepid maintenance programmer
improves the performance of the Stack by rewriting it not to use an ArrayList at all. Here's the
new lean-and-mean version:

```
class Stack
{
    private int       topOfStack = -1;
    private Object[] theData     = new Object[1000];

    public void push( Object article )
    {   theData[ ++topOfStack ] = article;
    }

    public Object pop()
    {   Object popped = theData[ topOfStack-- ];
        theData[topOfStack] = null; // prevent memory leak
        return popped;
    }

    public void pushMany( Object[] articles )
    {   assert (topOfStack + articles.length) < theData.length;
        System.arraycopy(articles, 0, theData, topOfStack+1,
                                            articles.length);
        topOfStack += articles.length;
    }

    public int size()   // current stack size.
    {   return topOfStack + 1;
    }
}
```

Notice that pushMany() no longer calls push() multiple times—it just does a block transfer.

The new version of Stack works just fine; in fact, it's *better* (or at least, faster) than the previous version. Unfortunately, the MonitorableStack derived class *doesn't* work any more, since it won't correctly track stack usage if pushMany() is called. The derived-class version of push() is no longer called by the inherited pushMany() method, so the highWaterMark is no longer updated by pushMany(). Stack is a fragile base class.

Let's imagine you can fix this problem by providing the following pushMany() implementation in MonitorableStack:

```
public void pushMany( Object[] articles )
{   for( int i = 0; i < articles.length; ++i )
        push( articles[i] );
}
```

This version explicitly calls the local push() override, so you've "fixed" the problem, but note that similar problems may exist in all the other overrides of Stack, so you'll have to examine *all* of them to make sure they still work.

Now let's imagine that a new requirement emerges—you need to empty a stack without explicitly popping the items. You go back into the Stack declaration and add the following:

```
public void discardAll()
{   stack = new Object[1000];
    topOfStack = -1;
}
```

Again, adding a method seems both safe and reasonable. You wouldn't expect derived-class (or any other) code to break if you simply add a base-class method, since no derived class could possibly leverage the previously nonexistent addition. Unfortunately, this reasonable-seeming modification to the base-class definition has broken the derived classes yet again. Since discardAll() doesn't call pop(), the high- and low-water marks in MonitorableStack are not updated if the entire stack is discarded.

So how can you structure the code so fragile base classes are less likely to exist? You'll find a clue in the work you had to do. Every time you modified the base class, you had to override all the base-class methods in the derived classes and provide derived-class versions. If you find yourself overriding everything, you should really be implementing an interface, not extending a base class.

Under interface inheritance, there's no inherited functionality to go bad on you. If Stack were an interface, implemented by both a SimpleStack and a MonitorableStack, then the code would be much more robust.

Listing 2-1 provides an interface-based solution. This solution has the same flexibility as the implementation-inheritance solution: You can write your code in terms of the Stack abstraction without having to worry about what kind of concrete stack you're actually manipulating. You can also use an interface reference to access objects of various classes polymorphically. Since the two implementations must provide versions of everything in the public interface, however, it's much more difficult to get things wrong.

Note that I'm *not* saying that implementation inheritance is "bad," but rather that it's a potential maintenance problem. Implementation inheritance is fundamental to OO systems, and you can't (in fact, don't want to) eliminate it altogether. I *am* saying that implementation inheritance is risky, and you have to consider the consequences before using it.

Generally, it's safer to implement an interface using a delegation model as I've done with the MonitorableStack in Listing 2.1. (You delegate interface operations to a contained object of what would otherwise be the base class.) Both of these strategies are viable ways to incorporate inheritance into your system.

But, as with any design decision, you are making a trade-off by using a delegation model. The delegation model is harder to do. You're giving up implementation convenience to eliminate a potential fragile-base-class bug. On the other hand, being able to use inherited functionality is a real time-saver, and these small "pass-through" methods increase the code size and impact maintainability. It's your decision whether you're willing to take the risk of a difficult-to-find bug emerging down the line in order to save you a few lines of code now. Sometimes it's worth the risk—the base class may have 200 methods, and you'd have to implement all of them in the delegation model. That's a lot of work to do.

Listing 2-1. *Eliminating Fragile Base Classes Using Interfaces*

```
 1  import java.util.*;
 2
 3  interface Stack
 4  {
 5      void    push( Object o );
 6      Object  pop();
 7      void    pushMany( Object[] articles );
 8      int     size();
 9  }
10
11  class SimpleStack implements Stack
12  {
13      private int        topOfStack = 0;
14      private ArrayList theData     = new ArrayList();
15
16      public void push( Object article )
17      {   theData.add( topOfStack++, article );
18      }
19
20      public Object pop()
21      {   return theData.remove( --topOfStack );
22      }
23
24      public void pushMany( Object[] articles )
25      {   for( int i = 0; i < articles.length; ++i )
26              push( articles[i] );
27      }
28
29      public int size()    // current stack size.
30      {   return theData.size();
31      }
```

```
32  }
33
34  class MonitorableStack implements Stack
35  {
36      private int highWaterMark = 0;
37      private int lowWaterMark  = 0;
38
39      SimpleStack stack = new SimpleStack();
40
41      public void push( Object o )
42      {   stack.push(o);
43
44          if( stack.size() > highWaterMark )
45              highWaterMark = stack.size();
46      }
47
48      public Object pop()
49      {
50          Object returnValue = stack.pop();
51          if( stack.size() < lowWaterMark )
52              lowWaterMark = stack.size();
53          return returnValue;
54      }
55
56      public void pushMany( Object[] articles )
57      {   for( int i = 0; i < articles.length; ++i )
58              push( articles[i] );
59
60          if( stack.size() > highWaterMark )
61              highWaterMark = stack.size();
62      }
63
64      public int  maximumSize() { return highWaterMark; }
65      public int  minimumSize() { return lowWaterMark;  }
66      public void resetMarks () { highWaterMark = lowWaterMark = size(); }
67      public int  size()        { return stack.size(); }
68  }
```

Multiple Inheritance

Languages that support *multiple inheritance* let you have the equivalent of multiple extends relationships in a class definition. If extends is "bad," surely multiple extends relationships are worse, but occasionally the moral equivalent of multiple inheritance is legitimately useful. For example, in the next chapter I'll introduce the concept of a "menu site"—a frame window that has a menu bar. The main window of my application *is* both a frame window (a JFrame) and a MenuSite. A frame that acts as a menu site has all the properties of both base classes, so multiple inheritance seems reasonable in this context.

I've implemented this feature using interfaces and the delegation model I discussed in the previous section. (My class extends JFrame and implements the MenuSite interface, delegating all MenuSite operations to a default-implementation object.) Conceptually, this solution accomplishes the same thing as multiple inheritance. Since this delegation-based solution is in common use, you could call this architecture the Multiple Inheritance design pattern.

Here's the general form of the pattern:

```
interface Base
{   void f();

    static class Implementation implements Base
    {   public void f(){/*...*/}
    }
}


// Effectively extend both Something and Base.Implementation:

class Derived extends Something implements Base
{   Base delegate = new Base.Implementation();
    public void f()
    {   delegate.f();
    }
}
```

The implement/delegate idiom, like inheritance, has the benefit of not having to write the base-class code more than once. I'm using encapsulation of a default version rather than derivation from that default version to achieve that end. On the downside, I have to access the default implementation through a trivial accessor method in the encapsulating class, such as the one on the first line in f(), above. Similarly, the MonitorableStack.push(...) method (on line 41 of Listing 2-1) has to call the equivalent method in SimpleStack. Programmers grumble about having to write these one-liners, but writing an extra line of code is a trivial price to pay for eliminating a fragile base class. C++ programmers will also note that the implement/delegate idiom eliminates all of C++'s multiple-inheritance-related problems (such as implementation ambiguity).

Frameworks

A discussion of fragile base classes wouldn't be complete without a mention of framework-based programming. Frameworks such as Microsoft's Foundation Class (MFC) library have become a popular way of building class libraries. Though MFC itself is mercifully fading away, the structure of MFC has been entombed in countless Microsoft shops where the programmers assume that if Microsoft does it that way, it must be good.

A *framework* typically starts out with a library of half-baked classes that don't do everything they need to do; but, rather, they rely on a derived class to provide key functionality that's needed for the base class to operate properly. A good example in Java is the paint() method of the AWT Component class, which represents a rectangular area of the screen. Component defines paint(), but you're expected to override paint() in the derived class to actually draw something on the screen. The paint() method is effectively a placeholder for the rendering code, and the real version of paint() must be provided by a derived class. Most frameworks are comprised almost entirely of these partially implemented base classes.

This derivation-based architecture is unpleasant for several reasons. The fragile-base-class issue I've been discussing is one of these. The proliferation of classes required to get the framework to work is an even more compelling problem. Since you have to override paint() to draw a window, each different window requires a derived class that overrides paint() to draw that window. You must derive a unique class from Component for every window that has to paint itself in some unique way. A program with 15 different windows may require 15 different Component derivatives.

One of my rules of thumb in OO estimation is that a class takes, on average, two to three weeks to fully implement in Java (including documentation and debugging) and longer in C++. The more classes you have, the longer it takes to write your program.

Here's another perspective on the proliferation-of-classes problem: The customization-via-derivation strategy just doesn't work if the hierarchy is at all deep. Consider the class hierarchy in Figure 2-1. The Editor class handles basic text manipulation. It accepts keystrokes and modifies an internal buffer in response to those keystrokes. The actual buffer update is performed by the (protected) updateBuffer() method, which is passed keystrokes and updates the buffer appropriately. In theory, you can change the way that particular keystrokes are interpreted by overriding this method (Custom Editor in gray in Figure 2-1).

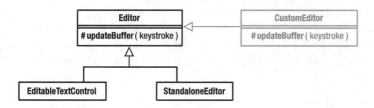

Figure 2-1. *A failure of Template Method*

Unfortunately, the new behavior is available to only those classes that extend Custom Editor, not to any existing classes that extend Editor itself. You'll have to derive classes from Editor, Editable Text Control, and Standalone Editor to get the new key mappings to be universally supported. You've doubled the size of this part of the class hierarchy. It would be nice to inject a class between Editor and its derivatives, but you'd have to change the source code to do that, and you may not have the source code. Design patterns such as Strategy, which I'll discuss later in this chapter and in Chapter 4, can solve this problem nicely, but a pure derivation-based approach to customization won't often work.

The Template-Method and Factory-Method Patterns

The updateBuffer() in Figure 2-1 is an example of the **Template-Method** pattern. In Template Method, base-class code calls an overridable placeholder method, the real implementation of which is supplied by the derived class. The base-class version may be *abstract*, or it may actually implement a reasonable default operation that the derived class will customize.

Template Method is best used in moderation; an entire class "framework" that depends on derivation-based customization is brittle in the extreme. The base classes are just too fragile. When I was programming in MFC, I had to rewrite all my applications every time

Microsoft released a new version. Often the code compiled just fine but didn't work anymore because some base-class method had changed. Template Method is not used in any of the code I supply in this book.

It's a telling condemnation of Template Method that most of the Java-library code works pretty well "out of the box" and that the Java libraries are more useful than MFC ever was. You can extend the Java classes if you need to customize them for an off-the-wall application, but they work just fine without modification for the vast majority of applications. This sort of it-works-out-of-the-box structure is just better than a derivation-based framework. It's easier to maintain, it's easier to use, and it doesn't put your code at risk if a vendor-supplied class changes its implementation.

Template Method is also an example of how fine the line between "idiom" and "pattern" can sometimes be. You can easily argue that the Template Method is just a trivial use of polymorphism and shouldn't be glorified by the exalted title of *pattern*.

One reason for discussing Template Method in the current chapter is that you can use a trivial variant of Template Method to create objects that instantiate an unknown concrete class. The **Factory-Method** pattern describes nothing more than a Template Method that creates an object whose concrete class isn't known to the base class. The declared return value of the Factory Method is some interface that the created object implements. Factory Method describes another way to hide concrete-class names from base-class code. (Factory Method is an unfortunate choice of name. People have a natural tendency to call any method that creates an object a *factory method*, but these creational methods are not the Factory-Method pattern.)

Swing's JEditorPane class provides an example of Factory Method that demonstrates both what's right and what's wrong with Swing. JEditorPane implements a text-control widget that can display HTML and, as such, is incredibly useful. For example, the following code pops up a frame that displays some simple HTML text:

```java
JFrame       mainFrame   = new JFrame();
JEditorPane pane         = new JEditorPane();

pane.setContentType ( "text/html" );
pane.setEditable    ( false );
pane.setText
(
    "<html>" +
    "<head>" +
    "</head>" +
    "<body>" +
        "<center><b>Hello</b> <i>World</i></center>" +
    "</body>" +
    "</html>"
);
mainFrame.setContentPane(pane);
mainFrame.setDefaultCloseOperation(JFrame.EXIT_ON_CLOSE);
mainFrame.pack();
mainFrame.show();
```

All you need do is set the content type to `"text/html"` to get the `JEditorPane` to interpret the tags for you.

The flip side of `JEditorPane` is that its underlying design is so complex that it's excruciating to change its behavior in even trivial ways. The problem I wanted to solve was client-side-UI layout. Swing's layout-manager mechanism can be difficult to use for laying out nontrivial UIs. Looking at Java's JavaServer Pages (JSP) system, I thought, "how nice it would be to do most of my layout in HTML but have a simple mechanism (such as JSP custom tags) to call in custom controls where I needed them." Essentially, I wanted a `Panel` whose layout could be specified in HTML (with custom tags). I called this class `MarkupPanel` because its layout could be specified with a markup language (HTML + custom tags).

I looked, first, at solving this problem by creating a custom `LayoutManager`, but I abandoned this approach for two reasons: I didn't want to build an HTML parser, and it was difficult to associate the `Component` objects that I dropped into the `Container` with specific locations in the HTML that specified the layout. I decided to create my panel by modifying the `JEditorPane`, which did most of what I wanted already, to support custom tags. Listing 2-2 shows a stripped-down version of the real `MarkupClass`. I've added support for a `<today>` tag, which displays today's date on the output screen, rather than implementing the generic mechanism I actually use. Even in its stripped-down form, you get a feel for the work involved in modifying the class to accept custom tags. It's not a pretty picture.

HTML parsing is done by something called an `EditorKit` that's used internally by the `JEditorPane`. To recognize a custom tag, you have to provide your own `EditorKit`. You do this by passing the `JEditorPane` object a `setEditorKit(myCustomKit)` message, and the most convenient way to do that is to extend `JEditorKit` and set things up in the constructor (Listing 2-2, line 15). By default the `JEditorKit` uses an `EditorKit` extension called `HTMLEditorKit`, which does almost all the necessary work.

The main thing you have to change is something called a `ViewFactory`, which the `JEditorKit` uses to build the visible representation of the HTML page. I've created an `HTMLEditorKit` derivative called `MarkupPanelEditorKit` that returns my custom view factory to the `JEditorPane` (Listing 2-2, line 21).

The `CustomViewFactory` (Listing 2-2, line 29) overrides a single method, `create()`. Every time the `JEditorPane` recognizes a new HTML element in the input, it calls `create()`, passing it an `Element` object that represents the element actually found. The `create()` method extracts the tag name from the `Element`. If the tag is a `<today>` tag (recognized on line 40), `create()` returns an instance of yet another class: a `View`, whose `createComponent()` method returns the `Component` that's actually displayed on the screen in place of the `<today>` tag.

Whew! As I said, Swing is not an example of simplicity and clarity in program design. This is an awful lot of complexity for an obvious modification. Swing's architecture is, I think, way too complex for what it does. One of the reasons for this overcomplexity is that someone went crazy with patterns without considering whether the resulting system was usable. I wouldn't disagree if you argued that Factory Method was not the best choice of patterns in the previous code.

Be that as it may, this code demonstrates an abundance of Factory Method reifications—the pattern is used thee times in an overlapping fashion.

Figure 2-2 shows the structure of the system. The design patterns are indicated using the *collaboration* symbol: a dashed oval labeled with the pattern name. The lines that connect to the oval indicate the classes that participate in the pattern, each of which is said to fill some *role*. The role names are standardized—they're part of the formal pattern description in the

Gang-of-Four book, for example. The roles taken on by some class are identified in UML by putting the names at the end of the line that comes out of the collaboration symbol.

Look at the first of the Factory Method reifications: By default, an HTMLEditorKit creates an HTMLEditorKit.HTMLFactory by calling getViewFactory() (the Factory Method). Markup-PanelEditorKit extends HTMLEditorKit and overrides the Factory Method (getViewFactory()) to return an extension of the default HTMLEditorKit.HTMLFactory class.

In this reification, HTMLEditorKit has the role of Creator. HTMLEditorKit.HTMLFactory has the role of Product, and the two derived classes, MarkupPanelEditorKit and CustomViewFactory, have the roles of Concrete Creator and Concrete Product.

Now shift focus and look at the classes and patterns from a slightly different perspective. In the second reification of Factory Method, HTMLEditorKit.HTMLFactory and ComponentView have the roles of Creator and Product. The Factory Method is create(). I extend HTMLEditorKit.HTML-Factory to create the Concrete Creator, CustomViewFactory, whose override of create() manufactures the Concrete Product: the anonymous inner class that extends ComponentView.

Now refocus again. In the third reification, ComponentView and the anonymous inner class have the roles of Creator and Product. The Factory Method is createComponent(). I extend ComponentView to create the Concrete Creator, the anonymous inner class, whose override of createComponent() manufactures the Concrete Product: a JLabel.

So, depending on how you look at it, HTMLEditorKit.HTMLFactory is either a Product or a Creator, and CustomViewFactory is either a Concrete Product or a Concrete Creator. By the same token, ComponentView is itself either a Creator or a Product, and so on.

Listing 2-2. *Using the Factory Method*

```
1   import java.awt.*;
2   import javax.swing.*;
3   import javax.swing.text.*;
4   import javax.swing.text.html.*;
5   import java.util.Date;
6   import java.text.DateFormat;
7
8   public class MarkupPanel extends JEditorPane
9   {
10      public MarkupPanel()
11      {   registerEditorKitForContentType( "text/html",
12                      "com.holub.ui.MarkupPanel$MarkupPanelEditorKit" );
13          setEditorKitForContentType(
14                      "text/html",new MarkupPanelEditorKit() );
15          setEditorKit( new MarkupPanelEditorKit() );
16
17          setContentType          ( "text/html" );
18          setEditable             ( false );
19      }
20
21      public class MarkupPanelEditorKit extends HTMLEditorKit
22      {
23          public ViewFactory getViewFactory()
```

```
24              {   return new CustomViewFactory();
25              }
26              //...
27          }
28
29          private final class CustomViewFactory extends HTMLEditorKit.HTMLFactory
30          {
31              public View create(Element element)
32              {   HTML.Tag kind = (HTML.Tag)(
33                              element.getAttributes().getAttribute(
34                                  javax.swing.text.StyleConstants.NameAttribute) );
35
36                  if(    kind instanceof HTML.UnknownTag
37                    && element.getAttributes().getAttribute(HTML.Attribute.ENDTAG)
38                                                                      ==null)
39                  {   // <today> tag
40                      if( element.getName().equals("today") )
41                      {   return new ComponentView(element)
42                          {   protected Component createComponent()
43                              {   DateFormat formatter = DateFormat.
44                                          getDateInstance(DateFormat.MEDIUM);
45                                  return new JLabel( formatter.format(;
46                                                      new Date() ) );
47                              }
48                          };
49                      }
50                  }
51                  return super.create(element);
52              }
53          }
54  }
```

If you're appalled by the complexity of this system, you're not alone. Factory Method is just a bad choice of architecture. It takes way too much work to add a custom tag, an obvious modification to any HTML parser. You'll see many other design patterns in subsequent chapters (such as Strategy) that would have been better choices.

If you're mystified by why things are so complex, consider that the Swing text packages are extraordinarily flexible. In fact, they're way more flexible than they need to be for any applications I've ever written. (I've been told there are actually requirements for this level of complexity in real programs, but I haven't seen it.) Many designers fall into the trap of making up requirements because something *may* have to work in a certain way (as compared to requirements actually demanded by real users). This trap leads to code that's more complex than it needs to be, and this complexity dramatically impacts the system's maintainability and ease of use.

In my experience, the degree of flexibility built into Swing is a bogus requirement—a "feature" that nobody actually asked for or needed. Though some systems indeed need to be this complex, I have a hard time even imagining why I would need the level of flexibility that

Swing provides, and the complexity increases development time with no obvious payback. In strong support of my claim that nobody needs to customize Swing to this degree is that nobody (who I know, at least) actually does it. Though you can argue that nobody can figure out *how* to do it, you can also argue that nobody has been lobbying for making customization easier.

I'll finish up with Factory Method by noting that the pattern forces you to use implementation inheritance just to get control over object creation. This is really a bogus use of extends because the derived class doesn't really extend the base class; it adds no new functionality, for example. This inappropriate use of the extends relationship leads to the fragile-base-class problem I discussed earlier.

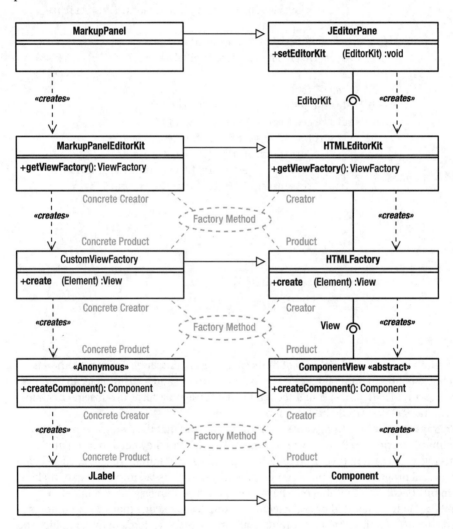

Figure 2-2. *Overlapping uses of Factory Method in* MarkupPanel

Summing Up Fragile Base Classes

I published an early version of parts of this chapter on JavaWorld, and I know from the responses there that many JavaWorld readers have discounted at least some of what I've just said because they've come up with workarounds for the problem. That is, you have a "solution" to the problem, so the issue is somehow invalid.

If that's the case, you're missing the point.

You should write your code so you don't need to even think about these sorts of "solutions." The problem with fragile base classes is that you are forced to worry about these sorts of "solutions" all the time, even after you think you have a debugged, functional class. No "solution" is permanent, since someone can come along and add a method to the base class that breaks all the derived classes. (Again, imagine that clear() wasn't part of the original ArrayList class but was added after you wrote the Stack class. The addition seemed harmless, but it broke your Stack implementation.) The only real solution to the adding-a-malicious-method problem is encapsulation.

If you've come up with a solution that works, great. My point is that that's what you should have done to begin with, and that many of the design patterns discussed later in this book are elegant solutions to the fragile-base-class problem. All the Gang-of-Four-design-pattern solutions depend on encapsulation and interfaces, however.

In general, it's best to avoid concrete base classes and extends relationships. My rule of thumb is that 80 percent of my code at minimum should be written in terms of interfaces. I never use a reference to a HashMap, for example; I use references to the Map interface. (I'm using the word *interface* loosely here. An InputStream is effectively an interface when you look at how it's used, even though it's implemented as an abstract class.)

The more abstraction you add, the greater the flexibility. In today's business environment, where requirements change regularly as the program is under development, this flexibility is essential. Moreover, most of the "agile" development methodologies (such as Crystal and Extreme Programming) simply won't work unless the code is written in the abstract. On the other hand, flexibility typically comes at a cost: more complexity. Swing, I think, can be improved by making it less flexible, which would make it simpler to program and easier to maintain. Trade-offs always exist.

If you examine the Gang-of-Four patterns closely, you'll see that a significant number of them provide ways to eliminate implementation inheritance in favor of interface inheritance, and that's a common characteristic of many patterns you find. By definition, successful design patterns are extracted from well-written, easy-to-maintain code, and it's telling that so much of this well-written, easy-to-maintain code avoids implementation inheritance like the plague.

Also bear in mind that extends is sometimes the best solution to a problem (see the next section). I know I've spent a lot of time arguing strongly against using extends, but that's not to say that implementation inheritance is never valuable. Use extends with care, however, and only in situations where the fragility issue is outweighed by other considerations. As is the case with every design trade-off, you should weigh both the good and the bad points of every alternative and choose the alternative that has the most going for it. Implementation inheritance is certainly convenient and is often the simplest solution to a problem. Nonetheless, the base class *is* fragile, and you can always get inheritance without extends by implementing an interface that defines methods that access a contained instance of a default implementation.

When *extends* Is Appropriate

Having thoroughly vilified the extends relationship, let's talk about when it's appropriate to use it.

One good use of extends is in class *normalization* (a term I've borrowed from database design). A normalized class hierarchy concentrates into base classes code that would otherwise be implemented identically in multiple derived classes. Let's explore this issue in some depth.

Though this book is not about the object-oriented design process, the way in which you go about producing a design can have a large effect on the quality of the result, and it's important to discuss the process, at least superficially, so that you can see how extends relationships end up in the model.

Bad designs tend to be created inside out. The designer starts by creating a towering edifice of a static model (a giant "class diagram") without any thought as to how those classes will actually be used in the actual program. The result is an ungainly mess—ten times larger than necessary, impossible to implement, and probably unusable without serious modification in the real program.

In practice, the class diagram should be little more than a convenient way of annotating information that you discover elsewhere in the design process. It's an artifact of the process, not a driving force. Done properly, OO design involves the following steps:

1. Learn the "problem domain" (accounting, order processing, and so on).

2. Talk to your users to figure out the problems they need to solve.

3. Identify use cases—stand-alone tasks performed by an end user that have some useful outcome—that cover all these problems.

4. Figure out the activities you need to do to accomplish the goals established in the use case.

5. Create a "dynamic model" that shows how a bunch of objects will send messages to one another at runtime to perform the activities identified in the previous step.

While you're modeling dynamically, create a class diagram that shows how the objects interact. For example, if an object of class A sends a message to an object of class B, then the class diagram will show an association between these classes and a "operation" in the class representing the receiving object.

Working this way, the static model is as lightweight as possible. It contains only those operations that are actually used in the design. Only those associations that need to exist actually exist.

So where does implementation inheritance (extends) come into the picture? It's often the case that you notice that certain kinds of objects use only a subset of the operations in a given class. Whenever you see a subset, you should think "normalization." All operations that are used by *all* the objects in the system should be defined in a common base class. All operations that are used by only a subset of the objects in a class should be defined in a class that extends that "normalized" base class. Adding derivation, then, is a design activity that occurs well into the design process, after you've done enough dynamic modeling that you can identify the common operations. It's a way of concentrating common operations into a shared base class. So, normalization is one quite reasonable use of implementation inheritance.

Now let's discuss the "is-a" relationship. Many books teach that you can use the phrase " is a" to recognize inheritance relationships. If you can say that "an employee *is a* manager," then the Manager class should derive from Employee. "Is a" works well when reading a class-hierarchy diagram. ("A HashSet 'is a' Collection.") It's not a great design tool, however.

Don't be thrown by the English language here. Simply because a real-world manager *is* an employee does not mean that you have Employee and Manager classes or that these classes have *any* relationship with each other in your model, much less an extends relationship. You could just as easily say that "this employee has management responsibilities" (which implies some sort of encapsulation) as say that "a manager is an employee" (which implies derivation).

I can think of several valid ways to associate Manager and Employee classes, but each way makes sense in only one context: If Employee and Manager do the same thing—have the same operations implemented in the same way—then they're really the same class. Employees could be distinguished from managers by how they're stored (the Employee objects in some list have managerial permissions), by an internal attribute, or by some other mechanism. Don't confuse an employee in a managerial role (in other words, an instance of Employee that's referenced by a variable called manager) with a Manager class.

If the two classes perform identical operations but do so differently, then there should be a common interface that each class implements. For example, Employee could be an interface that is implemented in different ways by both the Manager and Engineer classes.

If the two classes have no operations in common, then they are completely distinct, and no extends or implements relationship exists at all. For example, Employees may fill out time-sheets, and Managers may authorize them. No operations exist.[2]

If one of the classes adds a few operations to the other (a Manager does everything an Employee does, plus a bit), then extends may be appropriate.

The key to the inheritance structure is in the *operations* that are performed, whether these operations are shared, and so on.

The other issue affecting the should-I-use-extends decision is compile-time type checking. If you want the compiler to guarantee that certain operations can be executed only at certain times, then use extends. For example, if a Manager extends Employee, then you can't perform managerial operations in methods that are passed Employee objects. This restriction is usually a good thing, but if there's a reasonable default thing to do (nothing, for example), then it may make sense to dispense with the derivation and put a few empty methods in the base class. Simple class hierarchies are easier to build and maintain than complicated ones.

Of course, you could accomplish the same thing with interfaces. If a Manager was an Employee that implemented the Managerial interface, then you could pass around references to Managerial objects when appropriate and pass around Employee references when Managerial capabilities weren't needed. I'd probably decide (between extends and implements) by looking at the complexity of the two solutions, choosing the simpler one.

---

2. Don't confuse the object model with the physical users. It's reasonable for the same person to log on sometimes in the role of Manager and other times in the role of Employee. The object model concerns itself with the roles that the physical users take on, not with the users themselves.

I'll mention one caveat: You don't want any base-class methods that do nothing but throw exceptions. This practice moves compile-time errors into runtime and results in buggier programs. Sometimes the class hierarchy is simplified enough so that a runtime error is okay, but not often. For example, the methods of the various Java Collection classes that throw UnsupportedOperationException are reasonable, but only because it's unlikely you'll see this exception thrown once the code is debugged. (I've been told that the reason Unsupported-OperationException exists is that assertions weren't part of the language when the collections were designed, which is fair enough. To my mind, UnsupportedOperationException should extend AssertionError, since it's really identifying a problem that should be found at debug time.)

Getting Rid of *extends*

So let's say you're refactoring your system (improving its structure without changing its external behavior) and you notice that you need an interface where what you have now is a class. How do you do it?

Let's start from the beginning. Here's your existing class:

```
class Employee
{   //...
    public void youAreFired()
    {   // lots of code
    }
}
```

and there's a lot of code scattered through the system that looks something like this:

```
Employee fred = new Employee();
//...
fred.youAreFired();
```

Follow these steps:

1. Create an interface that has the same name as the existing class, like so:

   ```
   interface Employee
   {   void youAreFired();
   }
   ```

2. Rename the existing class, like so:

   ```
   class Peon implements Employee // used to be Employee
   {   public void youAreFired()
       {   // lots of code
       }
   }
   ```

Now comes the hard part. You need to change every place that you create an Employee using new. The obvious modification simply replaces new Employee() with new Peon(), but that change will put you in the same position you were in when you started. If you need to change the interface or class name again, you'll still have to go back and change a lot of code. You really want to get rid of that new altogether, or at least hide it.

Factories and Singletons

One good strategy for avoiding the must-change-all-new-invocations problem is to use the **Abstract-Factory** pattern, which is usually combined with a second creational pattern, **Singleton**, when it's implemented. Abstract Factory is something of a building-block pattern, since many other patterns rely on Abstract Factories for at least some of their implementation. I'll introduce the pattern now, and you'll see many applications of it in subsequent chapters.

The common theme to all reifications of Abstract Factory is that you use a Factory to create an object whose exact type you don't know. You *do* know the interfaces that the created object implements, but you don't know the created object's actual class. Listing 2-3 shows a workable example. (The UML is in Figure 2-3, though I don't expect you to understand this diagram fully yet.) Using the Employee.Factory, you can replace all calls to new Employee() with Employee.Factory.create(). Since the create() method can return an instance of any class that implements the Employee interface, your code is isolated from any knowledge of the implementation class. You can change this class to some other Employee implementer without affecting your code.

Listing 2-3. *A Workable Factory Implementation*

```
1  public interface Employee
2  {   void youAreFired();
3  }
4
5  public static class EmployeeFactory
6  {   private Factory(){/*empty*/}
7
8      public static Employee create()
9      {   return new Peon();
10     }
11 }
12
13 /*package*/ class Peon implements Employee
14 {   public void youAreFired()
15     {   // lots of code
16     }
17 }
```

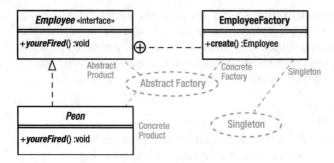

Figure 2-3. *Factory structure*

Note in Listing 2-3 that I've made the "concrete class" (Peon) package access to limit its scope. Since I expect users of the Peon to get instances via EmployeeFactory.create(), and I expect them to access the instances through only the Employee interface, no one needs to be able to access Peon at all.

I could restrict access to the concrete class even further by making it a private inner class of the factory, like this:

```
public static class EmployeeFactory
{   private EmployeeFactory(){/*empty*/}

    public static Employee create()
    {   return new Peon();
    }

    private static class Peon implements Employee
    {   public void youAreFired()
        {   // lots of code
        }
    }
}
```

Now, nobody (including classes in the same package as EmployeeFactory) can instantiate Peon objects directly.

It's also interesting to look at the following anonymous-inner-class version of the factory:

```
public static class EmployeeFactory
{   private Factory(){/*empty*/}

    public static Employee create()
    {   return new Employee()
        {   public void youAreFired()
            {   // lots of code
            }
        }
    }
}
```

In this version, the concrete-class name is so private that you—the programmer—don't even know what it is.

I'm just touching the surface of Abstract Factory for now. I'll explore this pattern a bit further later in the current chapter.

The other design pattern in Listing 2-3 is Singleton. A Singleton is a one-of-a-kind object; only one instance of it will ever exist. You must be able to access the Singleton globally, in the same way that you could call new globally. Anything that satisfies these two requirements (uniqueness [or at least a constrained number of instances] and global access) is a reification of Singleton. In the current example, the `Employee.Factory` object is a Singleton because it meets both conditions of the pattern.

It's often the case that Singleton is used to get an Abstract Factory, which is in turn used to get an object whose actual class is unknown. You'll see several examples of this melding of Singleton and Abstract Factory in the Java libraries. For example, the following returns a Singleton:

```
Runtime.getRuntime()
```

Here is another example from the java.awt package. In the following call, the `Toolkit.getDefaultToolkit()` call returns a Singleton implementer of the `Toolkit` interface:

```
ButtonPeer peer = Toolkit.getDefaultToolkit().createButton(b);
```

This `Toolkit` object is itself an Abstract Factory of objects that implements the `ButtonPeer` interface.

Returning to the UML diagram in Figure 2-3, you can see that `Employee.Factory` participates simultaneously in both Abstract Factory and Singleton.

Singleton

Now let's look at the patterns I just used in more depth, starting with Singleton.

Java has lots of Singletons in its libraries, such as the `Toolkit` object just described. Every time you call getDefaultToolkit(), you get the same object back. Although `Toolkit` is actually an abstract class, it's effectively an interface because you can't instantiate a `ToolKit` explicitly. The fact that methods are actually defined in the abstract class doesn't matter. It's functioning as an interface. You could, of course, create an interface made up of the abstract methods, implement that interface in a class, and then extend the class, but whether you use that approach or use an abstract class is really an implementation-level decision that doesn't impact the design at all.

Another example of Singleton is the following:

```
Runtime runtimeEnvironment = Runtime.getRuntime();
```

Again, every time you call getRuntime(), you get the same object back.

You'll look at lots of possible reifications of Singleton in subsequent chapters, but returning to the one in Listing 2-3, the easiest way to deal with the Singleton's global-access requirement is to make everything static. That way, I can say something such as `Employee.Factory.create()` to create an `Employee` without needing the equivalent of a static getRuntime() method.

The main point of confusion with the make-everything-static reification of Singleton is the illusion that there's no object, per se, only a class. In Java, though, the line between a class and an object is a fine one. A class comprised solely of static methods and fields is indistin-guishable from an object. It has state (the static fields) and behavior (you can send messages to it that are handled by the static methods). It's an object.

Moreover, the class actually *is* an object with a runtime presence: For every class, there's a *class object*—an implicit Class class instance that holds metadata about the class (a list of the class's methods, for example), among other things. In broad terms, the class object is created by the JVM when it loads the .class file, and it remains in existence as long as you can access or create objects of the class. The class object is itself a Singleton: There's only one instance that represents a given class, and you can access the instance globally through MyClassName.class or by calling Class.forName("MyClass"). Interestingly, in this particular reification of Singleton, many instances of the Class class exist, but they're all unique.

Returning to the code, the Employee.Factory Singleton in Listing 2-3 has one nonstatic method: a private constructor. Because the constructor is inaccessible, any attempts to call new Employee.Factory() kick out a compiler error, thereby guaranteeing that only one object exists.

Threading Issues in Singleton

The everything-is-static approach is nice, but it's not workable in many situations. If every-thing is static, you need to know enough at compile time to fully specify it. It's not often the case that you have this much information. Consider the Toolkit Singleton, which needs to know the operating system that the program is actually executing under in order to instantiate itself correctly.

Also, you don't have much reason to derive a class from an everything-is-static variant of Singleton since there are no overridable methods. If you anticipate that someone will want to use derivation to modify the behavior of (or add methods to) a Singleton, then you have to use the classic Gang-of-Four approach, discussed next.

It's often the case that the Singleton class is abstract and the runtime instantiation returned by createInstance() or the equivalent is an unknown class that extends the abstract class. Many possible classes could be derived from the Singleton class, each instantiated in different circum-stances. You can use the everything-is-static reification of Singleton only when you'll never want to derive a class from the Singleton—when there is only one possible implementation.

You can solve these problems with the "classic" Gang-of-Four implementation of Singleton, which allows for runtime initialization. The "classic" reification of Singleton looks like this:

```
1   class Singleton
2   {   private static Singleton instance = null;
3       public static instance()
4       {   if( instance == null )
5           {   instance = new Singleton();
6           }
7           return instance;
8       }
9       //...
10  }
```

Lots of threading issues are associated with classic Singletons, the first of which being accessor synchronization. The following will eventually happen in a multithreaded scenario:

1. Thread 1 calls instance(), executes test on line 4, and is preempted by a clock tick before it gets to new.

2. Thread 2 calls instance() and gets all the way through the method, thereby creating the instance.

3. Thread 3 now wakes up, thinks that the instance doesn't exist yet (it finished the test *before* it was suspended), and makes a second instance of the Singleton.

You can solve the problem by synchronizing instance(), but then you have the (admittedly minor) overhead of synchronization every time you access the Singleton. You *really* need to synchronize only once, the first time the accessor method is called.

The easy solution is to use a static initializer. Here's the general structure:

```
class Singleton2
{   private static Singleton instance = new Singleton();
    public instance() { return instance; }

    //...
}
```

The explanation of why static initializers work is actually pretty complicated, but the Java Language Specification guarantees that a class will not be initialized twice, so the JVM is required to guarantee that the initializer is run in a thread-safe fashion.

The only time the static-initializer approach isn't workable is when initialization information must be passed into the constructor at runtime. Consider a database-connection Singleton that must be initialized to hold the URL of the server. You need to establish the URL quite early, but you don't want to open the connection until you actually need it. For example, I could put the following in main(...):

```
public static void main( String[] args )
{   //...
    Connection.pointTo( new URL(args[i]) );
    //...
}
```

Elsewhere in the program, I get access to the connection by calling this:

```
Connection c = Connection.instance();
```

I don't want the connection to be opened until the first call to instance(), and I don't want to pass the URL into every call to instance(). I can't initialize the URL in a static initializer because I don't know what URL to use at class-load time.

I can solve the problem with a "classic" Gang-of-Four Singleton, like this:

```
class Connection
{   private static URL server;
    public static pointAt( URL server ){ this.server = server; }

    private Connection()
    {   //...
        establishConnectionTo( server );
        //...
    }

    private static Connection instance;
    public synchronized static Connection instance()
    {   if( instance == null )
            instance = new Connection();
        return connection();
    }
}
```

Double-Checked Locking (Don't Do It)

The main problem with the classic Singleton approach is synchronization overhead. The synchronized keyword does something useful only on the first call. Usually, this extra overhead is trivial, but it may not be if access is heavily contested.

Unfortunately, the "solution" to this problem that's used most often—called Double-Checked Locking (DCL)—*doesn't work* with JVM versions prior to 1.5. Listing 2-4 shows the idiom. Generally, you shouldn't use DCL because you have no guarantee that the JVM your program is using will support it correctly (it has been said that getting rid of double-checked locking is like trying to stamp out cockroaches; for every 10 you squash, 1,000 more are lurking under the sink.) My advice is this: if you come across a double-checked lock in legacy code, *immediately* replace it with solutions such as those discussed in the previous section.

Listing 2-4. *Double-Checked Locking*

```
 1  class DoubleChecked
 2  {   private static volatile DoubleChecked instance = null;
 3      private static Object lock = new Object();
 4
 5      public static DoubleChecked instance()
 6      {   if( instance == null )
 7              synchronized( lock )
 8              {   if( instance == null )
 9                      instance = new DoubleChecked();
10              }
11          }
12          return instance;
13      }
14  }
```

The intent of DCL in the context of a Singleton is to synchronize only during creation, when `instance` is `null`. You have to check twice because a thread could be preempted just after the first test but before synchronization completes (between lines 6 and 7 in Listing 2-4). In this case, a second thread could then come along and create the object. The first thread would wake up and, without the second test, would create a second object.

The reason why DCL doesn't work is complicated and has to do with the way with something called a *memory barrier* works in the hardware. Though DCL is intuitive, your intuition is most likely wrong. I've listed a few articles on DCL and why it doesn't work on the web page mentioned in the preface (`http://www.holub.com/goodies/patterns/`). It's been my experience that many programmers don't understand the DCL problem, even when they read about it. Every time I've written something on this subject, I've received dozens of messages from too-clever programmers who think they've come up with a solution. They're all wrong. None of these so-called solutions work. Please don't send them to me. The only universal solutions (which work across all JVMs) is either to synchronize the accessor or to use a static initializer.

Note, by the way, that Listing 2-4 should work correctly starting with Java version 1.5, running under Sun's HotSpot JVM, provided that you remember to include the `volatile` keyword in the `instance` declaration on line 2. DCL won't work with earlier versions of Java and probably won't work with other JVMs. It's best to avoid DCL altogether.

Killing a Singleton

The only topic left to discuss about Singletons is how to get rid of the things. Imagine a Singleton that wraps a global (outside-of-the-program) resource such as a database connection. How do you close the connection gracefully? Of course, the socket will be slammed shut when the program terminates; slamming the door closed is not exactly graceful, but it must be handled nonetheless.

First, let's look at what you *can't* do.

You can't send a `close()` message to the Singleton object, because you have no way to guarantee that someone won't need the Singleton after you've closed it.

You can't use a finalizer to clean up the resource. Finalizers just don't work. Finalizers are called only if the garbage collector reclaims the memory used by the object. You have absolutely no guarantee that a finalizer will ever be called. (It won't be called if the object is waiting to be reclaimed when the program shuts down, for example.) Finalizers are also nasty to use. They can slow down the garbage collector by an order of magnitude or more. The finalizer semantics have thread-related problems that make it possible for an object to be used by a thread after it has been finalized. My general advice about finalizer is: don't use them.

Java provides only one viable way to shut down a Singleton that uses global resources— the `Runtime.addShutdownHook(...)` method—and that method works only if the program shuts down normally.

A "shutdown hook" is an initialized, but dormant, thread that's executed when the program shuts down, after all the user threads have terminated. Memory referenced from the shutdown-hook object will not be garbage collected until the hook runs. Listing 2-5 shows the boilerplate code. The `objectClosed` (set on line 10 and tested in all the public methods) makes sure that an error is printed on the console window if someone tries to use the Singleton while shutdown is in progress.

Listing 2-5. *Shutting Down a Singleton*

```
1  class Singleton
2  {   private static   Singleton   instance      = new Singleton();
3          private volatile boolean    objectClosed = false;
4
5          private Singleton()
6          {   Runtime.getRuntime().addShutdownHook
7              (   new Thread()
8                  {   public void run()
9                      {   objectClosed = true;
10                         // Code that clean's up global resources
11                     }
12                 }
13             );
14
15             // Code goes here to initialize global
16             // resources.
17         }
18
19         public static Singleton instance()
20         {   return instance;
21         }
22
23         public void method()
24         {   if( objectClosed )
25                 throw new Exception("Tried to use Singleton after shut down");
26             //...
27         }
28 }
```

Note, by the way, that the `Runtime.getRuntime()` call on line 6 of Listing 2-5 is another example of a classic Gang-of-Four Singleton. It's a `static` method that creates an object the first time it's called and returns the same object every time it's called.

If you use the everything-is-static reification, establish the hook in a static-initializer block, as follows:

```
class StaticSingleton
{   static
    {   Runtime.getRuntime().addShutdownHook
        (   new Thread()
            {   public void run()
                {   // Code that cleans up global resources.
                }
            }
        );

        // Code goes here to initialize global resources.
    }
}
```

The shutdown hook isn't an ideal solution. It's possible for the program to be terminated abnormally (in Unix, with a `kill -9`, for example), in which case the hook never executes. If you register several shutdown hooks, all the shutdown hooks can run concurrently, and you have no way to predict the order in which they'll be started. It's possible, then, to have dead-lock problems in the hooks that hang the VM and prevent it from terminating. Finally, if you use a Singleton in a shutdown hook, you run the risk of creating a zombie Singleton that rises from the dead.

Abstract Factory

If you can remember back that far, I started out talking about Singleton working in concert with a second pattern, Abstract Factory, to create objects, so let's explore Abstract Factories a bit further. I'll present the classic reification now, but you'll see *lots* of this pattern in subsequent chapters.

The `Employee.Factory` object in Listing 2-3 (page 59) is a Singleton, but it's also a factory of Peon objects. The actual class of the object returned from `Employee.Factory.create()` is unknown to the caller—a requirement of the Abstract Factory pattern. All you know about the returned object is the interfaces that it implements (in this case, `Employee`). Consequently, you can modify the concrete Peon class at will—even change its name—without impacting any surrounding code.

Of course, changing the `Employee` interface in an "unsafe" way—removing methods or modifying method arguments, for example—is hard work. Adding methods to the interface is usually safe, however, and that's the downside of interface-based programming generally. You have to be careful when you're designing your interfaces.

If you look up Abstract Factory in Appendix A, you'll see that the `Employee.Factory` is not a classic reification (though it's probably the most commonplace variant). A good example of a classic Abstract Factory in Java is in the `Collection` class, which serves as an `Iterator` factory. Consider this code:

```
void g()
{   Collection stuff = new LinkedList();
    //...
    f( stuff );
}


void client( Collection c )
{   for( Iterator i = c.iterator(); c.hasNext() ; )
        doSomething( i.next() );
}
```

Not only is the product (the `Iterator`) abstract—in the sense that you don't know its actual class, only the interface it implements—but the iterator factory (the `Collection`) is abstract too. Listing 2-6 shows a stripped-down version of this system, and Figure 2-4 shows the associated UML. `Collection` and `Iterator` are both interfaces (which have the roles of

Abstract Factory and Abstract Product in the design pattern). Collection is an Abstract
Factory of things that implement Iterator, the Abstract Product. LinkedList has the role of
Concrete Factory, which is the class that actually does the creating, and it creates an object
that has the role of Concrete Product (some class whose name you don't know that implements the Iterator interface). Collection also demonstrates another characteristic of the
Abstract Factory pattern. Abstract Factories create one of a "family" of related classes. The
family of classes in this case is the family of iterators. A given abstract factory can create
several different Iterator derivatives depending on which Concrete Factory (data structure)
you're actually talking to at any given moment.

The main benefit of Abstract Factory is that the isolation it gives you from the creation
means you can program strictly in terms of interfaces. The client() method doesn't know that
it's dealing with a LinkedList, and it doesn't know what sort of Iterator it's using. Everything
is abstract. This structure gives you enormous flexibility. You can pass any sort of Collection
to client()—even instances of classes that don't exist when you wrote the client() method—
and client() doesn't care.

Listing 2-6. *A Classic Abstract Factory* (Collection)

```
 1   interface Collection
 2   {   Iterator iterator();
 3       //...
 4   }
 5
 6   interface Iterator
 7   {   Object next();
 8       boolean hasNext();
 9       //...
10   }
11
12   class Tree
13   {   public Iterator iterator()
14       {   return new Walker();
15       }
16
17       private class Walker implements Iterator
18       {   public Object    next()   { /*...*/ return null;  }
19           public boolean  hasNext(){ /*...*/ return false; }
20       }
21   }
```

Let's move back to the Factory object in Listing 2-3 (on page 59). It differs from the classic
reification in that it leaves out the Abstract Factory interface entirely (a commonplace variant
when the Factory is also a Singleton). Employee.Factory is the Concrete Factory. It still produces
an Abstract Product, however: the Employee derivative (Peon) is the Concrete Product.

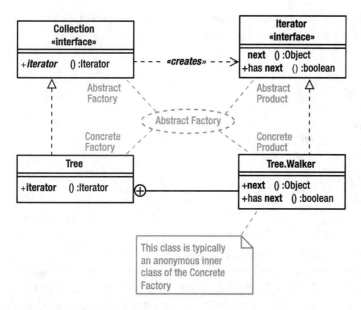

Figure 2-4. *Structure of a classic Abstract Factory* (Collection*)*

Let's fiddle a bit more with our solution and *really* make the product abstract. Consider this variation:

```
interface Employee
{   void youAreFired();

    public static class Factory
    {   private Factory(){ }

        static Employee create()
        {   return new Employee()
            {   public void youAreFired()
                {   // lots of code
                }
            }
        }
    }
}
```

I've simplified things (always good) by using an anonymous inner class rather than a named one. The anonymous-inner-class mechanism lets me leverage the language to enforce the Concrete-Product-is-unknown rule. *I* don't even know the actual name of the inner class. As before, the structure of the code has changed, but I still have a reasonable reification of Abstract Factory and Singleton. The structure of the system has only a loose correlation to the underlying pattern.

How about yet another variant? I don't like saying `Employee.Factory.create()`. I'd rather say `Employee.create()`, which is shorter. I can do that by changing the interface into an abstract class, like so:

```
abstract class  Employee
{   abstract void youAreFired();
    static Employee create()
    {   return new Employee()
        {   public void youAreFired()
            {   // lots of code
            }
        }
    }
}
```

This reification has a big disadvantage—it's a class, so it will use up the extends relationship. On the other hand, all the methods except create() are abstract, so you don't have a fragile-base-class problem. The fact that I've declared the class using abstract class rather than interface is just an implementation issue; from a design perspective, Employee is an interface, regardless of the syntax I use to declare the thing. One advantage to the abstract-class approach is that the Singleton-ness is enforced by the compiler, since new Employee() is illegal on an abstract class. It would certainly be nice if Java supported static methods in interfaces, but it doesn't.

This example demonstrates two main design-pattern issues. First, the classes you've been looking at reify two patterns simultaneously. Factory has two roles: Concrete Factory in the Abstract Factory pattern and Singleton in the Singleton pattern. That's two patterns in one class. Next, you've looked at several possible reifications, but they're all legitimate reifications of the same patterns. A tenuous connection exists between a pattern and the structure of the reification.

Pattern Stew

While we're on the subject of Abstract Factory, let's look at another interesting example from Java that illustrates the things-change-when-you-refocus issue I discussed in Chapter 1. Consider the following code, which dumps the main page of my web site to the console verbatim. (It doesn't interpret the HTML at all; it just prints it on the screen.)

```
URL url = new URL("http://www.holub.com/index.html");

URLConnection connection = url.openConnection();

connection.setDoInput(true);
connection.setDoOutput(false);
connection.connect();

InputStream in = connection.getInputStream();
```

```
int c;
while( (c = in.read()) != -1 )
{   System.out.print( (char)c );
}
```

The code in Listing 2-7 shows a simplified implementation of the classes used in this example. Figure 2-5 shows the associated UML.

Here you see two overlapping reifications of Abstract Factory. The URL class is a Concrete Factory of objects that implement URLConnection (the Abstract Product). The actual concrete class for the current example is HttpURLConnection (the Concrete Product). But in another context—if a different protocol were specified in the URL constructor, for example—the factory would produce a different derivative (FtpURLConnection, and so on). Since all possible Concrete Products implement URLConnection, the client code doesn't care what class is actually created. This reification is different from the one in the Gang-of-Four book in that it's missing an interface in the Abstract-Factory role.

Refocusing, the URLConnection is itself an Abstract Factory of InputStream derivatives. (InputStream is actually an abstract class, but it's always used as an interface.) In the current context, an InputStream derivative that understands HTTP is returned, but again, a different sort of stream (one that understands FTP, for example) would be returned in a different context. This reification is a classic reification of the Gang-of-Four pattern.

Listing 2-7. *A Stripped-Down* URLConnection *Implementation*

```
1   interface URLConnection
2   {   void setDoInput  (boolean on);
3       void setDoOutput (boolean on);
4       void connect     ();
5
6       InputStream getInputStream();
7   }
8
9   abstract class InputStream  // used as interface
10  {   public abstract int read();
11  }
12
13  class URL
14  {   private String spec;
15
16      public URL( String spec ){ this.spec = spec; }
17
18      public URLConnection openConnection()
19      {   return new HttpURLConnection(this);
20      }
21  }
```

```
22
23   class HttpURLConnection implements URLConnection
24   {   public HttpURLConnection(URL toHere) { /*...*/ }
25       public InputStream getInputStream()
26       {   return new InputStream()
27           {   public int read()
28               {   // code goes here to read using the HTTP Protocol
29                   return -1;
30               }
31           };
32       }
33
34       public void setDoInput  (boolean on)   { /*...*/ }
35       public void setDoOutput (boolean on)   { /*...*/ }
36       public void connect     (          )   { /*...*/ }
37   }
```

The main point of this exercise is to solidify the notion of focus. When you focus on the design in different ways, you see different patterns. In Figure 2-5, the URLConnecction class has two roles (Abstract Factory and Abstract Product), depending on how you focus. The overlapping combination of patterns, and simultaneous participation of a single class in multiple patterns, is commonplace.

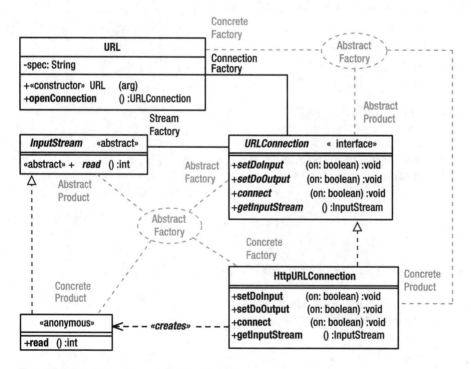

Figure 2-5. *Design patterns in* URLConnection

Dynamic Creation in a Factory

The URL/URLConnection system has another interesting facet. How does the URL object know which sort of URLConnection derivative to create? You could use code such as the following:

```java
public class URL
{   private String spec;

    public URL( String spec )
    {   this.spec = spec;
    }

    public URLConnection openConnection()
    {
        if     ( spec.startsWith("http:") ) return new HttpURLConnection();
        else if( spec.startsWith("ftp:") )  return new FtpURLConnection();
        //...
        else
            throw new IllegalArgumentException("Unknown Protocol");
    }
}

class     HttpURLConnection implements URLConnection { /*...*/ }
class     FtpURLConnection  implements URLConnection { /*...*/ }
interface URLConnection                              { /*...*/ }
```

The only problem with this approach is long-term flexibility. I'd like to be able to add support for new protocols without having to modify the existing code at all. In fact, I want to be able to add new protocols without even shutting down a running application. This sort of flexibility is particularly important in server-side applications, where you need to modify the server's behavior without *bouncing* it (shutting down and then restarting the server).

Java, fortunately, provides you with an easy solution to this problem. The code in Listing 2-8 uses dynamic creation to manufacture a class of the correct type. The first few lines of openConnection() create a string that holds a class name representing the connection. The class name is formed by extracting the protocol (everything to the left of the colon) in the URL specification, converting the first character of the protocol to upper-case, prefixing a package name, and appending the string "URLConnection". For example, given new URL("*xxx*://www.holub.com"), the openConnection() method manufactures the class name com.holub.protocols.*Xxx*URLConnection.

The openConnection() method then calls Class.forName() to create the class object for the class whose name you've just synthesized (an example of Singleton). Finally, openConnection() passes the class object a newInstance() message to instantiate an instance of the class (an example of Abstract Factory: Class has the role of Abstract Factory, the Class instance that represents the synthesized name is in the Concrete-Factory role, Object has the role of Abstract Product, and the created instance has the role of Concrete Product). Note that the created object must implement a known interface (URLConnection) for all this stuff to work.

Listing 2-8. *Dynamic Instantiation*

```
1   import java.io.IOException;
2
3   public class URL
4   {   private String spec;
5
6       public URL( String spec )
7       {   this.spec = spec;
8       }
9
10      public URLConnection openConnection() throws IOException
11      {
12          // Assemble the class name by prefixing a package
13          // and appending URLConnection to the protocol.
14          // The first character of the protocol is mapped to
15          // uppercase.
16
17          StringBuffer name   = new StringBuffer( "com.holub.protocols." );
18          String       prefix = spec.substring( 0, spec.indexOf(":"));
19
20          name.append( Character.toUpperCase(prefix.charAt(0)) );
21          name.append( prefix.substring(1) );
22          name.append( "URLConnection" );
23
24          String className = name.toString();
25
26          // Manufacture an object of the class whose name we just
27          // assembled:
28
29          try
30          {   Class factory = Class.forName( className );
31              return (URLConnection)( factory.newInstance() );
32          }
33          catch( Exception e )
34          {
35              // Throw an IOException whose message is the one
36              // associated with the exception that got us here.
37
38              IOException toThrow = new IOException();
39              toThrow.initCause( e );
40              throw toThrow;
41          }
42      }
43  }
44
```

```
45  class HttpURLConnection implements URLConnection
46  {   //...
47  }
48
49  class FtpURLConnection implements URLConnection
50  {   //...
51  }
52
53  interface URLConnection
54  {   //...
55  }
```

Another example of the same structure is Java's `Toolkit` Singleton, which uses dynamic creation to manufacture a `Toolkit` derivative that knows about the current operating environment. The `getDefaultToolkit()` method uses `System.getProperty(...)` to learn the operating-system name and then assembles an appropriate class name using that string.

The main advantage of the dynamic-creation strategy is that the name of the class that handles a protocol doesn't need to be known at runtime. If I need to add support for a new protocol, all I need do is create a class that implements `URLConnection` whose name starts with the protocol name. I then compile the class and move the .class file to the directory associated with the *com.holub.protocols* package. That's it. I'm done. No recompile. No server bounce. The next time the user specifies a URL for the new protocol, the server instantiates and loads the new class.

The main downside of dynamic creation is that it's difficult to pass arguments to the object's constructor. You can do that using the Introspection API methods of the `Class` class, but it requires a lot of complicated code that I don't want to go into here.

Command and Strategy

Another useful pattern for creating objects in an abstract way is **Strategy**, which is a specialization of the more general pattern **Command**.

Command is a building-block pattern upon which almost all the Gang-of-Four Behavioral patterns rely. You'll see many variants throughout the book.

The basic idea of Command is to pass around knowledge of how to do something by encapsulating that knowledge within an object. In C or C++, you'd pass around an algorithm by writing a function that implements the algorithm and then pass a *function pointer*—a syntactic mechanism that allows a programmer to call a function if the programmer knows the function's address—its location in memory. If you've programmed in C, you'll be reminded of the `qsort()` function.

You don't need function pointers in object-oriented systems, because you can pass around an algorithm by passing around an object that implements the algorithm. (Typically you'd pass an interface reference to the method that used the algorithm, and the method executes the algorithm by calling an interface method.)

One basic-to-Java use of Command is in threading. The following code shows a way to run a bit of code on its own thread that emphasizes the use of the Command pattern:

```
class CommandObject implements Runnable
{   public void run()
    {   // stuff to do on the thread goes here
    }
};


Thread controller = new Thread( new CommandObject() );
controller.start(); // fire up the thread
```

You pass the Thread object a Command object that encapsulates the code that runs on the thread. This way, the Thread object can be completely generic—it needs to know how to create and otherwise manage threads, but it doesn't need to know what sort of work the thread will perform. The controller object executes the code by calling run(). One of the main character-istics of the Command pattern is that the "client" class—the class that uses the Command object—doesn't have any idea what the Command object is going to do.

You can use Command, itself, in more sophisticated ways to solve complex problems such as "undo" systems. I'll come back to the pattern in Chapter 4. For now, I want to move on to a simple variant on Command: Strategy. The idea is simple: Use a Command object to define a strategy for performing some operation and pass the strategy into the object at runtime. You can often use Strategy instead of implementation inheritance if you're extending a class solely to change behavior.

Strategy is used all over the place in Java. Consider the array-sorting problem, as solved in the Arrays utility. You can sort an array into reverse order like this:

```
public void main( String[] args )
{
    // sort the command-line arguments:

    Arrays.sort
    (   args,
        new Comparator()
        {   public int compare( Object o1, Object o2 )
            {
                // By using a minus sign to reverse the sign
                // of the result, "larger" items will be
                // treated as if they're "smaller."

                return -( o1.compareTo(o2) );
            }
        }
    );
}
```

You pass into the sort method an object that defines a strategy for comparing two array elements. The sort method compares objects by delegating to the Strategy object. Listing 2-9 shows a Shell sort implementation that uses Strategy for comparison purposes. shellSort(...) delegates to the Strategy object on line 29.

Listing 2-9. *Sorters.java: Using Strategy*

```
1   package com.holub.tools;
2
3   import java.util.Comparator;
4
5   /** Various sort algorithms */
6
7   public class Sorters
8   {   /** A Straightforward implementation of Shell sort. This sorting
9        *   algorighm works in O(n<sup>1.2</sup>) time, and is faster than
10       *   Java's Arrays.sort(...) method for small
11       *   arrays. The algorithm is described by Robert Sedgewick in
12       *   <em>Algorithms in Java, Third Edition, Parts 1-4</em>
13       *   (Reading: Addison-Wesley, 2003 [ISBN 0-201-36120-5]), pp. 300-308,
14       *   and in most other algorithms books.
15       */
16
17      public static void shellSort(Object[] base, Comparator compareStrategy)
18      {   int     i, j;
19          int     gap;
20          Object  p1, p2;
21
22          for( gap=1; gap <= base.length; gap = 3*gap + 1 )
23              ;
24
25          for( gap /= 3;  gap > 0  ; gap /= 3 )
26              for( i = gap; i < base.length; i++ )
27                  for( j = i-gap; j >= 0 ; j -= gap )
28                  {
29                      if( compareStrategy.compare( base[j], base[j+gap] ) <= 0 )
30                          break;
31
32                      Object t    = base[j];
33                      base[j]     = base[j+gap];
34                      base[j+gap] = t;
35                  }
36      }
37
38      //...
39
```

```
40      private static class Test
41      {   public static void main( String[] args )
42          {
43              String array[] = { "b", "d", "e", "a", "c" };
44              Sorters.shellSort
45              (   array,
46                  new Comparator()
47                  {   public int compare( Object o1, Object o2 )
48                      {   // sort in reverse order
49                          return -( ((String)o1).compareTo((String)o2) );
50                      }
51                  }
52              );
53
54              for( int i = 0; i < array.length; ++i )
55                  System.out.println( array[i] );
56          }
57      }
58  }
```

Another good example of Strategy in Java is the LayoutManager used by java.awt.Container and its derivatives. You add visual objects to a container, which it lays out by delegating to a Strategy object that handles the layout. For example, the following code lays out four buttons side by side:

```
Frame container = new Frame();
container.setLayout( new FlowLayout() );
container.add( new Button("1") );
container.add( new Button("2") );
container.add( new Button("3") );
container.add( new Button("3") );
```

You can lay the buttons out in a two-by-two grid like this:

```
Frame container = new Frame();
container.setLayout( new GridLayout(2,2) );
container.add( new Button("1") );
container.add( new Button("2") );
container.add( new Button("3") );
container.add( new Button("3") );
```

If you were using implementation inheritance rather than Strategy, you'd have to have a FlowFrame class that extended Frame and did flow-style layout and another GridFrame class that extended Frame and did grid-style layout. Using the LayoutManager Strategy object (which implements the LayoutManager interface but doesn't extend anything) lets you eliminate the implementation inheritance and simplify the implementation.

Strategy provides a good alternative to Factory Method. Rather than use implementation inheritance to override a creation method, use a Strategy object use to create the auxiliary objects. If I were king, I would rewrite the JEditorPane to work like this:

```
interface ProxyCreator
{   JComponent proxy( String tagName, Properties tagArguments );
}


MyJEditorPane pane = new MyJEditorPane();
pane.setProxyCreator
(   new ProxyCreator()
    {   public JComponent proxy( Sting tagName, Properties tagArguments )
        {
            /** Return a JComponent that replaces the tag
            *  on the page
            */
        }
    }
);
```

MyJEditorPane would look like this:

```
public class MyJEditorPane
{   private ProxyCreator default =
        new ProxyCreator()
        {   public JComponent proxy( Sting tagName, Properties tagArguments )
            {
                /** Return a JComponent that replaces the tag
                *  on the page
                */
            }
        }

    public setProxyCreator( ProxyCreator creationStrategy )
    {   default = creationStrategy;
    }

    private void buildPage( String html_input )
    {   //...
        JComponent proxy = factory.proxy( tagName, tagArguments );
        //...
    }
}
```

Every time MyJEditorPane encounters a tag, it calls the ProxyCreator's proxy(...) method to get a JComponent to display in place of that tag. No implementation inheritance is required.

Summing Up

So, to sum up, as much as 80 percent of your code should be written in terms of interfaces, not concrete classes, to give you the flexibility you need to modify your program easily as requirements change. You've looked at the following patterns that help you create objects in such a way that you know the interfaces the object implements but not the actual class the object instantiates:

- **Singleton**: A one-of-a-kind object.

- **Abstract Factory**: A "factory" that creates a "family" of related objects. The concrete class of the object is hidden, though you know the interface it implements.

- **Template Method** A placeholder method at the base-class level that's overridden in a derived class.

- **Factory Method**: A Template Method that creates an object whose concrete class is unknown.

- **Command**: An object that encapsulates an unknown algorithm.

- **Strategy**: An object that encapsulates the strategy for solving a known problem. In the context of creation, pass the creating object a factory object that encapsulates the strategy for instantiating auxiliary classes.

Singleton, in particular, is deceptively simple. It's difficult to implement it correctly, and many reifications are in common use. You've also spent a lot of time looking at how the patterns merge and overlap in real code.

Of these four patterns, I don't use Template Method and Factory Method often because they depend on implementation inheritance with the associated fragile-base-class problems.

You'll look at other Creational patterns (to use the Gang-of-Four term) in context later in the book, but Singleton and Abstract Factory are used the most often. You'll see lots of different applications of both of these patterns.

CHAPTER 3

■ ■ ■

The Game of Life

This chapter provides an in-depth look at an implementation of John Conway's Game of Life—probably the most widely implemented application on the planet. You'll look at this particular program because my version applies ten distinct design patterns, all jumbled together as they are in the real world. At the same time, the program isn't so large as to be impossible to understand.

I can't really devote enough space in this chapter to give Life it's due, but reams have been written on the subject. I've set up a web page at http://www.holub.com/software/life/ that lists various links to Life resources and also provides an applet version of the game (written by Alan Hensel). You can find the source code for the implementation discussed in this chapter on the same web page.

I strongly recommend you play with the game before you continue; otherwise, a lot of what I'm about to talk about will be incomprehensible.

My implementation of Life uses the Java client-side GUI library (Swing) heavily, and I'm assuming some familiarity with that library. You don't need to be an expert Swing programmer, but I'm assuming you know the basics. If you've never used Swing, you should work through the Swing Tutorial on the Sun web site (http://java.sun.com/docs/books/tutorial/uiswing/).

This chapter has a lot of code in it. I don't expect you to read every line—I've called out the important stuff in the text. I'm often frustrated by books that don't show entire programs, however. It seems like the code I'm interested in is never there. Consequently, I've risked putting too much code in the text in order to show you the complete program. Feel free to skim if you're bored or overwhelmed by the sheer volume of the stuff.

Finally, the code in this chapter is toy code (not the case with the SQL interpreter in the next chapter, which is production code). Consequently, I let myself get rather carried away with the patterns. The point of the exercise it to learn how design patterns work, however, not to write the best possible implementation of Life.

Get a Life

Life is a simple cellular automaton like the ones discussed in Chapter 1. Among other things, Life models organic patterns of behavior—cell growth in a petri dish or embers in a fire, for example. It can also behave in interesting programmatic ways. You can, for example, make a Life game behave like a Turing machine (so in theory, it could mimic any computer.) An anthropologist friend of mine says that some of the patterns remind her of behavioral patterns within human societies. Life also demonstrates "emergent" behavior—the behavior of the system as a whole can't be predicted solely by looking at the behavior of the objects that comprise the system (and is much more interesting than the component-level behavior).

The standard game board is a large rectilinear grid. Each cell has eight neighbors.

1	2	3
8	●	4
7	6	5

A cell is either "dead" or "alive." You "seed" the game by marking cells as alive, and then you set things going. Two passes are made every time an internal clock ticks. In the first pass, the cells determine their next state by examining their neighbor's state. In the second pass, the cells transition to the previously computed state. Here are the rules:

- A dead cell comes alive when it has exactly three live neighbors. In the following examples, the cells containing black dots are alive, and the cells marked with hollow circles will come alive on the next tick.

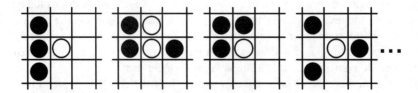

- A cell stays alive if it has exactly two or three neighbors. In the following examples, the cells containing black dots will stay alive.

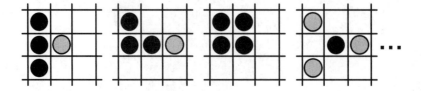

- Otherwise, the cell dies from either loneliness or overcrowding. In the following examples, the gray cells will die on the next tick (the example on the left from overcrowding, the others from loneliness).

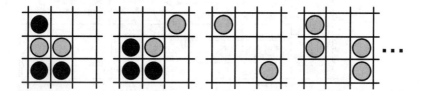

That's it. Not much in the way of rules, but depending on how it's seeded, the game board exhibits remarkable, very lifelike, behavior. The simplest example of interesting behavior is a *glider*, demonstrated by the following seed state (frame 1, on the left) and four subsequent game states. After the first two ticks (in frame 3), the glider has flipped itself symmetrically (along the diagonal axis) and moved itself down one row. After the fourth tick (frame 5), it flips back and moves over one column. It's now back in its original configuration but is offset diagonally by one cell from the starting position. Since the original configuration of cells is now restored, the pattern repeats indefinitely, and the group of cells glides toward the lower-right corner of the screen. When you look at the screen, you tend to think of the glider as an object that's moving across the board, but that's not what's going on at all. The real situation is just cells turning themselves on and off based on their neighbor's state. The cells have no notions at all of gliders or of what's happening on the board as a whole.

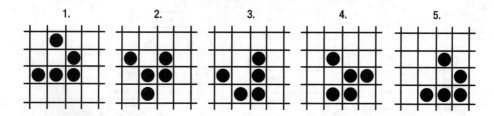

Hensel's Life applet at `http://www.holub.com/software/life/` demonstrates a bunch of interesting behaviors. Click the Empty Universe button and then click Open to open a catalog of preseeded Life games. The other buttons on the page bring up and run preseeded Life games that demonstrates a few of the more interesting patterns.

Charting the Structure of Life

I've sketched the static structure of my implementation of Life in Figure 3-1. Though I'd normally start designing with the dynamic model, I've found that when you're trying to understand (rather than design) an application, a good grasp of the static structure of the system is an important precursor to drilling into the messaging. I'll talk about the dynamic model as I drill into the patterns.

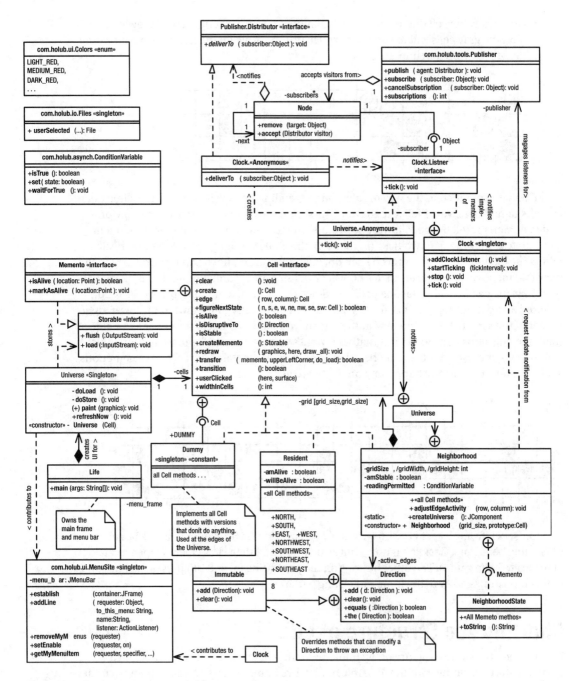

Figure 3-1. *The static structure of Life*

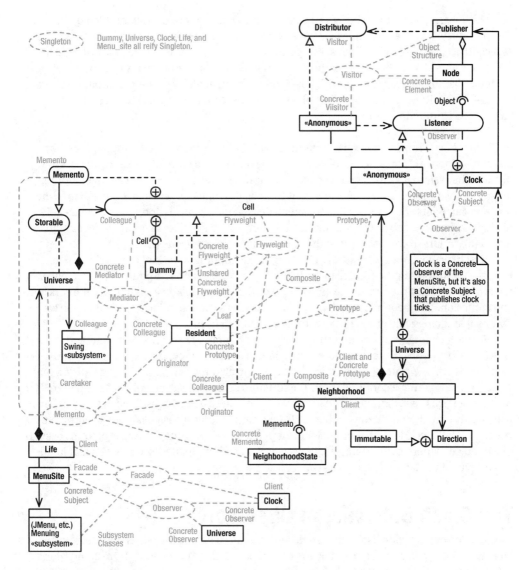

Figure 3-2. *The design patterns in Life*

Figure 3-1 shows a lot of classes, but I'll present them in small doses so you can see how they work together. Perhaps more interesting than the class diagram is Figure 3-2, which shows the static structure with the extraneous details stripped out and the main design patterns identified. I've put the interfaces into lozenges so that you can pick them out easily. I've also tried to keep the classes more or less in the same relative positions as they are in Figure 3-1, so you can correlate the two diagrams easily. You may want to bookmark these two diagrams; I'll be referring to them regularly. I call this variant of a class diagram a *patterns diagram*, which is not an official UML term. I find patterns diagrams to be quite useful in understanding a program's structure.

This diagram has a lot of design patterns—nine significant ones—all jumbled up in complicated ways. The Cell interface, for example, participates in four design patterns. The Neighborhood class participates in seven patterns! This is not the neat picture you'd expect from the Gang-of-Four book, but it represents the real world pretty accurately. Though Figure 3-2 looks like so much spaghetti, we'll take it one pattern at a time. (The real situation is even worse—I've omitted several "building-block" patterns from the diagram because it was already too cluttered.)

Don't panic.

When I first showed these diagrams to my wife Deirdre, who's also a programmer, her initial reaction was "that's so complicated I don't want to deal with it." Once we started going through the system, as I'll do with you as the chapter unfolds, her reaction changed to "this diagram is really rich." By "rich," she meant that the drawing conveys a lot of useful information in a compact form—it's dense. Density in design documents is good. A knowledgeable reader can glean an enormous amount from Figure 3-2 in a glance; this same information would take hours to convey without the vocabulary supplied by the patterns.

That transition, from "complicated" to "rich" is an important one and is typical of what happens when you start being able to apply the patterns with ease. The patterns let you make sense of the overall structure, so the appearance of complexity falls away along with the concomitant confusion. The incomprehensible becomes clear. As a client of mine once said, "I don't see how people can possibly program OO without a picture in front of them."

Figure 3-2 contains other interesting facets. For example, Flyweight, Composite, and Prototype (all in the middle of the figure) are almost identical structurally. The same three classes, along with their associated relationships, participate in all three patterns. If all you had was the static structure, you'd be confused, since the structure could indicate any of the three patterns, or perhaps none of them. Simply because you have a certain structure doesn't mean that you have a pattern. My point is one I made in Chapter 1—you can't identify a design pattern solely by static structure. You have to know the intent of the designer as well. Also, note how the patterns overlap. The notion of pattern cut-and-paste is nonsensical on its face—patterns just don't occur in the sort of splendid isolation that allows a clean paste operation.

The Clock Subsystem: Observer

Now let's look at the code itself. I'll start describing the classes at the edges of the system—looking at the ancillary pieces used by the core abstractions. These pieces form stand-alone subsystems, so they're easy to look at in isolation.

You'll see the clock subsystem in the upper-right corners of Figures 3-1 and 3-2. The first pattern it uses is **Observer**. Clock uses Observer to fire periodic clock-tick events at interested parties (in this case, the Universe via an anonymous inner class).

Observer is also used in Java's menuing system, which I'll need to talk about anyway, so I may as well cover it now. Figure 3-3 shows Java's menuing system.

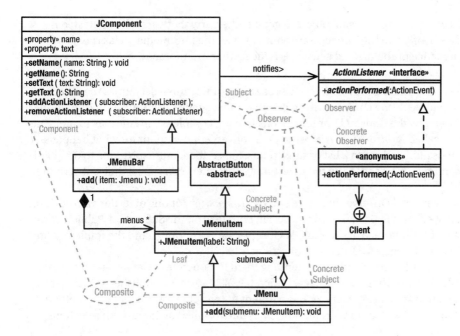

Figure 3-3. *Java's menuing subsystem (simplified)*

The main intent of Observer is to decouple an object that's interested in some event from the originator of that event. In the menuing system, the event occurs when you click a menu item, and whoever is interested in that event needs to find out when the item is selected.

The best way to see the notification-related problems that Observer solves is to look at the wrong way to do it: an implementation-inheritance based solution.

```
class BadJMenuItem
{   abstract void itemSelected();
}

class myMenuItem extends BadJMenuItem
{   public void itemSelected()
    {   // do whatever you'd do when the item is selected.
    }
}
```

This approach has two difficulties:

- You have to derive a class from BadJMenuItem for every menu item in the system, perhaps requiring hundreds of classes, all of which could be fragile.

- When a menu item is selected, you can notify only objects in the visual subsystem (in other words, BadJMenuItem derivatives). More often than not, the object that needs to be notified is some "business object" in the program, however. (In the case of Life, the Clock object needs to be notified when the user selects a new clock speed.) Passing the notification through a visual object to get it to the party that's actually interested is needless work, and the unnecessary complexity of the intermediary class creates a maintenance problem. I'll discuss this issue further in a moment.

Observer—the pattern the real JMenuItem uses for notification—decouples the object interested in the event (the Observer) from the object that sends the notification (the Notifier, called the *Subject* by the Gang of Four for reasons that are completely mysterious to me). This pattern is also called *Publish/Subscribe*, which is a convenient metaphor for what happens. A publisher sends publications to a list of subscribers. Subscribers must subscribe to the publications by sending a message to the publisher, and subscribers can cancel their subscription at any time.

In the reification of Observer in Figure 3-3, the JComponent (or one of its derivatives) is the Subject/Publisher. That is, JMenuItem or JMenu can both take on the Subject (or Publisher) role. The ActionListener interface has the role of Observer (or Subscriber), and the implementing class has the role of Concrete Observer/Subscriber.

A Subject publishes notifications by sending them to Concrete Observers as an argument to some method of the Observer interface. Concretely, a JComponent publishes actionEvents by sending them to ActionListeners as an argument to the actionPerformed(...) method.

Here's the code that sets up a simple Observer that's notified of menu-item selections:

```
class Subscriber implements ActionListener
{   public void actionPerformed(ActionEvent e)
    {   // do whatever you do when the menu item is selected.
    }
}
```

You "subscribe" like this:

```
JMenuItem lineItem = new JMenuItem("Foo");
//...
lineItem.addActionListener( new Subscriber() );

JMenuBar menuBar = new JMenuBar();  // add the item to the menu bar
menuBar.add( lineItem );
```

Thereafter, when the user selects the menu item, the Subject notifies the Concrete Observer by calling one or more of the methods in the Observer interface. In concrete terms, the JComponent (the publisher) sends notifications to the its ActionListeners (the subscribers) by sending each of them an actionPerformed() message. It's important to note that the menu bar on which the menu item resides is not involved in the notification process. Notifications go directly from the publisher to the subscriber. This way you don't need to create and maintain intermediary "mediator" objects that do nothing but relay messages.

The current JMenuItem subscriber is little more than a Command object (discussed in Chapter 2) that's passed into the Publisher, which invokes the methods of the Observer interface to send an event to a subscriber. The code that actually notifies the subscribers is encapsulated in the Command object.

The JComponent class implements the publication mechanism by keeping a list of subscribers. (Other reifications may implement the subscription mechanism in the Concrete

Subject, in which case JComponent could look more like the classic Gang-of-Four reification where the Subject is an interface.)

A more realistic example of Observer uses an anonymous inner class as the Concrete Subject/Subscriber.

```
class Client
{   volatile boolean menuItemSelected = false;

    public Client( JMenu topMenu )
    {   // Add an item to the topMenu, and arrange to be notified when it
        // is selected:

        JMenuItem myItem = new JMenuItem( "Hello" );
        myItem.addActionListener
        (   new ActionListener()
            {   public void actionPerformed( ActionEvent e )
                {   menuItemSelected = true;                // process selection
                }
            }
        );

        topMenu.add( myItem );
    }
}
```

This anonymous-inner-class version seemed, at first, pretty strange to me. Once I got used to the weird syntax, I came to prefer the anonymous-inner-class style because it lets me put all three parts of the Observer pattern (the publisher reference, the subscriber reference, and the activity to perform on publication) in one place. It's rather like a for statement, which lets you put all the parameters of loop control in one place.

Observer simplifies the code by passing the notification directly to the interested client, rather than through some visual intermediary.

Now let's apply the Observer pattern to Life. The Clock class, shown in Listing 3-1, uses Observer to notify a subscriber (the Universe object) of clock-tick events. The Clock has the role of Subject/Publisher. The Concrete Observer/Subscriber role is filled by any class that implements the Listener (Observer) interface (Listing 3-1, line 93). In this example, the Observer interface defines only one method (void tick()), but the pattern doesn't prohibit more complex interfaces.

The Universe object (the Concrete Observer/Subscriber) subscribes to the "tick" event like this:

```
Clock.instance().addClockListener
(   new Clock.Listener()
    {   public void tick()
        {   // code to handle a clock tick goes here
        }
    }
);
```

Clock is a Singleton, a reference to which is fetched by Clock.instance(). (The complete code from which the previous snippet is extracted is in Listing 3-7, which I'll discuss later in the chapter. If you want to skip ahead, the previous code is on line 1 of Listing 3-7, p. 142.)

The anonymous Clock.Listener derivative has the role of Concrete Observer/Subscriber. (In Figure 3-1, this anonymous Clock.Listener derivative is the one immediately to the left of the Clock class—the one that's connected to the Neighborhood indirectly via the Universe.)

It's actually arguable whether the Universe is the Concrete Observer or the anonymous inner class that actually receives the message is the Concrete Observer. Conceptually, it's the Universe, but physically, it's the inner-class object. In the UML, the inner-class-ness of the declaration is indicated by the circle with the plus in it, and the arrow indicates that messages are sent from the event handler object to the Universe object in the course of handling the tick.

As an aside, notice in the earlier code that Clock is a "classic" Gang-of-Four Singleton—only one instance of it exists, and it's accessed through a static accessor method that creates the instance (Clock.instance()). The private constructor (Listing 3-1, line 21) guarantees uniqueness, and the accessor method is declared on line 27. This Singleton can't be reified using the everything-is-static or the make-the-instance-reference-static mechanism because the clock constructor modifies the look of the menu bar, and the constructor cannot do that until the menu bar exists. When I tried to use one of the simpler reifications, I found that the Clock Singleton was being created too early, so the menu wasn't being set up properly. A "classic" Singleton solves the problem.

The Concrete Observer/Subscriber (the Universe instance) registers itself with the Publisher by calling addClockListener() (Listing 3-1, line 89), which delegates to an object of class Publisher, which we'll look at momentarily. The Universe object starts the clock by calling Clock.instance().startTicking(), and thereafter, the listener is notified at periodic intervals. (The tick() method of the registered listener is called.)

The tick management is handled by a java.util.Timer object declared on Listing 3-1, line 14. This is yet another example of Observer. The startTicking method on line 39 passes a scheduleAtFixedRate() message to a TimerTask object, whose run() method is called every time the timer "expires." This particular timer is set up to be recurrent, so it expires (and calls run()) at periodic intervals determined by the millisecondsBetweenTicks argument.

Listing 3-1. *Clock.java: The* Clock *Class*

```
 1   package com.holub.life;
 2
 3   import java.awt.*;
 4   import java.awt.event.*;
 5   import javax.swing.*;
 6   import java.util.*;
 7   import java.util.Timer;        // overrides java.awt.timer
 8   import com.holub.ui.MenuSite;
 9   import com.holub.tools.Publisher;
10
11   /**...*/
12
13   public class Clock
14   {   private Timer            clock        = new Timer();
```

```
15      private TimerTask        tick        = null;
16
17      // The clock can't be an everything-is-static Singleton because
18      // it creates a menu, and it can't do that until the menus
19      // are established.
20      //
21      private Clock()
22      {   createMenus();
23      }
24
25      private static Clock instance;
26
27      public synchronized static Clock instance()
28      {   if( instance == null )
29              instance = new Clock();
30          return instance;
31      }
32
33      /** Start up the clock.
34       *  @param millisecondsBetweenTicks The number of milliseconds between
35       *                         ticks. A value of 0 indicates that
36       *                         the clock should be stopped.
37       */
38
39      public void startTicking( int millisecondsBetweenTicks )
40      {   if(tick != null)
41          {   tick.cancel();
42              tick=null;
43          }
44
45          if( millisecondsBetweenTicks > 0 )
46          {   tick =  new TimerTask()
47                      {   public void run(){ tick(); }
48                      };
49              clock.scheduleAtFixedRate( tick, 0, millisecondsBetweenTicks);
50          }
51      }
52
53      public void stop()
54      {   startTicking( 0 );
55      }
56
57      private void createMenus()
58      {
59          // First set up a single listener that will handle all the
60          // menu-selection events except "Exit"
61
```

```
62            ActionListener modifier =
63                new ActionListener()
64                {   public void actionPerformed(ActionEvent e)
65                    {
66                        String name = ((JMenuItem)e.getSource()).getName();
67                        char toDo = name.charAt(0);
68
69                        if( toDo=='T' )
70                            tick();                        // single tick
71                        else
72                            startTicking(    toDo=='A' ? 500:        // agonizing
73                                             toDo=='S' ? 150:        // slow
74                                             toDo=='M' ? 70 :        // medium
75                                             toDo=='F' ? 30 : 0 ); // fast
76                    }
77                };
78
79        MenuSite.addLine(this,"Go","Halt",                    modifier);
80        MenuSite.addLine(this,"Go","Tick (Single Step)",modifier);
81        MenuSite.addLine(this,"Go","Agonizing",           modifier);
82        MenuSite.addLine(this,"Go","Slow",                modifier);
83        MenuSite.addLine(this,"Go","Medium",              modifier);
84        MenuSite.addLine(this,"Go","Fast",                modifier);
85    }
86
87    private Publisher publisher = new Publisher();
88
89    public void addClockListener( Listener observer )
90    {   publisher.subscribe(observer);
91    }
92
93    public interface Listener
94    {   void tick();
95    }
96
97    public void tick()
98    {   publisher.publish
99        (   new Publisher.Distributor()
100            {   public void deliverTo( Object subscriber )
101                {   ((Listener)subscriber).tick();
102                }
103            }
104        );
105    }
106 }
```

Implementing Observer: The *Publisher* Class

It turns out that Observer can be surprisingly difficult to implement, particularly in an environment such as Swing, where several threads may interact.

Swing notifications, such as menu-selection events, are processed on an "event" thread that's created by the Swing subsystem. Many Swing applications are single threaded in that main() does nothing but create a few windows and then terminate. All actual processing is done on the Swing event thread in response to some user input action. Nonetheless, I've worked on several systems where the main object model was running on the main thread (among others) and creating Swing user-interface elements on the fly. Since the Swing notifications are issued from the Swing event thread, Swing sends lots of asynchronous messages to the main object model at unpredictable times. Since the Swing code on the event-handler thread and the code on the main thread can access the same objects simultaneously, a collision is unavoidable unless you synchronize properly.

The Swing event thread is not directly accessible to you, so unless you add or remove subscribers in event handlers (possible but unlikely), it's possible for the subscriber list to be modified on a user thread while notifications are in progress on the Swing event thread. Since both threads are accessing the same subscriber list, you're in trouble.

Unfortunately, a publisher implementation such as the following just won't work in this environment.

```
class Publisher1
{   ArrayList subscribers = new ArrayList();

    public synchronized void subscribe( Runnable subscriber )
    {   subscribers.add( subscriber );
    }

    public synchronized void cancelSubscription( Runnable subscriber )
    {   subscribers.remove( subscriber);
    }

    private synchronized void fireEvent()   // notify all subscribers
    {   for( int i = 0; i < subscribers.size(); ++i )
            ((Runnable) subscribers.get(i) ).run();
    }
}
```

It's reasonable that the subscriber list be modified during notification, and the notification cycle could take some time. You don't know how long it will take for run() to run, since that code is provided by the client class. Locking the subscribe() method during the entire notification period may "starve" the thread that's trying to subscribe because notifications could happen one after the other, and the subscribing thread may never be able to get in.

If you remove the synchronization from fireEvent() to eliminate the "starvation," then you introduce an equally nasty problem. The fireEvent() method can execute on one thread while the subscribe() or cancel() method executes on a different thread. Without synchronization, it's possible for the list to be accessed in the middle of a modification, corrupting the subscribers list as a consequence.

Turning the tables, again, there's something to be said in favor of synchronizing every-thing. In an unsynchronized situation, if the subscribers you add while notifications are in progress are tacked onto the end of the list, the subscriber can be notified of an event that happened before it subscribed! The event happens, notifications start and are preempted, the new subscriber is added, and then the subscriber is notified. The synchronized version of fireEvent() doesn't have this problem.

So what's a mother to do? You have several approaches. The first is to use the Collection interface rather than a concrete-class name (which I had to do earlier to be able to call get()) and use an Iterator to traverse the list.

```
class Publisher2
{   private Collection subscribers = new LinkedList();

    public synchronized void subscribe( Runnable subscriber )
    {   subscribers.add( subscriber );
    }

    public synchronized void cancelSubscription( Runnable subscriber )
    {   subscribers.remove( subscriber);
    }

    private void fireEvent()
    {   for( Iterator i = subscribers.iterator(); i.hasNext(); )
            ((Runnable) i.next() ).run();
    }
}
```

I'm leveraging the fact that add(...) and remove(...) throw an exception if they're called while an iterations in progress. Therefore, attempts to register a listener while notifications are going on will result in an exception toss, and the thread that attempted to add the listener will have to try again later. This solution is obviously not ideal: it dumps too much work on the shoulders of the calling object.

Another approach uses copying.

```
class Publisher3
{   private Collection subscribers = new LinkedList();

    public synchronized void subscribe( Runnable subscriber )
    {   subscribers.add( subscriber );
    }

    public synchronized void cancelSubscription( Runnable subscriber )
    {   subscribers.remove( subscriber);
    }

    private void fireEvent()
    {   Collection localCopy;
```

```
        synchronized( this )
        {   localCopy = subscribers.clone();
        }

        for( Iterator i = subscribers.iterator(); i.hasNext(); )
            ((Runnable) i.next() ).run();
    }
}
```

I've used clone() to make a copy of the subscriber list. (I must synchronize while copying.) Then I notify the subscribers from the copy. Since the original list isn't used during notification, I can now modify that list without impacting the notification process. This approach solves the problems I've been discussing, but it introduces a few new ones.

First, it's possible for the publisher to notify a subscriber after the subscriber has canceled its subscription (because notifications are being made from the copy). This problem exists in all the Swing observers and is a problem with Observer generally. In practice, observers are rarely removed, so this problem is probably not worth solving. If you know that a notification can arrive after removal, then you can write the code defensively.

The second copying-related problem is worth putting some effort into. It's just unacceptable to make a copy every time an event is fired, which can be frequently. It's better to make copies only when subscribers cancel their subscriptions, which happens rarely in practice.

The Publisher class (Listing 3-3, later) solves the too-much-copying problem elegantly (if I do say so myself). Listing 3-2 shows an excerpt from the Clock class that shows you how it handles Observer. The addClockListener(...) method just delegates to the Publisher. The tick() method, which is called every time the clock "ticks," notifies all the observers. It does this by passing a Command object that actually does the notification to the Publisher. That is, the Publisher calls the Distributor() derivative's deliverTo() method multiple times, passing it a different subscriber on the list each time.

Because the Command object encapsulates the knowledge of how to notify an Observer, the Publisher can delegate the mechanics of notification to the Command object. The Publisher doesn't need to know how to actually notify subscribers.

The subscriber-specific information is in the Command object, not the Publisher. The Publisher manages the list of subscribers, and it knows that Distributor derivatives know how to notify subscribers, so the Publisher can delegate the notification process to the Distributor. This way, the Publisher doesn't need to know anything about the Clock.Listener interface.

Listing 3-2. *Implementing Observer with a* Publisher *Object*

```
1  private Publisher publisher = new Publisher();
2
3  public interface Listener
4  {   void tick();
5  }
6
7  public void addClockListener( Listener l )
8  {   publisher.subscribe(l);
9  }
10
```

```
11  public void tick()
12  {   publisher.publish
13        (   new Publisher.Distributor()
14            {   public void deliverTo( Object subscriber )
15                {   ((Listener)subscriber).tick();
16                }
17            }
18        );
19  }
```

Turning to Listing 3-3, the Publisher object maintains a linked list of subscribers. (The head-of-list reference is declared on line 117.) I've implemented the linked list myself rather than using the LinkedList class, primarily because LinkedList doesn't support operations I need (appending a list segment to another list, for example). My original implementation was actually built around LinkedList, but the implementation was large, messy, and hard to maintain. A singly linked list is trivial to implement in any event, and I saw no point in writing bad code solely to support an existing data-structure class.

Each node in the list is represented by an instance of the Node class (Listing 3-3, line 92), which holds references to the subscriber and the next Node in the list. The constructor both creates a new node and links that node into the list, at its head. I pass the constructor references to both the new subscriber and the current head-of-list pointer. The node puts itself at the head of the list by initializing its next reference to the old head reference. The subscribe() method (Listing 3-3, line 133) sets the head-of-list reference to the newly created Node object. All the fields of Node are final, so the Node is an "immutable" object. It cannot change once it's created. Consequently, it's safe for multiple threads to access a given Node object simultaneously with no need for synchronization.

The top part of Figure 3-4 shows the message flow (I'll discuss the bottom part of this figure in the "Implementing Observer: The *Publisher* Class" section). When an event occurs, the client class calls the publish() method on line 128. The publish() method just traverses the list from head to tail, asking each subscriber to "accept" the deliveryAgent Command object that was passed as an argument to publish(...).

Looking at the Node's accept(...) method (Listing 3-3, line 112), you'll see that all accept() does is ask the deliveryAgent to actually do the work of notification (by calling deliverTo(...)). The deliveryAgent actually notifies the subscriber that the event occurred. By using a Command object to hide the notification mechanics, I move those mechanics out of the Publisher itself, making it much more flexible. I'll have more to say on this issue in the next section.

As a design aside, since the Node class is an inner class of Publisher, you could argue reasonably that I should dispense with the accept() method entirely and modify the publish(...) method to invoke deliverTo directly, as follows:

```
public void publish( Distributor deliveryAgent )
{   for(Node cursor = subscribers; cursor != null; cursor = cursor.next)
        deliveryAgent.deliverTo( cursor.subscriber );
}
```

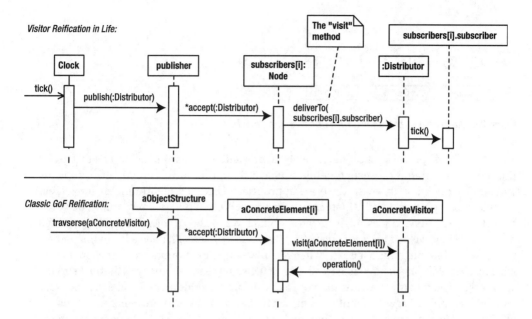

Figure 3-4. *The dynamic behavior of Visitor*

This change would simplify the code, but when I put on my designer hat, I don't like it that the Publisher object accesses a private field of Node (subscriber) as if it were public. Simply because Java permits this sort of back-door access of inner classes does not mean that it's a good thing—it strengthens the coupling relationships between the two classes unneces-sarily. I like to treat inner classes such as Node as if they were top-level classes with respect to access. If you do let an outer-class method violate the inner-class's declared access privilege, at least do it with your eyes open, knowing that you're trading off a bit of maintainability to trivially simplify the code. (Sometimes—when the inner class is effectively a C-like struct with no methods—direct access is reasonable. I'll permit myself to do this only when the inner class is declared private, however.)

Getting back to the publication process, remember from a few paragraphs back that Node objects are immutable—they can't be modified after creation—and new Node objects are inserted at the head of the list. The ramifications of this add-to-head-of-list strategy are signif-icant when notifications are in progress. Figure 3-5 shows the situation that occurs when one thread calls subscribe(d) just after another thread calls publish(...). The list is being modi-fied while notifications are in progress. The new node (in gray) was not in the list when publi-cation begins, so the first subscriber to be notified is c. All subscribers to the right of c are also notified as the Publisher traverses the list, but d may as well not be in the list, at least for the purposes of this particular notification. It's perfectly safe, then, to add nodes to the list while publication is in progress, and I haven't had to copy the list (or synchronize anything) to achieve this safety.

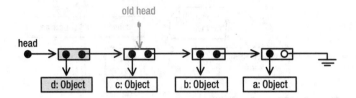

Figure 3-5. *Adding a subscriber while notifications are in progress*

The removal process is a bit more involved, primarily because I'm using a recursive algorithm. Many programmers seem to think recursive algorithms are inherently "bad" (opaque and inefficient), but in this case, the use is appropriate. Recursive algorithms are indeed hard to understand at times, but the inefficiency argument is often bogus. For example, because the list in the present code is singly linked, I would have to keep a stack of references to all the nodes that I have visited because once I find the node to delete, I'll need a list of that node's predecessors. Keeping this list is trivial in a recursive implementation—the list elements are just local variables in each recursive call. Doing the same thing manually with some sort of stack would use roughly the same memory as the recursive solution and make the code larger and more complex. I saw no point in using a mechanism that was more complex and no more efficient (at least in terms of space) than the recursive one simply to eliminate the recursion. I could also have solved the need-to-know-your-predecessor's-problem by making the list doubly linked, but that would also have added a bunch of unnecessary complexity. Figure 3-6 shows "before" and "after" pictures of the removal process. In the "before" image, I am removing node b (in gray). The bottom image shows what things look like after the remove. Interestingly, I have added two nodes but haven't actually removed anything. Any traversals that were in progress in the original list will continue as if nothing had happened, because nothing has happened to the original list. I've also moved the head pointer to the newly added far-left node. New traversals will begin at the new head-of-list reference, so they will not include the node I removed. Once any ongoing traversals complete, there will be no external references to any of the nodes in the dashed box, so they will all be garbage collected.

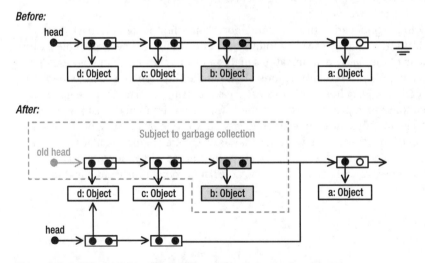

Figure 3-6. *Adding a subscriber while notifications are in progress*

Looking at the code, the recursion simplifies the code at the expense of clarity. The cancelSubscription() method (Listing 3-3, line 137) just delegates to the head-of-list node's remove() method (Listing 3-3, line 101). This recursive method first traverses down to the node to delete. It then starts returning back up to the original call. It does nothing with the node to delete, but as it returns it creates the new nodes for everything to the left of the deleted one and initializes the new nodes to point at the original subscribers.

Listing 3-3. *Publisher.java: A Subscription Manager*

```
1   package com.holub.tools;
2
3   /*********************************************************************
4    * This class replaces the Multicaster class that's described in
5    * <i>Taming Java Threads</i>. It's better in almost every way
6    * (It's smaller, simpler, faster, etc.). The primary difference
7    * between this class and the original is that I've based
8    * it on a linked-list, and I've used a Strategy object to
9    * define how to notify listeners, thereby making the interface
10   * much more flexible.
11   * <p>
12   * Publisher class provides an efficient thread-safe means of
13   * notifying listeners of an event. The list of listeners can be
14   * modified while notifications are in progress, but all listeners
15   * that are registered at the time the event occurs are notified (and
16   * only those listeners are notified). The ideas in this class are taken
17   * from the Java's AWTEventMulticaster class, but I use an (iterative)
18   * linked-list structure rather than a (recursive) tree-based structure
19   * for my implementation. The observers are notified in the opposite
20   * order that they were added.
21   * <p>
22   * Here's an example of how you might use it:
23   * <PRE>
24   *   class EventGenerator
25   * {   interface Listener
26   *     {   notify( String why );
27   *     }
28   *
29   *     private Publisher publisher = new Publisher();
30   *
31   *     public void addEventListener( Listener l )
32   *     {   publisher.subscribe(l);
33   *     }
34   *
35   *     public void removeEventListener ( Listener l )
36   *     {   publisher.cancelSubscription(l);
37   *     }
38   *     public void someEventHasHappend(final String reason)
```

```
39   *      {    publisher.publish
40   *           (    new Publisher.Distributor()
41   *                {    public void deliverTo( Object subscriber )
42   *                     {    ((Listener)subscriber).notify(reason);
43   *                     }
44   *                }
45   *           );
46   *      }
47   *  }
48   * </PRE>
49   * Since you're specifying what a notification looks like
50   * by defining a Listener interface, and then also defining
51   * the message passing symantics (inside the Distributor derivative),
52   * you have complete control over what the interface looks like.
53   
     . . .
74   */
75
76  public class Publisher
77  {
78      public interface Distributor
79      {   void deliverTo( Object subscriber );     // the Visitor pattern's
80      }                                            // "visit" method.
81
82      // The Node class is immutable. Once it's created, it can't
83      // be modified. Immutable classes have the property that, in
84      // a multithreaded system, access does not have to be
85      // synchronized, because they're read-only.
86      //
87      // This particular class is really a struct so I'm allowing direct
88      // access to the fields. Since it's private, I can play
89      // fast and loose with the encapsulation without significantly
90      // impacting the maintainability of the code.
91
92      private class Node
93      {   public final Object subscriber;
94          public final Node    next;
95
96          private Node( Object subscriber, Node next )
97          {   this.subscriber = subscriber;
98              this.next       = next;
99          }
100
101         public Node remove( Object target )
102         {   if( target == subscriber )
103                 return next;
104
```

```
105              if( next == null )                      // target is not in list
106                  throw new java.util.NoSuchElementException
107                                          (target.toString());
108
109              return new Node(subscriber, next.remove(target));
110          }
111
112          public  void accept( Distributor deliveryAgent ) // deliveryAgent is
113          {   deliveryAgent.deliverTo( subscriber );      // a "visitor"
114          }
115      }
116
117      private volatile Node subscribers = null;
118
119      /** Publish an event using the deliveryAgent. Note that this
120       *  method isn't synchronized (and doesn't have to be). Those
121       *  subscribers that are on the list at the time the publish
122       *  operation is initiated will be notified. (So, in theory,
123       *  it's possible for an object that cancels its subscription
124       *  to nonetheless be notified.) There's no universally "good"
125       *  solution to this problem.
126       */
127
128      public void publish( Distributor deliveryAgent )
129      {   for(Node cursor = subscribers; cursor != null; cursor = cursor.next)
130              cursor.accept( deliveryAgent );
131      }
132
133      public void subscribe( Object subscriber )
134      {   subscribers = new Node( subscriber, subscribers );
135      }
136
137      public void cancelSubscription( Object subscriber )
138      {   subscribers = subscribers.remove( subscriber );
139      }
140
141      //-------------------------------------------------------------------
142      private static class Test
143      {
144          static final StringBuffer actualResults   = new StringBuffer();
145          static final StringBuffer expectedResults = new StringBuffer();
146
147          interface Observer
148          {   void notify( String arg );
149          }
150
151          static class Notifier
```

```
152          {   private Publisher publisher = new Publisher();
153
154              public void addObserver( Observer l )
155              {   publisher.subscribe(l);
156              }
157
158              public void removeObserver ( Observer l )
159              {   publisher.cancelSubscription(l);
160              }
161
162              public void fire( final String arg )
163              {   publisher.publish
164                  (   new Publisher.Distributor()
165                      {   public void deliverTo( Object subscriber )
166                          {   ((Observer)subscriber).notify(arg);
167                          }
168                      }
169                  );
170              }
171          }
172
173          public static void main( String[] args )
174          {
175              Notifier source = new Notifier();
176              int     errors = 0;
177
178              Observer listener1 =
179                  new Observer()
180                  {   public void notify( String arg )
181                      {   actualResults.append( "1[" + arg + "]" );
182                      }
183                  };
184
185              Observer listener2 =
186                  new Observer()
187                  {   public void notify( String arg )
188                      {   actualResults.append( "2[" + arg + "]" );
189                      }
190                  };
191
192              source.addObserver( listener1 );
193              source.addObserver( listener2 );
194
195              source.fire("a");
196              source.fire("b");
197
198              expectedResults.append("2[a]");
```

```
199             expectedResults.append("1[a]");
200             expectedResults.append("2[b]");
201             expectedResults.append("1[b]");
202
203             source.removeObserver( listener1 );
204
205             try
206             {   source.removeObserver(listener1);
207                 System.err.print("Removed nonexistent node!");
208                 ++errors;
209             }
210             catch( java.util.NoSuchElementException e )
211             {   // should throw an exception, which we'll catch
212                 // (and ignore) here.
213             }
214
215             expectedResults.append("2[c]");
216             source.fire("c");
217
218             if( !expectedResults.toString().equals(actualResults.toString()) )
219             {
220                 System.err.print("add/remove/fire failure.\n");
221                 System.err.print("Expected:[");
222                 System.err.print( expectedResults.toString() );
223                 System.err.print("]\nActual:  [");
224                 System.err.print( actualResults.toString() );
225                 System.err.print("]");
226                 ++errors;
227             }
228
229             source.removeObserver( listener2 );
230             source.fire("Hello World");
231             try
232             {   source.removeObserver( listener2 );
233                 System.err.println("Undetected illegal removal.");
234                 ++errors;
235             }
236             catch( Exception e ) { /*everything's okay, do nothing*/ }
237
238             if( errors == 0 )
239                 System.err.println("com.holub.tools.Publisher: OKAY");
240             System.exit( errors );
241         }
242     }
243 }
```

The Clock Subsystem: The Visitor Pattern

Now let's refocus on the `Publisher` from the design-pattern perspective. The notion of passing to every node of some data structure a Command object that either uses or modifies that node is immortalized in the **Visitor** pattern.

Here are the roles that the various Life classes take on within the pattern:

- **Clock** is the Client.

- **Publisher** is the Object Structure.

- **Distributor** is the Visitor interface.

- **Node** is the contained Element.

- **Node.accept()** is the "accept" request.

- **deliverTo()** is the "visit" request.

- An anonymous **Distributor** derivative created by **Clock** is the Concrete Visitor.

Figure 3-4, which you looked at earlier, shows the UML for both the actual reification and the "classic" Gang-of-Four reification of Visitor. In the `Publisher` reification at the top of the Figure, an external "client" (the `Clock`) does something to or with the objects in some container (the `Publisher`) by passing a Visitor object (a class that implements `Distributor`) to that container. The container handles the traversal, asking each object to "accept" the visitor. The object then turns around and passes a "visit" method to each visitor, passing it an interface to itself or equivalent.

This reification has only one difference between it and the "classic" Gang-of-Four reification: The Visitor object in the "classic" version is passed a reference to the accepting Element, and the visitor then turns around and performs some operation on that Element. In other words, the visitor is passed a reference to the Element that it must access. Otherwise, the Visitor wouldn't know how to send messages to the Element. (If you can remember back that far, the Car-and-Map example in Chapter 1 uses the same strategy. In fact, a car is a Visitor to the Road Element.) In the `Publisher` reification, however, the `Node` Element exposes one of its fields (the `subscriber` reference) to the `Distributor` Visitor by passing it as an argument to the Visitor's `deliverTo(...)` method.

One other reification of Visitor needs mentioning. Instead of passing the Visitor a reference to the Element itself or passing the Visitor one or more fields of Element, you can pass the Visitor a reference to an interface that provides restricted access to the Element. In other words, the interface in the Element role can represent a subset of the interface to the actual object. This way the Element object can tightly control what the Visitor can do to it.

Another common extension involves heterogeneous lists. The `Publisher` class's Visitor interface (`Distributor`) is trivial, having only one method. If the Object Structure is heterogeneous, it's reasonable for the Visitor interface to implement several versions of the "visit" request, one for each Element type. It's also reasonable for the Element (the `Node`) to implement some interface so that the traversal code can be decoupled from the actual element type. For example:

```
interface Visitor
{   public visit( NodeType           aNode );
    public visit( AnotherNodeType    aNode );
    public visit( YetAnotherNodeType aNode );
}
```

This way the Concrete Visitor doesn't have to guess which possible node type it's dealing with.

Whew! That's pretty complicated. Fortunately, Visitor is as hard as it gets. Visitor is one of the most complicated—and hardest to understand—Gang-of-Four patterns, but it's pretty useful when applied correctly. Now that you, I hope, understand the mechanics, let's look at why I used Visitor at all.

Java has a class called AWTEventMulticaster that works a lot like the Publisher class. Using it, you can make a list of literally any listener that's supported by AWT. Here's how you'd implement a list of ActionListener objects:

```
public myComponent extends Component
{
    ActionListener subscribers = null;

    public synchronized void addActionListener(ActionListener subscriber)
    {   subscribers = AWTEventMulticaster.add(subscribers, subscriber);
    }

    public synchronized void removeActionListener(ActionListener subscriber)
    {   subscribers = AWTEventMulticaster.remove(subscribers, subscriber);
    }

    public void fire()
    {   if (subscribers != null)
            subscribers.actionPerformed(new ActionEvent(/*...*/));
    }
}
```

Here's how you'd implement a list of TextListener objects:

```
public myComponent extends Component
{
    TextListener subscribers - null;

    public synchronized void addTextListener(TextListener subscriber)
    {   subscribers = AWTEventMulticaster.add(subscribers, subscriber);
    }

    public synchronized void removeTextListener(TextListener subscriber)
    {   subscribers = AWTEventMulticaster.remove(subscribers, subscriber);
    }
```

```
   public void fire()
   {   if (subscribers != null)
           subscribers.textValueChanged(new TextEvent(/*...*/));
   }
}
```

The chameleon-like adaptability comes from AWTEventMulticaster implementing literally every listener interface supported by AWT and of course, implementing all the methods of every listener interface. That's a lot of work, it's hard to maintain, and the class carries around the baggage of implementing dozens of methods, only one of which is typically used in a given application.

The general problem that AWTEventMulticaster is trying to solve is how to implement a generalized event publisher where the various event handlers take arbitrary arguments and return arbitrary values. AWTEventMulticaster solves the problem by implementing all the event handlers that the designers could imagine, but that's a lot of work and requires modification of the original class if you need to add a handler that you didn't imagine.

Returning your thoughts to the Publisher, I am solving the same problem as the designers of AWTEventMulticaster. I want to be able to publish arbitrary events to arbitrary subscribers. I could apply the same kitchen-sink mentality to the Publisher by supporting a few generic interfaces. Here's one possibility that can handle three types of subscribers, each of which can handle a different number of arguments in the event-notification method:

```
class BruteForcePublisher
{
    Node head = null;

    interface Subscriber0
    {   public void eventFired();
    }
    interface Subscriber1
    {   public void eventFired(Object arg1);
    }
    interface Subscriber2
    {   public void eventFired(Object arg1, Object arg2);
    }

    class Node
    {   //...
        private Object  subscriber;
        private Node    next;

        public void fire()
        {   ((Subscriber0)subscriber).eventFired();
        }

        public void fire(Object arg1 )
        {   ((Subscriber1)subscriber).eventFired(arg1);
        }
```

```
        public void fire(Object arg1, Object arg2)
        {   ((Subscriber2)subscriber).eventFired(arg1,arg2);
        }
    }

    public void fire()
    {   for( Node current = head; current != null; current = current.next )
            current.fire();
    }

    public void fire(Object arg1)
    {   for( Node current = head; current != null; current = current.next )
            current.fire(arg1);
    }

    public void fire(Object arg1, Object arg2)
    {   for( Node current = head; current != null; current = current.next )
            current.fire(arg1, arg2);
    }
}
```

Even if you can stomach that all the arguments have to be declared as Object so can't be type checked, this solution has a lot of problems. What if I want to add a subscriber whose interface requires two methods? I'd have to add the following to my class definition:

```
class BruteForcePublisherV2
{
    //...

    interface Subscriber1x2
    {   public void event1Fired(Object arg1, Object arg2);
        public void event2Fired(Object arg1, Object arg2);
    }

    class Node
    {   //...
        public void fire2(  Object e1Arg1, Object e1Arg2,
                            Object e2Arg1, Object e2Arg2)
        {   ((Subscriber2)subscriber).event1Fired(e1Arg1, e1Arg2);
            ((Subscriber2)subscriber).event2Fired(e2Arg1, e2Arg2);
        }
    }

    //...

    public void fire( Object e1Arg1, Object e1Arg2,
                      Object e2Arg1, Object e2Arg2 )
```

```
    {    for( Node current = head; current != null; current = current.next )
             current.fire(e1Arg1, e1Arg2, e2Arg1, e2Arg2);
    }
}
```

In fact, every time I need to add another event type, I need to add a new interface and two methods to the class. This is way too much work.

To the rescue comes the Visitor pattern. The basic idea is that you often traverse collections of objects passing messages to the object that comprise the collection. In the current example, I'm traversing a list of subscribers, passing event notifications to each subscriber. The problem with this naive implementation is that I need to add a method to the data-structure element (the Node) every time I add a new event type to the system, but the odds of calling that particular method in a given chunk of code is small.

Visitor solves the problem with a Command object. The idea is to pass the Node a Command object (the Visitor) that understands how to notify a particular kind of listener. This way the Node doesn't have to support every possible listener type. You saw this process earlier in Listing 3-2.

The main downside of Visitor, other than its obvious complexity, is that the Visitor is external to the Node but nonetheless can modify or otherwise accesses what would normally be `private` components of the Node. This violation of encapsulation flies in the face of one of the central precepts of OO systems: data abstraction. A Visitor can access the Element strictly through a public interface, however, and I strongly recommend you do that whenever possible.

It's also difficult to maintain Visitor-based systems because changes to the Nodes require parallel changes in the Visitor interface and all its derivatives. It's exactly this rippling effect of a change that OO systems are designed to avoid. Use Visitor only when the interface is expected to be stable.

The Menuing Subsystem: Composite

Now let's move to the menuing subsystem in the lower-left corner of Figures 3-1 and 3-2 on pages 84 and 85.

The first pattern of interest in the menuing system is **Composite**. I'll explain how Composite is used now. You'll see how it's implemented in Life later.

Composite simplifies the management of a hierarchy of similar objects by letting a container treat everything that it contains identically, even if the contained objects are actually instances of different classes. If you look at a containment hierarchy as a kind of tree, the containers are the interior nodes.

Composite is used extensively in the current Life implementation, but Java's menuing system provides a scaled-down example, so let's start there. Figure 3-7 and Figure 3-8 show the two menus that my Life implementation supports, and Figure 3-9 shows the containment hierarchy for these menus. (Figure 3-9 also shows—in gray at the bottom—how you can hook a submenu into the system.)

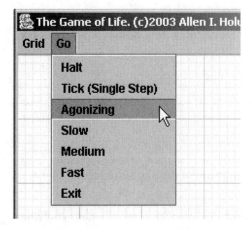

Figure 3-7. *Life's Go menu*

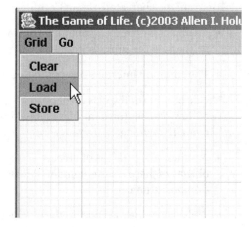

Figure 3-8. *Life's Grid menu*

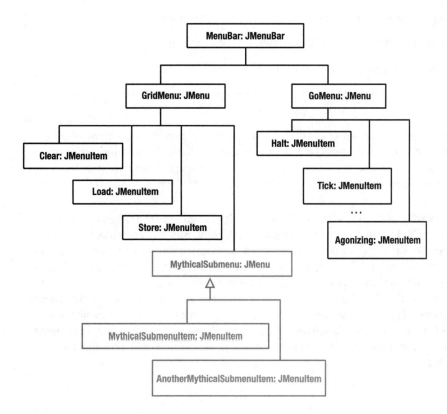

Figure 3-9. *The menu containment hierarchy*

Here are the characteristics of Composite:

- An object hierarchy is split up into two main classes of objects, both of which typically implement the same interface.

- The common interface serves the role of Component.

- One or more of the classes of objects in the hierarchy serve in the role of Leaf—objects of these classes form the leaves (terminate the branches) of the object tree. They don't contain anything.

- Another of the classes of objects in the hierarchy serve in the role of Composite— objects of these classes contain objects that implement the same interface as do the Composite objects.

- When you write the code for the Composite, you don't need to know whether a contained object is a Leaf or another Composite because you can access them through the interface they both implement. The code is much simpler to write as a consequence.

The following translates the general description to the menuing system:

- The menu hierarchy consists of JMenuItem and JMenu objects.

- The JMenuItem serves in the role of Leaf.

- The JMenu serves in the role of Composite. JMenu extends JMenuItem, so a JMenu is a JMenuItem.

- The programmers who wrote the code to handle menus don't need to know whether a menu item is a Leaf (a JMenuItem) or a Composite (a JMenu representing a submenu) because the two can be treated identically. That is, a menu can contain both JMenu and JMenuItem objects, but the JMenu can be treated as a JMenuItem.

This example differs from the "classic" Gang-of-Four example in that JMenuItem serves in two roles. It acts simultaneously as the Component interface and a Leaf node. In a "classic" reification, JMenuItem and JMenu would implement a common interface, and JMenu would not extend JMenuItem. Neither architecture is superior to the other; both are legitimate reifications of the pattern—two different ways to accomplish the same objective.

You'll notice that the AWT Component/Container hierarchy also satisfies these requirements so reifies Composite. Figure 3-10 shows the UML. A Container is a Component, as are all the leaf nodes, such as Button, that don't contain anything. A container can lay out its subcomponents without regard to their actual class, since all the subcomponents implement the (effective) Component interface.

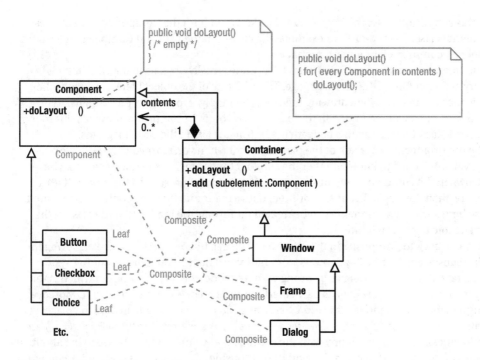

Figure 3-10. *The AWT component-container system*

A directory system is another a natural example of Composite. (A *directory* is a file that contains other files, including subdirectories. In Unix/Linux systems, a directory is literally a file, in fact. You can open it, read its contents, and so on.)

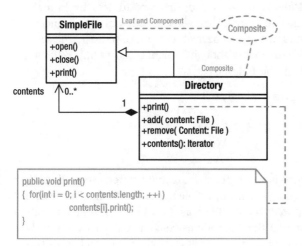

In this simple example, the SimpleFile class serves in both the Component and the Leaf roles. (In the "classic" Gang-of-Four example, the classes in the Leaf and Composite roles both implement a common Component interface.)

One common source of confusion with Composite is really obvious in the UML for a Directory at the bottom of the previous page. The structure of the object hierarchy inverts the class-hierarchy structure. When drawing the object hierarchy, a root node is a container, typically shown at the top of the tree, with the leaf nodes below it. In composite, however, this root node is a subclass, typically shown beneath the leaf-node class in the UML diagrams.

The important characteristic of the pattern is that when you're traversing a directory system, you don't need to know whether the subdirectories are files or subdirectories. The code shown in the comment, previously, just sends a print() message to the object. If it's a SimpleFile, then the single filename is printed. If it's a Directory, then its contents are printed. Because both sorts of components can be treated uniformly, the methods of the class in the Composite role are easy to write.

I'll come back to Composite in the context of Life in a bit, but let's continue exploring the menuing subsystem. Listing 3-4 demonstrates how you'd have to build the menuing system using the raw APIs. A lot of things can wrong with this code, the most obvious of which is that it's way too long. None of the code is particularly complicated, but there's a lot of it. Moreover, building a menu is a repetitive task, and when you build menus by hand all over the place, you have lots of repetitive code. ProtoUniverse.addMenus(...) and ProtoClock.addMenus(...) are almost identical. I'm also not happy with the clutter. I really don't want to be worrying about the details of the menu APIs when I'm working on "business" classes (classes that implement key design abstractions).

A more serious problem, from a design point of view, is that a ProtoUniverse is what's called a *key abstraction* of the design (a "business" object). Its characteristics are determined by the problem definition, and it's part of the user's mental model of the problem. ProtoClock and Neighborhood are also key abstractions. To say that a Neigborhood is a Frame or a Menu Contributor is nonsensical. You don't talk about your next-door "framers" (unless they're in the construction trade). You talk about your neighbors. Similarly, you don't say you live in a nice Menu Contributor; you live in a nice neighborhood. For derivation to make sense in a design, the subclass must be the same thing as the superclass, though it might behave a little differently.

The basic drill for adding a menu item is as follows:

```
JMenuItem item = new JMenuItem( "Visible Text" );
item.setName("someInternalName");
item.addActionListener( handlerToCallWhenItemSelected )
containingMenu.add( item );
```

The "name" you establish with setName is an arbitrary string that's stored internally in the JComponent. (All JComponents have one.) The name is not visible to the user at all. (The visible label—called the *text*—is either passed into the constructor, as shown here, or set with a call to setText()). The point of an internal "name" is that the visible text could change over time, but the internal name won't. I use the internal name, not the visible label, when I decide which menu item was selected (in the switch statement on line 65 of Listing 3-4, for example).

One thorny problem emerges when you look at the code in Listing 3-4 really closely. That cast on line 20 is ugly. I want to be able to create a UI at this level using the Composite pattern. A JFrame is a JComponent that holds other JComponents: I want to be able to treat all subwindows as JComponent objects. I need that cast to exercise the MenuContributor abilities of the ProtoUniverse, however. You should avoid casts generally—they're a source of runtime errors. Were JComponent an interface rather than a class, I could neatly solve the problem by changing the ProtoUniverse declaration to read as follows:

```
class ProtoUniverse extends JPanel
            implements Cell, JComponent, MenuContributor
```

But JComponent isn't an interface, so I'm stuck. I can't change the source code for AWT and Swing. This difficulty demonstrates why it's a good idea to use interfaces from Day One.

Another "solution" to the cast problem also doesn't work: Make MenuContributor an abstract class that extends JComponent to add a few methods, and then define all my references as references to this new class. The ProtoClock contributes to the menu but doesn't display a UI, however. I don't want a ProtoClock to carry around the literal and metaphorical baggage of a JComponent, so deriving it from JComponent is inappropriate.

Short of a major refactor of AWT/Swing, no ideal solution exists to this problem, so I'll just let the cast stand for now.

Listing 3-4. *Building a Menuing System with the Raw APIs*

```
1   import javax.swing.*;
2   import java.awt.*;
3   import java.awt.event.*;
4
5   interface MenuContributor
6   {   void addMenus( JMenuBar menuBar );
7   }
8
9   class Menus extends JFrame
10  {
11      public Menus()
12      {
13
14          JComponent       theUniverse   = new ProtoUniverse();
15          MenuContributor theClock       = new ProtoClock();
16          //...
17
18          JMenuBar menuBar = new JMenuBar();
19          theClock.                     addMenus( menuBar );
20          ((MenuContributor)theUniverse).addMenus( menuBar );
21
22          JMenuItem exit = new JMenuItem("Exit");
23          exit.addActionListener
24          (   new ActionListener()
25              {   public void actionPerformed(ActionEvent e)
26                  {   System.exit(0);
27                  }
28              }
```

```
29              );
30              menuBar.add(exit);
31
32              menuBar.setVisible(true);
33              setJMenuBar( menuBar );
34
35              getContentPane().add( theUniverse );
36              setDefaultCloseOperation( EXIT_ON_CLOSE );
37              pack();
38              setSize( 200, 200 );
39              show();
40          }
41
42      public static void main( String[] args )
43      {   new Menus();
44      }
45  }
46
47  class ProtoClock implements MenuContributor
48  {   //...
49
50      public void addMenus( JMenuBar menuBar )
51      {
52          JMenuItem halt = new JMenuItem("Halt");
53          JMenuItem slow = new JMenuItem("Slow");
54          JMenuItem fast = new JMenuItem("Fast");
55          //...
56
57          halt.setName( "halt" );
58          slow.setName( "slow" );
59          fast.setName( "fast" );
60
61          ActionListener handler =
62              new ActionListener()
63              {   public void actionPerformed(ActionEvent e)44
64                  {   String name = ((JMenuItem)e.getSource()).getName();
65                      switch( name.charAt(0) )
66                      {
67                      case 'h':   setClockSpeed( 0 ); break;
68                      case 'f':   setClockSpeed( 500 );   break;
69                      case 's':   setClockSpeed( 250 );   break;
70                      }
71                  }
72              };
73
74          halt.addActionListener( handler );
75          slow.addActionListener( handler );
```

```
76              fast.addActionListener( handler );
77
78              JMenu go = new JMenu( "Go" );
79              go.add( halt );
80              go.add( slow );
81              go.add( fast );
82
83              menuBar.add( go );
84          }
85
86      private void setClockSpeed( int speed )
87      {   System.out.println( "Changing speed to " + speed );
88      }
89  }
90
91  class ProtoUniverse extends JPanel implements Cell, MenuContributor
92  {   //...
93      public void addMenus( JMenuBar menuBar )
94      {
95          JMenuItem clear = new JMenuItem("Clear");
96          JMenuItem load  = new JMenuItem("Load");
97          JMenuItem store = new JMenuItem("Store");
98          //...
99
100         clear.setName( "clear" );
101         load.setName( "load" );
102         store.setName( "store" );
103
104         ActionListener handler =
105             new ActionListener()
106             {   public void actionPerformed(ActionEvent e)
107                 {   String name = ((JMenuItem)e.getSource()).getName();
108                     switch( name.charAt(0) )
109                     {
110                     case 'c':   clearGrid();    break;
111                     case 'l':   loadGrid(); break;
112                     case 's':   storeGrid();    break;
113                     }
114                 }
115             };
116
117         clear.addActionListener( handler );
118         load.addActionListener ( handler );
119         store.addActionListener( handler );
120
121         JMenu grid = new JMenu( "Grid" );
122         grid.add( clear );
```

```
123          grid.add( load );
124          grid.add( store );
125
126          menuBar.add( grid );
127
128     }
129
130     // stubs:
131
132     private void clearGrid(){ System.out.println("clear"); }
133     private void loadGrid() { System.out.println("load");    }
134     private void storeGrid(){ System.out.println("store"); }
135 }
136
137 interface Cell
138 {   //...
139 }
140
```

The Menuing Subsystem: Facade and Bridge

Now that you know how the underlying menuing system works, you're ready to look at the actual code (MenuSite.java in Listing 3-6, on page 123).

The MenuSite is an example of the **Facade** design pattern. The point of Facade is to make it easier to access a complex system via a simple one. The main problem with the raw menuing APIs I just discussed is that it's just too complicated to build a menuing system. You need to create lots of classes, nest them together properly, and hook up listeners. All this work does nothing but clutter up the code unnecessarily and make the code hard to maintain. The main point of the MenuSite Facade is to hide this complexity and let you build a menu with a few simple method calls.

This particular Facade also nicely solves a few OO-design issues. You'll remember (I hope) from Chapter 1 that it's best for objects to create their own user interfaces so as not to expose implementation information to a UI-builder object. Put another way, a screen in an object-oriented user interface is typically an aggregate of smaller user interfaces that individual objects in the system provide. This way, when you change an object's structure, you also change the way that it presents itself. If both the business and presentation logic are in the same class definition, then the scope of your change is limited to that class definition. You don't have to go out and find all the screen-builder classes and change them too.

Implementing this aggregate-UI structure can be vexing with any menuing system, which are typically treated procedurally as a monolithic object. It's reasonable, however, for an object to want to add menu items that are related to itself to the main menu bar. For example, Life's Clock class needs to add a menu that handles changes in clock speed. Nothing else in the system is particularly interested in that menu, so the Clock should create (and install) it.[1]

---

1. This user-interface architecture, by the way, is not Model/View/Controller. It's called Presentation/ Action/Control and is discussed in the book *A System of Patterns: Pattern-Oriented Software Architecture* by Buschmann, et. al. (John Wiley & Sons, 1996).

A great example of this sort of object structure is in Microsoft's Object-Linking-and-Embedding In-Place-Activation system. (I'm not particularly happy with the way that Microsoft implemented their architecture, but the concepts are solid.) When you want to put a numeric table into a Microsoft Word document, you select Insert:Object:Microsoft Excel Worksheet from the main menu. Word launches Excel, and the two programs negotiate how to share a common user interface. Word gives Excel a portion of the screen to work with (into which Excel puts its spreadsheet UI) and Excel puts menu items onto the main Word menu bar. While you're working on the spreadsheet, you're actually talking to the "Excel" object through a user interface created by that object. Excel also pops up various toolbars and other UI elements.

When you click outside Excel's window, the Excel object shuts down. Excel removes all its pop-up windows, removes from the menu bar any items that it added, and returns to Word an image to display in place of the Excel-generated user interface. Finally, Excel returns a "blob" of data to Word—a byte array that Word keeps for Excel until the next activation.

This "blob" of data is an example of the **Memento** pattern, which I'll discuss in greater depth later in this chapter. The data blob is the Memento, Excel is the Originator, and Word is the Caretaker. The point of Memento is that the Caretaker (Word) has no idea what's in the Memento—Word certainly can't manipulate the stored spreadsheet. The Caretaker (Word) just holds onto the Memento until the Originator (Excel) needs it again.

Returning to the UI issues, the Excel object creates its own user interface but integrates this UI into an existing framework UI managed by Word. OLE activation is a great example of object-oriented structure. Some high-level object owns the application's main frame and menu bar, but the actual UI is an aggregation of smaller user interfaces contributed by various objects in the system. The point of this structure is to isolate the objects' implementations from the rest of the system. When Microsoft comes out with a new version of Excel that has new UI requirements, it does not have to modify Word at all. The UI changes are concentrated in Excel itself. The same reasoning applies to smaller objects; when you need to make a structural change to the object that impacts the UI (such as adding a new clock speed), all the changes are concentrated in a single class definition (the Clock), and you don't need to change anything in the encapsulating program.

The *MenuSite*

The current Life implementation solves the menuing problem by using a class (MenuSite) that allows you to approach the menuing system in an object-oriented way. The point of the MenuSite class is twofold: to simplify the interface to the menuing system and to make it easy for objects to contribute to a shared menu bar. The notion of talking to an entire subsystem (or at least a group of related classes) through a single simple interface is embodied in the **Facade** design pattern. Facade provides a simple way to perform some task that would otherwise be complicated. It's perfectly reasonable to make a Facade that simplifies one aspect of what a subsystem does, but elsewhere in your code, you'd talk to the subsystem directly, without using the Facade. A Facade doesn't necessarily isolate you from changes to subsystem. Nonetheless, a Facade can provide this isolation if you're careful to access subsystem classes through only the

Facade. The Bridge design pattern (discussed in a subsequent chapter) can force subsystem isolation by prohibiting direct access to subsystem classes. That is, a Facade provides assistance with a subsystem while a Bridge isolates you from that subsystem completely.

Since the MenuSite interface is key, let's look at how to use it. You must first "bind" it to a top-level frame window. The Life class (Listing 3-5) does it on line 26 with the following method call:

```
MenuSite.establish( this );
```

The Life object does only two things: It creates the main frame and installs the MenuSite into it, and (on line 30) it creates the game board (the Universe) and installs it in the frame. It's often the case that an OO system's main() does nothing but create a few high-level objects, hook them together, and terminate. Remember, an OO system is a network of cooperating objects. There's no spider in the middle of the web pulling the strands. Put another way, there's no "god" class that controls the workings of the program.

Listing 3-5. *Life.java*

```
1   package com.holub.life;
2
3   import java.awt.*;
4   import javax.swing.*;
5   import com.holub.ui.MenuSite;
6
7   /*****************************************************************
8    * An implementation of Conway's Game of Life.
9    * @author Allen I. Holub
10   */
11
12  public final class Life extends JFrame
13  {
14      private static JComponent universe;
15
16      public static void main( String[] arguments )
17      {   new Life();
18      }
19
20      private Life()
21      {   super( "The Game of Life. "
22                      +"&copy;2003 Allen I. Holub <http://www.holub.com>");
23
24          // Must establish the MenuSite very early in case
25          // a subcomponent puts menus on it.
26          MenuSite.establish( this );
27
28          setDefaultCloseOperation  ( EXIT_ON_CLOSE        );
29          getContentPane().setLayout ( new BorderLayout()   );
30          getContentPane().add( Universe.instance(), BorderLayout.CENTER);
```

```
31
32          pack();
33          setVisible( true );
34      }
35  }
```

The MenuSite object is an everything-is-static Singleton. That means you can have only one menu bar in a program. I thought about allowing multiple menu bars, but the problem of finding a particular menu site turned out to be pretty complicated, so I took the easy way out. I'm willing to concede the point if you think my decision was too limiting.

Once the site is established, any object can add or remove menus by calling static methods. The Clock class's createMenus method (Listing 3-1, line 57, reproduced next) sets up the menus for the Clock object to use. The method starts by creating a single ActionListener object—a Concrete Observer that is shared by most of the line items on the menu. This particular observer starts up a java.util.Timer object at the speed indicated by the selected item:

```
ActionListener modifier =
    new ActionListener()
    {   public void actionPerformed(ActionEvent e)
        {
            String name = ((JMenuItem)e.getSource()).getName();
            char toDo = name.charAt(0);

            if( toDo=='T' )
                tick();                     // single tick
            else
                startTicking(    toDo=='A' ? 500:      // agonizing
                                 toDo=='S' ? 150:      // slow
                                 toDo=='M' ? 70 :      // medium
                                 toDo=='F' ? 30 : 0 ); // fast
        }
    };
```

The method then sets up the menus by calling MenuSite.addLine(...) several times (reproduced next). The first argument identifies the object that "owns" the menu item. The second argument specifies the menu to which the item is added. In this case, it's added to the Go menu on the main menu bar. Since no Go menu exists, The MenuSite automatically creates the new Menu and places it on the menu bar. The third argument is the "name" of this partic ular line item. (Menu items, like all Components, have both an invisible "name" and a visible "text" attribute. By default, the MenuSite uses the same string for both purposes.) The final argument is the Observer to notify when a user selects this menu item.

```
MenuSite.addLine(this,"Go","Halt",                modifier);
MenuSite.addLine(this,"Go","Tick (Single Step)",modifier);
MenuSite.addLine(this,"Go","Agonizing",           modifier);
MenuSite.addLine(this,"Go","Slow",                modifier);
MenuSite.addLine(this,"Go","Medium",              modifier);
MenuSite.addLine(this,"Go","Fast",                modifier);
```

It's not done here, but if the `Clock` object wanted to remove all the menu items that it added, it could call this:

`MenuSite.removeMyMenus(this);`

Similarly, the `Clock` can disable all the menu items it adds by calling this:

`MenuSite.setEnable(this, false);`

The point of this structure, again, is that it makes it easy for a particular object to manage only those menu items that it's interested in and for the rest of the system to not care about how a given object is using the menu. Table 3-1 shows the remainder of the documentation for `MenuSite`.

Listing 3-6 shows the entire source code for `MenuSite`. The implementation of this Facade doesn't have any design patterns, so I won't spend any time on it. (This isn't a book on GUI building, after all.) The main point of including the entire listing in this book is to demonstrate how much complexity the Facade is hiding. This complex mess would be in the midst of your code were the Facade not there. You'll find several pages of code that demonstrates how to use a `MenuSite` in the `MenuSite.Test.main(...)` method, starting on line 548 of Listing 3-6. If you want to skip the listing, turn to page 139.

Table 3-1. `MenuSite` *Documentation*

`public static void establish(JFrame container)`: Establishes a `JFrame` as the program's menu site. This method must be called before any of the other menu-site methods may be called. (Most of these will throw a `NullPointerException` if you try.)

`public static void addMenu(Object requester, String menuSpecifier)`: Creates and adds an empty menu to the menu bar. Menus are generally created by `addLine(...)`. This method is provided for situations where one requester creates a menu structure and other requesters add line items to this structure. The requesters that added the line items can remove those items without removing the menu that contained the items.

Menus are inserted on the menu bar just to the left of the Help menu. (The "help" menu [a menu whose name is the string help—case is ignored] is special in that it always appears on the far right of the menu bar.) Use `addLine(...)` to add line items to the menu. This method does the name-to-label substitution described in `addLine(...)`as well. As in `addLine(...)`, the name string also defines the (visible) label if no mapping is found.

If the requested menu already exists, this method silently does nothing.

Parameters:
  requester: The object that "owns" this menu. All menus (and line items) added by a specific requester are removed by a single `removeMyMenus(...)` call. The requester need not be the actual object that adds the menu—there may not be a single one—it is simply used to identify a group of menu items that will be removed in bulk. All items that have the same requester object are removed at once.

menuSpecifier: The menu to create. A simple specifier (with no colons in it) creates an item on the menu bar itself. Submenus are specified using the syntax main:sub. For example, the following call creates a New submenu under the File menu:

```
addMenu( this, "File:New" )
```

If the supermenu (in this example, File) doesn't exist, it's created. You can have more than one colon if you want to go down more than one level (for example, Edit:Text:Size). Up to six levels below the menu bar (six colons) are supported. (If you have more than that, you should seriously reconsider your menu structure.) Intermediate menus are added as necessary.

---

public static void addLine(Object requester, String toThisMenu, String name, Action-Listener observer): Adds a line item to a menu. The menu is created if it does not already exist. This method is the preferred way to both create menus and add line items to existing menus. See addMenu(...) for the rules of menu creation.

The name parameter is used for both the name and visible text, but you can specify text different from the name by calling addMapping(...) (which can also be used to define shortcuts).

Parameters:

requester: The object that requested that this line item be added.

name: The (hidden) name text for this item. When there's no name map (see addMapping(...)), the same string is used for both the name and the label; otherwise the name argument specifies the name only, and the associated label (and shortcut) is taken from the map.

Use the name "-" to place a separator into a menu. The listener argument is not used in this case and can be null.

toThisMenu: The specifier of the menu to which you're adding the line item. (See addMenu(...) for a discussion of specifiers.) The specified menu is created if it doesn't already exist.

listener: The ActionListener to notify when the menu item is selected.

---

public static void removeMyMenus(Object requester): Removes all items that were added by this requester. For the time being, the case of "foreign" items being placed on a menu created by another requester is not handled. Consider a program in which two objects both add an item to the File menu. The first object to add an item will be the official "owner" of the menu, since it created the menu. When you call removeMyMenus() for this first object, you want to remove the line item it added to the File menu, but you don't want to remove the File menu itself because it's not empty. Right now, the only solution to this problem is for a third requester to create the menu itself using addMenu(...)

---

continues

public static void setEnable(Object requester, boolean enable): Disables or enables all menus and menu items added by a specific requester. You can disable a single menu item by using this:

```
MenuSite.getMyMenuItem(requester,"parent:spec","name").setEnabled(false);
```

Parameters:

enable: Set this to true to enable all the requester's menu items.

---

public static JMenuItem getMyMenuItem(Object requester, String menuSpecifier, String name): Gets a menu item for external modification.

Parameters:

requester: The object that inserted the menu or item.

menuSpecifier: The menu specifier passed to the original addMenu(...) or addLine(...) call.

name: The name passed to addLine(...); should be null if you want a menu rather than a line item within the menu.

Returns:

The underlying JMenu or JMenuItem. Returns null if the item doesn't exist.

---

public static void mapNames(URL table) throws IOException: Establishes a "map" of (hidden) names to (visible) labels and shortcuts. Establishing a map changes the behavior of addLine(...) and addMenu(...) in that the specified ("text") label and shortcut are installed automatically for all names specified in the table. A map must be specified before the item named in the map are added to the menu site. You may call this method multiple times to load multiple maps, but the "name" component of each entry must be unique across all maps.

Parameters:

table: A Properties-style file that maps named keys to labels, along with an optional shortcut. The general form is as follows:

```
name1 = label One; C
name2 = label Two; Alt X
```

You can specify the shortcut in one of two ways. If it's a single character, as in the first example, the platform-default modifier is used. For example, in the first example, the shortcut will be a Ctrl+C in Windows, Command+C on the Mac, and so on. Otherwise, the shortcut specifier must take the form described in javax.swing.KeyStroke.getKeyStroke(String). For example:

- F1
- control DELETE
- typed a
- alt shift released X
- alt shift X

Names such as DELETE and F1 are shorthand for VK_DELETE and VK_F1. (You can find the complete set of VK_X constants in the java.awt.event.KeyEvent class.) You can use any of these "virtual" keys simply by removing the VK_.

F10 is hard-mapped to display the main menu (so that you can navigate the menus with the arrow keys, I assume). You could probably defeat this behavior with a key binding, but it's easier to just accept it as a fait accompli and not try to define F10 as a keyboard shortcut.

The input file is a standard Properties file, which is assumed to be ISO 8859-1 (not Unicode) encoded. ASCII works just fine, but see Properties.load(java.io.InputStream) for a full description of the file format.

---

public static void addMapping(String name, String label, String shortcut): Adds a name-to-label mapping manually. A mapping must be specified before the item is added to the menu site.

Parameters:

name: The menu-item name passed to addMenu(...) or addLine(...).

label: The visible label for that item.

shortcut: The shortcut, if any. Should be an empty string ("") if no shortcut is required. See mapNames(java.net.URL) for information on how to form this string.

Listing 3-6. *MenuSite.java*

```java
1   package com.holub.ui;
2
3   import java.io.*;
4   import java.util.*;
5   import java.util.logging.*;
6   import java.util.regex.*;
7   import java.net.*;
8   import java.awt.*;
9   import java.awt.event.*;
10  import javax.swing.*;
11
12  /**...*/
13
14  public final class MenuSite
15  {
16      private static JFrame      menuFrame  = null;
17      private static JMenuBar    menuBar    = null;
18
19      /**...*/
20      private static Map requesters = new HashMap();
21
22      /**...*/
```

```
23        private static Properties nameMap;
24
25        /**...*/
26        private static Pattern shortcutExtractor =
27                    Pattern.compile(
28                        "\\s*([^;]+?)\\s*"                // value
29                        +"(;\\s*([^\\s].*?))?\\s*$" );   // ; shortcut
30
31        /**...*/
32        private static Pattern submenuExtractor =
33                    Pattern.compile( "(.*?)(?::(.*?))?"
34                        + "(?::(.*?))?"
35                        + "(?::(.*?))?"
36                        + "(?::(.*?))?"
37                        + "(?::(.*?))?"
38                        + "(?::(.*?))?" );
39
40        /**...*/
41
42        private static final LinkedList menuBarContents =
43                                            new LinkedList();
44
45        /**...*/
46        private MenuSite()
47
48        /**...*/
49
50        private static boolean valid()
51        {   assert menuFrame != null : "MenuSite not established";
52            assert menuBar   != null : "MenuSite not established";
53            return true;
54        }
55
56        /**...*/
57        public synchronized static void establish(JFrame container)
58        {
59            assert container != null;
60            assert menuFrame == null:
61                            "Tried to establish more than one MenuSite";
62
63            menuFrame = container;
64            menuFrame.setJMenuBar( menuBar = new JMenuBar() );
65
66            assert valid();
67        }
68
69        /**...*/
```

```
70      public static void addMenu( Object requester, String menuSpecifier )
71      {   createSubmenuByName( requester, menuSpecifier );
72      }
73
74      /**...*/
75      public static void addLine( Object requester,
76                                  String toThisMenu,
77                                  String name,
78                                  ActionListener listener)
79      {
80          assert requester  != null: "null requester" ;
81          assert name       != null: "null item"      ;
82          assert toThisMenu != null: "null toThisMenu";
83          assert valid();
84
85          // The "element" field is here only so that we don't create
86          // a menu if the assertion in the else clause fires.
87          // Otherwise, we could just create the items in the
88          // if and else clauses.
89
90          Component element;
91
92          if( name.equals("-") )
93              element = new JSeparator();
94          else
95          {   assert listener != null: "null listener";
96
97              JMenuItem lineItem = new JMenuItem(name);
98              lineItem.setName( name );
99              lineItem.addActionListener( listener );
100             setLabelAndShortcut( lineItem );
101
102             element = lineItem;
103         }
104
105         JMenu found = createSubmenuByName( requester, toThisMenu );
106         if( found==null )
107             throw new IllegalArgumentException(
108                         "addLine() can't find menu ("+ toThisMenu +")" );
109
110         Item item = new Item(element, found, toThisMenu );
111         menusAddedBy(requester).add( item );
112         item.attachYourselfToYourParent();
113     }
114
115     /**...*/
116
```

```
117    public static void removeMyMenus( Object requester )
118    {
119        assert requester != null;
120        assert valid();
121
122        Collection allItems=(Collection)( requesters.remove(requester) );
123
124        if( allItems != null )
125        {   Iterator i = allItems.iterator();
126            while( i.hasNext() )
127            {   Item current = (Item) i.next();
128                current.detachYourselfFromYourParent();
129            }
130        }
131    }
132
133    /**...*/
134    public static void setEnable(Object requester, boolean enable)
135    {
136        assert requester != null;
137        assert valid();
138
139        Collection allItems = (Collection)( requesters.get(requester) );
140
141        if( allItems != null )
142        {
143            Iterator i = allItems.iterator();
144            while( i.hasNext() )
145            {   Item current = (Item) i.next();
146                current.setEnableAttribute(enable);
147            }
148        }
149    }
150
151    /**...*/
152
153    public static JMenuItem getMyMenuItem(Object requester,
154                                    String menuSpecifier, String name)
155    {
156        assert requester      != null;
157        assert menuSpecifier  != null;
158        assert valid();
159
160        Collection allItems = (Collection)( requesters.get(requester) );
161
162        if( allItems != null )
163        {   Iterator i = allItems.iterator();
```

```
164            while( i.hasNext() )
165            {   Item current = (Item) i.next();
166                if( current.specifiedBy( menuSpecifier ) )
167                {   if( current.item() instanceof JSeparator )
168                        continue;
169
170                    if( name==null && current.item() instanceof JMenu )
171                        return (JMenu)( current.item() );
172
173                    if(((JMenuItem)current.item()).getName().equals(name))
174                        return (JMenuItem) current.item();
175                }
176            }
177        }
178        return null;
179    }
180
181
182    //===============================================================
183    //          Private support methods and classes            |
184    //===============================================================
185
186    /**...*/
187    private static JMenu createSubmenuByName( Object requester,
188                                              String menuSpecifier )
189    {
190        assert requester != null;
191        assert menuSpecifier != null;
192        assert valid();
193
194        Matcher m = submenuExtractor.matcher(menuSpecifier);
195        if( !m.matches() )
196            throw new IllegalArgumentException(
197                                "Malformed menu specifier.");
198
199        // If it's null, then start the search at the menu bar;
200        // otherwise start the search at the menu addressed by "parent"
201
202        JMenuItem   child  = null;
203        MenuElement parent = menuBar;
204        String      childName;
205
206        for(int i=1; (childName = m.group(i++)) != null; parent=child )
207        {
208            child = getSubmenuByName(childName,parent.getSubElements());
209
210            if( child != null )
```

```
211                 {   if( !(child instanceof JMenu) ) // it's a line item!
212                         throw new IllegalArgumentException(
213                             "Specifier identifes line item, not menu.");
214                 }
215             else // it doesn't exist, create it
216             {
217                 child = new JMenu       (childName);
218                 child.setName          (childName );
219                 setLabelAndShortcut (child );
220
221                 Item item = new Item(child, parent, menuSpecifier );
222                 menusAddedBy(requester).add(item);
223                 item.attachYourselfToYourParent();
224             }
225         }
226
227         return (JMenu)child; // the earlier instanceof guarantees safety
228     }
229
230     /**...*/
231
232     private static JMenuItem getSubmenuByName( String name,
233                                         MenuElement[] contents )
234     {
235         JMenuItem found = null;
236         for( int i = 0; found==null && i < contents.length ; ++i )
237         {
238             // This is not documented, but the system creates internal
239             // pop-up menus for empty submenus. If we come across one of
240             // these, then look for "name" in the pop-up's contents. This
241             // would be a lot easier if PopupMenu and JMenuItem
242             // implemented a common interface, but they don't.
243             // I can't use a class adapter to make them appear to
244             // implement a common interface because the JPopupWindows
245             // are manufactured by Swing, not by me.
246
247             if( contents[i] instanceof JPopupMenu )
248                 found = getSubmenuByName( name,
249                             ((JPopupMenu)contents[i]).getSubElements());
250
251             else if( ((JMenuItem) contents[i]).getName().equals(name) )
252                 found = (JMenuItem) contents[i];
253         }
254         return found;
255     }
256
257     /**...*/
```

```
258
259    public static void mapNames(URL table) throws IOException
260    {   if( nameMap == null )
261            nameMap = new Properties();
262        nameMap.load( table.openStream() );
263    }
264
265    /**...*/
266
267    public static void addMapping( String name, String label,
268                                                    String shortcut)
269    {   if( nameMap == null )
270            nameMap = new Properties();
271        nameMap.put( name, label + ";" + shortcut );
272    }
273
274    /**...*/
275    private static void setLabelAndShortcut( JMenuItem item )
276    {   String name = item.getName();
277        if( name == null )
278            return;
279
280        String label;
281        if( nameMap != null
282                && (label= (String)(nameMap.get(name))) != null )
283        {
284            Matcher m = shortcutExtractor.matcher(label);
285            if( !m.matches() )  // Malformed input line
286            {
287                item.setText( name );
288                Logger.getLogger("com.holub.ui").warning
289                (
290                    "Bad "
291                    +"name-to-label map entry:"
292                    + "\n\tinput=[" + name + "=" + label + "]"
293                    + "\n\tSetting label to " + name
294                );
295            }
296            else
297            {   item.setText( m.group(1) );
298
299                String shortcut = m.group(3);
300
301                if( shortcut != null )
302                {   if( shortcut.length() == 1 )
303                    {   item.setAccelerator
304                        ( KeyStroke.getKeyStroke
```

```
305                        ( shortcut.toUpperCase().charAt(0),
306                          Toolkit.getDefaultToolkit().
307                                        getMenuShortcutKeyMask(),
308                          false
309                        )
310                     );
311                 }
312              else
313              {  KeyStroke key=KeyStroke.getKeyStroke(shortcut);
314                 if( key != null )
315                     item.setAccelerator( key );
316                 else
317                 {  Logger.getLogger("com.holub.ui").warning
318                    ( "Malformed shortcut parent specification "
319                       + "in MenuSite map file: "
320                       + shortcut
321                    );
322                 }
323              }
324           }
325        }
326     }
327  }
328
329  /**...*/
330  private static Collection menusAddedBy( Object requester )
331  {
332      assert requester  != null: "Bad argument"  ;
333      assert requesters != null: "No requesters" ;
334      assert valid();
335
336      Collection menus = (Collection)( requesters.get(requester) );
337      if( menus == null )
338      {   menus = new LinkedList();
339          requesters.put( requester, menus );
340      }
341      return menus;
342  }
343
344  /**...*/
345  private static final class Item
346  {
347      // private JMenuItem  item;
348      private Component  item;
349
350      private String      parentSpecification; // of JMenu or of
351                                                // JMenuItem's parent
```

```
352        private MenuElement parent;              // JMenu or JMenuBar
353        private boolean     isHelpMenu;
354
355        public String toString()
356        {   StringBuffer b = new StringBuffer(parentSpecification);
357            if( item instanceof JMenuItem )
358            {   JMenuItem i = (JMenuItem)item;
359                b.append(":");
360                b.append(i.getName());
361                b.append(" (");
362                b.append(i.getText());
363                b.append(")");
364            }
365            return b.toString();
366        }
367
368        /*-------------------------------------------------------------*/
369
370        private boolean valid()
371        {   assert item     != null : "item is null" ;
372            assert parent   != null : "parent is null" ;
373            return true;
374        }
375
376        /**...*/
377
378        public Item( Component item, MenuElement parent,
379                                        String parentSpecification )
380        {   assert parent != null;
381            assert parent instanceof JMenu || parent instanceof JMenuBar
382                            : "Parent must be JMenu or JMenuBar";
383
384            this.item            = item;
385            this.parent          = parent;
386            this.parentSpecification = parentSpecification;
387            this.isHelpMenu  =
388                    ( item instanceof JMenuItem )
389                && ( item.getName().compareToIgnoreCase("help")==0 );
390
391            assert valid();
392        }
393
394        public boolean specifiedBy( String specifier )
395        {   return parentSpecification.equals( specifier );
396        }
397
398        public Component item()
```

```
399          {   return item;
400          }
401
402          /**...*/
403
404          public final void attachYourselfToYourParent()
405          {   assert valid();
406
407              if( parent instanceof JMenu )
408              {   ((JMenu)parent).add( item );
409              }
410              else if( menuBarContents.size() <= 0 )
411              {   menuBarContents.add( this );
412                  ((JMenuBar)parent).add( item );
413              }
414              else
415              {   Item last = (Item)(menuBarContents.getLast());
416                  if( !last.isHelpMenu )
417                  {
418                      menuBarContents.addLast(this);
419                      ((JMenuBar)parent).add( item );
420                  }
421                  else    // remove the help menu, add the new
422                  {       // item, then put the help menu back
423                          // (following the new item).
424
425                      menuBarContents.removeLast();
426                      menuBarContents.add( this );
427                      menuBarContents.add( last );
428
429                      if( parent == menuBar )
430                          parent = regenerateMenuBar();
431                  }
432              }
433          }
434
435          /**...*/
436          public void detachYourselfFromYourParent()
437          {   assert valid();
438
439              if( parent instanceof JMenu )
440              {   ((JMenu)parent).remove( item );
441              }
442              else // the parent's the menu bar.
443              {
444                  menuBar.remove( item );
445                  menuBarContents.remove( this );
```

```
446                    regenerateMenuBar(); // without me on it
447
448                    parent = null;
449                }
450        }
451
452        /**...*/
453
454        public void setEnableAttribute( boolean on )
455        {   if( item instanceof JMenuItem )
456            {   JMenuItem item = (JMenuItem) this.item;
457                item.setEnabled( on );
458            }
459        }
460
461        /**...*/
462        private JMenuBar regenerateMenuBar()
463        {   assert valid();
464
465            // Create the new menu bar and populate it from
466            // the current content's list.
467
468            menuBar = new JMenuBar();
469            ListIterator i = menuBarContents.listIterator(0);
470            while( i.hasNext() )
471                menuBar.add( ((Item)(i.next())).item );
472
473            // Replace the old menu bar with the new one.
474            // Calling setVisible causes the menu bar to be
475            // redrawn with a minimum amount of flicker. Without
476            // it, the redraw doesn't happen at all.
477
478            menuFrame.setJMenuBar( menuBar );
479            menuFrame.setVisible( true );
480            return menuBar;
481        }
482    }
483
484    /**...*/
485
486    private static class Debug
487    {
488        public interface Visitor
489        {   public void visit(JMenu e,int depth);
490        }
491
492        private static int traversalDepth = -1;
```

```
493
494        /**...*/
495
496        public static void visitPostorder( MenuElement me, Visitor v )
497        {
498            // If it's actually a JMenuItem (as compared to a
499            // JMenuItem derivative such as a JMenu), then it's
500            // a leaf node and has no children.
501
502            if( me.getClass() != JMenuItem.class )
503            {   MenuElement[] contents = me.getSubElements();
504                for( int i=0; i < contents.length; ++i )
505                {
506                    if( contents[i].getClass() != JMenuItem.class )
507                    {   ++traversalDepth;
508                        visitPostorder( contents[i], v );
509                        if( !(contents[i] instanceof JPopupMenu) )
510                            v.visit((JMenu)contents[i], traversalDepth);
511                        --traversalDepth;
512                    }
513
514                }
515            }
516        }
517    }
518
519    /**...*/
520    public static class Test extends JFrame
521    {
522        static Test instance; // = new Test();
523        static boolean isDisabled1 = false;
524        static boolean isDisabled2 = false;
525
526        Test()
527        {
528            setSize( 400, 200 );
529            addWindowListener
530            (   new WindowAdapter()
531                {   public void windowClosing( WindowEvent e )
532                    {   System.exit(1);
533                    }
534                }
535            );
536            MenuSite.establish( this );
537            show();
538        }
539
```

```
540        //----------------------------------------------------------------
541        static class RemoveListener implements ActionListener
542        {   public void actionPerformed( ActionEvent e )
543            {   MenuSite.removeMyMenus( instance );
544            }
545        }
546        //----------------------------------------------------------------
547
548        static public void main( String[] args ) throws Exception
549        {
550            com.holub.tools.Log.toScreen("com.holub.ui");
551            UIManager.setLookAndFeel(
552                UIManager.getSystemLookAndFeelClassName() );
553
554            instance = new Test();
555
556            // Create a generic reporter.
557
558            ActionListener reportIt =
559                    new ActionListener()
560                    {   public void actionPerformed(ActionEvent e)
561                        {   JMenuItem item = (JMenuItem)(e.getSource());
562                            System.out.println( item.getText() );
563                        }
564                    };
565
566
567            // Create the File menu first.
568
569            ActionListener terminator =
570                new ActionListener()
571                {   public void actionPerformed( ActionEvent e )
572                    {   System.exit(0);
573                    }
574                };
575
576            // Make the file menu with its own ID so that the removal
577            // test in the main menu doesn't remove it.
578
579            Object fileId = new Object();
580            MenuSite.addMenu(fileId, "File" );
581            MenuSite.addLine(fileId, "File", "Quit", terminator);
582            MenuSite.addLine(fileId, "File", "Bye",  terminator);
583
584            // Now, make a few more menus.
585
586            MenuSite.addMenu(instance, "Main" );
```

```
587            MenuSite.addLine
588            (   instance, "Main", "Add Line Item to Menu",
589                new ActionListener()
590                {   public void actionPerformed( ActionEvent e )
591                    {   MenuSite.addLine(instance, "Main",
592                            "Remove Main and Help menus",
593                            new ActionListener()
594                            { public void actionPerformed(ActionEvent e)
595                                { MenuSite.removeMyMenus(instance);
596                                }
597                            }
598                        );
599                    }
600                }
601            );
602
603            //-----------------------------------------------------------
604            MenuSite.addLine( instance, "Main", "-", null );
605            //-----------------------------------------------------------
606            final Object disable1 = new Object();
607
608            MenuSite.addLine(   instance, "Main", "Toggle1",
609                new ActionListener()
610                {   public void actionPerformed( ActionEvent e )
611                    {   isDisabled1 = !isDisabled1;
612                        MenuSite.setEnable( disable1, !isDisabled1 );
613                        MenuSite.getMyMenuItem(instance,
614                                                "Main", "Toggle1").
615                        setText
616                        (   isDisabled1 ? "Enable following Item"
617                                        : "Disable following Item"
618                        );
619
620                    }
621                }
622            );
623            MenuSite.getMyMenuItem(instance, "Main", "Toggle1").
624                                setText("Disable following Item");
625
626            MenuSite.addLine(disable1, "Main", "Disableable", reportIt);
627
628            // - - - - - - - - - - - - - - - - - - - - - - - - - - - - -
629            final Object disable2 = new Object();
630
631            MenuSite.addLine(   instance, "Main", "Toggle2",
632                new ActionListener()
633                {   public void actionPerformed( ActionEvent e )
```

```
634                     {   isDisabled2 = !isDisabled2;
635                         MenuSite.setEnable( disable2, !isDisabled2 );
636                         MenuSite.getMyMenuItem(instance,
637                                         "Main", "Toggle2").
638                             setText
639                             (   isDisabled2 ? "Enable following Item"
640                                         : "Disable following Item"
641                             );
642                     }
643                 }
644             );
645         MenuSite.getMyMenuItem(instance, "Main", "Toggle2").
646                         setText("Disable following Item");
647         MenuSite.addLine(disable2, "Main", "Disableable", reportIt);
648
649         //--------------------------------------------------------
650
651         // Check that a single line item can be removed
652
653         final Object id = new Object();
654
655         MenuSite.addLine( id, "Main", "-", null );
656         MenuSite.addLine
657         (   id, "Main", "Remove this item & separator line",
658             new ActionListener()
659             {   public void actionPerformed( ActionEvent e )
660                 {   MenuSite.removeMyMenus( id );
661                 }
662             }
663         );
664
665         // Check out submenus. Create two of them, one in two
666         // steps and the other in a single step. Then add items
667         // that remove the submenus to make sure that removal works
668         // correctly.
669
670         MenuSite.addLine(instance,"Main", "-", null );
671         MenuSite.addLine(instance,
672                 "Main:Submenu1", "Submenu One Item", reportIt );
673         MenuSite.addLine(instance,
674                 "Main:Submenu2", "Submenu Two Item", reportIt );
675         MenuSite.addLine(instance,
676                 "Main:Submenu3", "Submenu Three Item", reportIt );
677         MenuSite.addLine(instance,
678                 "Main:Submenu2:SubSubmenu2",
679                 "Sub-Submenu Two Item", reportIt );
680
```

```
681             MenuSite.addLine(instance,
682                     "Main:Submenu3:SubSubmenu3",
683                     "Sub-Submenu Three Item", reportIt );
684
685             MenuSite.addLine(instance,
686                     "Main:Submenu3:SubSubmenu3:SubSubSubmenu3",
687                     "Sub-Sub-Submenu Three Item", reportIt );
688
689             MenuSite.addLine(instance, "Main", "-", null );
690
691             // Check that the map file works correctly.
692             // Items 5 and 6 are deliberately malformed in the map
693             // file and will cause an error to be logged.
694             // item.7 doesn't exist in the file.
695
696             MenuSite.mapNames(
697                 new URL("file://c:/src/com/holub/ui/test/menu.map.txt"));
698
699             MenuSite.addLine( instance, "Main", "item.1", reportIt );
700             MenuSite.addLine( instance, "Main", "item.2", reportIt );
701             MenuSite.addLine( instance, "Main", "item.3", reportIt );
702             MenuSite.addLine( instance, "Main", "item.4", reportIt );
703             MenuSite.addLine( instance, "Main", "item.5", reportIt );
704             MenuSite.addLine( instance, "Main", "item.6", reportIt );
705             MenuSite.addLine( instance, "Main", "item.7", reportIt );
706
707             // Create a help menu. Do it in the middle of things
708             // to make sure that it ends up on the far right.
709             // Use all three mechanisms for adding menu items directly
710             // using the menu's "name," and using the menu's "text").
711
712             MenuSite.addLine( instance, "Help", "Get Help", reportIt );
713
714             // Create a second "requester" and have it add a Removal
715             // menu with the name RemovalMenu. Picking that menu
716             // will remove only the menu for the current requester.
717             // Do this after doing the help menu to make sure that
718             // it's inserted in the right place.
719
720             final Object x = new Object();
721             MenuSite.addLine
722             (   x,
723                 "Removal", "Select to Remove Removal menu",
724                 new ActionListener()
725                 {   public void actionPerformed(ActionEvent e)
726                     {   MenuSite.removeMyMenus(x);
727                     }
728                 }
```

```
729                    );
730              }
731         }
732   }
733
```

The Core Classes

This section contains four listings that I'll be presenting in depth in the next few sections. The classes in these listings all participate in the same set of patterns, so it's best to put them together in one place. I don't expect you to read them now, however. Bookmark the subsections and refer to them later, then skip ahead to page 161.

This section really shows you one of the significant disadvantages of a hard-core design-pattern approach. My implementation of Life is probably the most complicated implementation of life ever written—way too complicated, given what it does. ("If it's that complicated, it must be wrong!") If you go nuts with the patterns and lose track of what you're actually trying to accomplish, you can introduce so much complexity into the code as to render it almost useless.

My goal in writing this code was as much to demonstrate design patterns as it was to build an optimal Life implementation, however. The SQL interpreter in the next chapter does not have this problem—it is production code.

The *Universe* Class

Listing 3-7 shows Universe.java.

Listing 3-7. *Universe.java*

```java
1    package com.holub.life;
2
3    import java.io.*;
4
5    import java.awt.*;
6    import javax.swing.*;
7    import java.awt.event.*;
8
9    import com.holub.io.Files;
10   import com.holub.ui.MenuSite;
11
12   import com.holub.life.Cell;
13   import com.holub.life.Storable;
14   import com.holub.life.Clock;
15   import com.holub.life.Neighborhood;
16   import com.holub.life.Resident;
17
18   /**
19    * The Universe is a mediator that sits between the Swing
```

```
20    * event model and the Life classes. It is also a Singleton,
21    * accessed via Universe.instance(). It handles all
22    * Swing events and translates them into requests to the
23    * outermost Neighborhood. It also creates the Composite
24    * Neighborhood.
25    */
26
27   public class Universe extends JPanel
28   {   private          final Cell      outermostCell;
29       private static  final Universe  theInstance = new Universe();
30
31       /** The default height and width of a Neighborhood in cells.
32        *  If it's too big, you'll run too slowly because
33        *  you have to update the entire block as a unit, so there's more
34        *  to do. If it's too small, you have too many blocks to check.
35        *  I've found that 8 is a good compromise.
36        */
37       private static final int  DEFAULT_GRID_SIZE = 8;
38
39       /** The size of the smallest "atomic" cell&mdash;a Resident object.
40        *  This size is extrinsic to a Resident (It's passed into the
41        *  Resident's "draw yourself" method.
42        */
43       private static final int  DEFAULT_CELL_SIZE = 8;
44
45       // The constructor is private so that the universe can be created
46       // only by an outer-class method [Neighborhood.createUniverse()].
47
48       private Universe()
49       {   // Create the nested Cells that comprise the "universe." A bug
50           // in the current implementation causes the program to fail
51           // miserably if the overall size of the grid is too big to fit
52           // on the screen.
53
54           outermostCell = new Neighborhood
55                           (   DEFAULT_GRID_SIZE,
56                               new Neighborhood
57                               (   DEFAULT_GRID_SIZE,
58                                   new Resident()
59                               )
60                           );
61
62           final Dimension PREFERRED_SIZE =
63                           new Dimension
64                           ( outermostCell.widthInCells() * DEFAULT_CELL_SIZE,
65                             outermostCell.widthInCells() * DEFAULT_CELL_SIZE
66                           );
67
```

```
68      addComponentListener
69      (   new ComponentAdapter()
70          {   public void componentResized(ComponentEvent e)
71              {
72                      // Make sure that the cells fit evenly into the
73                      // total grid size so that each cell will be the
74                      // same size. For example, in a 64x64 grid, the
75                      // total size must be an even multiple of 63.
76
77                      Rectangle bounds = getBounds();
78                      bounds.height /= outermostCell.widthInCells();
79                      bounds.height *= outermostCell.widthInCells();
80                      bounds.width  =  bounds.height;
81                      setBounds( bounds );
82              }
83          }
84      );
85
86      setBackground   ( Color.white    );
87      setPreferredSize( PREFERRED_SIZE );
88      setMaximumSize  ( PREFERRED_SIZE );
89      setMinimumSize  ( PREFERRED_SIZE );
90      setOpaque       ( true           );
91
92      addMouseListener
93      (   new MouseAdapter()
94          {   public void mousePressed(MouseEvent e)
95              {   Rectangle bounds = getBounds();
96                  bounds.x = 0;
97                  bounds.y = 0;
98                  outermostCell.userClicked(e.getPoint(),bounds);
99                  repaint();
100             }
101         }
102     );
103
104     MenuSite.addLine( this, "Grid", "Clear",
105         new ActionListener()
106         {   public void actionPerformed(ActionEvent e)
107             {   outermostCell.clear();
108                 repaint();
109             }
110         }
111     );
112
113     MenuSite.addLine
114     (   this, "Grid", "Load",
```

```
115                   new ActionListener()
116                   {   public void actionPerformed(ActionEvent e)
117                       {   doLoad();
118                       }
119                   }
120            );
121
122            MenuSite.addLine
123            (   this, "Grid", "Store",
124                new ActionListener()
125                {   public void actionPerformed(ActionEvent e)
126                    {   doStore();
127                    }
128                }
129            );
130
131            MenuSite.addLine
132            (   this, "Grid", "Exit",
133                new ActionListener()
134                {   public void actionPerformed(ActionEvent e)
135                    {   System.exit(0);
136                    }
137                }
138            );
139
140            Clock.instance().addClockListener
141            (   new Clock.Listener()
142                {   public void tick()
143                    {   if( outermostCell.figureNextState
144                             ( Cell.DUMMY,Cell.DUMMY,Cell.DUMMY,Cell.DUMMY,
145                               Cell.DUMMY,Cell.DUMMY,Cell.DUMMY,Cell.DUMMY
146                             )
147                          )
148                        {   if( outermostCell.transition() )
149                               refreshNow();
150                        }
151                    }
152                }
153            );
154        }
155
156        /** Singleton Accessor. The Universe object itself is manufactured
157         *  in Neighborhood.createUniverse()
158         */
159
160        public static Universe instance()
161        {   return theInstance;
```

```
162     }
163
164     private void doLoad()
165     {   try
166         {
167             FileInputStream in = new FileInputStream(
168                 Files.userSelected(".",".life","Life File","Load"));
169
170             Clock.instance().stop();        // stop the game and
171             outermostCell.clear();          // clear the board.
172
173             Storable memento = outermostCell.createMemento();
174             memento.load( in );
175             outermostCell.transfer( memento, new Point(0,0), Cell.LOAD );
176
177             in.close();
178         }
179         catch( IOException theException )
180         {   JOptionPane.showMessageDialog( null, "Read Failed!",
181                 "The Game of Life", JOptionPane.ERROR_MESSAGE);
182         }
183         repaint();
184     }
185
186     private void doStore()
187     {   try
188         {
189             FileOutputStream out = new FileOutputStream(
190                 Files.userSelected(".",".life","Life File","Write"));
191
192             Clock.instance().stop();        // stop the game
193
194             Storable memento = outermostCell.createMemento();
195             outermostCell.transfer( memento, new Point(0,0), Cell.STORE );
196             memento.flush(out);
197
198             out.close();
199         }
200         catch( IOException theException )
201         {   JOptionPane.showMessageDialog( null, "Write Failed!",
202                 "The Game of Life", JOptionPane.ERROR_MESSAGE);
203         }
204     }
205
206     /** Override paint to ask the outermost Neighborhood
207      *  (and any subcells) to draw themselves recursively.
208      *  All knowledge of screen size is also encapsulated.
```

```
209          *   (The size is passed into the outermost <code>Cell</code>.)
210          */
211
212     public void paint(Graphics g)
213     {
214         Rectangle panelBounds = getBounds();
215         Rectangle clipBounds  = g.getClipBounds();
216
217         // The panel bounds is relative to the upper-left
218         // corner of the screen. Pretend that it's at (0,0)
219         panelBounds.x = 0;
220         panelBounds.y = 0;
221         outermostCell.redraw(g, panelBounds, true);
222     }
223
224     /** Force a screen refresh by queuing a request on
225      *  the Swing event queue. This is an example of the
226      *  Active Object pattern (not covered by the Gang of Four).
227      *  This method is called on every clock tick. Note that
228      *  the redraw() method on a given <code>Cell</code>
229      *  does nothing if the <code>Cell</code> doesn't
230      *  have to be refreshed.
231      */
232
233     private void refreshNow()
234     {   SwingUtilities.invokeLater
235         (   new Runnable()
236             {   public void run()
237                 {   Graphics g = getGraphics();
238                     if( g == null )     // Universe not displayable
239                         return;
240                     try
241                     {
242                         Rectangle panelBounds = getBounds();
243                         panelBounds.x = 0;
244                         panelBounds.y = 0;
245                         outermostCell.redraw(g, panelBounds, false);
246                     }
247                     finally
248                     {   g.dispose();
249                     }
250                 }
251             }
252         );
253     }
254 }
```

The *Cell* Interface

Listing 3-8 shows Cell.java.

Listing 3-8. *Cell.java*

```
1   package com.holub.life;
2   import java.awt.*;
3
4   import com.holub.life.Storable;
5
6   /**...*/
7
8   public interface Cell
9   {
10      /** Figure out the next state of the cell, given the specified
11       *  neighbors.
12       *  @return true if the cell is unstable (changed state).
13       */
14      boolean figureNextState(    Cell north,     Cell south,
15                                  Cell east,      Cell west,
16                                  Cell northeast, Cell northwest,
17                                  Cell southeast, Cell southwest );
18
19      /** Access a specific contained cell located at the edge of the
20       *  composite cell.
21       *  @param row      The requested row. Must be on the edge of
22       *                  the block.
23       *  @param column   The requested column. Must be on the edge
24       *                  of the block.
25       *  @return true    if the state changed.
26       */
27      Cell edge( int row, int column );
28
29      /** Transition to the state computed by the most recent call to
30       *  {@link #figureNextState}
31       *  @return true if a changed of state happened during the transition.
32       */
33      boolean transition();
34
35      /** Redraw yourself in the indicated
36       *  rectangle on the indicated Graphics object if necessary. This
37       *  method is meant for a conditional redraw, where some of the
38       *  cells might not be refreshed (if they haven't changed state,
39       *  for example).
40       *  @param g redraw using this graphics,
41       *  @param here a rectangle that describes the bounds of the
42       *  current cell.
```

```
43        *  @parem drawAll if true, draw an entire compound cell;
44        *  otherwise, draw only the subcells that need to be redrawn.
45        */
46
47        void redraw(Graphics g, Rectangle here, boolean drawAll);
48
49        /** A user has clicked somewhere within you.
50         *  @param here The position of the click relative to the bounding
51         *              rectangle of the current Cell.
52         */
53
54        void userClicked(Point here, Rectangle surface);
55
56        /** Return true if this cell or any subcells are alive.
57         */
58        boolean isAlive();
59
60        /** Return the specified width plus the current cell's width
61         */
62        int widthInCells();
63
64        /** Return a fresh (newly created) object identical to yourself
65         *  in content.
66         */
67        Cell create();
68
69        /** Returns a Direction indicated the directions of the cells
70         *  that have changed state.
71         *  @return A Direction object that indicates the edge or edges
72         *          on which a change has occurred.
73         */
74
75        Direction isDisruptiveTo();
76
77        /** Set the cell and all subcells into a "dead" state.
78         */
79
80        void clear();
81
82        /**
83         *  The Memento interface stores the state
84         *  of a cell and all its subcells for future restoration.
85         */
86
87        interface Memento extends Storable
88        {   /** On creation of the memento, indicate that a cell is
89             *  alive.
```

```
90          */
91          void markAsAlive    (Point location);
92
93          /** On restoration of a cell from a memento, indicate that
94           *  a cell is alive.
95           */
96          boolean isAlive (Point location);
97      }
98
99      /**  This method is used internally to save or restore the state
100      *    of a cell from a memento.
101      *    @return true if this cell was modified by the transfer.
102      */
103     boolean transfer( Storable memento, Point upperLeftCorner,
104                                             boolean doLoad );
105
106     /** Possible value for the "load" argument to transfer() */
107     public static boolean STORE = false;
108
109     /** Possible value for the "load" argument to transfer() */
110     public static boolean LOAD = true;
111
112     /** This method is used by container of the outermost cell.
113      *  It is not used internally. It need be implemented only by
114      *  whatever class defines the outermost cell in the universe.
115      *  Other cell implementations should throw an
116      *  UnsupportedOperationException when this method is called.
117      */
118     Storable createMemento();
119
120     /** The DUMMY Singleton represents a permanently dead (thus stable)
121      *  cell. It's used for the edges of the grid. It's a Singleton.
122      *  The Dummy class is private, but it is accessed through
123      *  the public DUMMY field, declared below. I'd like this
124      *  class to be private, but the JLS doesn't allow private
125      *  members in an interface.
126      */
127
128     public static final Cell DUMMY = new Cell()
129     {
130         public boolean figureNextState(Cell n,  Cell s,  Cell e,  Cell w,
131                                     Cell ne, Cell nw, Cell se, Cell sw)
132                                         {return true;            }
133
134         public Cell      edge(int r, int c) {return this;        }
135         public boolean   isAlive()          {return false;       }
136         public Cell      create()           {return this;        }
```

```
137        public Direction isDisruptiveTo()    {return Direction.NONE;   }
138        public void      clear()             {                         }
139        public int       widthInCells()      {return 0;                }
140        public boolean   transition()        {return false;            }
141
142        public void userClicked(Point h, Rectangle s                  )
143        public void redraw      (Graphics g, Rectangle here,
144                                                  boolean drawAll    )
145
146        public boolean transfer( Storable m, Point ul, boolean load )
147        {   return false;
148        }
149
150        public Storable createMemento()
151        {   throw new UnsupportedOperationException(
152                    "Cannot create memento of dummy block");
153        }
154    };
155  }
```

The *Resident* Class

Listing 3-9 Shows Resident.java.

Listing 3-9. *Resident.java*

```
1   package com.holub.life;
2
3   import java.awt.*;
4   import javax.swing.*;
5   import com.holub.ui.Colors; // Contains constants specifying various
6                               // colors not defined in java.awt.Color.
7   import com.holub.life.Cell;
8   import com.holub.life.Storable;
9   import com.holub.life.Direction;
10  import com.holub.life.Neighborhood;
11  import com.holub.life.Universe;
12
13  /**...*/
14
15  public final class Resident implements Cell
16  {
17      private static final Color BORDER_COLOR = Colors.DARK_YELLOW;
18      private static final Color LIVE_COLOR   = Color.RED;
19      private static final Color DEAD_COLOR   = Colors.LIGHT_YELLOW;
20
21      private boolean amAlive    = false;
22      private boolean willBeAlive = false;
```

```
23
24      private boolean isStable(){return amAlive == willBeAlive; }
25
26      /** figure the next state.
27       *  @return true if the cell is not stable (will change state on the
28       *  next transition().
29       */
30      public boolean figureNextState(
31                              Cell north,      Cell south,
32                              Cell east,       Cell west,
33                              Cell northeast, Cell northwest,
34                              Cell southeast, Cell southwest )
35      {
36          verify( north,      "north"    );
37          verify( south,      "south"    );
38          verify( east,       "east"     );
39          verify( west,       "west"     );
40          verify( northeast, "northeast" );
41          verify( northwest, "northwest" );
42          verify( southeast, "southeast" );
43          verify( southwest, "southwest" );
44
45          int neighbors = 0;
46
47          if( north.    isAlive()) ++neighbors;
48          if( south.    isAlive()) ++neighbors;
49          if( east.     isAlive()) ++neighbors;
50          if( west.     isAlive()) ++neighbors;
51          if( northeast.isAlive()) ++neighbors;
52          if( northwest.isAlive()) ++neighbors;
53          if( southeast.isAlive()) ++neighbors;
54          if( southwest.isAlive()) ++neighbors;
55
56          willBeAlive = (neighbors==3 || (amAlive && neighbors==2));
57          return !isStable();
58      }
59
60      private void verify( Cell c, String direction )
61      {   assert (c instanceof Resident) || (c == Cell.DUMMY)
62                  : "incorrect type for " + direction +  ": " +
63                      c.getClass().getName();
64      }
65
66      /** This cell is monetary, so it's at every edge of itself. It's
67       *  an internal error for any position except for (0,0) to be
68       *  requsted since the width is 1.
69       */
```

```
70      public Cell edge(int row, int column)
71      {   assert row==0 && column==0;
72          return this;
73      }
74
75      public boolean transition()
76      {   boolean changed = isStable();
77          amAlive = willBeAlive;
78          return changed;
79      }
80
81      public void redraw(Graphics g, Rectangle here, boolean drawAll)
82      {   g = g.create();
83          g.setColor(amAlive ? LIVE_COLOR : DEAD_COLOR );
84          g.fillRect(here.x+1, here.y+1, here.width-1, here.height-1);
85
86          // Doesn't draw a line on the far right and bottom of the
87          // grid, but that's life, so to speak. It's not worth the
88          // code for the special case.
89
90          g.setColor( BORDER_COLOR );
91          g.drawLine( here.x, here.y, here.x, here.y + here.height );
92          g.drawLine( here.x, here.y, here.x + here.width, here.y );
93          g.dispose();
94      }
95
96      public void userClicked(Point here, Rectangle surface)
97      {   amAlive = !amAlive;
98      }
99
100     public void    clear()           {amAlive = willBeAlive = false; }
101     public boolean isAlive()         {return amAlive;                }
102     public Cell    create()          {return new Resident();         }
103     public int     widthInCells()    {return 1;}
104
105     public Direction isDisruptiveTo()
106     {   return isStable() ? Direction.NONE : Direction.ALL ;
107     }
108
109     public boolean transfer(Storable blob,Point upperLeft,boolean doLoad)
110     {
111         Memento memento = (Memento)blob;
112         if( doLoad )
113         {   if( amAlive = willBeAlive = memento.isAlive(upperLeft) )
114                 return true;
115         }
116         else if( amAlive )                     // store only live cells
```

```
117              memento.markAsAlive( upperLeft );
118
119          return false;
120      }
121
122      /** Mementos must be created by Neighborhood objects. Throw an
123       *  exception if anybody tries to do it here.
124       */
125      public Storable createMemento()
126      {   throw new UnsupportedOperationException(
127                      "May not create memento of a unitary cell");
128      }
129 }
```

The *Neighborhood* Class

Listing 3-10 shows Neighborhood.java.

Listing 3-10. *Neighborhood.java*

```
1   package com.holub.life;
2
3   import java.awt.*;
4   import java.awt.event.*;
5   import java.util.*;
6   import java.io.*;
7   import javax.swing.*;
8
9   import com.holub.io.Files;
10  import com.holub.life.Cell;
11  import com.holub.ui.MenuSite;
12  import com.holub.ui.Colors;
13  import com.holub.asynch.ConditionVariable;
14
15  import com.holub.life.Cell;
16  import com.holub.life.Clock;
17  import com.holub.life.Direction;
18  import com.holub.life.Storable;
19
20  import com.holub.io.P;
21
22  /**...*/
23
24  public final class Neighborhood implements Cell
25  {
26      /** Block if reading is not permitted because the grid is
27       *  transitioning to the next state. Only one lock is
28       *  used (for the outermost neighborhood) since all updates
29       *  must be requested through the outermost neighborhood.
```

```
30          */
31          private static final ConditionVariable readingPermitted =
32                                              new ConditionVariable(true);
33
34          /** Returns true only if none of the cells in the Neighborhood
35           *  changed state during the last transition.
36           */
37
38          private boolean amActive = false;
39
40          /** The actual grid of Cells contained within this neighborhood. */
41          private final Cell[][] grid;
42
43          /** The neighborhood is square, so gridSize is both the horizontal
44           *  and vertical size.
45           */
46          private final int      gridSize;
47
48          /** Create a new Neigborhood containing gridSize-by-gridSize
49           *  clones of the prototype. The Prototype is deliberately
50           *  not put into the grid.
51           */
52
53          public Neighborhood(int gridSize, Cell prototype)
54          {
55              this.gridSize = gridSize;
56              this.grid = new Cell[gridSize][gridSize];
57
58              for( int row = 0; row < gridSize; ++row )
59                  for( int column = 0; column < gridSize; ++column )
60                      grid[row][column] = prototype.create();
61          }
62
63          /** The "clone" method used to create copies of the current
64           *  neighborhood. This method is called from the containing
65           *  neighborhood's constructor. (The current neighborhood
66           *  is passed into the containing-neighborhood constructor
67           *  as the "prototype" argument.
68           */
69
70          public Cell create()
71          {   return new Neighborhood(gridSize, grid[0][0]);
72          }
73
74          /** Became stable on the last clock tick. One more refresh is
75           *  required.
76           */
77
78          private boolean oneLastRefreshRequired = false;
```

```
79
80      /** Shows the direction of the cells along the edge of the block
81       *  that will change  state in the next transition. For example,
82       *  if the upper-left corner has changed, then the current
83       *  Cell is disruptive in the NORTH, WEST, and NORTHWEST directions.
84       *  If this is the case, the neighboring
85       *  cells may need to be updated, even if they were previously
86       *  stable.
87       */
88      public  Direction isDisruptiveTo(){ return activeEdges; }
89      private Direction activeEdges = new Direction( Direction.NONE );
90
91      /** Figures the next state of the current neighborhood and the
92       *  contained neighborhoods (or cells). Does not transition to the
93       *  next state, however. Note that the neighboring cells are passed
94       *  in as arguments rather than being stored internally&mdash;an
95       *  example of the Flyweight pattern.
96       *
97       *  @see #transition
98       *  @param north        The neighbor to our north
99       *  @param south        The neighbor to our south
100      *  @param east         The neighbor to our east
101      *  @param west         The neighbor to our west
102      *  @param northeast    The neighbor to our northeast
103      *  @param northwest    The neighbor to our northwest
104      *  @param southeast    The neighbor to our southeast
105      *  @param southwest    The neighbor to our southwest
106      *
107      *  @return true if this neighborhood (i.e. any of it's cells)
108      *              will change state in the next transition.
109      */
110
111     public boolean figureNextState( Cell north,     Cell south,
112                                     Cell east,      Cell west,
113                                     Cell northeast, Cell northwest,
114                                     Cell southeast, Cell southwest )
115     {
116         boolean nothingHappened = true;
117
118         // Is some ajacent neighborhood active on the edge
119         // that ajoins me?
120
121         if(     amActive
122             || north     .isDisruptiveTo().the( Direction.SOUTH     )
123             || south     .isDisruptiveTo().the( Direction.NORTH     )
124             || east      .isDisruptiveTo().the( Direction.WEST      )
125             || west      .isDisruptiveTo().the( Direction.EAST      )
126             || northeast.isDisruptiveTo().the( Direction.SOUTHWEST )
127             || northwest.isDisruptiveTo().the( Direction.SOUTHEAST )
```

```
128                 || southeast.isDisruptiveTo().the( Direction.NORTHWEST )
129                 || southwest.isDisruptiveTo().the( Direction.NORTHEAST )
130            )
131            {
132            Cell    northCell,      southCell,
133                    eastCell,       westCell,
134                    northeastCell, northwestCell,
135                    southeastCell, southwestCell;
136
137            activeEdges.clear();
138
139            for( int row = 0; row < gridSize; ++row )
140            {   for( int column = 0; column < gridSize; ++column )
141                {
142                    // Get the current cell's eight neighbors
143
144                    if(row == 0 )
145                    {   northwestCell = (column==0)
146                            ? northwest.edge(gridSize-1,gridSize-1)
147                            : north.edge    (gridSize-1,column-1)
148                            ;
149
150                        northCell= north.edge(gridSize-1,column);
151
152                        northeastCell = (column == gridSize-1 )
153                            ? northeast.edge (gridSize-1, 0)
154                            : north.edge     (gridSize-1, column+1)
155                            ;
156                    }
157                    else
158                    {   northwestCell  = (column == 0)
159                            ? west.edge(row-1, gridSize-1)
160                            : grid[row-1][column-1]
161                            ;
162
163                        northCell = grid[row-1][column];
164
165                        northeastCell = (column == gridSize-1)
166                            ? east.edge(row-1, 0)
167                            : grid[row-1][column+1]
168                            ;
169                    }
170
171                    westCell = (column == 0)
172                            ? west.edge( row, gridSize-1)
173                            : grid[row][column-1]
174                            ;
175
176                    eastCell = (column == gridSize-1)
```

```
177                        ? east.edge(row, 0)
178                        : grid[row][column+1]
179                        ;
180
181             if(row == gridSize-1)
182             {    southwestCell = ( column==0 )
183                        ? southwest.edge(0,gridSize-1)
184                        : south.edge(0,column-1)
185                        ;
186
187                 southCell = south.edge(0,column);
188
189                 southeastCell = (column == gridSize-1 )
190                        ? southeast.edge(0,0)
191                        : south.edge(0, column+1)
192                        ;
193             }
194             else
195             {    southwestCell  = (column == 0)
196                        ? west.edge(row+1, gridSize-1)
197                        : grid[row+1][column-1]
198                        ;
199
200                 southCell = grid[row+1][column];
201
202                 southeastCell = (column == gridSize-1)
203                        ? east.edge(row+1, 0)
204                        : grid[row+1][column+1]
205                        ;
206             }
207
208             // Tell the cell to change its state. If
209             // the cell changed (the figureNextState request
210             // returned false), then mark the current block as
211             // unstable. Also, if the unstable cell is on the
212             // edge of the block modify activeEdges to
213             //  indicate which edge or edges changed.
214
215             if( grid[row][column].figureNextState
216                 ( northCell,     southCell,
217                   eastCell,      westCell,
218                   northeastCell, northwestCell,
219                   southeastCell, southwestCell
220                 )
221             )
222             {    nothingHappened = false;
223             }
224         }
225     }
```

```
226            }
227
228            if( amActive && nothingHappened )
229                oneLastRefreshRequired = true;
230
231            amActive = !nothingHappened;
232            return amActive;
233        }
234
235
236        /** Transition the neighborhood to the previously-computed
237         *  state.
238         *  @return true if the transition actually changed anything.
239         *  @see #figureNextState
240         */
241        public boolean transition()
242        {
243            // The condition variable is set and reset only by the
244            // outermost neighborhood. It's actually incorrect
245            // for an inner block to touch it because the whole
246            // board has to be locked for edge cells in a subblock
247            // to compute their next state correctly. There's no
248            // race condition since the only place that transition()
249            // is called is from the clock tick, and recursively
250            // from here. As long as the recompute time is less
251            // than the tick interval, everything's copasetic.
252
253            boolean someSubcellChangedState = false;
254
255            if( ++nestingLevel == 0 )
256                readingPermitted.set(false);
257
258            for( int row = 0; row < gridSize; ++row )
259                for( int column = 0; column < gridSize; ++column )
260                    if( grid[row][column].transition() )
261                    {   rememberThatCellAtEdgeChangedState(row, column);
262                        someSubcellChangedState = true;
263                    }
264
265            if( nestingLevel-- == 0 )
266                readingPermitted.set(true);
267
268            return someSubcellChangedState;
269        }
270        // The following variable is used only by the transition()
271        // method. Since Java doesn't support static local variables,
272        // I am forced to declare it in class scope, but I deliberately
273        // don't put it up at the top of the class definition because
274        // it's not really an attribute of the class&mdash;it's just
```

```java
275     // an implemenation detail of the immediately preceding
276     // method.
277     //
278     private static int nestingLevel = -1;
279
280
281     /** Modifies activeEdges to indicate whether the addition
282      *  of the cell at (row,column) makes an edge active.
283      */
284     private void rememberThatCellAtEdgeChangedState(int row,int column)
285     {
286         if( row == 0 )
287         {   activeEdges.add( Direction.NORTH );
288
289             if(column==0)
290                 activeEdges.add( Direction.NORTHWEST );
291             else if(column==gridSize-1)
292                 activeEdges.add( Direction.NORTHEAST );
293         }
294         else if( row == gridSize-1 )
295         {   activeEdges.add( Direction.SOUTH );
296
297             if(column==0)
298                 activeEdges.add( Direction.SOUTHWEST );
299             else if(column==gridSize-1)
300                 activeEdges.add( Direction.SOUTHEAST );
301         }
302
303         if( column == 0 )
304         {   activeEdges.add( Direction.WEST );
305         }
306         else if( column == gridSize-1 )
307         {   activeEdges.add( Direction.EAST );
308         }
309         // else it's an internal cell. Do nothing.
310     }
311
312     /** Redraw the current neighborhood only if necessary (something
313      *  changed in the last transition).
314      *
315      *  @param g Draw onto this graphics.
316      *  @param here Bounding rectangle for current Neighborhood.
317      *  @param drawAll force a redraw, even if nothing has changed.
318      *  @see #transition
319      */
320
321     public void redraw(Graphics g, Rectangle here, boolean drawAll)
322     {
323         // If the current neighborhood is stable (nothing changed
```

```
324        // in the last transition stage), then there's nothing
325        // to do. Just return. Otherwise, update the current block
326        // and all sub-blocks. Since this algorithm is applied
327        // recursively to subblocks, only those blocks that actually
328        // need to update will actually do so.
329
330
331        if( !amActive && !oneLastRefreshRequired && !drawAll )
332            return;
333        try
334        {
335            oneLastRefreshRequired = false;
336            int compoundWidth = here.width;
337            Rectangle subcell = new Rectangle( here.x, here.y,
338                                               here.width  / gridSize,
339                                               here.height / gridSize );
340
341            // Check to see if we can paint. If not, just return. If
342            // so, actually wait for permission (in case there's
343            // a race condition, then paint.
344
345            if( !readingPermitted.isTrue() )
346                return;
347
348            readingPermitted.waitForTrue();
349
350            for( int row = 0; row < gridSize; ++row )
351            {   for( int column = 0; column < gridSize; ++column )
352                {   grid[row][column].redraw( g, subcell, drawAll );
353                    subcell.translate( subcell.width, 0);
354                }
355                subcell.translate(-compoundWidth, subcell.height);
356            }
357
358            g = g.create();
359            g.setColor( Colors.LIGHT_ORANGE );
360            g.drawRect( here.x, here.y, here.width, here.height );
361
362            if( amActive )
363            {   g.setColor( Color.BLUE );
364                g.drawRect( here.x+1,      here.y+1,
365                            here.width-2, here.height-2 );
366            }
367
368            g.dispose();
369        }
370        catch( InterruptedException e )
371        {   // thrown from waitForTrue. Just
372            // ignore it, since not printing is a
```

```
373                 // reasonable reaction to an interrupt.
374             }
375     }
376
377     /** Return the edge cell in the indicated row and column.
378      */
379     public Cell edge(int row, int column)
380     {   assert   (row    == 0 || row    == gridSize-1)
381               || (column == 0 || column == gridSize-1)
382               : "central cell requested from edge()";
383
384         return grid[row][column];
385     }
386
387     /** Notification of a mouse click. The point is relative to the
388      * upper-left corner of the surface.
389      */
390     public void userClicked(Point here, Rectangle surface)
391     {
392         int pixelsPerCell = surface.width / gridSize ;
393         int row           = here.y        / pixelsPerCell ;
394         int column        = here.x        / pixelsPerCell ;
395         int rowOffset     = here.y        % pixelsPerCell ;
396         int columnOffset  = here.x        % pixelsPerCell ;
397
398         Point position = new Point( columnOffset, rowOffset );
399         Rectangle subcell = new Rectangle(  0, 0, pixelsPerCell,
400                                                   pixelsPerCell );
401
402         grid[row][column].userClicked(position, subcell);
403         amActive = true;
404         rememberThatCellAtEdgeChangedState(row, column);
405     }
406
407     public boolean isAlive()
408     {   return true;
409     }
410
411     public int widthInCells()
412     {   return gridSize * grid[0][0].widthInCells();
413     }
414
415     public void clear()
416     {   activeEdges.clear();
417
418         for( int row = 0; row < gridSize; ++row )
419             for( int column = 0; column < gridSize; ++column )
420                 grid[row][column].clear();
421
```

```
422            amActive = false;
423        }
424
425        public boolean transfer(Storable memento, Point corner,
426                                                    boolean load)
427        {   int   subcellWidth = grid[0][0].widthInCells();
428            int   myWidth       = widthInCells();
429            Point upperLeft = new Point( corner );
430
431            for( int row = 0; row < gridSize; ++row )
432            {   for( int column = 0; column < gridSize; ++column )
433                {   if(grid[row][column].transfer(memento,upperLeft,load))
434                        amActive = true;
435
436                    Direction d =
437                            grid[row][column].isDisruptiveTo();
438
439                    if( !d.equals( Direction.NONE ) )
440                        activeEdges.add(d);
441
442                    upperLeft.translate( subcellWidth, 0);
443                }
444                upperLeft.translate(-myWidth, subcellWidth );
445            }
446            return amActive;
447        }
448
449        public Storable createMemento()
450        {   Memento m = new NeighborhoodState();
451            transfer(m, new Point(0,0), Cell.STORE);
452            return m;
453        }
454
455        /**
456         * The NeighborhoodState stores the state of this neighborhood
457         * and all its sub-neighborhoods. For the moment, I'm storing
458         * state with serialization, but a future modification might
459         * rewrite load() and flush() to use XML.
460         */
461
462        private static class NeighborhoodState implements Cell.Memento
463        {   Collection liveCells = new LinkedList();
464
465            public NeighborhoodState( InputStream in ) throws IOException
466                                                    { load(in); }
467            public NeighborhoodState(               ){               }
468
469            public void load( InputStream in ) throws IOException
470            {   try
471                {   ObjectInputStream source = new ObjectInputStream( in );
```

```
472                         liveCells = (Collection)( source.readObject() );
473                     }
474                 catch(ClassNotFoundException e)
475                 {   // This exception shouldn't be rethrown as
476                     // a ClassNotFoundException because the
477                     // outside world shouldn't know (or care) that we're
478                     // using serialization to load the object. Nothing
479                     // wrong with treating it as an I/O error, however.
480
481                     throw new IOException(
482                             "Internal Error: Class not found on load");
483                 }
484             }
485
486         public void flush( OutputStream out ) throws IOException
487         {   ObjectOutputStream sink = new ObjectOutputStream(out);
488             sink.writeObject( liveCells );
489         }
490
491         public void markAsAlive(Point location)
492         {   liveCells.add( new Point( location ) );
493         }
494
495         public boolean isAlive(Point location)
496         {   return liveCells.contains(location);
497         }
498
499         public String toString()
500         {   StringBuffer b = new StringBuffer();
501
502             b.append("NeighborhoodState:\n");
503             for( Iterator i = liveCells.iterator(); i.hasNext() ;)
504                 b.append( ((Point) i.next()).toString() + "\n" );
505             return b.toString();
506         }
507     }
508 }
```

Mediator

The Life object instantiates only one Life-related class: the Universe. The instantiation
(Listing 3-7 line 30) looks like this:

```
getContentPane().add( Universe.instance(), BorderLayout.CENTER);
```

As far as the Life class is concerned, the Universe is just a JComponent of some sort. The
Life class has a single responsibility: main-frame creation. The only thing it cares about is that
the Universe can be added to a JFrame. Since the Universe class extends JComponent, Life can
just treat it as a JComponent. This way I can completely rework the user interface without
impacting the code in the Life class.

The Universe class is declared in Listing 3-7. It's a Singleton with a private constructor that uses the declare-the-instance-as-static reification of the pattern. (The instance reference is declared on line 29, and the instance() method on line 160 returns this reference.) This method is called from only one place (the Life-class constructor), so it could be replaced by a simple constructor, but then the one-of-a-kind nature of the Universe object wouldn't be guaranteed.

The main purpose of the Universe is to serve as in intermediary between the Swing subsystem and the Life subsystem. As such, the Universe is an example of the **Mediator** pattern. ("Intermediary" would have been a better choice of pattern name.)

The main intent of Mediator is to coordinate the interaction between two different subsystems so that these subsystems don't have to interact directly with each other. Mediator also helps isolate subsystems—I may want swap out Swing to run Life on the Palm Pilot, for example—but the main responsibility of Mediator is to mediate a complex message flow.

A Mediator does not need to encapsulate all subsystem interaction, but the more interaction it encapsulates, the better the isolation between subsystems (at the cost of heavier coupling to the mediator subsystem, of course). If all interaction is through the mediator, then you can swap out an entire subsystem without affecting any of the other collaborators. In Life, I chose for the Universe to encapsulate all interaction with Swing except painting. The Resident and Neighborhood object paint themselves on the screen using Java's Graphics class, which is effectively a Mediator in its own right (sitting between your program and the underlying operating-system objects such as the Windows "device context"). The Universe mediator encapsulates all event management: It intercepts all UI events that come out of Swing and translates them into messages that the Life subsystem understands. For example, the universe sets itself up to receive mouse-click messages on line 92 of Listing 3-7. It translates these into mouseClicked(...) messages, which are sent to the outermost cell. The only events Universe doesn't handle are the menuing events fielded by the clock subsystem, which, as you saw earlier, is built as a stand-alone subsystem so handles its own menuing, and so on.

The mediator is bidirectional (it passes messages from Life to Swing as well as the other way around). For example, a clock tick causes the Universe to ask Swing to refresh the screen if any of the cells changed state.

The Universe also controls a user interface of its own. It sets up and manages the single JPanel on which all the cells are drawn. So the Life classes are isolated from window maintenance and sizing as well. The Universe also sets up and manages the Grid menu that clears the game board loads previously stored game states.

People often confuse Mediator with Facade. One way to tell the difference is that the users of a Mediator don't know anything about the other subsystems to which the Mediator talks (the "Colleagues"). The Life classes don't know or care that the Universe is talking to Swing. They get messages from the mediator but are unaware of the stimulus that causes the mediator to send the message. The MenuSite facade, on the other hand, doesn't hide that you're talking to the menuing subsystem; all it does is hide the complexity of that communication. Mediator may or may not simplify anything—that's not its main purpose; rather, Mediator effectively hides the existence of the other subsystem. Mediators are very active, hiding complex interactions such as event handling. Facades tend to be more passive, expanding a single message into the multiple messages required for some piece of work. Mediators are usually bidirectional, with messages flowing in both directions from the Colleagues. Facades tend to be one-directional: messages flow from the Clients into the Facade, but not in the other direction.

Composite Revisited

Now let's examine the classes that comprise the Life subsystem. Most of the real work happens in the Cell interface and Neighborhood and Resident classes, which reify several design patterns. Since you've already looked at Composite, let's start there.

The Cell interface (Listing 3-8) has the role of Component in the Composite pattern. Objects of the Resident class (Listing 3-9) comprise the Leaves in the pattern. They represent individual cells in the game. Objects of the Neighborhood class (Listing 3-10) comprise the Composites in the pattern. They comprise the interior nodes of the hierarchy.

The Neighborhood objects hold a two-dimensional array (8×8 in the current version) of Cells, declared as follows on line 41 of Listing 3-10:

```
private final Cell[][] grid;
```

Since the array is declared in terms of the Cell interface, it can hold both Resident and Neighborhood objects. Life's user interface makes this structure visible. Figure 3-11 shows the object hierarchy, and Figure 3-12 shows the UI for the entire Life "universe" (the entire grid of cells), seeded with a glider in the upper-right corner. A Neighborhood object (whose UI is the entire window) contains an 8×8 grid of Neighborhood objects (delimited on the UI by darker lines), each of which holds an 8×8 grid of Resident objects. I could nest even further to make a larger grid (a Neighborhood of Neighborhoods of Neighborhoods of Residents, for example).

What the Composite structure gives you is the ability to write the Neighborhood class in such a way that it doesn't care whether it contains a grid of Neighborhood objects or a grid of Resident objects. They all implement the Cell interface, so they can be treated identically using that interface. For example, when you ask a Neighborhood to draw itself, it asks the contained Cells to draw themselves, and then the Neighborhood draws a darker line around the entire grid of Cells. This process goes on recursively through any sub-Neighborhood objects, until you get down to the Resident, which draws itself as a yellow square with a border on two adjacent sides. If you were looking only at the drawing mechanism, this organization seems overly complex, but we'll look at other advantages shortly.

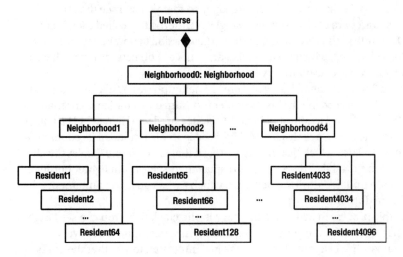

Figure 3-11. *The object hierarchy of Life*

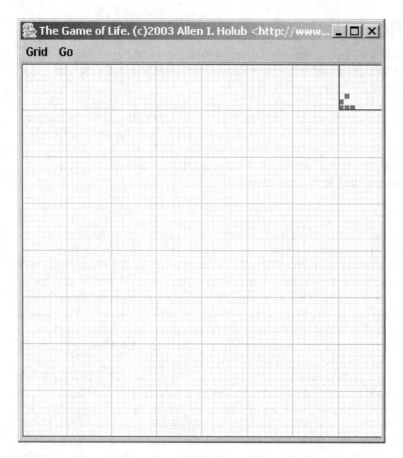

Figure 3-12. *The game board seeded with a glider*

The grid (deliberately) looks like a piece of graph paper so that you can see the object structure. The smallest squares are each drawn by a single `Cell` derivative called a `Resident`. The `Resident` has the Leaf role in the Composite pattern. (Leaves don't contain anything but their own state.) The `Neighborhood`, which holds an 8×8 array of `Cell` objects, draws itself with a darker border so that you can see its boundary.

The reason I'm using `Composite` at all is to get more efficient updates. You'll have noticed in Figure 3-12, that the `Neighborhood` that holds the glider is outlined in a darker color than the other `Neighborhoods`. Every `Cell` has a notion of "stability" associated with it. A `Cell` is stable if it will not change state on the next clock tick. A `Neighborhood` is stable if none of its contained `Cells` will change state on the next clock tick. A `Neighborhood` that is not stable displays itself with a dark-blue border. Stable `Neighborhood` objects display themselves with lighter borders. Only the unstable `Cells` are updated during clock ticks, which saves you a vast amount of work, since most `Cells` are dormant.

Figure 3-13 shows this process in action (each image is one clock tick). You can see `Neighborhood` objects become unstable as the glider moves into them. Interestingly, not every `Neighborhood` that contains a live cell is unstable; you're just interested in whether the `Cells` will change state, not whether they're in the "alive" state.

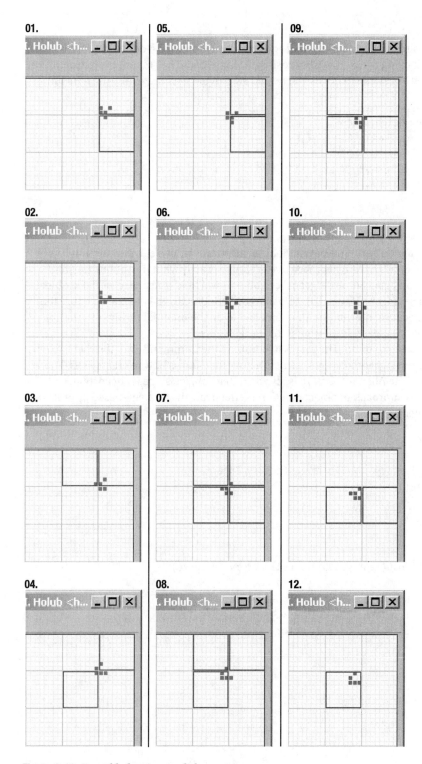

Figure 3-13. *Board behavior as glider moves*

Prototype

You can see Composite in action in Neighborhood.java by following a clock tick through the system. I'll start by looking at how the Composite grid is created. The Universe constructor (on line 48) uses the following code to create the nested system of Cells that comprises the life universe:

```
outermostCell = new Neighborhood
                (   DEFAULT_GRID_SIZE,
                    new Neighborhood
                    (   DEFAULT_GRID_SIZE,
                        new Resident()
                    )
                );
```

To see what's going on here, you have to look at the Neighborhood constructor, but let's analyze the problem first. The Neighborhood doesn't know exactly what it contains (beyond that it contains Cell objects). Some Neighborhood objects will hold other Neighborhood objects, but others will hold Resident objects. The Neighborhood nonetheless has to manufacture the contained objects, because information that's needed to do the manufacturing (for example, the number of objects to create) is internal to the Neighborhood.

Two solutions spring to mind. The first is to combine the Command and Abstract Factory patterns; you pass the Neighborhood an Abstract Factory that knows how to create cells. The code is shown below. The Abstract Factory is also a Strategy object, since it encapsulates a creation strategy. This approach to object creation is effectively the Strategy-based approach I discussed in Chapter 2.

```
class Neighborhood
{
    interface CellFactory    // Abstract Factory Interface
    {   Cell create();
    }

    //...

    public Neighborhood( int gridSize, CellFactory factory )
    {   //...
        for( int row = 0; row < gridSize; ++row )
            for( int column = 0; column < gridSize; ++column )
                grid[row][column] = factory.create();
    }
}

//...

class Universe
{   //...
```

```
// Pass the Neighborhood constructor an anonymous-inner-class
// Concrete Factory that produces a <nobr><code>Cell</code></nobr> derivative.
// (Cell is the Abstract product and either Neighborhood
// or  Resident is the Concrete Product).

outermostCell = new Neighborhood
                (   DEFAULT_GRID_SIZE,
                    new Creator()
                    {   public Cell creator()
                        {   return new Neighborhood
                            (   DEFAULT_GRID_SIZE,
                                new Creator()
                                {   public Cell creator()
                                    {   return new Resident();
                                    }
                                }
                            )
                        }
                    }
                );
}
```

The main problem with this approach is that it's too complicated. You need an unnecessary interface (`CellFactory`), and the initialization of `outermostCell` is hideous.

The second problem is that the object you need to create may not be in a default, newly constructed state. For example, consider a runtime-customizable user interface. You can store a list of all the changes that a user has made from the default UI-object state. When you create every UI object, though, you'll have to first manufacture it and then modify its state to reflect the user preferences. You can sometimes do this modification in a constructor, but UI widgets are often provided by a third party (or by Sun as part of Java), and you don't have the option of hacking up the source code to support user customization. The create-then-modify strategy can also be quite time consuming, and the after-the-fact modifications complicates the code considerably. (A Factory is pretty much mandatory, for example.)

Here's another example: I have a generic server-side socket handler (written before the `SocketFactory` was added to Java—nowadays I'd use a `SocketFactory`). My socket handler listens on the main socket, and when a client connects, it creates a `ClientConnection` Command object to handle the actual communication with the client. Using a Command object means I don't have to use implementation inheritance to change the way the socket handler works. I just pass it an instance of some class that implements the `ClientConnection` interface. The problem is that the socket handler has to manufacture a `ClientConnection` object every time a client connects. (It actually makes a pool of `ClientConnection` objects and reuses them, but that's just an implementation detail.) I could solve this problem by passing in a `ClientConnectionFactory` object, but that approach has the same problems as the earlier example.

To the rescue comes the **Prototype** pattern: when all you have is a reference to an interface, and you need to make many instances of the referenced object, then clone them.

To solve the UI problem using Prototype, you'd serialize a user-customized version of a UI component to the disk. The next time you ran the program, you'd reload the serialized version and then make copies of that prototype object rather than calling new.

To solve the socket-connection problem, you'd pass the socket-handler constructor a prototype ClientConnection object. The socket handler will just clone the prototype on an as-needed basis.

The Neighborhood constructor uses Prototype to create subcells, using the following code:

```
public Neighborhood(int gridSize, Cell prototype)
{
    this.gridSize = gridSize;
    this.grid = new Cell[gridSize][gridSize];

    for( int row = 0; row < gridSize; ++row )
        for( int column = 0; column < gridSize; ++column )
            grid[row][column] = prototype.create();
}
```

Prototype lets you remove all knowledge of the concrete Cell-derivative type from the Neighborhood: it's passed a prototype Cell, which in practice is either a Resident or another Neighborhood, and it populates itself with clones of the prototype.

I opted to use a create() method rather than a clone() override to get type safety; clone() returns Object, so you have to cast its return value. A call to clone() works just fine if you didn't mind the cast.

Composite Redux

Moving back to Composite, having populated the Neighborhood, you now need to pass messages to the cells. I'll use the clock-tick activities as an example. Figure 3-14 shows the clock-tick-initiated message flow. (The remainder of this section explains the diagram.)

The Universe Mediator translates clock ticks into the messages that cause the board to update. It subscribes to the clock-tick message as follows (Listing 3-7, line 1):

```
Clock.instance().addClockListener
(   new Clock.Listener()
    {   public void tick()
        {   if( outermostCell.figureNextState
                    ( Cell.DUMMY,Cell.DUMMY,Cell.DUMMY,Cell.DUMMY,
                      Cell.DUMMY,Cell.DUMMY,Cell.DUMMY,Cell.DUMMY
                    )
            )
            {   if( outermostCell.transition() )
                    refreshNow();
            }
        }
    }
);
```

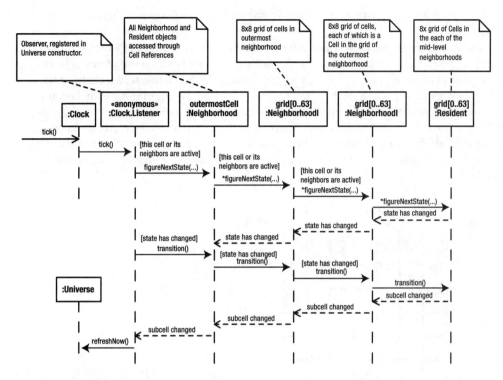

Figure 3-14. *The messages that follow a clock tick*

The message handler (tick()) passes a figureNextState() message to the outermost cell. If any of the contained cells think they may need to change state in the next pass, figureNextState() returns true, and the tick handler sends transition() message to the outermost cell to force a transition to the next state. Finally, refreshNow() is called to force a screen refresh if any of the contained cells actually changed state.

Starting with the Resident, the figureNextState() method (Listing 3-9, line 30) is passed references to its neighbors (more on these references later); it counts the number of live neighbors, and it determines its next state based on the neighbor count. In the second pass, the transition() method (Listing 3-9, line 75) just moves to that state. The transition() method also remembers whether it changed state for reasons that will become clear in a moment.

At the Composite level, I'll explain transition() first because it's simpler. Bear in mind as you read the following that the main Composite-related issue is that the Neighborhood doesn't have to know whether it contains other Neighborhood objects or whether it contains Resident objects. The high-level behavior (Listing 3-10, line 241) is identical. The Neighborhood just relays the message to its contained cells.

```
for( int row = 0; row < gridSize; ++row )
    for( int column = 0; column < gridSize; ++column )
        if( grid[row][column].transition() )
        {   rememberThatCellAtEdgeChangedState(row, column);
            someSubcellChangedState = true;
        }
```

If the subcell changed state, then the Neighborhood object remembers this and reports it to the caller.

The Neighborhood also keeps track of whether any cells at the edge of this Neighborhood have changed state, but unlike the Resident, the Neighborhood needs to keep track of which edges of the neighborhood are active. (A Resident doesn't bother because, if it changes state, all the edges are active.) Adjacent Neighborhoods need the active-edge information because the states of subcells at the adjacent-Neighborhood's edges may need to change state if cells in this Neighborhood are actively changing. Figure 3-15 illustrates the issues. A change in cell C, for example, affects three adjacent neighborhoods (shown in grey): when cell C changes state, the cell in the southwest corner of the northeast neighborhood may need to change state as well.

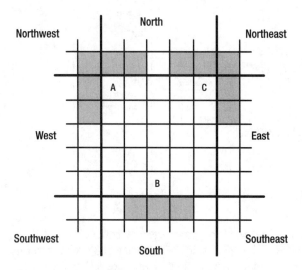

Figure 3-15. *Edge activity affects other neighborhoods*

The rememberThatCellAtEdgeChangedState() method (Listing 3-10, line 284) keeps track of things in a Direction object called activeEdges.

The Direction class (Listing 3-11) defines a simple wrapper around a bit map. The add(...) method sets a bit. The has(...) method tests that a bit is set. The oddly named the() method works just like has(). It's there so that the following call reads like English.

```
northNeighbor.isDisruptiveTo().the( Direction.SOUTH );
```

The isDisruptiveTo method (Listing 3-10, line 88) returns the activeEdges Direction you saw earlier—the one that's modified during the transition process to identify the edges of the Neighborhood that contains cells that have changed state in the current transition.

Listing 3-11. *Direction.java*

```
1  package com.holub.life;
2
3  /**...*/
4
```

```
 5  public class Direction
 6  {   private int map = BITS_NONE;
 7
 8      private static final int BITS_NORTH     = 0x0001;
 9      private static final int BITS_SOUTH     = 0x0002;
10      private static final int BITS_EAST      = 0x0004;
11      private static final int BITS_WEST      = 0x0008;
12      private static final int BITS_NORTHEAST = 0x0010;
13      private static final int BITS_NORTHWEST = 0x0020;
14      private static final int BITS_SOUTHEAST = 0x0040;
15      private static final int BITS_SOUTHWEST = 0x0080;
16      private static final int BITS_ALL       = 0x00ff;
17      private static final int BITS_NONE      = 0x0000;
18
19      // Various directions. Note that since we're talking
20      // about the edges of a grid, NORTH | WEST and NORTHWEST are
21      // different things. NORTH means that anything along the NORTH
22      // edge is active; ditto for WEST and the west edge. NORTHWEST
23      // means that the cell in the NORTHWEST corner is active.
24      // If the NORTHWEST corner is active, the NORTH and WEST
25      // edges will also be active, but the converse is not true.
26
27      public static final Direction NORTH     = new Immutable(BITS_NORTH);
28      public static final Direction SOUTH     = new Immutable(BITS_SOUTH);
29      public static final Direction EAST      = new Immutable(BITS_EAST);
30      public static final Direction WEST      = new Immutable(BITS_WEST);
31      public static final Direction NORTHEAST = new Immutable(BITS_NORTHEAST);
32      public static final Direction NORTHWEST = new Immutable(BITS_NORTHWEST);
33      public static final Direction SOUTHEAST = new Immutable(BITS_SOUTHEAST);
34      public static final Direction SOUTHWEST = new Immutable(BITS_SOUTHWEST);
35      public static final Direction ALL       = new Immutable(BITS_ALL);
36      public static final Direction NONE      = new Immutable(BITS_NONE);
37
38      public  Direction()             {                }
39      public  Direction( Direction d ){  map = d.map; }
40      private Direction( int bits    ){  map = bits;  }
41
42      public boolean  equals( Direction d ){ return d.map == map; }
43      public void     clear (             ){ map = BITS_NONE;      }
44      public void     add   ( Direction d ){ map |= d.map;         }
45      public boolean  has   ( Direction d ){ return the(d);              }
46      public boolean  the   ( Direction d ){ return (map & d.map)==d.map; }
47
48      private static final class Immutable extends Direction
49      {
50          private static final String message =
51              "May not modify Direction constant (Direction.NORTH, etc.)";
52
```

```
53          private Immutable(int bits){ super(bits); }
54
55          public void clear()
56          {    throw new UnsupportedOperationException(message);
57          }
58
59          public void add( Direction d )
60          {    throw new UnsupportedOperationException(message);
61          }
62      }
63  }
```

The Direction implementation has a couple of other issues. Note that the bit values declared at the top of the class definition are not exposed to the outside world. The add(...) method, for example, takes a Direction argument, not an int that holds a bit mask. If I allowed an int argument, it would be possible for a careless programmer to pass a nonsense value into add(...). Passing a Direction makes it impossible to pass add(...) a bad value.

The other interesting facet of the Direction class is the Immutable variant (Listing 3-11, line 48). Immutable extends Direction, overriding all methods that can modify a Direction object to throw exceptions. The prebuilt Direction objects (NORTH, SOUTH, and so on) are all instances of Immutable because a user of these objects shouldn't be modifying them. By using Immutable, I guarantee that the object can't be modified rather than leaving it up to the good-will of the programmer. (Design note: It's been argued that I got things backward here—that a subclass shouldn't refuse to do something that the base-class contract says that it can do. It's a reasonable point, but I don't see how inverting things changes the situation.)

The Immutable class is also an example of a situation where a design-pattern solution would add more complexity than it's worth. You could implement immutability with the Decorator pattern, described in Chapter Four, but the subclass is an inner class of the class that it's extending, and it is a trivial extension to boot, so problems such as fragile base classes are immaterial.

Also note that Direction is not a Singleton because there will be many instances of it, and you can create a Direction using new. On the other hand, the eight predefined directions are very Singleton-like in their behavior. In his book *Pattern Hatching* (Addison-Wesley, 1998), John Vlissides—one of the Gang of Four—pointed out that a Singleton doesn't actually have to be limited to a single instance, as long as the number of instances is constrained. It is reasonable for a Singleton reification to manage a constrained set of instances rather than a single instance, in the same way that Direction manages a set of eight predefined Direction objects. Nonetheless, it's difficult to tell whether Direction is a Singleton simply by looking only at its structure. The public constructor is the only clue to its non-Singleton-ness.

Flyweight

The obvious way to implement Life would be to make each Cell a JButton derivative. That way, when you were setting up a pattern on the grid, you could bring a cell to life simply by clicking on it, the normal button-press mechanism can be leveraged to handle the change of appearance and state. You could arrange the buttons that represented the cells using a large JFrame and a GridLayout object. In this naive implementation, each button would also hold references to all eight neighbors. Though this approach is by far the easiest to implement, it's impractical. Swing components are "lightweight" only in the sense that there's no underlying OS window backing them. Looking at the JSDK 1.4.1 sources

- The JButton class holds two nonstatic fields.

- The AbstractButton superclass holds 28 nonstatic fields.

- The JComponent superclass holds 23 nonstatic fields.

- The Container superclass holds 23 nonstatic fields.

- The Component superclass holds 48 nonstatic fields.

That's 124 fields total—496 bytes. About half of these fields are references to other objects that are also good sized and hold references to even more objects. Let's guess conservatively and assume that each of these referenced objects requires 50 bytes, yielding another 3,100 bytes. You also need to add 8 pointers to the Cell's neighbors and a boolean to remember the current cell state (36 bytes). So, the grand total is 3,632 bytes per button. To make the math easy, let's assume that the life "Universe" is a 1024×1024 grid of cells. That's an even 1,048,576 cells. Multiplying by the cell size, you get 3.6 gigabytes (3,632MB) of memory required to hold the grid. Odds are, you don't have that much core memory in your machine, which means that the array will have to be stored in virtual memory and paged into core as the program runs. This paging is an extremely time-consuming process. The net result would be excruciatingly slow performance.

Obviously, the obvious approach won't work.

I've solved the problem by combining Composite with another design pattern, **Flyweight**.

The notion of a flyweight is tied closely to the definition of an object. If you've read somewhere that an object is a bundle of data and a set of "method" functions that access the data, then you've been misled. This sort of description is typical of a procedural programmer who's new to objects, but it's fundamentally incorrect. An object is defined primarily by what it does, by the messages that it can handle. The object will typically have some sort of internal state represented by a set of fields, but the way in which this state is implemented internally has absolutely nothing to do with what the object is. All that should matter are the methods.

Don't be confused here by the notion of "attributes." At the risk of repeating something I said in Chapter 1, an *attribute* is a characteristic of an object that serves to distinguish a class of objects from another class of objects. A "salary" attribute, for example, distinguishes one class of people (employee) from other classes of people (volunteer, consultant, former dot-com-er, and so on). The most important attributes of the object are the methods—the set of messages that the object can handle. Other attributes serve as a design aid that tells you whether a method makes sense. (Asking a volunteer to printYourSalary() won't do anything useful since a volunteer doesn't have a salary attribute.)

Simply because an object has an attribute does not mean that it has an associated field. *Synthesized* attributes are computed at runtime, not stored in the object, for example. A salary attribute, may be inferred from a pay grade, a title, years of employment, or some other measure that was stored as a field. It may be computed from a complex formula that involved fields, method calls, and database lookups.

The attribute-related issue that concerns the Flyweight pattern is that all the attributes of some class of object may be synthesized. The fact that the class has no fields in it does not impact its "object-ness" in any way, as long as it has responsibilities (and the methods needed to exercise those responsibilities). Moreover, it's often debatable where a particular attribute should be stored. Take the Neighborhood and Resident as a case in point. It's reasonable for a Resident to know its size and position on the screen. By the same token, it's equally reasonable for a Neighborhood to know the size and positions of all the Cells it contains. Generally, you'd put this information into the Resident class because it would be easier for a Resident object to draw itself. It's not "wrong," however, for a Neighborhood object to synthesize a Cell's size and position and pass that information to a contained Cell. If done properly (by accessing subcells through an interface), a design that moves the size and location of an element into the container doesn't tighten the coupling at all.

When a class of objects allows a container class to hold data that could just as easily be stored in the contained object, then the data is called *extrinsic data*. For example, the figureNextState() method of the Cell interface you looked at earlier is passed references to the Cell's eight neighbors. The neighbor references could be contained inside the Cell, but that would take too much space at runtime. By the same token, it's perfectly reasonable that a container such as a Neighborhood would be able to synthesize the eight neighbor references when it asks a subcell to figure its next state. Since they're external to a Resident, the neighbor references are considered extrinsic. The Cell's size and location information are also synthesized by the surrounding Cell, so they are also extrinsic. In fact, only two fields of the Resident class are not extrinsic: the amAlive and willBeAlive fields (declared on lines 21 and 22 of Listing 3-9). The current implementation stores this information in boolean fields, but I could save even more space by setting and clearing bits in a byte instead of using two booleans.

The Cell, then, is a Flyweight. (*Flyweight* is a term for a boxer who weighs less than 112 pounds.) Most of a Flyweight's state information is extrinsic. You can see how the extrinsic data in a flyweight works by following a mouse click from the Universe (which manages the only window in the system) to the Resident that has to service the click. Figure 3-16, explained shortly, shows how the messages propagate when the mouse is clicked from the position shown in Figure 3-17 (ten cells from both the top and left edge of the universe).

A Resident isn't a window because of the memory requirements, and its size and location are extrinsic for the same reason. The mouse-click handler in the Universe class (Listing 3-7, line 92) sends the outermost cell a userClicked() message, passing as arguments the window-relative position of the mouse "hot spot" and a bounding rectangle—a Rectangle whose horizontal and vertical size is the size of the window and whose upper-left corner is at position (0,0). The outermost cell is actually being passed the size of itself (the outermost cell is as big as the whole window) and the location within itself of the mouse click.

Since the outermost cell is a Neighborhood, this call gets you to the userClicked() override in the Neighborhood class (Listing 3-10, line 390). This override relays the message to its subcells. First it figures out which subcell contains the click position. pixelsPerCell holds the number of pixels in a subcell (the container cell width divided by the number of cells.) Using this information and the click location, the override determines which subcell needs to be informed of the click and relays the message to that subcell only.

The important thing to notice is that the calling method passes the subcell a rectangle that identifies the subcell's size (the number of pixels in a single subcell), and the calling method modifies the click position to be relative to the subcell's bounding rectangle.

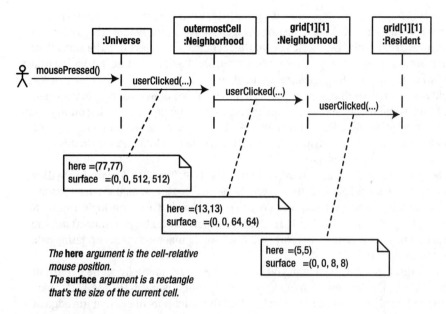

Figure 3-16. *The messages that follow a mouse click*

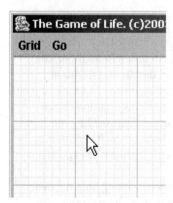

Figure 3-17. *Mouse position for scenario in Figure 3-16*

Since the outermost Neighborhood contains other Neighborhood objects, this first call to userClicked(...) (on line 402) is actually recursive. It's received by the contained Neighborhood object. This contained object, then, does the same work, scaling the size of the rectangle down even further and moving the position to be relative to its subcell's bounding rectangle. The method calls userClicked(...) again, but this time the contained Cell is a Resident, so you end up in the override in Listing 3-9, line 96. The Resident doesn't care where, within itself, the click occurred, so the Resident version of userClicked(...) ignores its arguments. The method just inverts its amAlive state.

Screen painting happens in a similar way. The Universe sends redraw(...) messages to the outermost cell on lines 221 and 245 of Listing 3-7, getting you to the Neighborhood override in Listing 3-10, line 321. This override scales down the rectangle and relays it to the subcell (on line 352), which eventually gets you to the Resident override (Listing 3-9, line 81), which draws one cell in yellow or red, depending on whether it's alive.

You should note two other things in this code. A Neighborhood draws a darker-than-usual border around itself when it's not stable. This is the code that generated the moving outlines you looked at earlier as the glider flew across the universe. This last example is another example of why it's a good thing for an object to display its own UI. It would be a lot harder to do this "outlining" in an external rendering class.

Also, the Neighborhood's redraw(...) override (Listing 3-10, line 321) doesn't do anything if the test at the top succeeds. That is, if the current Neighborhood is stable, then the version on the screen is just fine, so the Neighborhood doesn't redraw itself. This same logic applies to the figureNextState() (Listing 3-10, line 111). If the Neighborhood is stable, it doesn't ask the contained cells to figure their states. This way, you don't waste machine cycles updating cells that don't need to be updated.

To finish with this aspect of Flyweight, you can see the dark underbelly of the pattern in the Neighborhood class's implementation of figureNextState() (Listing 3-10, line 111). This method is made hideously complicated by the fact that the neighbors of cells on the edge of a Neighborhood are in a different Neighborhood object. All that nasty code after line 144 of Listing 3-10 is just figuring out which neighborhood holds the adjacent cell. None of this complexity would be necessary if the cells held their own neighbor pointers, but getting rid of this excess baggage was the whole point of using Flyweight to begin with.

The figureNextState() method makes many calls to edge(...), which returns a cell on the edge of an adjacent Neighborhood. The edge() method looks an awful lot like one of the getters I disparaged earlier in this chapter, so some explanation is in order. Remember, the basic argument against getters is that they expose implementation details and negatively impact maintainability. Here, however, the cells are a fundamental attribute of a Neighborhood. The fact that a Neighborhood is made up of Cells is one of the key defining characteristics (attributes) of a neighborhood. As I mentioned in Chapter 1, occasionally providing method-level access to a core attribute is at times okay, and this is one of those times. It would be a serious error to expose how the Neighborhood stores the cells, but it's harmless to expose the fact that the Neighborhood simply contains cells.

Moreover, edge(...) is called only by other Neighborhood objects. Passing data between two identical objects doesn't impact maintenance one iota, since they both instantiate the same class definition. Normally, I'd make a method such as edge(...) private to ensure that it wasn't called from foreign classes, but I can't do that here because the Composite pattern mandates access through the Cell interface. I could get around this problem by dispensing with the Cell interface, making edge(...) private, and redefining Resident to extend Neighborhood and override all the public methods. Although this reorganization lets me restrict access to edge(...), it's unacceptable for a Cell to carry around all the baggage of a Neighborhood (the array of subcells, for example) when it's not using that baggage.

Flyweight Pools

Returning to the clock-tick handler, as follows, the Universe passes the outermost cell eight references to the Cell.DUMMY object:

```
Clock.instance().addClockListener
(   new Clock.Listener()
    {   public void tick()
        {   if( outermostCell.figureNextState
                    ( Cell.DUMMY,Cell.DUMMY,Cell.DUMMY,Cell.DUMMY,
                      Cell.DUMMY,Cell.DUMMY,Cell.DUMMY,Cell.DUMMY
                    )
                )
            {   if( outermostCell.transition() )
                    refreshNow();
            }
        }
    }
);
```

This code is a simplistic example of *flyweight pooling*, the other main characteristic of the Flyweight pattern. Rather than create eight identical flyweights, I use eight references to a single flyweight. (In fact, the DUMMY object actually masquerades as 256 instances of Cell, since the eight references passed into figureNextState() are themselves treated as Neighborhood objects, each of which uses the same DUMMY objects as the cells on the edge of its Neighborhood.) Conceptually, the entire grid that comprises the Life universe is bordered by DUMMY objects, but these objects on the border are all actually the same object.

The DUMMY object is defined using the anonymous-inner-class mechanism in the Cell interface (Listing 3-8, line 128). It implements a dead cell that does nothing. By passing it into the outermost Cell of the composite, this cell is effectively surrounded by "dummy" objects. Using an anonymous inner class makes the actual class definition inaccessible.

The DUMMY object, by the way, is yet another Singleton. The instance is manufactured in the DUMMY declaration on line 128 of Listing 3-8. The Singleton is accessed globally using Cell.DUMMY instead of an accessor method. Only one instance of the class can possibly exist since the class itself is defined using the anonymous inner-class mechanism. You can't create another instance using new because you don't have a class name to use.

A better example of Flyweight pooling is Java's BorderFactory class. The javax.Swing.Border defines a Flyweight, albeit a big one. The Border interface defines a paint method that uses four variables to render the border. Here's the prototype for that method:

```
void paintBorder(Component c, Graphics g, int x, int y, int width, int height)
```

Since all these arguments could just as well be attributes of the class that implements Border, these arguments really define the Border's extrinsic data. Making these fields extrinsic yields an important benefit. A single Border object can draw borders around any numbers of components. For example, I can put a three-pixel EmptyBorder around several components with the following code:

```
Border threePixelPadding = new EmptyBorder( 3, 3, 3, 3 );

JButton hello   = new JButton("Hello");
JButton goodbye = new JButton("Goodbye");

hello.setBorder( threePixelPadding );
goodbye.setBorder( threePixelPadding );
```

The extrinsic information needed to render the border is passed into the `Border` three-`PixelPadding` object when it's time to do the drawing.

Since the border is so flexible, and since most `Border` objects are used around many components, there's no real need to use `new` to make a `Border` derivative with certain characteristics every time you need one. That is, it's better to use the same `Border` object everywhere rather than to create many identical objects. You want to cache a single instance and use the instance in the cache.

Swing accomplishes caching with an Abstract Factory: `BorderFactory`. Use it like this:

```
JButton hello   = new JButton("Hello");
JButton goodbye = new JButton("Goodbye");

hello.setBorder  ( BorderFactory.createEmptyBorder(3,3,3,3) );
goodbye.setBorder( BorderFactory.createEmptyBorder(3,3,3,3) );
```

If I were implementing `BorderFactory`, I'd do it as a flyweight pool. The first time I was asked for a three-pixel-wide empty border, I would have the `BorderFactory` manufacture it. Subsequent requests for `Border` objects with the same characteristics would return the same object. Only one three-pixel-wide-empty-`Border` object would exist. (Swing gives no guarantee that the `BorderFactory` actually works this way, so you can't safely do things such as use `==` to compare factory-generated objects—something that you could do if being a flyweight pool was part of the object's contract.)

So far, this code is just a reification of Abstract Factory that's used to create Singletons. (You can argue with me about whether the manufactured `Border` objects are indeed Singletons, but I think of them in a similar light as the `Class`-object Singleton.) What makes the `BorderFactory` a Flyweight pool is that the Singleton that's managed by the factory is a flyweight, and the purpose of the factory is to limit the number of flyweight instances to the minimal set.

Memento

One final design pattern exists in Life: **Memento**. I briefly discussed Memento in the context of OLE in-place activation back in the section "The Menuing System: Facade and Bridge." The idea of a memento is that some object (an Originator) needs another object (a Caretaker) to hold the Originator's state. The Originator encapsulates that state into a black box (a Memento), which the Caretaker stores. The Caretaker cannot modify the state of the Originator by manipulating the Memento, however. To enforce the black-box nature of a Memento, it is often represented physically as a byte array or an `Object` whose concrete class is unknown to the Caretaker.

You'll remember that OLE container uses Memento to store the state of the in-place activated object. When Excel (the Originator) shuts down, it passes its state to Word as a memento—a byte array that Word stored until Excel needed it again. Since Word (the Caretaker) has no idea what's in that byte array, Word can't do anything with the Memento but store it. Another good example is a web-browser cookie—a chunk of data provided by the server that the browser holds onto until it talks to that server again. The browser has no idea what's in the cookie—it's the Caretaker.

A Caretaker can store the memento as a blob in a database, by serializing it to disk or just by holding it in memory until the Originator needs it again.

Though you may think you can use Memento to implement "undo," it's not usually suitable for that purpose. Simply restoring some piece of the program to a previous state doesn't undo any "side effects" of the original operation. For example, if an object updates a database during some operation, simply restoring the object to its former state does not reverse the database update. In any event, the memento may not store actual state information; it may contain some "key" you use to get the actual state information. In JSP, for example, the cookie holds a "session ID" that's used to find the actual session state in the server. There's not enough information in the cookie itself to do anything like an undo operation. The Command pattern, discussed in Chapter Four, solves the undo problem.

In the case of Life, I wanted to be able to save the state of a Life universe (all of the cells) so that I could seed a complex pattern onto the board only once and then load the pattern back into the game at some future time. I wanted to isolate the mechanics of storage and retrieval in my Universe mediator, so I implemented persistence by having the Universe ask the Cells for a memento that the Universe stores and retrieves.

I applied two levels of interfaces in Life's implementation of Memento to guarantee the black-box quality of the Memento itself. At the Universe level everything is done in terms of the Storable interface (Listing 3-12). It has only two methods, load(...) and flush(...), which do the obvious.

If you look back at the Universe (Listing 3-7), you'll see that it sets up menu handlers that store and load the entire game board (on line 113). These handlers call doStore() and doLoad() to do the actual work.

The doStore method (Listing 3-7, line 186) uses Abstract Factory to create a Memento.

```
Storable memento = outermostCell.memento();
```

(This Abstract Factory isn't called out in Figure 3-2 simply because there wasn't enough room to cram it in, so I've put it in Figure 3-18. Cell is an Abstract Factory of Storable Abstract Products. Neighborhood is the Concrete Factory of NeighborhoodState Concrete Products.) doStore() then asks the outermost cell to transfer its state into the memento. Finally, it asks the memento to flush itself out to the disk.

The doLoad() method (Listing 3-7, line 164) is basically the same as doStore(). It reverses the disk access and transfer operations, however. It first loads the memento from the disk and then asks the outermost cell to import the memento into itself.

At the Caretaker level (the Universe) the Memento is a black box—a Storable object of some sort that knows how to load and store itself. The Universe can't change the state of the data in the memento.

Listing 3-12. *Storable.java*

```
1  package com.holub.life;
2  import java.io.*;
3
4  /**...*/
5
6  public interface Storable
7  {    void load ( InputStream in   ) throws IOException;
8       void flush( OutputStream out ) throws IOException;
9  }
```

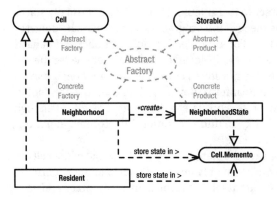

Figure 3-18. *Life's mementos*

Moving into the concrete classes, at the Life level, access to the Memento is through the Cell.Memento interface (Listing 3-8, line 87), implemented by the Neighborhood.Neighborhood-State class (Listing 3-10, line 462). NeighborhoodState implements the Storable interface to serialize itself out to the disk and back in using the built-in serialization system. At some point, I plan to replace the serialization with XML so that I can build seed files in an ASCII editor, but for the time being, serialization will do. Note that this change to an XML format involves a localized change in the NeighborhoodState class; it affects no other classes. NeighborhoodState encapsulates a linked list of points, each identifying a live cell on the board. All cells not in the list are dead. A Resident object marks itself as alive by calling markAsAlive, which simply adds a point to the list. When loading from the Memento, a Resident asks if it isAlive(), and if an affirmative answer comes back, the Resident object sets its state to "alive" (in the transfer(...) overload, Listing 3-9, line 109).

This implementation of Memento seems complex, but it has two important characteristics: I can change the way in which the game state is stored by changing only one class (Neighborhood-State), and, because I have isolated the Memento generation from the file system in the mediator, I can change the location of the stored Memento without changing anything except the Universe class. All likely changes are localized to a single class.

Loose Ends

Listings 3-13, 3-14, and 3-15 contain the remaining classes in the Game of Life.

The Colors interface (Listing 3-13) contains nothing but symbolic constants that alias various java.awt.Color values I use regularly. Use this interface like a Singleton. That is, use Colors.DARK_RED to access the dark-red Color. Don't implement the Colors interface to use DARK_RED without the prefix. Many Java programs do implement interfaces to access static data in this way, but I don't think much of that practice from a design point of view. An employee is not a color (which implies extends), and employees do not support messages that are passed to colors generally (which implies implements), so an Employee class should not implement Colors. It's better to think of Colors as a kind of multiway Singleton that provides global access to a constrained set of objects. Just use the fields directly.

The `Files` utility contains only one method that makes it a little easier to display a file-chooser dialog. When you want a user-selected file, you call this:

```
File in = Files.userSelected(".",".txt","Text File","Open");
```

The method takes care of the mechanics of getting the dialog box displayed. This class is a simplistic example of Facade.

Finally, the `ConditionVariable` class in Listing 3-15 is a roll-your-own threading primitive that corrects an omission in Java's `wait()` method. One of the main problems with `wait()` is that the thing you're waiting on has no notification state. That is, a thread that needs to wait for some event to occur may not want to be suspended if the event has already occurred when the thread calls `wait()`. `ConditionVariable` solves the problem by incorporating a `boolean` that's checked prior to issuing the `wait()` request. Think of a condition variable as a `boolean` that represents a condition of some sort. If the condition is false, then you wait for it to become true. If the condition is true, then you'll never wait at all. You create a condition variable in the `false` state like this:

```
ConditionVariable eventHappened = new ConditionVariable( false );
```

You can issue the following call to wait for the condition to become true:

```
eventHappened.waitForTrue();
```

When the event does happen, the event handler sets the condition variable to the true state as follows:

```
eventHappened.set( true );
```

Any waiting threads are released, and all subsequent calls to `eventHappened.waitForTrue()` return immediately without blocking. If you need the threads to start waiting for the condition variable again, set it back to a false state as follows:

```
eventHappened.set( false );
```

`ConditionVariable` is another simple Facade, simplifying a tiny bit of behavior of Java's threading subsystem.

I use a condition variable in Life to make sure that the activities associated with a clock tick don't overlap. The semaphore (`readingPermitted`) is declared at the top of the `Neighborhood` class (Listing 3-10, line 31). The reading-permitted state is set and cleared in the `Neighborhood`'s `transition()` override (Listing 3-10, line 241). Finally, the `Neighborhood`'s `redraw` override does nothing if reading is not permitted (Listing 3-10, line 345). The `waitForTrue()` on the line following this last test is just insurance that handles a potential race condition in the code.

Listing 3-13. *Colors.java*

```
1  // &copy; 2003 Allen I Holub. All rights reserved.
2  package com.holub.ui;
3  import java.awt.*;
4
5  /*  The Colors interface contains nothing but symbolic constants for various
6   *  color values that I use regularly. The names are self explanatory.
7   */
```

```
 8
 9   /**...*/
10
11   public interface Colors
12   {
13   /**...*/ static final Color DARK_RED       = new Color(0x99, 0x00, 0x00);
14   /**...*/ static final Color MEDIUM_RED     = new Color(0xcc, 0x00, 0x00);
15   /**...*/ static final Color LIGHT_RED      = new Color(0xff, 0x00, 0x00);
16
17   /**...*/ static final Color DARK_ORANGE    = new Color(0xff, 0x66, 0x00);
18   /**...*/ static final Color MEDIUM_ORANGE  = new Color(0xff, 0x99, 0x00);
19   /**...*/ static final Color LIGHT_ORANGE   = new Color(0xff, 0xcc, 0x00);
20   /**...*/ static final Color ORANGE         = new Color(0xff, 0x99, 0x00);
21
22   /**...*/ static final Color OCHRE          = new Color(0xcc, 0x99, 0x00);
23   /**...*/ static final Color DARK_YELLOW    = new Color(0xff, 0xff, 0x00);
24   /**...*/ static final Color MEDIUM_YELLOW  = new Color(0xff, 0xff, 0x99);
25   /**...*/ static final Color LIGHT_YELLOW   = new Color(0xff, 0xff, 0xdd);
26
27   /**...*/ static final Color DARK_GREEN     = new Color(0x00, 0x66, 0x00);
28   /**...*/ static final Color MEDIUM_GREEN   = new Color(0x00, 0x99, 0x00);
29   /**...*/ static final Color LIGHT_GREEN    = new Color(0x00, 0xff, 0x00);
30   /**...*/ static final Color GREEN          = MEDIUM_GREEN;
31
32   /**...*/ static final Color DARK_BLUE      = new Color(0x00, 0x00, 0x99);
33   /**...*/ static final Color MEDIUM_BLUE    = new Color(0x00, 0x00, 0xcc);
34   /**...*/ static final Color LIGHT_BLUE     = new Color(0x00, 0x00, 0xff);
35
36   /**...*/ static final Color DARK_PURPLE    = new Color(0x99, 0x00, 0x99);
37   /**...*/ static final Color MEDIUM_PURPLE  = new Color(0xcc, 0x00, 0xff);
38   /**...*/ static final Color LIGHT_PURPLE   = new Color(0xcc, 0x99, 0xff);
39   /**...*/ static final Color PURPLE         = MEDIUM_PURPLE;
40   }
```

Listing 3-14. *Files.java*

```
 1   package com.holub.io;
 2
 3   import java.io.*;
 4   import javax.swing.*;
 5   import javax.swing.filechooser.FileFilter; // disambiguate from java.io version
 6
 7   /**...*/
 8
 9   public class Files
10   {
11       /** Throw up a file chooser and return the file that the user selects.
12        *  @param extension File extension you're looking for. Use null if
13        *                   any will do.
```

```
14       *   @param description the description of what the extension means.
15       *                    Not used if "extension" is null.
16       *   @param selectButtonText Replaces the "Open" on the chooser button.
17       *   @param startHere Name of initial directory in which to look.
18       *   @return the selected file.
19       *   @throws FileNotFoundException if the user didn't select a file. I've
20       *            done this rather than returning null so that it's easy to
21       *            do the following:
22       *   <PRE>
23       *   FileInputStream in =
24       *       new FileInputStream(
25       *                   Files.userSelected(".",".txt","Text File","Open"));
26       *   </PRE>
27       */
28
29      public static File userSelected( final String startHere,
30                          final String extension,
31                          final String description,
32                          final String selectButtonText )
33                                   throws FileNotFoundException
34      {   FileFilter filter =
35              new FileFilter()
36              {   public boolean accept(File f)
37                  {   return f.isDirectory()
38                              || (extension != null
39                                      && f.getName().endsWith(extension) );
40                  }
41                  public String getDescription()
42                  {   return description;
43                  }
44              };
45
46          JFileChooser chooser = new JFileChooser(startHere);
47          chooser.setFileFilter(filter);
48
49          int result = chooser.showDialog(null,selectButtonText);
50          if(result == JFileChooser.APPROVE_OPTION)
51              return chooser.getSelectedFile();
52
53          throw new FileNotFoundException("No file selected by user");
54      }
55
56      static class Test
57      {
58          public static void main(String[] args)
59          {
60              try
```

```
61                     {   File f=Files.userSelected(".",".test","Test File","Select!");
62                         System.out.println( "Selected " + f.getName() );
63                     }
64                     catch( FileNotFoundException e)
65                     {   System.out.println( "No file selected" );
66                     }
67                     System.exit(0); // Required to stop AWT thread & shut down.
68                 }
69             }
70  }
```

Listing 3-15. *ConditionVariable.java*

```
1   package com.holub.asynch;
2
3   /**
4    *  This class is a simplified version of the com.asynch.Condition
5    *  class. Use it to wait for some condition to become true:
6    *  <PRE>
7    *  ConditionVariable hellFreezesOver = new ConditionVariable(false);
8    *
9    *  Thread 1:
10   *      hellFreezesOver.waitForTrue();
11   *
12   *  Thread 2:
13   *      hellFrezesOver.set(true);
14   *  </PRE>
15   *  Unlike <code>wait()</code> you will not be suspended at all if you
16   *  wait on a true condition variable. You can call <code>set(false)</code>,
17   *  to put the variable back into a false condition (thereby forcing
18   *  threads to wait for it to become true, again).
19   */
20
21  public class ConditionVariable
22  {
23      private volatile boolean isTrue;
24
25      public ConditionVariable( boolean isTrue ){ this.isTrue = isTrue; }
26
27      public synchronized boolean isTrue()
28      {   return isTrue;
29      }
30
31      public synchronized void set( boolean how )
32      {   if( (isTrue = how) == true )
33              notifyAll();
34      }
```

```
35
36      public final synchronized void waitForTrue() throws InterruptedException
37      {   while( !isTrue )
38              wait();
39      }
40  }
```

Summing Up

Whew! That's 11 design patterns—the 9 pictured in Figure 3-2 plus Command and Abstract Factory—used in a program that has only 20 classes and interfaces in it, some of which are trivial. Though Life is a small program, it nicely demonstrates how the patterns all work together in the real world. They never stand in splendid isolation, as they would appear in a catalog-based design-patterns book.

More important, if you factor out all of the text in this chapter that describes what the pattern is, you'll find that there's hardly anything left. That is, if you knew the patterns already, I could have explained the entire Life program to you in a couple pages. This economy of expression makes for very productive conversations.

One of the main reasons for doing design at all is improved communication (between programmers, between designers and programmers, between programmers and users, and so on). I hope I've shown you how effective the design-pattern vocabulary can be in achieving that end.

This chapter also shows you one of the significant disadvantages of a hard-core design-pattern approach. As I mentioned earlier, my implementation of Life is probably the most complicated implementation of Life ever written. As I said at the beginning of the chapter, this Game of Life is, after all, a toy, and I let myself go nuts with the patterns. The current implementation certainly shows how the patterns all interact to get work done, however, and that was one of the main things I was trying to show you.

CHAPTER 4

■ ■ ■

Implementing Embedded SQL

This chapter presents a complete subsystem that demonstrates all the remaining Gang-of-Four design patterns: a miniature SQL interpreter (and JDBC interface) that you can embed in your applications. This package is not a full-blown database but is a small in-memory database suitable for many client-side applications.

As was the case with the Game of Life game discussed in the previous chapter, I've set up a web page at http://www.holub.com/software/holubSQL/ that lists various links to SQL resources and provides an applet that lets you play with the interpreter I'm about to discuss. You can find the most recent version of the source code from this chapter on the same web page.

As was also the case with Life, I've opted to present a complete subsystem, so this chapter has a lot of code in it. As before, I don't expect you to read every line—I've called out the important stuff in the text.

With the exception of "The Interpreter Pattern" section, you don't need to know anything special to read this chapter. That section, which covers how the actual SQL interpreter and the parser that builds it works, is a doozy, though. After a lot of thought, I decided not to turn this chapter into a treatise on compiler writing, simply because the subject rarely comes up in normal programming. Moreover, the Interpreter Pattern section introduces only one design pattern, which is used only to build interpreters. If you're not going to build an interpreter, you can safely skip it (both the pattern and the section). If you're bold enough to proceed, however, I'm assuming (in that section only) that you know how write simple SQL statements, you know how to read an LL(1) BNF grammar, and you know how recursive-descent parsing works. The web page I just mentioned has links to SQL and JDBC resources if you need to learn that material, and it also links to a long introduction of formal grammars and recursive-descent parsing.

The Requirements

I originally wrote the small database engine in this chapter to handle the persistence layer for a client-side-only "shrink-wrap" application. My program used only a few tables and did only simple joins, and I didn't want the size, overhead, and maintenance problems of a "real" database. I also didn't need full-blown SQL—just a reasonable subset that supports table creation, modification, and simple queries (including joins) was sufficient. I didn't need views, triggers, functions, and the other niceties of a real database. I did, however, need the tables that comprised the database to be stored in some human-readable ASCII format such as comma-separated values (preferred) or XML, and none of the databases that I could find satisfied this last requirement.

I rolled my own database for other reasons as well. The database needed to be "embedded" into the rest of the program rather than being a stand-alone server. I just didn't want the hassle of installing (and maintaining) a stand-alone third-party database server that was likely to be an order of magnitude larger than the application itself. I wanted a small, lean implementation.

I wanted to talk to the database using JDBC so that I could replace it with something that was more fully featured if necessary. The database engine had to be written entirely in Java so that it was platform independent.

Finally, several times I've wanted to store a small amount of data in a database-like way, but without the overhead of an actual database. For example, it's handy to put configuration options into a database-like data structure so that you can issue queries against the configuration. Using a database to keep track of ten configuration options was just too much overhead, however. I wanted the data structures that underlie the SQL interpreter to be useable in their own right as a sort of "collection," but without the SQL.

I checked the web to see if there was anything that would do the job, but I couldn't find anything at the time, so I rolled up my sleeves and wrote my own. (I've subsequently discovered a couple small public-domain SQL interpreters, but that's life—it took less than two weeks to write the SQL engine you're about to examine, so I didn't waste any time.)

The Architecture

I approached the design of my small-database subsystem by breaking it into three distinct layers, each accessed through well-defined interfaces (see Figure 4-1). This use of interfaces to isolate subsystems from each other is a simple reification of the Bridge pattern, which I'll discuss in greater depth later in the current chapter. The basic idea of Bridge is to separate subsystems with a set of interfaces so you can modify one subsystem without impacting the other.

The data-storage layer manages the actual data that comprises a table and also handles persistence. This layer exposes two interfaces: Table (which defines access to the table itself) and Cursor, which provides an iterator across rows in the table (an object that lets you visit each row of the table in sequence).

The data-storage classes are wrapped in a SQL-engine layer, which implements the SQL interpreter and uses the underlying data-storage classes to manage the actual data. This layer exposes *result sets* (the set of rows that result from a SQL select operation) as Table objects, and you can examine the result set with a Cursor, so these two interfaces isolate both "faces" of the subsystem. (Like Janus, one face looks backward at the data-storage layer, and the other face looks forward at the JDBC layer.)

Finally, a JDBC-driver layer wraps the SQL engine with classes that implement the various interfaces required by JDBC, so you can access my simple database just like you would any other database. Using the JDBC Bridge also lets you easily replace my simple database with something that's more fully featured without having to modify your code. The JDBC layer completely hides the underlying Table and TableIterator interfaces. (You won't have to worry about JDBC-related stuff until you get to "The JDBC Layer" section toward the end of this chapter. Everything I discuss up to that point has nothing to do with JDBC. I'll explain how JDBC works when you get to that section, and when I do get to it, JDBC classes will be clearly indicated by using their fully qualified class names: java.sql.Xxx. If you don't see the java.sql, then the class is one of mine.)

The messaging between layers is effectively unidirectional. For example, the SQL engine knows about, and send messages to, the data-storage layer, but the data-storage layer knows nothing about the SQL engine and sends no messages to any of the objects that comprise the SQL engine. This one-way communication vastly simplifies maintenance because you know that the effects of a given change are limited. Since these three layers are completely independent of one another, I can also discuss them independently.

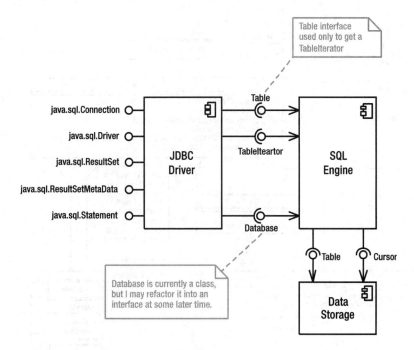

Figure 4-1. *Database-classes architecture*

The Data-Storage Layer

At the core of everything is the Table interface, its implementation (ConcreteTable), and various support classes and interfaces. As I did in the previous chapter, I'll start with a couple of monstrous figures, which will seem confusing at first but make sense as I discuss the program one bit at a time. Figure 4-2 shows the static structure of the classes that comprise the data-storage layer: the Table interface and all its implementations and supporting classes. Figure 4-3 shows the design patterns. As was the case with Life, there are almost as many patterns as there are classes, which is to say that several classes participate in more than one pattern. You should bookmark these figures so that you can refer to them as I discuss the various patterns.

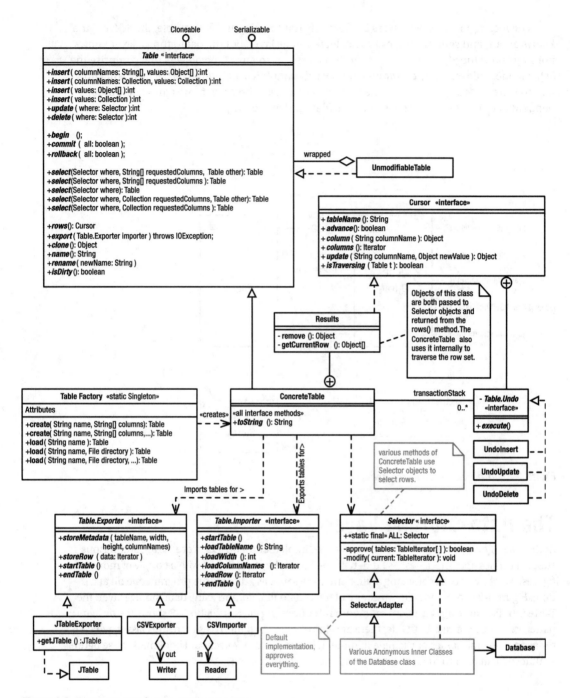

Figure 4-2. *Data-storage layer: static structure*

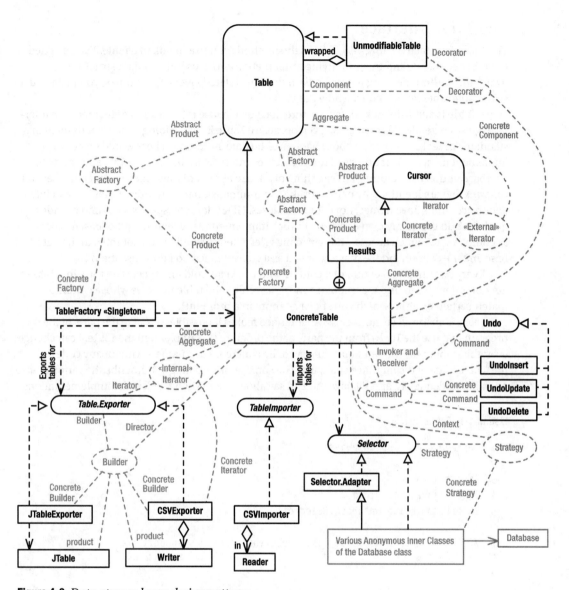

Figure 4-3. *Data-storage layer: design patterns*

The *Table* Interface

The Table interface (Listing 4-1) defines the methods you use to talk to a table. I've designed the Table so that it (and the underlying implementation) is useful as a data structure in its own right, without needing to wrap it with the SQL-related layers. Sometimes, you just need a searchable table rather than a whole database.

A Table is an in-memory data structure that you can use rather like a Collection. The interface doesn't extend Collection, however, because a Table is really doing a different thing than a standard Collection—they just both happen to be data structures. There would be no way to implement most of the methods of the Collection interface in the Table. A Table supports the database notion of a column. You can think of a Table as a set of *rows*, each of which has several *columns* that are identified by name. It's like a two-dimensional array, except that it's searchable and the columns have names, not column indexes. (JDBC lets you specify a column by index, but I don't do that in my own code, so I haven't implemented the feature. Index-based access—as compared to named access—has given me grief when I've had to add columns to the database and the column indexes have changed as a consequence, so I don't use them.)

Every *cell* (the intersection of a column and row) can hold an object. The rows in a Table are not ordered. You find a particular row by searching the table for rows whose columns match certain criteria (which you specify—more in a moment).

Table is an interface, not a class. An interface makes it possible to isolate the parts of the program that use the Table from the parts of the program that implement the Table. I can change everything about the implementation—even the concrete-class name—without any code on the "client" side of the interface changing. The comments in Listing 4-1 describe the various Table operations adequately, and I'll have more to say about them when I look at the implementations.

Listing 4-1. *Table.java*

```
1   package com.holub.database;
2
3   import java.io.*;
4   import java.util.*;
5   import com.holub.database.Selector;
6
7   /** A table is a database-like table that provides support for
8    *  queries.
9    */
10
11  public interface Table extends Serializable, Cloneable
12  {
13      /** Return a shallow copy of the table (the contents are not
14       *  copied.
15       */
16      Object clone() throws CloneNotSupportedException;
17
18      /** Return the table name that was passed to the constructor
19       *  (or read from the disk in the case of a table that
20       *  was loaded from the disk.) This is a "getter," but
21       *  it's a harmless one since it's just giving back a
```

```
22        *   piece of information that it was given.
23        */
24       String   name();
25
26       /** Rename the table to the indicated name. This method
27        *   can also be used for naming the anonymous table that's
28        *   returned from {@link #select select(...)}
29        *   or one of its variants.
30        */
31       void rename( String newName );
32
33       /** Return true if this table has changed since it was created.
34        *   This status isn't entirely accurate since it's possible
35        *   for a user to change some object that's in the table
36        *   without telling the table about the change, so a certain
37        *   amount of user discipline is required. Returns true
38        *   if you modify the table using a Table method (such as
39        *   update, insert, etc.). The dirty bit is cleared when
40        *   you export the table.
41        */
42       boolean isDirty();
43
44       /** Insert new values into the table corresponding to the
45        *   specified column names. For example, the value at
46        *   <code>values[i]</code> is put into the column specified
47        *   in <code>columnNames[i]</code>. Columns that are not
48        *   specified are initialized to <code>null</code>.
49        *
50        * @return the number of rows affected by the operation.
51        * @throws IndexOutOfBoundsException One of the requested columns
52        *                 doesn't exist in either table.
53        */
54       int  insert( String[] columnNames, Object[] values );
55
56       /** A convenience overload of {@link #insert(String[],Object[])} */
57
58       int  insert( Collection columnNames, Collection values );
59
60       /** In this version of insert, values must have as many elements as there
61        *   are columns, and the values must be in the order specified when the
62        *   Table was created.
63        * @return the number of rows affected by the operation.
64        */
65       int  insert( Object[]   values );
66
67       /** A convenience overload of {@link #insert(Object[])}
68        */
```

```
69
70      int  insert( Collection values );
71
72      /**
73       * Update cells in the table. The {@link Selector} object serves
74       * as a visitor whose <code>includeInSelect(...)</code> method
75       * is called for each row in the table. The return value is ignored,
76       * but the Selector can modify cells as it examines them. It's your
77       * responsibility not to modify primary-key and other constant
78       * fields.
79       * @return the number of rows affected by the operation.
80       */
81
82      int  update( Selector where );
83
84      /** Delete from the table all rows approved by the Selector.
85       * @return the number of rows affected by the operation.
86       */
87
88      int  delete( Selector where );
89
90      /** begin a transaction */
91      public void begin();
92
93      /** Commit a transaction.
94       *  @throw IllegalStateException if no {@link #begin} was issued.
95       *
96       *  @param all if false, commit only the innermost transaction,
97       *             otherwise commit all transactions at all levels.
98       *  @see #THIS_LEVEL
99       *  @see #ALL
100      */
101     public void commit( boolean all ) throws IllegalStateException;
102
103     /** Roll back a transaction.
104      *  @throw IllegalStateException if no {@link #begin} was issued.
105      *  @param all if false, commit only the innermost transaction,
106      *             otherwise commit all transactions at all levels.
107      *  @see #THIS_LEVEL
108      *  @see #ALL
109      */
110     public void rollback( boolean all ) throws IllegalStateException;
111
112     /** A convenience constant that makes calls to {@link #commit}
113      *  and {@link #rollback} more readable when used as an
114      *  argument to those methods.
115      *  Use <code>commit(Table.THIS_LEVEL)</code> rather than
```

```
116          *   <code>commit(false)</code>, for example.
117          */
118         public static final boolean THIS_LEVEL = false;
119
120         /** A convenience constant that makes calls to {@link #commit}
121          *  and {@link #rollback} more readable when used as an
122          *  argument to those methods.
123          *  Use <code>commit(Table.ALL)</code> rather than
124          *  <code>commit(true)</code>, for example.
125          */
126         public static final boolean ALL = true;
127
128         /**Described in the text on page 235*/
129
130         Table select(Selector where, String[] requestedColumns, Table[] other);
131
132         /** A more efficient version of
133          * <code>select(where, requestedColumns, null);</code>
134          */
135         Table select(Selector where, String[] requestedColumns );
136
137         /** A more efficient version of <code>select(where, null, null);</code>
138          */
139         Table select(Selector where);
140
141         /** A convenience method that translates Collections to arrays, then
142          *  calls {@link #select(Selector,String[],Table[])};
143          *  @param requestedColumns a collection of String objects
144          *               representing the desired columns.
145          *  @param other a collection of additional Table objects to join to
146          *               the current one for the purposes of this SELECT
147          *               operation.
148          */
149         Table select(Selector where, Collection requestedColumns,
150                                               Collection other);
151
152         /** Convenience method, translates Collection to String array, then
153          *  calls String-array version.
154          */
155         Table select(Selector where, Collection requestedColumns );
156
157         /** Return an iterator across the rows of the current table.
158          */
159         Cursor rows();
160
161         /** Build a representation of the Table using the
162          *  specified Exporter. Create an object from an
```

```
163      *  {@link Table.Importer} using the constructor with an
164      *  {@link Table.Importer} argument. The table's
165      *  "dirty" status is cleared (set false) on an export.
166      *  @see #isDirty
167      */
168     void export( Table.Exporter importer ) throws IOException;
169
170     /******************************************************************
171      * Used for exporting tables in various formats. Note that
172      * I can add methods to this interface if the representation
173      * requires it without impacting the Table's clients at all.
174      */
175     public interface Exporter
176     {   public void startTable()                  throws IOException;
177         public void storeMetadata(
178                     String tableName,
179                     int width,
180                     int height,
181                     Iterator columnNames )  throws IOException;
182         public void storeRow(Iterator data) throws IOException;
183         public void endTable()                    throws IOException;
184     }
185
186     /******************************************************************
187      * Used for importing tables in various formats.
188      * Methods are called in the following order:
189      * <ul>
190      * <li><code>start()</code></li>
191      * <li><code>loadTableName()</code></li>
192      * <li><code>loadWidth()</code></li>
193      * <li><code>loadColumnNames()</code></li>
194      * <li><code>loadRow()</code> (multiple times)</li>
195      * <li><code>done()</code></li>
196      * </ul>
197      */
198     public interface Importer
199     {   void     startTable()       throws IOException;
200         String   loadTableName()    throws IOException;
201         int      loadWidth()        throws IOException;
202         Iterator loadColumnNames()  throws IOException;
203         Iterator loadRow()          throws IOException;
204         void     endTable()         throws IOException;
205     }
206 }
```

The Bridge Pattern

The Table interface is part of the Bridge design pattern mentioned earlier. A **Bridge** separates subsystems from each other so that they can change independently. Unlike Facade (which you looked at in the previous chapter in the context of the menuing subsystem), a Bridge provides complete isolation between subsystems. Code on one side of the Bridge has no idea what's on the other side. (Facade, you'll remember, doesn't hide the subsystem—it just simplifies access to it.)

I'll explain Bridge by presenting several examples, shown in Figure 4-4. The top section shows Java's older AWT subsystem, and though you probably won't be familiar with it unless you're doing something such as PalmPilot programming, the architecture is a nice reification of the classic Gang-of-Four Bridge. The "client" classes (the ones that use java.awt.Window) can change completely without impacting the implementation of AWT. By the same token, the classes on the other side of the bridge (various "peer" classes that interface to the operating system's GUI layer) can change without impacting the client classes. AWT leverages this ability to change in order to make the GUI model platform independent, so your PalmPilot application's UI may well run on Windows, Linux, or some other operating system without modification.

The peer classes (the classes that implement the *xxx*Peer interfaces) are created at runtime using an Abstract Factory called java.awt.Toolkit. (Abstract Factory was discussed in Chapter 2, but to refresh your memory, a Collection is an Abstract Factory of Iterator objects. A Concrete Factory [ArrayList, for example] implements the Abstract-Factory interface to produce a Concrete Products [some implementation of Iterator whose class is unknown]. Other implementations of Collection may [or may not—you don't know or care] produce different Concrete Products that implement the same Iterator interface in a way that makes sense for that particular data structure.) Toolkit is an abstract class used as an interface. (It has to be abstract because it needs to contain a static method.) The Singleton pattern is used to fetch a concrete instance of the Toolkit "interface." That is, the Toolkit.getDefaultToolkit() method determines the operating environment at runtime (typically, by looking at a system property) and then instantiates a Toolkit implementer appropriate for that environment. I've shown the Windows and Motif variants in Figure 4-4, but a Toolkit implementation must exist for every environment on which a particular JVM runs.

The concrete Toolkit object acts as an Abstract Factory of "peer" objects. The peers are system-dependent implementers of various graphical objects. I've shown one such peer (the WindowPeer, which implements an unbordered stand-alone window) in Figure 4-4, but 27 peer interfaces exist and create the whole panoply of graphical objects (ButtonPeer, CanvasPeer, CheckboxPeer, and so on). For each of these interfaces, a system-dependent implementation exists that's manufactured by the system-dependent concrete Toolkit in response to one of its create*xxx*(...) methods. For example, the Windows Toolkit (sun.awt.windows.WToolkit) will produce a Windows-specific peer (sun.awt.windows.WWindowPeer) when you call Toolkit .createWindow(). The Motif Toolkit (sun.awt.windows.MToolkit) will produce a Motif-specific peer (sun.awt.motif.MWindowPeer) when you call Toolkit.createWindow().

The Abstract Factory I've just described is used in concert with the Bridge pattern to isolate the mechanics of switching subsystems. The java.awt.Window class understands Toolkits and peers. When you create a Window, that object creates the appropriate peer. As long as you program in terms of Window objects, you don't need to know that the peer exists. Consequently, everything on the other side of the bridge (all the peers) can change radically, even at runtime, without your program's side of the bridge being impacted. By the same token, none of the peer implementations knows or cares how they're used. Consequently, your program can change radically without the peer implementations knowing or caring.

It is commonplace for Abstract Factory and Bridge to be used together in the way I just described. You will rarely see a Bridge without an Abstract Factory helping to create the Concrete Implementor objects (for example, `WWindowPeer` and `MWindowPeer`).

Another example of Singleton, Abstract Factory, and Bridge working together includes the `java.text.NumberFormat` class, which is used to parse and print numbers in a `Locale`-specific way. When you call `NumberFormat.getInstance()`, you're using Singleton to access an Abstract Factory that creates some subclass of `NumberFormat` that understands the current `Locale`. The `NumberFormat` "interface" serves as a Bridge that isolates your program from the rather complicated subsystem that deals with `Locale`-specific formatting. That subsystem could change (to support new `Locale`s, for example), and your code wouldn't know it.

Now let's apply the notion of Bridge to the current problem. Referring again to Figure 4-4, the `Table` uses an Abstract-Factory/Bridge strategy much like AWT and `NumberFormat`, but things are simplified a bit. I'll cover the Abstract-Factory issues in the next section, but the figure shows a small bridge consisting of the `Database` class (the core of the SQL engine, which I'll describe shortly) and the `Table` interface. If you program in terms of `Database` objects, you don't know or care that the `Table` exists. It's possible, then, to completely change the underlying table implementation—even at runtime—without your code caring about the change. For example, at some future date I may introduce several kinds of `Table`s that store the underlying data in a way that's particularly efficient for a particular data set. The Bridge, however, isolates your code from that change.

I'll come back to Bridge (and to the third part of Figure 4-4) later in this chapter.

Creating a Table, Abstract Factory

Now let's look at the Abstract-Factory component of the `Table` creation process. The following code creates a `Table` named *people* whose rows have three columns named *last, first,* and *addrID* (for *address identifier*—not a particularly readable name, but short column names are good because they improve search times):

```
Table people  = TableFactory.create(
        "people",  new String[]{"last", "first", "addrId" } );
```

You can also create a table from data stored on the disk in comma-separated-value (CSV) format. The following call reads a table called *address* (which must be stored in a file named *address*) from the specified directory:

```
Table address = tableFactory.load( "address.csv", "c:/data/directory" );
```

The data is stored in CSV format, where every row of the table is on its own line and commas separate the column values from each other. Here's a short sample:

```
address
addrId, street, city,    state,  zip
0, 12 MyStreet,    Berkeley,  CA, 99998
1,  34 Quarry Ln.,  Bedrock,    AZ, 00000
```

The first line is the table name, the second line names the columns, and the remaining lines specify the rows.

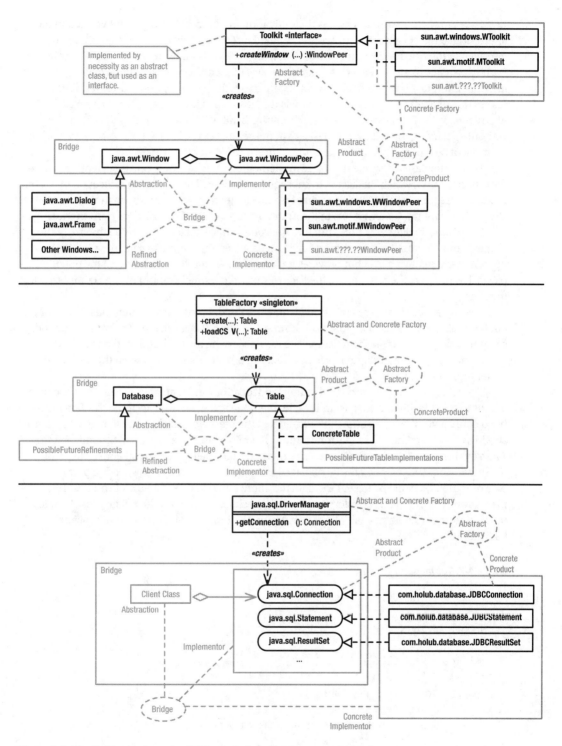

Figure 4-4. *The Bridge Pattern in AWT,* `com.holub.database,` *and JDBC*

The TableFactory demonstrates the reification of Abstract Factory that I've used most often. Unlike the classic reification (as embodied by Collection and Iterator), there's no interface in the Abstract Factory role of which Collection is an example. (More precisely, the TableFactory class serves as its own interface, as if Collection were an actual class, not an interface). You just have no need to complicate the code with a separate interface. What makes this reification an Abstract Factory is that it satisfies the same "intent" as a classic Abstract Factory: It provides a means of "creating families of related or dependant objects without specifying their concrete classes," to quote the Gang of Four. TableFactory is another example of how reifications of a particular pattern can differ in form.

This particular Factory creates Table implementers, of which only one is currently present—the ConcreteTable, which I'll discuss in subsequent sections. This particular reification of Abstract Factory is in some ways just the skeleton of a pattern, put in place primarily so that I can provide alternative Table implementations in the future. That is, this particular Factory isn't producing a "family" of objects right now but is put into the code to make it easy to increase the size of the "family" to some number greater than 1 if the need arises. Putting a small factory into the code up front has virtually no cost but provides for a lot of down-the-line flexibility, so the potential payback is high. On the other hand, the Factory does add a small amount of extra complexity to the code.

The TableFactory source code is in Listing 4-2. For the most part, its methods do nothing but hide calls to new. The load() method (Listing 4-2, line 57) is interesting in that the method can potentially load a table from various file formats on the disk. I'll explain the code in the load() method in greater depth in the next section, but let's look now at what the method does rather than how it does it.

The load() method is passed a filename and location, and it creates a Table from the data it finds in that file. Right now, it examines the filename extension to determine the data format, but it could just as easily examine the contents of the file. It's a trivial matter to make it load from an XML file rather than a CSV file, for example. It could even be passed a .sql file and load the Table by using the SQL. In other words, the method potentially isolates you completely from the underlying data format. The file read by the load() method may also specify a particular type of Table that could represent the data in a more efficient way than the current Table implementation, and the Factory could produce that specific Concrete Product. Since load() hides the complexity of creating a table, you can also think of TableFactory as a simple Facade |reification.

Listing 4-2. *TableFactory.java*

```
1   package com.holub.database;
2
3   import java.io.*;
4
5   public class TableFactory
6   {
7       /** Create an empty table.
8        *  @param name the table name
9        *  @param columns names of all the columns
10       *  @return the table
11       */
```

```java
12      public static Table create( String name, String[] columns )
13      {   return new ConcreteTable( name, columns );
14      }
15
16      /** Create a table from information provided by a
17       *  {@link Table.Importer} object.
18       */
19      public static Table create( Table.Importer importer )
20                                                          throws IOException
21      {   return new ConcreteTable( importer );
22      }
23
24      /** This convenience method is equivalent to
25       *  <code>load(name, new File(".") );</code>
26       *
27       *  @see #load(String,File)
28       */
29      public static Table load( String name ) throws IOException
30      {   return load( name, new File(".") );
31      }
32
33      /** This convenience method is equivalent to
34       *  <code>load(name, new File(location) );</code>
35       *
36       *  @see #load(String,File)
37       */
38      public static Table load( String name, String location )
39                                                          throws IOException
40      {   return load( name, new File(location) );
41      }
42
43      /* Create a table from some form stored on the disk.
44       *
45       * <p>At present, the filename extension is used to determine
46       * the data format, and only a comma-separated-value file
47       * is recognized (the filename must end in .csv).
48       *
49       * @param the filename. The table name is the string to the
50       *          left of the extension. For example, if the file
51       *          is "foo.csv," then the table name is "foo."
52       * @param the directory within which the file is found.
53       *
54       * @throws java.io.IOException if the filename extension is not
55       *          recognized.
56       */
57      public static Table load( String name, File directory )
58                                                          throws IOException
59      {
```

```
60            if( !(name.endsWith( ".csv" ) || name.endsWith( ".CSV" )) )
61                throw new java.io.IOException(
62                        "Filename (" +name+ ") does not end in "
63                        +"supported extension (.csv)" );
64
65            Reader in = new FileReader( new File( directory, name ));
66            Table loaded = new ConcreteTable( new CSVImporter( in ));
67            in.close();
68            return loaded;
69        }
70 }
```

Creating and Saving a Table: Passive Iterators and Builder

Now let's move onto the ConcreteTable implementation of Table. You can bring tables into
existence in two ways. A run-of-the-mill constructor is passed a table name and an array of
strings that define the column names. Here's an example:

```
Table t = new ConcreteTable( "table-name",
                             new String[]{ "column1", "column2" } );
```

The sources for ConcreteTable up to and including this constructor definition are in
Listing 4-3. The ConcreteTable represents the table as a list of arrays of Object (rowSet, line
32). The columnNames array (line 33) is an array of Strings that both define the column names
and organize the Object arrays that comprise the rows. A one-to-one relationship exists
between the index of a column name in the columnNames table and the index of the associated
data in one of the rowSet arrays. If you find the column name X at columnNames[i], then you
can find the associated data for column X at the ith position in one of these Object arrays.

The private indexOf method on line 49 is used internally to do this column-name-to-
index mapping. It's passed a column name and returns the associated index.

Note that everything is 0 indexed, which is intuitive to a Java programmer. Unfortunately,
SQL is 1 indexed, so you have to be careful if you implement any of the SQL methods that
specify column data using indexes. I've taken the coward's way out and have not implemented
any of the index-based JDBC methods. Be careful of off-by-one errors if you add these
methods to my implementation.

Of the other fields at the top of the class definition, tableName does the obvious, and
isDirty is true if the table has been modified. (I use this field to avoid unnecessary writes to
disk). I'll discuss transactionStack soon, when I discuss transaction processing.

Listing 4-3. *ConcreteTable.java: Simple Table Creation*

```
1  package com.holub.database;
2
3  import java.io.*;
4  import java.util.*;
5  import com.holub.tools.ArrayIterator;
6
7  /** The concrete class that implements the Table "interface."
8   * This class is not thread safe.
9   * Create instances of this class using {@link TableFactory} class,
```

```
10    *   not <code>new</code>.
11    *
12    *   <p>Note that a ConcreteTable is both serializable and "Cloneable,"
13    *   so you can easily store it onto the disk in binary form
14    *   or make a copy of it. Clone implements a shallow copy, however,
15    *   so it can be used to implement a rollback of an insert or delete,
16    *   but not an update.
17    */
18
19    /*package*/ class ConcreteTable implements Table
20    {
21        // Supporting clone() complicates the following declarations. In
22        // particular, the fields can't be final because they're modified
23        // in the clone() method. Also, the rows field has to be declared
24        // as a LinkedList (rather than a List) because Cloneable is made
25        // public at the LinkedList level. If you declare it as a List,
26        // you'll get an error message because clone()&mdash;for reasons that
27        // are mysterious to me&mdash;is declared protected in Object.
28        //
29        // Be sure to change the clone() method if you modify anything about
30        // any of these fields.
31
32        private LinkedList  rowSet = new LinkedList();
33        private String[]    columnNames;
34        private String      tableName;
35
36        private transient boolean    isDirty           = false;
37        private transient LinkedList transactionStack   = new LinkedList();
38
39        //-------------------------------------------------------------------
40        public ConcreteTable( String tableName, String[] columnNames )
41        {   this.tableName    = tableName;
42            this.columnNames = (String[]) columnNames.clone();
43        }
44
45        //-------------------------------------------------------------------
46        // Return the index of the named column. Throw an
47        // IndexOutOfBoundsException if the column doesn't exist.
48        //
49        private int indexOf( String columnName )
50        {   for( int i = 0; i < columnNames.length; ++i )
51                if( columnNames[i].equals( columnName ) )
52                    return i;
53
54            throw new IndexOutOfBoundsException(
55                    "Column ("+columnName+") doesn't exist in " + tableName );
56        }
```

The second constructor (shown in Listing 4-4) is more interesting. Here, the constructor is passed an object that implements the Table.Importer interface, defined on line 198 of Listing 4-1. The constructor uses the Importer to import data into an empty table. The source code is in Listing 4-4 (p. 196). As you can see, the constructor just calls the various methods of the Importer in sequence to get table *metadata* (the table name, column names, and so forth). It then calls loadRow() multiple times to load the rows.

Each call to loadRow() returns a standard java.util.Iterator, which iterates across the data representing a single row in left-to-right order. By using an iterator (rather than an array), I've isolated myself completely from the way that the row data is stored internally. The Iterator returned from the Importer could even synthesize the data internally.

The load process finishes up with a call to done().

Listing 4-4. *ConcreteTable.java Continued: Importing and Exporting*

```
57        //--------------------------------------------------------------------------
58        public ConcreteTable( Table.Importer importer ) throws IOException
59        {   importer.startTable();
60
61            tableName        =   importer.loadTableName();
62            int width        =   importer.loadWidth();
63            Iterator columns =   importer.loadColumnNames();
64
65            this.columnNames = new String[ width ];
66            for(int i = 0; columns.hasNext() ;)
67                columnNames[i++] = (String) columns.next();
68
69            while( (columns = importer.loadRow()) != null )
70            {   Object[] current = new Object[width];
71                for(int i = 0; columns.hasNext() ;)
72                    current[i++] = columns.next();
73                this.insert( current );
74            }
75            importer.endTable();
76        }
77        //--------------------------------------------------------------------------
78        public void export( Table.Exporter exporter ) throws IOException
79        {   exporter.startTable();
80            exporter.storeMetadata( tableName,
81                                    columnNames.length,
82                                    rowSet.size(),
83                                    new ArrayIterator(columnNames) );
84
85            for( Iterator i = rowSet.iterator(); i.hasNext(); )
86                exporter.storeRow( new ArrayIterator((Object[]) i.next()) );
87
88            exporter.endTable();
89            isDirty = false;
90        }
```

The CSVImporter class (Listing 4-5) demonstrates how to build an Importer. The following code shows a simplified version of how the TableFactory, discussed earlier, uses the CSVImporter to load a CSV file. The importer is created in the constructor call on the second line of the method. It's passed a Reader to use for input. The ConcreteTable constructor then calls the various methods of the CSVImporter to initialize the table.

```
public static Table loadCSV( String name, File directory ) throws IOException
{
    Reader in = new FileReader( new File( directory, name ));
    Table loaded = new ConcreteTable( new CSVImporter( in ));
    in.close();
    return loaded;
}
```

As you can see in Listing 4-5, there's not that much to building an importer. The startTable() method reads the table name first, and then it reads the metadata (the column names) from the second line and splits them into an array of String objects. The loadRow() method then reads the rows and then splits them. I'll discuss the ArrayIterator class called on line 30 in a moment.

Listing 4-5. *CSVImporter.java*

```
1   package com.holub.database;
2
3   import com.holub.tools.ArrayIterator;
4
5   import java.io.*;
6   import java.util.*;
7
8   public class CSVImporter implements Table.Importer
9   {   private BufferedReader  in;          // null once end-of-file reached
10          private String[]        columnNames;
11          private String          tableName;
12
13          public CSVImporter( Reader in )
14          {   this.in = in instanceof BufferedReader
15                          ? (BufferedReader)in
16                          : new BufferedReader(in)
17                          ;
18          }
19          public void startTable()            throws IOException
20          {   tableName   = in.readLine().trim();
21              columnNames = in.readLine().split("\\s*,\\s*");
22          }
23          public String loadTableName()       throws IOException
24          {   return tableName;
25          }
26          public int loadWidth()              throws IOException
27          {   return columnNames.length;
```

```
28      }
29      public Iterator loadColumnNames()    throws IOException
30      {    return new ArrayIterator(columnNames);
31      }
32
33      public Iterator loadRow()            throws IOException
34      {   Iterator row = null;
35          if( in != null )
36          {   String line = in.readLine();
37              if( line == null )
38                  in = null;
39              else
40                  row = new ArrayIterator( line.split("\\s*,\\s*"));
41          }
42          return row;
43      }
44
45      public void endTable() throws IOException
46  }
```

A more interesting importer is in Listing 4-6. The PeopleImporter loads a Table using the interactive UI pictured in Figure 4-5. You create a table that initializes itself interactively as follows:

```
Table t = TableFactory.create( new PeopleImporter() );
System.out.println( t.toString() );
System.exit(0);
```

My main intent is to illustrate the techniques used, so this class isn't really production quality, but it demonstrates an effective way to separate a UI from the "business object." I can completely change the structure of the user interface by changing the definition of the PeopleImporter. The Table implementation is completely unaffected by changes to the UI. In fact, the Table doesn't even know that it's being initialized from an interactive user interface.

Looking at the implementation, the getRowDataFromUser() method (Listing 4-6, line 46) creates the user interface, and the button handlers at the bottom of the method transfer the row data from the text-input fields to the rows LinkedList (declared on line 19). The balance of the class works much like the CSVImporter, but it transfers data from the rows array to the Table.

Figure 4-5. *The* PeopleImporter *user interface*

Listing 4-6. *PeopleImporter.java*

```
1   import com.holub.tools.ArrayIterator;
2   import com.holub.database.Table;
3   import com.holub.database.TableFactory;
4
5   import java.io.*;
6   import java.util.*;
7   import javax.swing.*;
8   import java.awt.*;
9   import java.awt.event.*;
10
11  /** A very simplistic demonstration of using Builder for
12   *  interactive input. Doesn't do validation, error detection,
13   *  etc. Also, I read all the user data, then import it to the
14   *  table, rather than reading the UI on a per-row basis.
15   */
16
17  public class PeopleImporter implements Table.Importer
18  {
19      private LinkedList rows = new LinkedList();
20
21      public void startTable()            throws IOException
22      {   getRowDataFromUser();
23      }
24      public String loadTableName()       throws IOException
25      {   return "people";
26      }
27      public int loadWidth()              throws IOException
28      {   return 3;
29      }
30      public Iterator loadColumnNames()   throws IOException
31      {   return new ArrayIterator(
32              new String[]{"first", "last", "addrID"});
33      }
34      public Iterator loadRow()           throws IOException
35      {   try
36          {   String[] row = (String[])( rows.removeFirst() );
37              return new ArrayIterator( row );
38          }
39          catch( NoSuchElementException e )
40          {   return null;
41          }
42      }
43
44      public void endTable() throws IOException
45
46      private void getRowDataFromUser()
```

```
47      {
48          final JTextField first  = new JTextField("              ");
49          final JTextField last   = new JTextField("              ");
50          final JDialog     ui     = new JDialog();
51
52          ui.setModal( true );
53          ui.getContentPane().setLayout( new GridLayout(3,1) );
54
55          JPanel panel = new JPanel();
56
57          panel.setLayout( new FlowLayout() );
58          panel.add( new JLabel("First Name:") );
59          panel.add( first );
60          ui.getContentPane().add( panel );
61
62          panel = new JPanel();
63
64          panel.setLayout( new FlowLayout() );
65          panel.add( new JLabel("Last Name:") );
66          panel.add( last );
67          ui.getContentPane().add( panel );
68
69          JButton done  = new JButton("Done");
70          JButton next  = new JButton("Next");
71              panel = new JPanel();
72
73          done.addActionListener
74          (   new ActionListener()
75              {   public void actionPerformed( ActionEvent e )
76                  {   rows.add
77                      (   new String[]{   first.getText().trim(),
78                                          last.getText().trim() }
79                      );
80                      ui.dispose();
81                  }
82              }
83          );
84
85          next.addActionListener
86          (   new ActionListener()
87              {   public void actionPerformed( ActionEvent e )
88                  {   rows.add
89                      (   new String[]{   first.getText().trim(),
90                                          last.getText().trim() }
91                      );
92                      first.setText("");
93                      last.setText("");
94                  }
```

```
95                    }
96                );
97              panel.add( next );
98              panel.add( done );
99              ui.getContentPane().add( panel );
100
101             ui.pack();
102             ui.show();
103         }
104
105         public static class Test
106         {   public static void main( String[] args ) throws IOException
107             {   Table t = TableFactory.create( new PeopleImporter() );
108                 System.out.println( t.toString() );
109                 System.exit(0);
110             }
111         }
112 }
```

The other method of interest in Listing 4-4 is the export() method, which exports the
table data similarly to the way the constructor imports the data. The export() method takes a
Table.Exporter argument and sends the Exporter the metadata and the rows. (The Exporter
interface is also an inner class of Table, defined on line 175 of Listing 4-1.)

As with the Importer constructor, the export() method first asks the Exporter to store the
table metadata, and then it passes the Exporter the rows one at a time. As was the case with
the Exporter constructor, the export() method passes the Exporter a java.util.Iterator
across the columns of a row rather than passing an Object array. This way, the Table implementor is not tied into a particular representation of the underlying data. (The ConcreteTable,
for example, isn't giving away the fact that it stores rows as Object arrays.)

The CSVExporter class in Listing 4-7 demonstrates how to build an Exporter. It's passed a
Writer and just writes the table data to that stream.

Listing 4-7. *CSVExporter.java*

```
1   package com.holub.database;
2
3   import java.io.*;
4   import java.util.*;
5
6   public class CSVExporter implements Table.Exporter
7   {   private final Writer out;
8       private       int    width;
9
10      public CSVExporter( Writer out )
11      {   this.out = out;
12      }
13
14      public void storeMetadata( String tableName,
```

```
15                                 int width,
16                                 int height,
17                                 Iterator columnNames ) throws IOException
18
19      {   this.width = width;
20          out.write(tableName == null ? "<anonymous>" : tableName );
21          out.write("\n");
22          storeRow( columnNames ); // comma-separated list of column IDs
23      }
24
25      public void storeRow( Iterator data ) throws IOException
26      {   int i = width;
27          while( data.hasNext() )
28          {   Object datum = data.next();
29
30              // Null columns are represented by an empty field
31              // (two commas in a row). There's nothing to write
32              // if the column data is null.
33              if( datum != null )
34                  out.write( datum.toString() );
35
36              if( --i > 0 )
37                  out.write(",\t");
38          }
39          out.write("\n");
40      }
41
42      public void startTable() throws IOException {/*nothing to do*/}
43      public void endTable()   throws IOException {/*nothing to do*/}
44  }
```

A more interesting example of an exporter is the JTableExporter in Listing 4-8, which builds the UI in Figure 4-6. The code that created the UI in the Test class is at the bottom of Listing 4-8 (line 45), but here's the essential stuff:

```
Table  people = ...;
JFrame frame  = ...;

JTableExporter tableBuilder = new JTableExporter();
people.export( tableBuilder );
frame.getContentPane().add(
        new JScrollPane( tableBuilder.getJTable() ) );
```

You pass the Table's export() method a JTableExporter() rather than a CSVExporter(). The JTableExporter() creates a JTable and populates it from the table data. You then extract the JTable from the exporter with the getJTable() call. (This "get" method is not really an accessor since the whole point of the JTableExporter is to create a JTable—I'm not giving away any surprising implementation details here.)

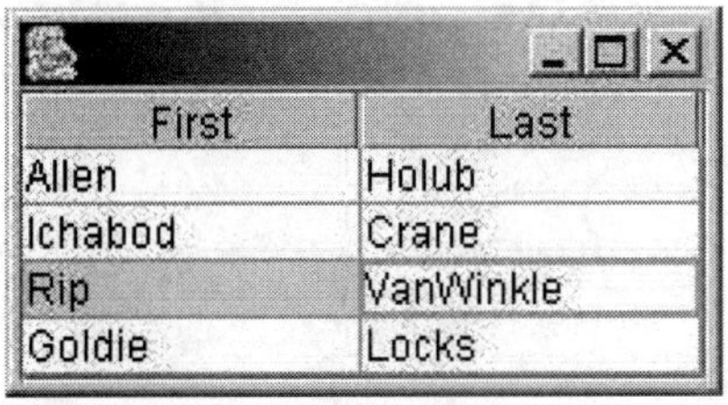

Figure 4-6. *The* JTableExporter *user interface*

Listing 4-8. *JTableExporter.java*

```
1   package com.holub.database;
2
3   import java.io.*;
4   import java.util.*;
5   import javax.swing.*;
6
7   public class JTableExporter implements Table.Exporter
8   {
9       private String[]    columnHeads;
10      private Object[][]  contents;
11      private int         rowIndex = 0;
12
13      public void startTable() throws IOException { rowIndex = 0; }
14
15      public void storeMetadata( String tableName,
16                                 int width,
17                                 int height,
18                                 Iterator columnNames ) throws IOException
19      {
20          contents    = new Object[height][width];
21          columnHeads = new String[width];
22
23          int columnIndex = 0;
24          while( columnNames.hasNext() )
25              columnHeads[columnIndex++] = columnNames.next().toString();
26      }
27
28      public void storeRow( Iterator data ) throws IOException
29      {   int columnIndex = 0;
30          while( data.hasNext() )
31              contents[rowIndex][columnIndex++] = data.next();
32          ++rowIndex;
33      }
34
35      public void endTable() throws IOException {/*nothing to do*/}
```

```
36
37     /** Return the Concrete Product of this builder&mdash;a JTable
38      *  initialized with the table data.
39      */
40     public JTable getJTable()
41     {   return new JTable( contents, columnHeads );
42     }
43
44     public static class Test
45     {   public static void main( String[] args ) throws IOException
46         {
47             Table people = TableFactory.create( "people",
48                             new String[]{ "First",   "Last"              } );
49             people.insert( new String[]{ "Allen",   "Holub"     } );
50             people.insert( new String[]{ "Ichabod", "Crane"     } );
51             people.insert( new String[]{ "Rip",     "VanWinkle" } );
52             people.insert( new String[]{ "Goldie",  "Locks"     } );
53
54             javax.swing.JFrame frame = new javax.swing.JFrame();
55             frame.setDefaultCloseOperation( JFrame.EXIT_ON_CLOSE );
56
57             JTableExporter tableBuilder = new JTableExporter();
58             people.export( tableBuilder );
59
60             frame.getContentPane().add(
61                     new JScrollPane( tableBuilder.getJTable() ) );
62             frame.pack();
63             frame.show();
64         }
65     }
66 }
```

The import/export code you've just been looking at is an example of the **Builder** design pattern. The basic idea of Builder is separate the code that creates an object from the object's internal representation so that the same construction process can be used to create different sorts of representations. Put another way, Builder separates a "business object" (an object that models some domain-level abstraction) from implementation-specific details such as how to display that business object on the screen or put it in a database. Using Builder, a domain-level object can create multiple representations of itself without having to be rewritten. The business object has the role of Director in the pattern, and objects in the role of Concrete-Builder (which implement the Builder interface) create the representation. In the current example, ConcreteTable is the Director, Table.Exporter is the Builder, and CSVExporter is the Concrete Builder.

To my mind Table.Importer is also a Builder (of Table objects) and CSVImporter is the matching Concrete Builder, though this way of looking at things is rather backward since I'm turning multiple representations into a single object rather than the other way around. The implementation is certainly similar, however.

As you saw in the PeopleImporter and JTableExporter classes, Builder nicely solves the object-oriented UI conundrum mentioned way back in Chapter 2. If an object can't expose implementation details (so you can't have getter and setter methods), then how do you create a user interface, particularly if an object has to represent itself in different ways to different subsystems? An object could have a method that returns a JComponent representation of itself or of some attribute of itself, but what if you're building a server-side UI and you need an HTML representation? What if you're talking to a database and you need an XML or SQL representation? Adding a billion methods to the class, one for each possible representation (getXML(), getJComponent(), getSQL(), getHTML(), and so on) isn't a viable solution—it's too much of a maintenance hassle to go into the class definition every time a new business requirement needs a new representation..

As you just saw, however, a Builder is perfectly able to accommodate disparate representations, and adding a new Builder doesn't require any modifications to the domain-level object at all. Any Table can be represented as a CSV list and also as a JComponent, all without having to modify the Table implementation. In fact, Builder provides a nice way to concentrate all the UI logic in a single place (the Concrete Builder) and to separate the UI logic from the "business logic" (all of which is in the Director).

Using Builder lets me support representations that don't need to exist when the program is first written. Adding XMLImporter and XMLExporter implementations of Table.Importer and Table.Exporter is an easy matter. Once I create these new classes, a Table can now store itself in XML format and load itself from an XML file. Moreover, I've added XML export/import to every Table implementation (all of which have to be Directors), not just ConcreteTable.

The only difficulty with Builder is in the design of the Builder interface itself. This interface has to have methods that accommodate all displayable state information. Consequently, a tight coupling relationship exists between the objects in the Director and Builder roles, simply because the Builder interface has to have methods that are "tuned" for use by the Director. It's possible that the Director could change in such a way that you would have to modify the Builder interface (and all the Concrete Builders, too) to accommodate the change. This problem is really the getter problem I discussed in Chapter 1. Builder, however, restricts the scope of the problem to a small number of classes (the Concrete Builders). I'd have a much worse situation if I were to put get/set methods in the Director (the Table). Unknown coupling relationships with random classes would be scattered all over the program. In any event, I haven't often needed to make those sorts of changes in practice.

Populating the Table

The next order of business is to put some data into the table. Several methods are provided for this purpose. The simplest method, shown below, inserts a new row into the table. It's up to you to assure that the order of array elements matches the order of columns specified when the table was created.

```
people.insert( new Object[]{ "Holub", "Allen", "1" } );
```

The foregoing method is delicate—it depends on a particular column ordering to work correctly. It's too easy to get the column ordering wrong. A second overload of insert(...) solves the problem by requiring both column names and their contents. The columns don't have to be in declaration order, but the two arrays much match. When firstArgument[i] specifies a column, secondArgument[i] must specify that column's contents. Here's an example:

```
people.insert( new String[]{ "addrId",    "first", "last"      },
               new Object[]{ "1",          "Fred",  "Flintstone"} );
```

Also, Collection versions of both methods exist. The following code creates a row from the Collection elements:

```
List rowData = new ArrayList();
rowData.add("Flintstone");
rowData.add("Wilma");
rowData.add("1")
people.insert(rowData);
```

The following codes does the same thing, but with rows specified in an arbitrary order:

```
List columnNames = new ArrayList();
columnNames.add("addrId");
columnNames.add("first");
columnNames.add("last");

List rowData = new ArrayList();
rowData.add("1")
rowData.add("Pebbles");
rowData.add("Flintstone");
people.insert( columnNames, rowData );
```

This last method seems to be of dubious value, but it turns out that a two-collection variant is quite useful when building the SQL interpreter, as you'll see later in the chapter.

Finally, I've provided a Map version where the keys are the column names and the values are the contents.

The source code for the methods that insert rows is in Listing 4-9. The overloads that don't take column-name arguments just add a new object array to the rowSet. The other methods go through the column names in sequence, determine the index in the object array associated with that column (using indexOf(...)), and put the appropriate data into the appropriate element of the Object array that represents the row.

The actual inserting of the object array into the list representing the table is done by the doInsert() method (Listing 4-9, line 148). I'll come back to the registerInsert(...) method that's called at the top of doInsert() in a moment, when I talk about the undo system. For now, note that all insert operations mark the table as "dirty." This boolean is initially false; it's marked true by all operations that modify the table, and it's reset to false by the export() method discussed earlier. A client class can determine the "dirty" state of the table by calling someTable.isDirty(). The SQL-engine layer uses this mechanism to avoid flushing to disk tables that have been read, but not modified, when you issue a SQL DUMP request.

The isDirty() method, by the way, is not a "get" method of the sort I was railing against in Chapter 1, even though it's implemented in the simplest possible way to return a private field:

```
public boolean isDirty(){ return isDirty; }
```

The fact that the "dirty" state is stored in a boolean, and that getDirty() returns that boolean, is just an implementation convenience. I'm not exposing any implementation details (there's no way that the client can determine how the table decides whether it's dirty), and since there's no setDirty(), there's no way for the "dirty" state to be corrupted from outside. I can change the implementation and represent the "dirty" state in some other way without impacting the interface or the classes that use the interface.

If you find this explanation confusing, think about the design process. I decided at design time that a "dirty" state was necessary, so I provided an isDirty() method in the interface. Later, I added the simplest implementation possible. This way of working is fundamentally different from starting with a isDirty field in the class and then adding getDirty() and setDirty() as a matter of course. It would be a serious error for a setDirty() method to exist because, where that method present, a client object could break a Table object by making the Table think it didn't need to be flushed to disk when it actually did; setDirty() has no valid use.

Listing 4-9. *ConcreteTable.java Continued: Inserting Rows*

```
91      //------------------------------------------------------------------
92      // Inserting
93      //
94      public int insert( String[] intoTheseColumns, Object[] values )
95      {
96          assert( intoTheseColumns.length == values.length )
97                  :"There must be exactly one value for "
98                  +"each specified column" ;
99
100         Object[] newRow = new Object[ width() ];
101
102         for( int i = 0; i < intoTheseColumns.length; ++i )
103             newRow[ indexOf(intoTheseColumns[i]) ] = values[i];
104
105         doInsert( newRow );
106         return 1;
107     }
108     //------------------------------------------------------------------
109     public int insert( Collection intoTheseColumns, Collection values )
110     {   assert( intoTheseColumns.size() == values.size() )
111                 :"There must be exactly one value for "
112                     +"each specified column" ;
113
114         Object[] newRow = new Object[ width() ];
115
116         Iterator v = values.iterator();
```

```
117            Iterator c = intoTheseColumns.iterator();
118            while( c.hasNext() && v.hasNext() )
119                newRow[ indexOf((String)c.next()) ] = v.next();
120
121            doInsert( newRow );
122            return 1;
123        }
124        //-------------------------------------------------------------------
125        public int insert( Map row )
126        {   // A map is considered to be "ordered,"  with the order defined
127            // as the order in which an iterator across a "view" returns
128            // values. My reading of this statement is that the iterator
129            // across the keySet() visits keys in the same order as the
130            // iterator across the values() visits the values.
131
132            return insert ( row.keySet(), row.values() );
133        }
134        //-------------------------------------------------------------------
135        public int insert( Object[] values )
136        {   assert values.length == width()
137                : "Values-array length (" + values.length + ") "
138                + "is not the same as table width (" + width() +")";
139
140            doInsert( (Object[]) values.clone() );
141            return 1;
142        }
143        //-------------------------------------------------------------------
144        public int insert( Collection values )
145        {   return insert( values.toArray() );
146        }
147        //-------------------------------------------------------------------
148        private void doInsert( Object[] newRow )
149        {
150            rowSet.add( newRow );
151            registerInsert( newRow );
152            isDirty = true;
153        }
```

Examining a Table: The Iterator Pattern

Now that you've populated the table, you may want to examine it. The design pattern is **Iterator**, of which Java's java.util.Iterator class is a familiar reification. The basic idea is that Iterator provides a way to access the elements of some *aggregate* object (some data structure) without exposing the internal representation of the aggregate. Java's Iterator is just one way to accomplish this end. Any reification that you invent that lets a client object examine an aggregate one element at a time is a reification of Iterator.

Another simple reification of Iterator is the ArrayIterator class, shown in Listing 4-10. This class just wraps an array with a class that implements the java.util.Iterator interface, so you can pass arrays to methods that take Iterator arguments. The ArrayIterator is also an example of the Adapter design pattern that I'll discuss later. ArrayIterator adapts an array object to implement an interface that an array doesn't normally implement.

Listing 4-10. *ArrayIterator.java*

```
1   package com.holub.tools;
2
3   import java.util.*;
4
5   /** A simple implementation of java.util.Iterator that enumerates
6    *  over arrays. Use this class when you want to isolate the
7    *  data structures used to hold some collection by passing an
8    *  Enumeration to some method.
9    * <!-- ... -->
10   * @author Allen I. Holub
11   */
12
13  public final class ArrayIterator implements Iterator
14  {
15      private int            position = 0;
16      private final Object[]  items;
17
18      public ArrayIterator(Object[] items){ this.items = items; }
19
20      public boolean hasNext()
21      {   return ( position < items.length );
22      }
23
24      public Object next()
25      {   if( position >= items.length )
26              throw new NoSuchElementException();
27          return items[ position++ ];
28      }
29
30      public void remove()
31      {   throw new UnsupportedOperationException(
32                              "ArrayIterator.remove()");
33      }
34
35      /** Not part of the Iterator interface, returns the data
36       *  set in array form. Modifying the returned array will
37       *  not affect the iteration at all.
38       */
39      public Object[] toArray()
```

```
40        {   return (Object[]) items.clone();
41        }
42  }
```

Though most iterators don't give you control over the order of traversal (the ArrayIterator just goes through the array elements in order), no requirement exists that an iterator visit nodes in any particular order. A ReverseArrayIterator could traverse from high to low indexes, for example. A tree class may have inOrderIterator(), preOrderIterator(), and postOrderIterator() methods, all of which returned objects that implemented the Iterator interface, but those objects would traverse the tree nodes "in order," root first or depth first. You can define an iterator to handle whatever ordering you like—even random ordering is okay—as long as the ordering is specified in the class contract. Some iterators—such as the tree iterators just discussed—may make requirements on the underlying data structure, however.

Iterators can also modify the underlying data structure. Some of the java.util.Iterator implementers support a remove() operation that lets you remove the current element from the underlying data structure, for example.

Iterator is used all over the ConcreteTable, but most important, it's used to examine or modify the rows. Listing 4-11 defines the Cursor interface used by the Table, but let's look at how it's used before looking at the code. The following method prints all the rows of the Table passed into the method as an argument:

```
public void print( Table someTable )
{
    Cursor current = someTable.rows();

    while( current.advance() )
    {   for( java.util.Iterator columns = current.columns(); columns.hasNext(); )
            System.out.print( (String) columns.next() + " " );
    }
}
```

The Cursor knows about columns, so you could print only the first- and last-name fields of some Table as follows:

```
public void printFirstAndLast( Table someTable )
{
    for(Cursor current = someTable.rows(); current.advance() ;)
    {
        System.out.print( current.column("first").toString() + " " +
                          current.column("last").toString()  + " "  );
    }
}
```

A Cursor can also update the contents of a row or delete the current row. (You actually modify the underlying table when you use these methods.) The following code changes the names of all people named Smith to Jones. It also deletes all rows representing people named Doe:

```java
public void modify( Table people )
{
    for( Cursor current = people.rows(); current.advance() ;)
    {   if( current.column("last").equals( "Smith" ) )
            current.update("last", "Jones" );

        else if( current.column("last").equals( "Doe" ) )
            current.delete();

    }
}
```

This functionality works properly with the transaction system that I'll discuss later in the chapter, so you can roll back modifications if necessary.

Listing 4-11. *Cursor.java*

```java
1   package com.holub.database;
2
3   import java.util.Iterator;
4   import java.util.NoSuchElementException;
5
6   /** The Cursor provides you with a way of examining the
7    *  tables that you create and the tables that are created
8    *  as a result of a select or join operation. This is
9    *  an "updateable" cursor, so you can modify columns or
10   *  delete rows via the cursor without problems. (Updates
11   *  and deletes done through the cursor <em>are</em> handled
12   *  properly with respect to the transactioning system, so
13   *  they can be committed or rolled back.)
14   */
15
16  public interface Cursor
17  {
18      /** Metadata method required by JDBC wrapper--Return the name
19       *  of the table across which we're iterating. I am deliberately
20       *  not allow access to the Table itself, because this would
21       *  allow uncontrolled modification of the table via the
22       *  iterator.
23       *  @return the name of the table or null if we're iterating
24       *          across a nameless table like the one created by
25       *          a select operation.
26       */
27      String tableName();
28
29      /** Advances to the next row, or if this iterator has never
30       *  been used, advances to the first row.
```

```
31      *  @throws NoSuchElementException if this call would advance
32      *          past the last row.
33      *  @return true if the iterator is positioned at a valid
34      *          element after the advance.
35      */
36     boolean advance() throws NoSuchElementException;
37
38     /** Return the contents of the requested column of the current
39      *  row. You should
40      *  treat the cells accessed through this method as read only
41      *  if you ever expect to use the table in a thread-safe
42      *  environment. Modify the table using {@link Table#update}.
43      *
44      *  @throws IndexOutOfBoundsException --- the requested column
45      *      doesn't exist.
46      */
47
48     Object column( String columnName );
49
50     /** Return a java.util.Iterator across all the columns in
51      *  the current row.
52      */
53     Iterator columns();
54
55     /** Return true if the iterator is traversing the
56      *  indicated table.
57      */
58     boolean isTraversing( Table t );
59
60     /** Replace the value of the indicated column of the current
61      *  row with the indicated new value.
62      *
63      *  @throws IllegalArgumentException if the newValue is
64      *          the same as the object that's being updated.
65      *
66      *  @return the former contents of the now-modified cell.
67      */
68     Object update( String columnName, Object newValue );
69
70     /** Delete the row at the current cursor position.
71      */
72     void delete();
73 }
```

The comments in Listing 4-11 describe the remainder of the methods in the interface adequately, so let's move onto the implementation in Listing 4-12.

Cursors are extracted from a Table using a classic Gang-of-Four Abstract Factory. The Table interface defines an Abstract Cursor Factory; the ConcreteTable, which implements that interface, is the Concrete Factory; the Cursor interface defines the Abstract Product; the Concrete Product an instance of the Results class on line 161 of Listing 4-12. As you saw in the earlier examples, you get a Cursor by calling rows() (Listing 4-12, line 157), which just instantiates and returns a Results object.

Looking at the implementation, the Results object traverses the List of rows using a standard java.util.Iterator. The advance() method on line 169 of Listing 4-12 just delegates to the Iterator, for example.

The interesting methods are update() and delete(), at the end of the listing. Other than do what their names imply, both methods set the table's "dirty" flag to indicate that something has changed. They also register the operation with the transaction-processing system (described on p. 226) by calling registerUpdate(...) or registerDelete(...).

Listing 4-12. *ConcreteTable.java Continued: Traversing and Modifying*

```
154     //-------------------------------------------------------------------------
155     // Traversing and cursor-based Updating and Deleting
156     //
157     public Cursor rows()
158     {   return new Results();
159     }
160     //-------------------------------------------------------------------------
161     private final class Results implements Cursor
162     {   private final Iterator rowIterator  = rowSet.iterator();
163         private      Object[] row           = null;
164
165         public String tableName()
166         {   return ConcreteTable.this.tableName;
167         }
168
169         public boolean advance()
170         {   if( rowIterator.hasNext() )
171             {   row = (Object[]) rowIterator.next();
172                 return true;
173             }
174             return false;
175         }
176
177         public Object column( String columnName )
178         {   return row[ indexOf(columnName) ];
179         }
180
181         public Iterator columns()
182         {   return new ArrayIterator( row );
183         }
184
```

```
185        public boolean isTraversing( Table t )
186        {   return t == ConcreteTable.this;
187        }
188
189        // This method is for use by the outer class only and is not part
190        // of the Cursor interface.
191        private Object[] cloneRow()
192        {   return (Object[])( row.clone() );
193        }
194
195        public Object update( String columnName, Object newValue )
196        {
197            int index = indexOf(columnName);
198
199            // The following test is required for undo to work correctly.
200            if( row[index] == newValue )
201                throw new IllegalArgumentException(
202                                        "May not replace object with itself");
203
204            Object oldValue = row[index];
205            row[index]      = newValue;
206            isDirty         = true;
207
208            registerUpdate( row, index, oldValue );
209            return oldValue;
210        }
211
212
213        public void delete()
214        {   Object[] oldRow = row;
215            rowIterator.remove();
216            isDirty = true;
217
218            registerDelete( oldRow );
219        }
220    }
```

Passive Iterators

The iterators we've been looking at are called *external* (or *active*) iterators because they're separate objects from the data structure they're traversing.

The storeRow() method of the Builder discussed in the previous section is an example of another sort of Iterator. Rather than creating an iterator object that's external to the data structure, the export() method effectively implements the traversal mechanism inside the data-structure class (the ConcreteTable). The export() method iterates by calling the Exporter's storeRow() method multiple times. We're still visiting every node in turn, so this is still the Iterator pattern, but things are now inside out.

This kind of iterator is known as an *internal* (or *passive*) iterator. The idea of a passive iterator is that you provide some data structure with a Command object, one method of which is called repetitively (once for each node) and is passed the "current" node.

Passive iterators are quite useful when the data structure is inherently difficult to traverse. Consider the case of a simple binary tree such as the one shown in Listing 4-13. A passive iterator is a simple recursive function, easy to write. The traverseInOrder method (Listing 4-13, line 31) demonstrates a passive iterator. This textbook recursive-traversal algorithm just passes each node to the Examiner object (declared just above this method, on line 23) in turn. You could print all the nodes of a tree like this:

```
Tree t = new Tree();
//...
t.traverse
(   new Examiner()
    {   public void examine( Object currentNode )
        {   System.out.println( currentNode.toString() );
        }
    }
);
```

Now consider the implementation of an active (external) iterator across a tree. The Tree class's iterator() method (line 49) returns a standard java.util.Iterator that visits every node of the tree in order. My main point in showing you this code is to show you how opaque this code is. The algorithm is short but difficult to both understand and write. (In essence, I use a stack to keep track of parent nodes as I traverse the tree.)

Listing 4-13. *Tree.java: A Simple Binary-Tree Implementation*

```
1   import java.util.*;
2
3   /** This class demonstrates how to make both internal and external
4    *  iterators across a binary tree. I've deliberately used a tree
5    *  rather than a linked list to make the external in-order iterator
6    *  more complicated.
7    */
8
9   public class Tree
10  {
11      private Node root = null;
12
13      private static class Node
14      {   public Node left, right;
15          public Object item;
16          public Node( Object item )
17          {   this.item = item;
18          }
19      }
20      //-------------------------------------------------------------------
```

```
21    // A Passive (internal) iterator
22    //
23    public interface Examiner
24    {   public void examine( Object currentNode );
25    }
26
27    public void traverse( Examiner client )
28    {   traverseInOrder( root, client );
29    }
30
31    private void traverseInOrder(Node current, Examiner client)
32    {   if( current == null )
33          return;
34
35      traverseInOrder(current.left,  client);
36      client.examine (current.item );
37      traverseInOrder(current.right, client);
38    }
39
40    public void add( Object item )
41    {   if( root == null )
42          root = new Node( item );
43      else
44          insertItem( root, item );
45    }
46    //-------------------------------------------------------------------
47    // An Active (external) iterator
48    //
49    public Iterator iterator()
50    {   return new Iterator()
51      {   private Node        current = root;
52          private LinkedList stack    = new LinkedList();
53
54          public Object next()
55          {
56            while( current != null )
57            {   stack.addFirst( current );
58                current = current.left;
59            }
60
61            if( stack.size() != 0 )
62            {   current = (Node)
63                        ( stack.removeFirst() );
64                Object toReturn=current.item;
65                current = current.right;
66                return toReturn;
67            }
```

```
68
69                        throw new NoSuchElementException();
70                    }
71
72            public boolean hasNext()
73            {    return !(current==null && stack.size()==0);
74            }
75
76            public void remove()
77            { throw new UnsupportedOperationException();
78            }
79        };
80    }
81    //------------------------------------------------------------------
82
83    private void insertItem( Node current, Object item )
84    { if(current.item.toString().compareTo(item.toString())>0)
85        {    if( current.left == null )
86                current.left = new Node(item);
87            else
88                insertItem( current.left, item );
89        }
90        else
91        {    if( current.right == null )
92                current.right = new Node(item);
93            else
94                insertItem( current.right, item );
95        }
96    }
97
98    public static void main( String[] args )
99    {    Tree t = new Tree();
100        t.add("D");
101        t.add("B");
102        t.add("F");
103        t.add("A");
104        t.add("C");
105        t.add("E");
106        t.add("G");
107
108        Iterator i = t.iterator();
109        while( i.hasNext() )
110            System.out.print( i.next().toString() );
111
112        System.out.println("");
113
114        t.traverse( new Examiner()
```

```
115                    { public void examine(Object o)
116                        { System.out.print( o.toString() );
117                        }
118                    } );
119          System.out.println("");
120      }
121  }
```

I'm not really done with the Iterator pattern because I haven't discussed the problems that iterators can cause in mulithreading situations, so I'll come back to them later in the current chapter. For now, I want to move onto the transaction-support subsystem.

Implementing Transactions (Undo) with the Command Pattern

The next interesting chunk of the ConcreteTable class is the "undo" subsystem that you need to support transactions. The design pattern here is the lowly Command pattern I discussed in Chapter 1. To refresh your memory, a Command object encapsulates knowledge of how to do some unspecified operation. For you C/C++ programmers, it's the object-oriented equivalent of a "function pointer," but rather than passing around a function that does something, you pass around an object who knows how to do it. The simplest reification of Command is Java's Runnable class, which encapsulates knowledge of what to do on a thread. You create a Command object like this:

```
Runnable backgroundTask = new Runnable()
                    { public void run()
                        {   System.out.println("Hello World");
                        }
                    };
```

and then pass it to a Thread object:

```
Thread controller = new Thread( backgroundTask );
```

You then start up the thread like this:

```
controller.start();
```

and the controller asks the Command object to do whatever it does by calling run().

That last statement is key to differentiating the Command pattern from some of the other design patterns that use Command objects (such as Strategy, discussed in Chapter 1 and later in this chapter). In Command, the Invoker (the Thread object) doesn't actually know what the Concrete Command object (backgroundTask) is going to do.

One of the more interesting uses of the Command pattern is in implementing an undo system. Since I use the Table to implement a database, it must be possible to *roll back* a transaction at the Table level. (JDBC doesn't actually require transactions, but I do.) Put another way, a modification to the Table may require several operations (inserts, updates, and so on), any one of which could fail for some reason. This group of logically connected operations forms a single transaction, and if any operation in the transaction fails, they all should fail. If you perform the first two operations of a transaction, for example, and the third operation then fails, then you must be able to undo the effect of the first two operations. This undo to the beginning of the transaction is called a *rollback*.

The complementary notion to a rollback is a *commit*. Once a transaction is committed, it becomes permanent. You can't roll it back anymore. Formally, once you begin a transaction, you can terminate the transaction by issuing a rollback request (which puts the table back into the state it was in when you issued the begin), or you commit the transaction.

The situation is made only marginally more complicated by the notion of nested transactions. Consider the following SQL:

```
BEGIN
    Operation-group A
    BEGIN
        Operation-group B
    ROLLBACK
    Operation-group C
COMMIT
```

The rollback causes the operations in Operation-group B to be ignored, so the result of the foregoing is to perform the operations in group A and C, but not B. On the other hand, the following SQL does nothing at all since the outermost transaction is rolled back:

```
BEGIN
    Operation-group A
    BEGIN
        Operation-group B
    COMMIT
    Operation-group C
ROLLBACK
```

Transaction processing can get a lot more complicated than what I've just described, but since my database is built on a single-user, single-process model and I'm doing only simple things with it, the transaction system I just described is adequate, so I won't go further into the topic.

One way to implement commit/rollback is to take a snapshot of the entire table every time you begin a transaction. A rollback restores the previous state from the snapshot. A commit just throws away the snapshot. You can implement nested transactions using a snapshot strategy by pushing a snapshot of the Table onto a stack every time you issue a BEGIN statement. You roll back by restoring the table to whatever state was remembered in the snapshot at the top of the stack. You commit a transaction simply by throwing away the snapshot at the top of the stack.

The main problem with a snapshot strategy for undo is that it's too inefficient in both time and memory. The other commonplace problem with snapshots (not really an issue here but often an issue in other applications) is that an operation may have side effects, and simply restoring an object or objects to a previous state doesn't undo the side effects. For example, consider an operation that both changes the internal state of the program but also modifies a database. The matching undo must not only put the program back into its original state, but also put the database back into its original state. A snapshot does only the former.

To your rescue comes a more sophisticated use of the Command pattern than the one I used earlier. I define an interface that a Table can use to request an undo operation (the Undo interface on line 224 of Listing 4-14). I then implement that interface with three separate classes (UndoInsert, UndoDelete, and UndoUpdate on lines 228, 238, and 248 of Listing 4-14). Taking UndoInsert as characteristic, you pass its constructor a reference to the inserted row. When the Table passes an execute() message to this object, it removes that row from the List that represents the table. The Invoker (the ConcreteTable object) doesn't actually know or care what the Concrete-Command objects (the Undo implementers) actually do, as long as the undo something.

Now that I've defined the Command objects, I need to organize them. The Undo stack was defined at the top of the class definition (Listing 4-3, line 37, previously) as follows:

```
private transient LinkedList transactionStack = new LinkedList();
```

The stack is actually a stack of lists, one list for each transaction level. Consider the following calls (which I've indented to show the transaction nesting).

```
 1  Table t new new ConcreteTable("x", "data"); // a single-column table
 2
 3  t.begin();
 4      t.insert( "data", "A" )
 5      t.insert( "data", "B" )
 6      t.begin();
 7          t.insert( "data", "C" )
 8          t.insert( "data", "D" )
 9      t.commit(false);
10  t.commit(false);
```

Transactioning is disabled until you issue the outermost begin() call: All operations are effectively committed when executed, and the transactionStack() is empty. Issuing a begin causes an empty list to be pushed onto the stack, and every insert, delete, or update operation will add a corresponding Undo object to the list at top of stack. The transactionStack will look like this just before the commit() on line 9, previously, is issued:

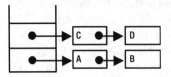

The four objects on the stack are instances of UndoInsert that remember the rows that they inserted. If a rollback() had been issued instead of the commit() on line 9, previously, the ConcreteTable would traverse the list of Undo objects at top of stack, asking each one to execute(), thereby undoing the operation. The list at top of stack is then discarded (so the A and B nodes are still on the stack). The commit() on line 9 doesn't execute anything, however. Rather, the ConcreteStack concatenates the operations in the list at the top of stack to the list just under it on the stack. After the first commit(), the transactionStack looks like this:

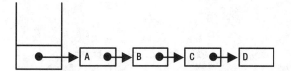

Again, if you issued a rollback at this juncture, the system would traverse the entire list asking each undo object to execute() and then discarding the list. Since this is a commit operation, though, the undo system just discards the list at the top of stack.

The implementation of this system starts on line 265 of Listing 4-14. The begin() method pushes a new list onto the stack. The register methods create the proper sort of undo object and add them to the end of the list at the top of stack. (Note that nothing is added if the stack is empty, because no begin has been issued in that case.) Finally, commit(...) and rollback(...) modify the list and execute Undo objects, as described previously.

Listing 4-14. *ConcreteTable.java Continued: Transaction Support*

```
221     //-------------------------------------------------------------------------
222     // Undo subsystem.
223     //
224     private interface Undo
225     {   void execute();
226     }
227     // - - - - - - - - - - - - - - - - - - - - - - - - - - - - - - - - - - -
228     private class UndoInsert implements Undo
229     {   private final Object[] insertedRow;
230         public UndoInsert( Object[] insertedRow )
231         {   this.insertedRow = insertedRow;
232         }
233         public void execute()
234         {   rowSet.remove( insertedRow );
235         }
236     }
237     // - - - - - - - - - - - - - - - - - - - - - - - - - - - - - - - - - - -
238     private class UndoDelete implements Undo
239     {   private final Object[] deletedRow;
240         public UndoDelete( Object[] deletedRow )
241         {   this.deletedRow = deletedRow;
242         }
243         public void execute()
244         {   rowSet.add( deletedRow );
245         }
246     }
247     // - - - - - - - - - - - - - - - - - - - - - - - - - - - - - - - - - - -
248     private class UndoUpdate implements Undo
249     {
250         private Object[] row;
```

```
251          private int cell;
252          private Object oldContents;
253
254          public UndoUpdate( Object[] row, int cell, Object oldContents )
255          {   this.row        = row;
256              this.cell       = cell;
257              this.oldContents = oldContents;
258          }
259
260          public void execute()
261          {   row[ cell ] = oldContents;
262          }
263      }
264      // - - - - - - - - - - - - - - - - - - - - - - - - - - - - - - - - -
265      public void begin()
266      {   transactionStack.addLast( new LinkedList() );
267      }
268      // - - - - - - - - - - - - - - - - - - - - - - - - - - - - - - - - - -
269      private void register( Undo op )
270      {   ((LinkedList) transactionStack.getLast()).addLast( op );
271      }
272      private void registerUpdate(Object[] row, int cell, Object oldContents)
273      {   if( !transactionStack.isEmpty() )
274              register( new UndoUpdate(row, cell, oldContents) );
275      }
276      private void registerDelete( Object[] oldRow )
277      {   if( !transactionStack.isEmpty() )
278              register( new UndoDelete(oldRow) );
279      }
280      private void registerInsert( Object[] newRow )
281      {   if( !transactionStack.isEmpty() )
282              register( new UndoInsert(newRow) );
283      }
284      // - - - - - - - - - - - - - - - - - - - - - - - - - - - - - - - - - - -
285      public void commit( boolean all ) throws IllegalStateException
286      {   if( transactionStack.isEmpty() )
287              throw new IllegalStateException("No BEGIN for COMMIT");
288          do
289          {   LinkedList currentLevel =
290                          (LinkedList) transactionStack.removeLast();
291
292              if( !transactionStack.isEmpty() )
293                  ((LinkedList)transactionStack.getLast())
294                                      .addAll(currentLevel);
295
296          } while( all && !transactionStack.isEmpty() );
297      }
```

```
298     // - - - - - - - - - - - - - - - - - - - - - - - - - - - - - - - - - - -
299     public void rollback( boolean all ) throws IllegalStateException
300     {   if( transactionStack.isEmpty() )
301             throw new IllegalStateException("No BEGIN for ROLLBACK");
302         do
303         {   LinkedList currentLevel =
304                         (LinkedList) transactionStack.removeLast();
305
306             while( !currentLevel.isEmpty() )
307                 ((Undo) currentLevel.removeLast()).execute();
308
309         } while( all && !transactionStack.isEmpty() );
310     }
311     // - - - - - - - - - - - - - - - - - - - - - - - - - - - - - - - - - -
```

Modifying a Table: The Strategy Pattern

Once you've built a table, you may want to change it. As you saw earlier, you can use a Cursor for this purpose, but that's sometimes inconvenient. Consequently, two methods are provided to do updates and deletes without using a Cursor explicitly.

By way of demonstration, the following code deletes everyone named Flintstone from the people table:

```
people.delete
(   new Selector.Adapter()
    {   public boolean approve( Cursor[] tables )
        {   return tables[0].column("lastName").equals("Flintstone");
        }
    }
);
```

The design pattern here is Strategy—introduced in Chapter 2. Pass into the Table an object that knows how to select rows: a Selector (that encapsulates a selection strategy). The delete method calls the Strategy object's approve() method as many times as there are rows, and approve() must return true if that row should be deleted. The one complication is that approve() is passed an array of Table objects rather than a single Table reference. In the current example, the array has only one Table in it, but you will see situations in a moment where that is not the case.

Update operations are done more-or-less like deletes, but you have to override a modify() method as well as the approve(...) method of the Selector. The following code moves everyone who lives in Arizona to California; it examines the entire "address" table and changes all rows whose "state" columns have the value "AZ" to "CA": The modify(...) method is passed a cursor that's prepositioned at the current row, and it updates the row through the cursor.

```
address.update
(   new Selector()
    {   public boolean approve( Cursor[] tables )
```

```
          {    return tables[0].column("state").equals("AZ");
          }
          public void modify( Cursor current )
          {    current.update("state", "AZ");
          }
     }
);
```

Astute readers (that's you, I'm sure) will notice that I extended Selector.Adapter in the earlier example, and I implemented the Selector interface directly in the latter example. Selector.Adapter implements Selector by providing default implementations of its two methods: approve() and modify(). This is the same naming and implementation strategy that's used by the AWT/Swing event model, which provides default implementations of the listener interfaces. (MouseAdapter implements MouseListener, for example.) This naming convention is unfortunate in that we're not reifying the Adapter design pattern, in spite of the class name. Don't get confused.

This code also demonstrates the passive (or internal) variant of the Iterator pattern that I discussed earlier. The approve(...) method of the Selector object is called for every row of the table. Since the traversal algorithm is in the Table, Selector is a passive iterator across Table objects. (I haven't shown this use of Iterator in Figure 4-2, only because there wasn't enough room to cram it in.)

The Selector interface is in Listing 4-15. The Selector.Adapter is declared as a static inner class of Selector (on line 49 of Listing 4-15). It approves everything and complains with an exception toss if it's used in an update() call. From a design point of view, I wrestled with the throw-an-exception strategy that I ended up using. As I mentioned earlier, I really dislike the notion of unsupported operations throwing exceptions because this structure effectively moves a compile-time error into runtime. The alternative was splitting the interface into two single-method interfaces, but I didn't like this solution any better because it complicates an otherwise trivial system. I wouldn't argue with you if you said that I made the wrong decision, however.

An instance of Selector.Adapter called ALL is declared at the end of the listing. This instance is used primarily in the "select" operations discussed in the following section, but you could use it as follows to delete all the rows of a table:

```
people.delete( Selector.ALL );
```

The implementations of update(...) and delete(...) are in Listing 4-16. All that these methods do is hide the iteration code and call the Strategy object's methods where appropriate.

Listing 4-15. *Selector.java*

```
1   package com.holub.database;
2
3   /** A Selector is a Strategy object that is used by
4    * {@link Table#select} to determine
5    * whether a particular row should be included in the result.
6    * The passed Cursor is positioned at the correct row,
```

```
 7   * and attempts to advance it will fail.
 8   */
 9
10  interface Selector
11  {
12      /** This method is passed rows from the tables being joined
13       *  and returns true if the aggregate row is approved for the
14       *  current operation. In a select, for example, "aproval"
15       *  means that the aggregate row should be included in the
16       *  result-set Table.
17       *  @param rows An array of iterators, one for the current
18       *              row in each table to be examined (The array will
19       *              have only one element unless a you're approving
20       *              rows in a join.) These iterators are already
21       *              positioned at the correct row. Attempts to
22       *              advance the iterator result in an exception
23       *              toss ({@link java.lang.IllegalStateException}).
24       *  @return true if the aggregate row should has been approved
25       *              for the current operation.
26       */
27      boolean approve( Cursor[] rows );
28
29      /** This method is called only when an update request for a
30       *  row is approved by {@link #approve approve(...)}. It should
31       *  replace the required cell with a new value.
32       *  You must do the replacement using the iterator's
33       *  {@link Cursor#update} method. A typical implementation
34       *  takes this form:
35       *  <PRE>
36       *  public Object modify( Cursor current )
37       *  {   return current.update( "columnName", "new-value" );
38       *  }
39       *  </PRE>
40       *  @param current     Iterator positioned at the row to modify
41       */
42      void modify( Cursor current );
43
44      /** An implementation of {@link Selector} whose approve method
45       *  approves everything, and whose replace() method throws an
46       *  {@link UnsupportedOperationException} if called. Useful
47       *  for creating selectors on the fly with anonymous inner classes.
48       */
49      public static class Adapter implements Selector
50      {   public boolean approve( Cursor[] tables )
51          {   return true;
52          }
53          public void modify( Cursor current )
```

```
54              {   throw new UnsupportedOperationException(
55                         "Can't use a Selector.Adapter in an update");
56              }
57          }
58
59      /** An instance of {@link Selector.Adapter),
60       *  pass Selector.ALL to the {@link Table}'s
61       *  {@link Table#select select(...)} or
62       *  {@link Table#delete delete(...)}  methods to select all rows
63       *  of the table. May not be used in an update operation.
64       */
65      public static final Selector ALL = new Selector.Adapter();
66
67  }
```

Listing 4-16. *ConcreteTable.java Continued: Updating and Deleting*

```
312         //-------------------------------------------------------------------
313         public int  update( Selector where )
314         {
315             Results  currentRow = (Results)rows();
316             Cursor[] envelope   = new Cursor[]{ currentRow };
317             int      updated    = 0;
318
319             while( currentRow.advance() )
320             {   if( where.approve(envelope) )
321                 {   where.modify(currentRow);
322                     ++updated;
323                 }
324             }
325
326             return updated;
327         }
328         //-------------------------------------------------------------------
329         public int  delete( Selector where )
330         {   int deleted = 0;
331
332             Results  currentRow = (Results) rows();
333             Cursor[] envelope   = new Cursor[]{ currentRow };
334
335             while( currentRow.advance() )
336             {   if( where.approve( envelope) )
337                 {   currentRow.delete();
338                     ++deleted;
339                 }
340             }
341             return deleted;
342         }
```

Selection and Joins

The final significant ability of Table is to do a SQL-like "select/join" operation. A simple select extracts from one table only those rows that satisfy some criterion. For example, the following code extracts from the people table those rows whose "lastName" column contains the value "Flintstone" (In SQL: SELECT * FROM people WHERE lastName="Flintstone"):

```
Selector flintstoneSelector =
    new Selector.Adapter()
    {   public boolean approve( Cursor[] tables )
            {   return tables[0].column("lastName").equals("Flintstone");
            }
    };

Table result = people.select( flintstoneSelector );
```

The select() method returns a Table (typically called a *result set*) that contains only the selected rows. This table differs from one you may declare in that it's "unmodifiable." Attempts to modify it result in an exception toss. You can make the table modifiable like this:

```
result = ((UnmodifiableTable)result).extract();
```

I'll explain this code further in a moment.

You can also get a result set that contains only specified columns of the selected rows. The following code extracts all people whose last name is Flintstone but includes only the first- and last-name columns in the result set (in SQL: SELECT first,last FROM people WHERE lastName="Flintstone"):

```
Table result = people.select(flintstoneSelector,
                    new String[]{"firstName", "lastName"}
```

Create a result set that contains selected columns of every row like this:

```
Table result = people.select(Selector.ALL,
                    new String[]{"firstName", "lastName"}
```

Finally, the following variant lets you specify the desired columns in a Collection rather than an array:

```
List columns = new ArrayList();
columns.add("firstName");
columns.add("lastName");

Table result = people.select(flintstoneSelector, columns);
```

Though selection is useful in and of itself, an even more powerful variant on selection is a "join" operation. The basic idea is to select simultaneously from multiple tables. The word *join* comes from the notion that you're joining multiple tables together to make one big virtual table and then selecting a row from that virtual table. It's well beyond the scope of this book to describe why joins are useful, but for those of you who know a little database stuff, this SQL

```
SELECT firstName, lastName, street, city, state, zip"
    FROM people, address
    WHERE people.addrId = address.addrId
```

is performed as follows:

```
String[] columns= new String[]{ "firstName","lastName",
                            "street","city","state","zip"};
Table [] tables = new Table[] { address };  // additional tables to
                                            // join to current table.
Table result=
    people.select
    (   new Selector.Adapter()
        {   public boolean approve( Cursor[] tables )
            {   return
                    tables[0].column("addrId"). /*people.addrId*/
                equals(tables[1].column("addrId")  /*=address.addrId*/ );
            }
        },
        columns,
        tables
    );
```

The array of Cursor objects passed into approve() is ordered identically to the array of Table objects that you pass into select(...).

Every possible combination of rows from the two tables is considered when the result set is built. (Formally, a result table holding every combination of rows from a set of source tables is said to be the *Cartesian product* of the source tables.) Given one table with the rows A, B, and C and a second table with the rows D and E, the following calls to approve() are made (where A, B, C, D, and E) are cursors positioned at the appropriate rows:

```
approve( Cursor[]{ A, D } );
approve( Cursor[]{ A, E } );
approve( Cursor[]{ B, D } );
approve( Cursor[]{ B, E } );
approve( Cursor[]{ C, D } );
approve( Cursor[]{ C, E } );
```

You can join any number of tables, but bear in mind that every time you add a table, you multiply the amount of work by the number of rows in the added table. (Joining two 5-row tables requires 25 calls to approve() [5×5]; joining three, 5-row tables requires 125 [5×5×5] approvals.) In a real database, you can do some clever work to reduce this overhead, but the number of tables always significantly increases the cost of the join operation.

An overload of this method lets you use Collection objects rather than arrays for the columns and tables arguments.

Listing 4-17 shows the code that implements the various select() overloads. From a design-pattern perspective, there's nothing interesting here. The select() overloads are just additional reifications of Strategy. From a programming perspective, the selectFromCartesian-Product(...) method on line 437 is worth examining. This is the method that does the actual join. It uses a recursive algorithm to assemble arrays of cursors representing each row of the Cartesian product and then passes that array off to your approve() method. The code is elegant (if I do say so myself), but the recursion makes it somewhat opaque.

Listing 4-17. *ConcreteTable.java Continued: Selection and Joins*

```
343        //----------------------------------------------------------------
344        public Table select( Selector where )
345        {   Table resultTable = new ConcreteTable( null,
346                                           (String[]) columnNames.clone() );
347
348            Results          currentRow  = (Results) rows();
349            Cursor[] envelope    = new Cursor[]{ currentRow };
350
351            while( currentRow.advance() )
352            {   if( where.approve(envelope) )
353                    resultTable.insert( (Object[]) currentRow.cloneRow() );
354            }
355            return new UnmodifiableTable(resultTable);
356        }
357        // - - - - - - - - - - - - - - - - - - - - - - - - - - - - - - - -
358        public Table select(Selector where, String[] requestedColumns )
359        {   if( requestedColumns  == null )
360                return select( where );
361
362            Table resultTable = new ConcreteTable( null,
363                                       (String[]) requestedColumns.clone() );
364
365            Results          currentRow  = (Results) rows();
366            Cursor[] envelope    = new Cursor[]{ currentRow };
367
368            while( currentRow.advance() )
369            {   if( where.approve(envelope) )
370                {   Object[] newRow = new Object[ requestedColumns.length ];
371                    for( int column=0; column < requestedColumns.length;
372                                                            ++column )
373                    {   newRow[column]=
374                            currentRow.column(requestedColumns[column]);
375                    }
376                    resultTable.insert( newRow );
377                }
378            }
379            return new UnmodifiableTable(resultTable);
```

```
380    }
381    // - - - - - - - - - - - - - - - - - - - - - - - - - - - - -
382    // This version of select does a join
383    //
384    public Table select( Selector where, String[]   requestedColumns,
385                                          Table[]    otherTables )
386    {
387        // If we're not doing a join, use the more efficient version
388        // of select().
389
390        if( otherTables == null || otherTables.length == 0)
391            return select( where, requestedColumns );
392
393        // Make the current table not be a special case by effectively
394        // prefixing it to the otherTables array.
395
396        Table[] allTables = new Table[ otherTables.length + 1 ];
397        allTables[0] = this;
398        System.arraycopy(otherTables, 0, allTables, 1, otherTables.length );
399
400        // Create places to hold the result of the join and to hold
401        // iterators for each table involved in the join.
402
403        Table    resultTable = new ConcreteTable(null,requestedColumns);
404        Cursor[] envelope    = new Cursor[allTables.length];
405
406        // Recursively compute the Cartesian product, adding to the
407        // resultTable all rows that the Selector approves
408
409        selectFromCartesianProduct( 0, where, requestedColumns,
410                                       allTables, envelope, resultTable );
411
412        return new UnmodifiableTable(resultTable);
413    }
414    // - - - - - - - - - - - - - - - - - - - - - - - - - - - - - - -
415    // Think of the Cartesian product as a kind of tree. That is
416    // given one table with rows A and B, and another table with rows
417    // C and D, you can look at the product like this:
418    //
419    //            root
420    //        _____|_____
421    //        |          |
422    //        A          B
423    //     ___|___    ___|___
424    //    |       |  |       |
425    //    C       D  C       D
426    //
```

```
427    // The tree is as deep as the number of tables we're joining.
428    // Every possible path from the root to a leaf represents one row
429    // in the Cartesian product. The current method effectively traverses
430    // this tree recursively without building an actual tree. It
431    // assembles an array of iterators (one for each table) positioned
432    // at the current place in the set of rows as it recurses to a leaf,
433    // and then asks the selector whether to approve that row.
434    // It then goes up a notch, advances the correct iterator, and
435    // recurses back down.
436    //
437    private static void selectFromCartesianProduct(
438                                    int          level,
439                                    Selector     where,
440                                    String[]     requestedColumns,
441                                    Table[]      allTables,
442                                    Cursor[] allIterators,
443                                    Table        resultTable )
444    {
445        allIterators[level] = allTables[level].rows();
446
447        while( allIterators[level].advance() )
448        {   // If we haven't reached the tips of the branches yet,
449            // go down one more level.
450
451            if( level < allIterators.length - 1 )
452                selectFromCartesianProduct(level+1, where,
453                                requestedColumns,
454                                allTables, allIterators, resultTable);
455
456            // If we are at the leaf level, then get approval for
457            // the fully-assembled row, and add the row to the table
458            // if it's approved.
459
460            if( level == allIterators.length - 1 )
461            {   if( where.approve(allIterators) )
462                    insertApprovedRows( resultTable,
463                                requestedColumns, allIterators );
464            }
465        }
466    }
467    // - - - - - - - - - - - - - - - - - - - - - - - - - - - - - - - -
468    // Insert an approved row into the result table:
469    //     for( every requested column )
470    //         for( every table in the join )
471    //             if the requested column is in the current table
472    //                 add the associated value to the result table
473    //
```

```
474        // Only one column with a given name is added, even if that column
475        // appears in multiple tables. Columns in tables at the beginning
476        // of the list take precedence over identically named columns that
477        // occur later in the list.
478        //
479        private static void insertApprovedRows( Table    resultTable,
480                                                String[] requestedColumns,
481                                                Cursor[] allTables )
482        {
483
484            Object[] resultRow = new Object[ requestedColumns.length ];
485
486            for( int i = 0; i < requestedColumns.length; ++i )
487            {   for( int table = 0; table < allTables.length; ++table )
488                {   try
489                    {   resultRow[i] =
490                            allTables[table].column(requestedColumns[i]);
491                        break;  // if the assignment worked, do the next column
492                    }
493                    catch(Exception e)
494                    {   // otherwise, try the next table
495                    }
496                }
497            }
498            resultTable.insert( /*requestedColumns,*/ resultRow );
499        }
500        // - - - - - - - - - - - - - - - - - - - - - - - - - - - - - - - - - - -
501        /**
502         * A collection variant on the array version. Just converts the collection
503         * to an array and then chains to the other version
504         * ({@linkplain #select(Selector,String[],Table[]) see}).
505         * @param requestedColumns the value returned from the {@link #toString}
506         *         method of the elements of this collection are used as the
507         *         column names.
508         * @param other Collection of tables to join to the current one,
509         *         <code>null</code>if none.
510         * @throws ClassCastException if any elements of the <code>other</code>
511         *         collection do not implement the {@link Table} interface.
512         */
513        public Table select(Selector where, Collection requestedColumns,
514                                                    Collection other)
515        {
516            String[] columnNames = null;
517            Table[]  otherTables = null;
518
519            if( requestedColumns != null )  // SELECT *
520            {
```

```
521                // Can't cast an Object[] to a String[], so make a copy to ensure
522                // type safety.
523
524                columnNames    = new String[ requestedColumns.size() ];
525                int     i      = 0;
526                Iterator column = requestedColumns.iterator();
527
528                while( column.hasNext() )
529                    columnNames[i++] = column.next().toString();
530            }
531
532        if( other != null )
533            otherTables = (Table[]) other.toArray( new Table[other.size()] );
534
535        return select( where, columnNames, otherTables );
536    }
537    // - - - - - - - - - - - - - - - - - - - - - - - - - - - - - - - - - - - -
538    public Table select(Selector where, Collection requestedColumns)
539    {   return select( where, requestedColumns, null );
540    }
```

Miscellany

The remainder of the ConcreteTable definition is in Listing 4-18. It contains a few house-keeping and workhorse methods (such as toString(), which returns a String representation of all the elements in the table). Listing 4-18 ends with a long unit-test class that has several examples of the calls I've been discussing. I like to put my unit tests into inner classes (which I always call Test) so that the test code will be in a separate .class file than the class I'm testing. I don't ship the test-class files with the product. Run the test using this:

```
java com.holub.database.ConcreteTable\$Test
```

(but omit the backslash if you're testing from a Windows "DOS box"). Normally, I like test classes such as this to print nothing at all if everything's okay, and I like to report the number of errors as the test-program's exit status. This way, I can automate the tests easily, and the result of running the test is a list of what went wrong. If you print too many "this is okay" messages, you'll lose the error messages in the clutter.

The problem with this approach is that the inner-class unit test has access to parts of the class that a normal "client" wouldn't be able to see. I am careful, when I use this unit-test strategy, to pretend that I do not have this special access. Of course, you can guarantee that you don't have access by putting your tests in a separate class in a separate package, but then the test code is in a different directory and is harder to augment if you change the interface to the class.

Having said all that, I haven't followed my usual testing guidelines in the current situation. I test by redirecting the output of the program to a file and then using the Unix diff utility to compare that output with an expected-output file. I test the class by running the following shell script, which prints the words *PASSED* or *FAILED*, depending on whether the actual output matches the expected output:

```
java com.holub.database.ConcreteTable\$Test > $TMP/ConcreteTable.test.tmp

diff $TMP/ConcreteTable.test.tmp ConcreteTable.test.out
case $? in
(0) print ConcreteTable PASSED
    ;;
(1) print ConcreteTable FAILED
    ;;
(*) print Unknown diff failure
    ;;
esac
```

It's ugly, but it works.

Listing 4-18. *ConcreteTable.java Continued: Miscellany*

```
541      //-------------------------------------------------------------------
542      // Housekeeping stuff
543      //
544      public  String  name()            { return tableName;          }
545      public  void    rename(String s)  { tableName = s;             }
546      public  boolean isDirty()         { return isDirty;            }
547      private int     width()           { return columnNames.length; }
548      //-------------------------------------------------------------------
549      public Object clone() throws CloneNotSupportedException
550      {   ConcreteTable copy  = (ConcreteTable)  super.clone();
551          copy.rowSet       = (LinkedList)     rowSet.clone();
552          copy.columnNames  = (String[]) columnNames.clone();
553          copy.tableName    = tableName;
554          return copy;
555      }
556      //-------------------------------------------------------------------
557      public String toString()
558      {   StringBuffer out = new StringBuffer();
559
560          out.append( tableName == null ? "<anonymous>" : tableName );
561          out.append( "\n" );
562
563          for( int i = 0; i < columnNames.length; ++i )
564              out.append(columnNames[i] + "\t");
565          out.append("\n-----------------------------------------\n");
566
567          for( Cursor i = rows(); i.advance(); )
568          {   Iterator columns = i.columns();
569              while( columns.hasNext() )
570              {   Object next = columns.next();
571                  if( next == null )
```

```
572                         out.append( "null\t" );
573                 else
574                         out.append( next.toString() + "\t" );
575             }
576             out.append('\n');
577         }
578         return out.toString();
579     }
580
581     //-----------------------------------------------------------------
582     public final static class Test
583     {
584         public static void main(String[] args)
585         {   new Test().test();
586         }
587
588         Table people  = TableFactory.create(
589             "people",  new String[]{"last", "first", "addrId" } );
590
591         Table address = TableFactory.create(
592             "address", new String[]{"addrId","street","city","state","zip"});
593
594         public void report( Throwable t, String message )
595         {   System.out.println( message + " FAILED with exception toss" );
596             t.printStackTrace();
597             System.exit(1);
598         }
599
600         public void test()
601         {   try{ testInsert(); }catch(Throwable t){ report(t,"Insert"); }
602             try{ testUpdate(); }catch(Throwable t){ report(t,"Update"); }
603             try{ testDelete(); }catch(Throwable t){ report(t,"Delete"); }
604             try{ testSelect(); }catch(Throwable t){ report(t,"Select"); }
605             try{ testStore();  }catch(Throwable t){ report(t,"Store/Load");}
606             try{ testJoin();   }catch(Throwable t){ report(t,"Join"  ); }
607             try{ testUndo();   }catch(Throwable t){ report(t,"Undo"  ); }
608         }
609
610         public void testInsert()
611         {   people.insert(new Object[]{"Holub",     "Allen","1"          });
612             people.insert(new Object[]{"Flintstone","Wilma","2"          });
613             people.insert(new String[]{"addrId",    "first","last"      },
614                         new Object[]{"2",          "Fred", "Flintstone"});
615
616             address.insert( new Object[]{"1","123 MyStreet",
617                                             "Berkeley","CA","99999" } );
618
```

```
619                 List l = new ArrayList();
620                 l.add("2");
621                 l.add("123 Quarry Ln.");
622                 l.add("Bedrock ");
623                 l.add("XX");
624                 l.add("12345");
625                 assert( address.insert(l) == 1 );
626
627                 l.clear();
628                 l.add("3");
629                 l.add("Bogus");
630                 l.add("Bad");
631                 l.add("XX");
632                 l.add("12345");
633
634                 List c = new ArrayList();
635                 c.add("addrId");
636                 c.add("street");
637                 c.add("city");
638                 c.add("state");
639                 c.add("zip");
640                 assert( address.insert( c, l ) == 1);
641
642                 System.out.println( people.toString() );
643                 System.out.println( address.toString() );
644
645                 try
646                 {   people.insert( new Object[]{ "x" } );
647                     throw new AssertionError(
648                             "insert wrong number of fields test failed");
649                 }
650                 catch(Throwable t){ /* Failed correctly, do nothing */ }
651
652                 try
653                 {   people.insert( new String[]{ "?" }, new Object[]{ "y" });
654                     throw new AssertionError(
655                             "insert-nonexistent-field test failed");
656                 }
657                 catch(Exception t){ /* Failed correctly, do nothing */ }
658             }
659
660         public void testUpdate()
661         {   System.out.println("update set state='YY' where state='XX'" );
662             int updated = address.update
663             (   new Selector()
664                 {   public boolean approve( Cursor[] tables )
665                     {   return tables[0].column("state").equals("XX");
```

```
666                        }
667                    public void modify( Cursor current )
668                    {    current.update("state", "YY");
669                    }
670                }
671            );
672        print( address );
673        System.out.println( updated + " rows affected\n" );
674    }
675
676    public void testDelete()
677    {
678        System.out.println("delete where street='Bogus'" );
679        int deleted =
680        address.delete
681        (    new Selector.Adapter()
682            {    public boolean approve( Cursor[] tables )
683                {    return tables[0].column("street").equals("Bogus");
684                }
685            }
686        );
687        print( address );
688        System.out.println( deleted + " rows affected\n" );
689    }
690
691    public void testSelect()
692    {    Selector flintstoneSelector =
693            new Selector.Adapter()
694            {    public boolean approve( Cursor[] tables )
695                { return tables[0].column("last").equals("Flintstone");
696                }
697            };
698
699        // SELECT first, last FROM people WHERE last = "Flintstone"
700        // The collection version chains to the string version, so the
701        // following call tests both versions
702
703        List columns = new ArrayList();
704        columns.add("first");
705        columns.add("last");
706
707        Table result = people.select(flintstoneSelector, columns);
708        print( result );
709
710        // SELECT * FROM people WHERE last = "Flintstone"
711        result = people.select( flintstoneSelector );
712        print( result );
```

```
713
714            // Check that the result is indeed unmodifiable
715
716            try
717            {   result.insert( new Object[]{ "x", "y", "z" } );
718                throw new AssertionError(
719                            "Insert to Immutable Table test failed");
720            }
721            catch( Exception e ){ /*it failed correctly*/ }
722
723            try
724            {   result.update( flintstoneSelector );
725                throw new AssertionError(
726                            "Update of Immutable Table test failed");
727            }
728            catch( Exception e ){ /*it failed correctly*/ }
729
730            try
731            {   result.delete( flintstoneSelector );
732                throw new AssertionError(
733                            "Delete of Immutable Table test failed");
734            }
735            catch( Exception e ){ /*it failed correctly*/ }
736        }
737
738        public void testStore() throws IOException, ClassNotFoundException
739        {   // Flush the table to disk, then reread it.
740            // Subsequent tests that use the "people" table will
741            // fail if this operation fails.
742
743            Writer out = new FileWriter( "people" );
744            people.export( new CSVExporter(out) );
745            out.close();
746
747            Reader in = new FileReader( "people" );
748            people = new ConcreteTable( new CSVImporter(in) );
749            in.close();
750        }
751
752        public void testJoin()
753        {
754            // First test a two-way join
755
756            System.out.println("\nSELECT first,last,street,city,state,zip"
757                            +" FROM people, address"
758                            +" WHERE people.addrId = address.addrId");
759
```

```
760            // Collection version chains to String[] version,
761            // so this code tests both:
762            List columns = new ArrayList();
763            columns.add("first");
764            columns.add("last");
765            columns.add("street");
766            columns.add("city");
767            columns.add("state");
768            columns.add("zip");
769
770            List tables = new ArrayList();
771            tables.add( address );
772
773            Table result=    // WHERE people.addrID = address.addrID
774                people.select
775                (   new Selector.Adapter()
776                    {   public boolean approve( Cursor[] tables )
777                        {   return      tables[0].column("addrId")
778                                .equals( tables[1].column("addrId") );
779                        }
780                    },
781                    columns,
782                    tables
783                );
784
785        print( result );
786        System.out.println("");
787
788        // Now test a three-way join
789        //
790        System.out.println(
791                "\nSELECT first,last,street,city,state,zip,text"
792                +" FROM people, address, third"
793                +" WHERE (people.addrId = address.addrId)"
794                +" AND (people.addrId = third.addrId)");
795
796        Table third = TableFactory.create(
797                        "third", new String[]{"addrId","text"} );
798        third.insert ( new Object[]{ "1", "addrId=1" } );
799        third.insert ( new Object[]{ "2", "addrId=2" } );
800
801        result=
802        people.select
803        ( new Selector.Adapter()
804          { public boolean approve( Cursor[] tables )
805            { return
806              (tables[0].column("addrId")
```

```
807                              .equals(tables[1].column("addrId"))
808               &&
809             tables[0].column("addrId")
810                              .equals(tables[2].column("addrId"))
811           );
812        }
813      },
814
815      new String[]{"last", "first", "state", "text"},
816      new Table[]{ address, third }
817    );
818
819    System.out.println( result.toString() + "\n" );
820  }
821
822  public void testUndo()
823  {
824    // Verify that commit works properly
825    people.begin();
826    System.out.println(
827                  "begin/insert into people (Solo, Han, 5)");
828
829    people.insert( new Object[]{ "Solo", "Han", "5" } );
830    System.out.println( people.toString() );
831
832    people.begin();
833    System.out.println(
834          "begin/insert into people (Lea, Princess, 6)");
835
836    people.insert( new Object[]{ "Lea", "Princess", "6" } );
837    System.out.println( people.toString() );
838
839    System.out.println(  "commit(THIS_LEVEL)\n"
840                  +"rollback(Table.THIS_LEVEL)\n");
841    people.commit      (Table.THIS_LEVEL);
842    people.rollback    (Table.THIS_LEVEL);
843    System.out.println ( people.toString() );
844
845    // Now test that nested transactions work correctly.
846
847    System.out.println( people.toString() );
848
849    System.out.println("begin/insert into people (Vader,Darth, 4)");
850    people.begin();
851    people.insert( new Object[]{ "Vader","Darth", "4" } );
852    System.out.println( people.toString() );
853
```

```
854            System.out.println(
855                "begin/update people set last=Skywalker where last=Vader");
856
857            people.begin();
858            people.update
859            (   new Selector()
860                {   public boolean approve( Cursor[] tables )
861                    {   return tables[0].column("last").equals("Vader");
862                    }
863                    public void modify(Cursor current)
864                    {   current.update( "last", "Skywalker" );
865                    }
866                }
867            );
868            System.out.println( people.toString() );
869
870            System.out.println("delete from people where last=Skywalker");
871            people.delete
872            (   new Selector.Adapter()
873                {   public boolean approve( Cursor[] tables )
874                    { return tables[0].column("last").equals("Skywalker");
875                    }
876                }
877            );
878            System.out.println( people.toString() );
879
880            System.out.println(
881                    "rollback(Table.THIS_LEVEL) the delete and update");
882            people.rollback(Table.THIS_LEVEL);
883            System.out.println( people.toString() );
884
885            System.out.println("rollback(Table.THIS_LEVEL) insert");
886            people.rollback(Table.THIS_LEVEL);
887            System.out.println( people.toString() );
888        }
889
890        public void print( Table t )
891        {   // tests the table iterator
892            Cursor current = t.rows();
893            while( current.advance() )
894            {   for(Iterator columns = current.columns();columns.hasNext();)
895                    System.out.print( (String) columns.next() + " " );
896                System.out.println("");
897            }
898        }
899    }
900 }
```

Variants on the *Table*: The Decorator Pattern

If you look back at the various select() overrides in Listing 4-17, you'll notice that they all take the following form:

```
public Table select(...)
{
    Table resultTable = new ConcreteTable( ... );

    /* populate the resultTable... */

    return new UnmodifiableTable(resultTable);
}
```

They create a ConcreteTable, populate it, and then return an UnmodifiableTable that wraps the actual result table. Listing 4-19 shows the UnmodifiableTable class. As you can see, its methods are divided into two categories. The methods that can modify a Table (insert(), update(), delete()) all do nothing but throw an exception if called. The remainder of the methods just delegate to the wrapped table. Finally, the UnmodifiableTable adds an extract() method (Listing 4-19, line 88) that just returns the wrapped Table. (As it says in the comment preceding the method, this last method is somewhat problematic because it provides a way to get around the unmodifiability, but the SQL-engine layer requires it to implement the SELECT INTO request efficiently.)

Listing 4-19. *UnmodifiableTable.java*

```
1   package com.holub.database;
2   import java.io.*;
3   import java.util.*;
4
5   /** This decorator of the Table class just wraps another table,
6    *  but restricts access to methods that don't modify the table.
7    *  The following methods toss an
8    *  {@link UnsupportedOperationException} when called:
9    *  <PRE>
10   *  public void  insert( String[] columnNames, Object[] values )
11   *  public void  insert( Object[] values )
12   *  public void  update( Selector where )
13   *  public void  delete( Selector where )
14   *  public void  store ()
15   *  </PRE>
16   *  Other methods delegate to the wrapped Table. All methods of
17   *  the {@link Table} that are declared to return a
18   *  <code>Table</code> actually return an
19   *  <code>UnmodifiableTable</code>.
20   *  <p>
21   *  Refer to the {@link Table} interface for method documentation.
22   */
```

```
23
24  public class UnmodifiableTable implements Table
25  {    private Table wrapped;
26
27      public UnmodifiableTable( Table wrapped )
28      {    this.wrapped = wrapped;
29      }
30
31      /** Return an UnmodifiableTable that wraps a clone of the
32       * currently wrapped table. (A deep copy is used.)
33       */
34      public Object clone() throws CloneNotSupportedException
35      {    UnmodifiableTable copy = (UnmodifiableTable) super.clone();
36          copy.wrapped = (Table)( wrapped.clone() );
37          return copy;
38      }
39
40      public int  insert(String[] c, Object[] v    ){ illegal(); return 0;}
41      public int  insert(Object[] v                ){ illegal(); return 0;}
42      public int  insert(Collection c,Collection v ){ illegal(); return 0;}
43      public int  insert(Collection v              ){ illegal(); return 0;}
44      public int  update(Selector w                ){ illegal(); return 0;}
45      public int  delete( Selector w               ){ illegal(); return 0;}
46
47      public void begin    (              ){ illegal(); }
48      public void commit   (boolean all){ illegal(); }
49      public void rollback (boolean all){ illegal(); }
50
51      private final void illegal()
52      {    throw new UnsupportedOperationException();
53      }
54
55      public Table select(Selector w,String[] r,Table[] o)
56      {    return wrapped.select( w, r, o );
57      }
58      public Table select(Selector where, String[] requestedColumns)
59      {    return wrapped.select(where, requestedColumns );
60      }
61      public Table select(Selector where)
62      {    return wrapped.select(where);
63      }
64      public Table select(Selector w,Collection r,Collection o)
65      {    return wrapped.select( w, r, o );
66      }
67      public Table select(Selector w, Collection r)
68      {    return wrapped.select(w, r);
69      }
```

```
70      public Cursor rows()
71      {   return wrapped.rows();
72      }
73      public void  export(Table.Exporter exporter) throws IOException
74      {   wrapped.export(exporter);
75      }
76
77      public String    toString()     { return wrapped.toString();   }
78      public String    name()         { return wrapped.name();       }
79      public void      rename(String s){        wrapped.rename(s);    }
80      public boolean   isDirty()      { return wrapped.isDirty();     }
81
82      /** Extract the wrapped table. The existence of this method is
83       *  problematic, since it allows someone to defeat the unmodifiability
84       *  of the table. On the other hand, the wrapped table came in from
85       *  outside, so external access is possible through the reference
86       *  that was passed to the constructor. Use the method with care.
87       */
88      public Table extract(){ return wrapped; }
89  }
```

What I've done with UnmodifiableTable is used a wrapping strategy to do something that I could also have done using inheritance. My goal was to change the behavior of several of the methods of ConcreteTable so that the Table was effectively immutable. I was reluctant to put an isImmutable flag into the ConcreteTable and test the flag all over the place—that solution was just too complicated. I could also have derived a class and overridden the methods that modified the table to throw an exception, but that solution introduces a fragile-base scenario. (I could inadvertently add a method to the superclass that modified the table and forget to override that method in the subclass.) Finally, the derivation solution leaves open the potential for hard-to-maintain code that reports errors at runtime that should really be compile-time errors. (If I try to assign a Table to an UnmodifiableTable reference, I'll get a compile-time error.)

I solved the problem by replacing implementation inheritance with an interface inheritance/delegation strategy. I implement the same interface as the object that I'm wrapping (the object that would otherwise be the superclass) and delegate to the wrapped object when necessary.

This solution to the fragile-base-class problem, which allows me to change behavior without using extends, is an example of the **Decorator** pattern.

You've seen decorators if you've used Java's I/O classes. For example, if you need to read a compressed stream of bytes efficiently, you use a chain of decorators. Here, Decorator reduces a complex task to a set of simple tasks, each of which is implemented independently. You could implement a massive efficiently-read-a-compressed-stream class, but it's easier to break the problem into the following three distinct subproblems:

1. Reading bytes.

2. Making reads more efficient with buffering.

3. Decompressing a stream of bytes.

Java solves the first problem with three classes. You start with `FileInputStream`, instantiated like this:

```
try
{   InputStream in = new FileInputStream( "file.name" );
}
catch( IOException e )
{   System.err.println( "Couldn't open file.name" );
    e.printStackTrace();
}
```

You then add buffering with a decoration (or *wrapping*) strategy. You wrap the `InputStream` object with another `InputStream` implementer that buffers bytes. You ask the wrapper for a byte; it asks the wrapped stream for many bytes and returns the first one. The decorator wrapping goes like this:

```
try
{   InputStream in = new FileInputStream( "file.name" );
    in = new BufferedInputStream( in );
}
catch( IOException e )
{   System.err.println( "Couldn't open file.name" );
    e.printStackTrace();
}
```

Add decompression with another decorator, like so:

```
try
{   InputStream in = new FileInputStream( "file.name" );
    in = new BufferedInputStream( in );
    in = new GZipInputStream( in );
}
catch( IOException e )
{   System.err.println( "Couldn't open file.name" );
    e.printStackTrace();
}
```

You can add additional filtering by adding additional decorators.

This solution is very flexible. You can mix and match the decorators to get the features you need. More important, each of the decorators is itself relatively simple, because it solves only one problem. Consequently, the decorators are easy to write, debug, and modify without impacting the rest of the system. I could change the buffering algorithm by rewriting `BufferedInputStream`, for example, and not have to touch any of the other decorators (or any of the code that used them). I could also add new filter functionality simply by implementing a new decorator. (Classes such as `CipherInputStream` were added to Java in this way.)

Though Decorator can effectively decompose a complex problem into simple pieces, the main intent of Decorator is to provide an alternative to implementation inheritance when you would be tempted to use `extends` to modify base-class behavior or add a few minor methods.

In addition to the fragile-base-class problem discussed in Chapter 2, extends can add a lot of complexity when you need to change a lot of behavior. Consider Java's collection classes. By design, the collection classes are not thread safe. Collections are not often accessed from nonsynchronized methods, so making them thread safe is just wasting CPU time as the program runs. You do, occasionally, need a thread-safe collection, however. Figure 4-7 shows how you'd have to extend the core collection classes to add thread safety. (The new classes are in gray.) I've had to double the number of concrete classes in the system.

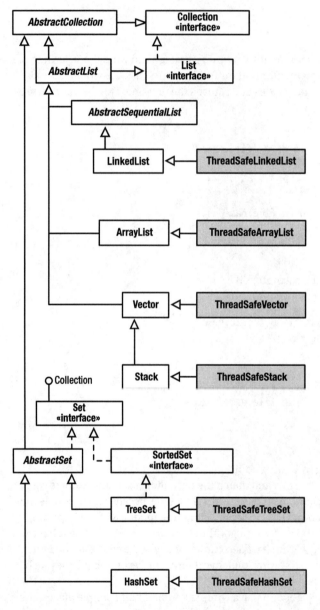

Figure 4-7. *Using implemenation inheritance to add thread safety to collections*

Now what if I want to add unmodifiable collections, perhaps by adding a lock() method that causes all the methods that would normally modify the collection to start throwing exceptions? When I use implementation inheritance for this modification, I have to double the number of concrete classes again. Figure 4-8 shows the result.

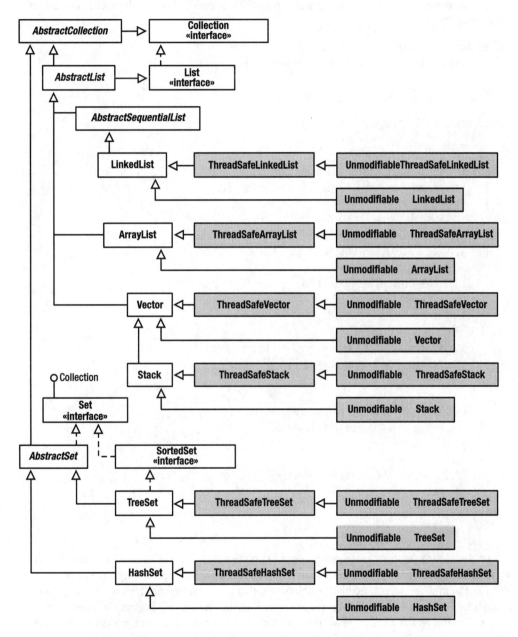

Figure 4-8. *Using implementation inheritance to add unmodifiability to collections*

With an inheritance-based solution, I have to double the number of concrete classes every time I add a new feature, assuming that I want to support every possible combination of features. I can leave off some combinations, of course, but those combinations will probably be the ones I need two weeks from now.

The designers of the Collection classes solved the thread-safety problem with a Decorator. Here's the code:

```
Collection threadSafe =
        Collections.synchronizedCollection( new LinkedList() );
```

The Collections class looks something like this:

```
public class Collections // utility
{
    //...
    public static Collection synchronizedCollection(final Collection wrapped)
    {   return new SynchronizedCollection(wrapped);
    }

    private static class SynchronizedCollection implements Collection
    {   private Collection unsafe;

        public SynchronizedCollection( Collection unsafe )
        {   this.unsafe = unsafe;
        }

        public synchronized boolean add( Object toAdd )
        {   return unsafe.add( toAdd );
        }

        public synchronized boolean remove( Object toAdd )
        {   return unsafe.remove( toAdd );
        ]

        // Implement synchronized version of all other Collection
        // methods here ...
    }
}
```

Collections is a utility class—a class made up of static "helper" methods that augment some existing class or library. Utilities are not Singletons because utilities don't behave like objects; they're just a bag full of functions. In this case, the Collections utility serves as a Concrete Factory of abstract Collection types. The ThreadSafeCollection class both is a Collection and wraps a Collection. The methods of ThreadSafeCollection are synchronized, however. Note that ThreadSafeCollection is private. The user of the Collections knows only that the object returned from unmodifiableCollection(...) implements Collection without allowing modifications to the backing collection. The concrete class name is unknown.

You can provide unmodifiable versions of a `Collection` with a similar wrapper, just as I did with the `UnmodifiableTable` class discussed at the beginning of this section.

You can get a synchronized unmodifiable collection with double wrapping, as follows:

```
Collection myList = new LinkedList();
//...
myList = Collections.synchronizedCollection
        (   Collections.unmodifiableCollection
            (   myList
            )
        );
```

The point of using Decorator is that I've added a grand total of two classes but accomplished the same thing that required 18 classes in an implementation-inheritance solution.

As I mentioned earlier, Java's I/O system uses Decorator heavily. Figure 4-9 shows enough of Java's input system that you can see the general structure. (I've left out the `Reader` classes, and so on.) I'll discuss the Adapter pattern shown in this figure at the end of the current chapter. For now, I want to focus on Decorator.

Structurally, all the Decorators contain an instance of some class that implements the same interface as the Decorator itself. I think of Decorator as the big-fish/little-fish pattern, as shown here. The big fish (the Decorator) swallows the little fish (the Concrete Component), but they're both fish (the Component). This is also the Gepetto (or Jonah) school of fish digestion: The little fish swims around happily in the big fish's stomach until it's disgorged. If a fisherman had caught the little fish just before it was swallowed (in other words, if you have a reference to a wrapped Component), then the fisherman could talk directly to the little fish by tying a tin can to the end of the fishing line and yelling into the can. (You can talk directly to a `LineNumberInputStream` that had been wrapped in another Decorator by keeping a reference to it, for example.) Finally, the bigger fish doesn't know whether it has swallowed a Concrete Component or another Decorator. They're all fish. Figure 4-10 shows the message flow during a write operation for the objects used in the previous `InputStream` example. Each of the Decorators gets its input from the wrapped object. This wrapped object could be another decorator or a Concrete Component; the Decorator knows nothing about that wrapped object other than the interface it implements. The order of wrapping is important. If the `BufferedInputStream` wrapped the `PushBackInputStream` in the earlier example, then a pushed-back character would effectively move to the end of the current buffer—the pushed-back characters would appear to be pushed back to random places in the input stream. Also note that since the `PushBackInputStream` wraps the `LineNumberInputStream`, pushing back a newline does not roll back the line number. On output, you want to compress before encrypting for efficiency reasons (the encryption algorithm is less efficient than the compression algorithm).

Also note that the `unread(...)` method that's used to push back characters is not defined in `InputStream`. Consequently, you can't access this functionality through an `InputStream` reference.

We're now done with the data-storage layer. Whew!

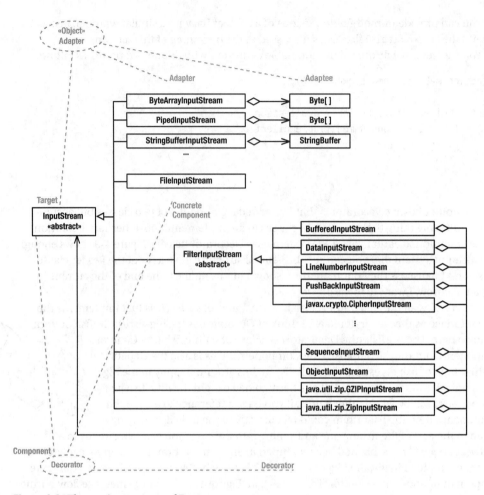

Figure 4-9. *The static structure of Decorator*

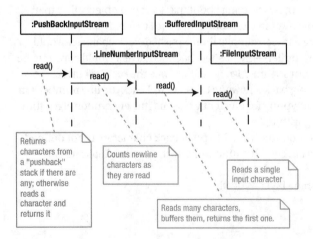

Figure 4-10. *The dynamic structure of Decorator*

Adding SQL to the Mix

(This is not the dreaded SQL-interpreter section, so don't skip over it.)

The Table classes are pretty useful in and of themselves. They provide a reasonably light-weight solution to the problem of an embedded database and could be better than something such as JDBC in situations where "lightweight" is mandatory—for database-like storage of configuration information without the overhead of a database, for example.

My main goal was to use a database as a persistence layer, however, and though I wanted the lightest-weight database I could get, I also wanted to be able to swap out that database with a more full-featured version should the need arise, all without having to modify any of my code. If I wrote code directly to the Table interface, then I'd have to modify that code to go to the JDBC interface required by a real database server.

It's tempting to implement a JDBC layer directly in terms of the Table interface (or, put another way, to implement the SQL interpreter inside the JDBC classes). JDBC has more complexity than I needed for the current application, though, and JDBC imposes a relatively complex structure that I didn't want to deal with quite yet. Consequently, I opted to go with a three-layer approach and wrap the Table with a simple SQL engine implemented with one primary class. This way I can focus on building the SQL interpreter without the complications of imposing the JDBC structure onto my interpreter. I also end up with a SQL-based table class that's easier to use than the JDBC classes.

The interpreter itself is good sized (about 50KB of byte code), and it certainly imposes a performance penalty on the system. A SQL where clause has to be reinterpreted with every row of a query, for example, as compared to executing a small Java method (probably inlined by the HotSpot JVM) on every row.

On the other hand, any SQL database will introduce similar inefficiencies. I wasn't doing all that much database access, and the ability to swap persistence layers without a rewrite was an important requirement.

I should also say that much of the work that I've done building the interpreter could be done using one of the Java "compiler-compilers" (such as JavaCUP at `http://www.cs.princeton.edu/~appel/modern/java/CUP/` or JavaCC at `https://javacc.dev.java.net/`). Without getting too much into the technical details, I would certainly use a compiler-compiler for implementing any language that was at all complicated. In the case of the small SQL subset that I'm implementing, the structure of the language lends itself to a parser technology called *recursive descent*, which can usually be hand built in such a way as to be more efficient than the generic, table-driven parsers created by tools such as CUP. Since the language was small, and minimum size and maximum efficiency were two of my design goals, I opted for a handcrafted approach, thinking that I could do a better job by hand than the tools could do. This may not actually be the case, however. I haven't implemented the language using a compiler-compiler and benchmarked the results against the hand-built version, so I really don't know. In any event, the hand-built version provides a few nice examples of design patterns.

So, back to the salt mines.

SQL-Engine Structure

Figure 4-11 and Figure 4-12 show the static structure of (and design patterns used by) the SQL-engine layer. As before, you may want to bookmark these figures so you can refer to them later.

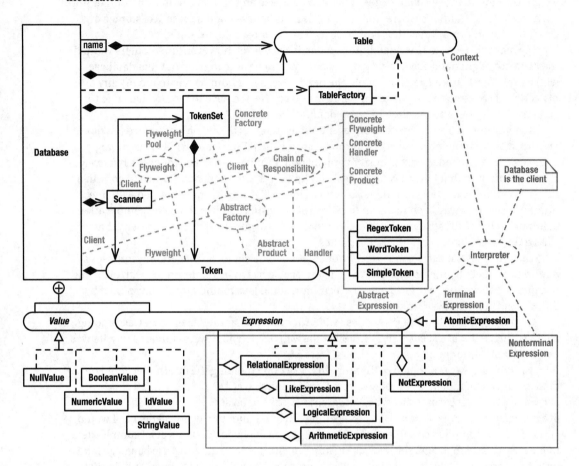

Figure 4-11. *SQL engine and JDBC layers: design patterns*

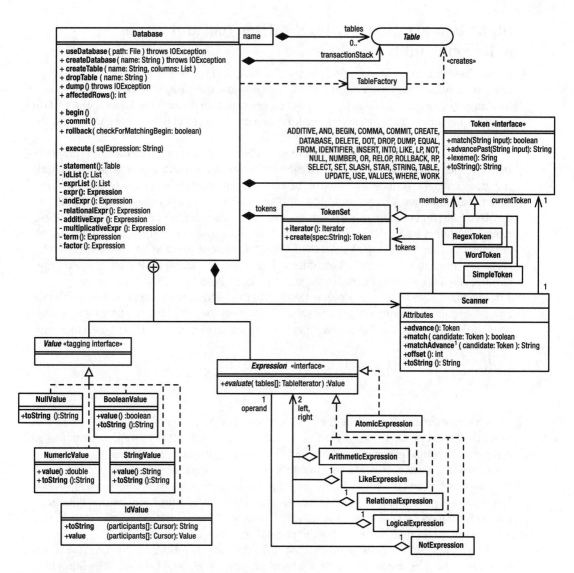

Figure 4-12. *SQL engine and JDBC layers: static structure*

Input Tokenization, Flyweight Revisited, and Chain of Responsibility

One of the requirements for a parser that is also a requirement for virtually any program that has to look at text-based input is input *tokenization*, or *scanning*, which is the process of breaking up a long input string into smaller pieces based on the way the input looks, and then representing those smaller strings as well-defined constants so you don't have to constantly rescan them.

In compilers, a *token* is the smallest meaningful lexical unit of the input. For example, a keyword such as while is a token, as are each of the various operators. A one-to-one relationship does not necessarily exist between the actual input characters and the token type. Identifiers, for example, are all represented by an IDENTIFIER token, even though the identifiers may consist of different combinations of characters. Sometimes, semantically similar operators are grouped together into a single token. For example, the <, >, <=, ==, and != operators could be grouped together into a single RELATIONAL_OPERATOR token. A scanner inputs a stream of characters and outputs a stream of token objects that represent that input. Put another way, the scanner extracts substrings of the input and translates these substrings into tokens.

The token objects must be unique. Every time the scanner encounters an identifier in the input, for example, it returns the same IDENTIFIER object that it did the last time it encountered an identifier. This way you can tell whether you've read an identifier with a simple statement such as this:

```
if( currentToken == IDENTIFIER )
    //...
```

An important attribute of the IDENTIFIER object (and of all tokens) is the input string that's associated with the token, called a *lexeme*. Once you get an IDENTIFIER token, for example, you can figure out which identifier you just read by examining the associated lexeme.

Given that a scanner always returns the same token object for a given input sequence, the scanner is a good example of a Flyweight-pool manager. The token objects themselves are Flyweights—the lexeme is the extrinsic data—and the scanner repeatedly returns the same token object for a particular input sequence. (I discussed Flyweights in Chapter 4. Go back and read about them if the preceding didn't make any sense.)

Java has a couple of generic tokenizers: java.util.StringTokenizer and java.io.StreamTokenizer. The former does only half of what a real scanner does: It breaks up the input into meaningful lexemes and return them to you, but it doesn't translate the lexemes into tokens. The StreamTokenizer does return tokens, but it recognizes only four of them: TT_EOF (end of file), TT_EOL (end of line), TT_NUMBER (a number), and TT_WORD (anything else). TT stands for *token type*. In the case of TT_NUMBER and TT_WORD, the associated lexemes can be examined via the nval and sval fields of the tokenizer (not a great design decision—public accessors would be better).

The StreamTokenizer is too limited for a compiler application, however. I want unique tokens for every keyword, for example. Lumping all the keywords and identifiers in the input into a single TT_WORD token is too coarse grained to be useful. A real scanner would return IDENTIFIER, WHILE, IF, and ELSE tokens as appropriate.

So, let's look at the more capable scanner used by the SQL engine. The first order of business is to define a set of tokens for the scanner to use. The individual tokens are responsible for recognizing the associated input lexemes. Tokens are always part of a set, so I didn't want anyone to create one without connecting it to an associated token set. Consequently, a TokenSet object serves as a Token factory. You create tokens as follows:

```
TokenSet tokens = new TokenSet();

Token   COMMA      = tokens.create( "','"               ),
        INPUT      = tokens.create( "INPUT"             ),
        IN         = tokens.create( "IN"                ),
        IDENTIFIER = tokens.create( "[a-zA-Z_][a-zA-Z_0-9]*" );
```

The argument to create() is a regular expression that describes the lexeme associated with this token. Surrounding the expression with single-quote marks causes all characters to be treated literally (rather than as regular-expression metacharacters. That is, the specification "'...'" is treated identically to the regular expression "\Q...\E". The closing quote is optional.

The TokenSet participates in several design patterns, but here it's in the Concrete Factory role of Abstract Factory. (There is no interface in the Abstract Factory role.) Token is the Abstract-Product interface, and implementers of the Token interface (which we'll look at shortly) are the Concrete Products.

The client class (the Database) doesn't know the actual classes of the Concrete Products: the Token objects returned from create(...). Nonetheless, the system supports three distinct Token subclasses that differ only in how efficient they are in processing the input string. That is, it's the job of each Token object to look at the input stream and tell whether the next few input characters match a lexeme associated with that token.

- A RegexToken uses Java's regular-expression system to match the input stream against the specification, so it is powerful but relatively inefficient. It is case insensitive.

- A SimpleToken matches tokens for which there is only one possible lexeme. Its recognizer, which just performs a literal match of the pattern against the input string, is by far the most efficient of the three token types. To make it as efficient as possible, the recognizer for a SimpleToken is not case insensitive (unlike the other two Token types). This inconsistency is, in some ways, a design flaw, but I was loath to slow down a recognizer that's used primarily for finding punctuation and operators. The factory uses a SimpleToken when the specifier passed to create(...) is either surrounded by single quotes or contains no regular-expression metacharacters.

- A WordToken is a SimpleToken that must be terminated at a "word boundary." (Either it must be followed by a character that's not legal in a Java identifier or it must be the last token in the input string.) The regular-expression subsystem isn't used for word tokens. The tokens are recognized in a case-insensitive way.

The TokenSet factory simplifies token creation by deciding which of the three Token implementers to create, based on what the specification looks like. In particular, if the string contains any of the regular-expression metacharacters and isn't surrounded by single-quote marks, RegexToken objects are created. In the case of quoted strings or strings that don't contain metacharacters, a WordToken is created if the specification ends in a character that's legal in a Java identifier; otherwise, it creates a SimpleToken.

Given a conflict in the lexemes (in other words, two Token specifications can match the same input sequence), the token that's created first takes precedence. In the earlier example, the INPUT token must be created before the IN token or the string "input" will be processed incorrectly. (An IN token will be recognized, and then an IDENTIFIER with the value "put" is recognized.) Similarly, IDENTIFIER has to come last; otherwise, it would suck up all the keywords.

The TokenSet reification of Abstract Factory omits the interface in the Abstract-Factory role. The downside of this incomplete reification is that you have to modify the source code for the TokenSet class if you add a new token type. You can create a token type simply by extending Token, of course, but you won't be able to create instances of your token via the factory unless you modify the factory as well. My main goal with this particular factory was to simplify the code, however. I just wanted to declare tokens without worrying about which Token subclass was needed for a particular input specification. Since I don't expect to add new token types, the lack of expansibility isn't a large concern (famous last words).

Moving onto the code, the Token class is in Listing 4-20, and the three implementations are in Listing 4-21 (SimpleToken.java), Listing 4-22 (WordToken.java), and Listing 4-23 (Regex-Token.java). SimpleToken (Listing 4-21) is the simplest, so let's start there. The constructor is passed a template input sequence. The match(String input) method returns true if the first characters on the input line match that template. The advancePast() method returns its argument with the lexeme removed from the front of it. Finally, lexeme() returns the most recently recognized lexeme.

The WordToken class in Listing 4-22 is only marginally more complicated. The match(...) method checks the input against the pattern, but it also looks to make sure that the character that follows couldn't occur in a Java identifier (in other words, is on a "word" boundary).

The RegexToken class in Listing 4-23 is the most complicated because it uses Java's regex package. It's a straightforward use of the Pattern and Matcher classes, but note that the pattern is compiled only once, when the RegexToken is created. As is the case in the other Token implementation, patterns are recognized in a case-insensitive way.

Listing 4-20. *Token.java*

```
1  package com.holub.text;
2
3  public interface Token
4  {   boolean match (String input, int offset);
5      String  lexeme( );
6  }
```

Listing 4-21. *SimpleToken.java*

```
1  package com.holub.text;
2
3  import java.util.*;
4  import java.util.regex.*;
5
6  /** Matches a simple symbol that doesn't have to be on a "word"
```

```
 7    *   boundary, punctuation, for example. SimpleToken
 8    *   is very efficient but does not recognize characters in
 9    *   a case-insensitive way, as does {@link WordToken} and
10    *   {@link RegexToken}.
11    */
12
13   public class SimpleToken implements Token
14   {
15       private final  String    pattern;
16
17       /** Create a token.
18        *  @param description a string that defines a literal-match lexeme.
19        */
20
21       public SimpleToken( String pattern )
22       {   this.pattern = pattern.toLowerCase();
23       }
24
25       public boolean match( String input, int offset )
26       {   return input.toLowerCase().startsWith( pattern, offset );
27       }
28
29       public String lexeme()  { return pattern; }
30       public String toString(){ return pattern; }
31   }
```

Listing 4-22. *WordToken.java*

```
 1   package com.holub.text;
 2
 3   import java.util.*;
 4   import java.util.regex.*;
 5
 6   /** Recognize a token that looks like a word. The match
 7    *   is case insensitive. To be recognized, the input
 8    *   must match the pattern passed to the constructor
 9    *   and must be followed by a non-letter-or-digit.
10    *   The returned lexeme is always all-lowercase
11    *   letters, regardless of what the actual input
12    *   looked like.
13    */
14
15   public class WordToken implements Token
16   {
17       private final String    pattern;
18
19       /** Create a token.
```

```
20      *  @param description a regular expression
21      *              ({@linkplain java.util.Pattern see}) that describes
22      *              the set of lexemes associated with this token.
23      */
24
25     public WordToken( String pattern )
26     {   this.pattern = pattern.toLowerCase();
27     }
28
29     public boolean match(String input, int offset)
30     {
31         // Check that the input matches the patter in a
32         // case-insensitive way. If you don't want case
33         // insenstivity, use the following, less-complicated code:
34         //
35         // if( !input.toLowerCase().startsWith(pattern, offset) )
36         //     return false;
37
38         if( (input.length() - offset) < pattern.length() )
39             return false;
40
41         String candidate = input.substring( offset,
42                                         offset+pattern.length() );
43         if( !candidate.equalsIgnoreCase(pattern) )
44             return false;
45
46         // Return true if the lexeme is at the end of the
47         // input string or if the character following the
48         // lexeme is not a letter or digit.
49
50         return     ((input.length() - offset) == pattern.length())
51                 || (!Character.isLetterOrDigit(
52                         input.charAt(offset + pattern.length()) ));
53     }
54
55     public String lexeme()  { return pattern; }
56     public String toString(){ return pattern; }
57 }
```

Listing 4-23. *RegexToken.java*

```
1  package com.holub.text;
2
3  import java.util.*;
4  import java.util.regex.*;
5
```

```
 6  /** Matches a token specified using a regular expression
 7   */
 8
 9  public class RegexToken implements Token
10  {
11      private          Matcher      matcher;
12      private final    Pattern      pattern;
13      private final    String       id;
14
15      /** Create a token.
16       *  @param description a regular expression
17       *              ({@linkplain java.util.Pattern see}) that describes
18       *              the set of lexemes associated with this token.
19       *              The expression is case insensitive, so the
20       *              expression "ABC" also recognizes "abc".
21       */
22      public RegexToken(String description)
23      {   id = description;
24          pattern = Pattern.compile(description, Pattern.CASE_INSENSITIVE);
25      }
26
27      public boolean match(String input, int offset)
28      {   matcher = pattern.matcher( input.substring(offset) );
29          return matcher.lookingAt();
30      }
31
32      public String lexeme()  { return matcher.group(); }
33      public String toString(){ return id; }
34  }
```

The `tokenSet` class is in Listing 4-24. Its members field (Listing 4-24, line 8) holds the members of the Flyweight pool (the previously created tokens).

The `create(...)` method (Listing 4-24, line 39) adds all the tokens that it creates to this collection. It also decides which subclass of Token to create by examining the input specification.

You can get an `java.util.Iterator` across all the Flyweights in the pool by calling `iterator()` (Listing 4-24, line 15). Note that this iterator is guaranteed to present the Token objects in the same order that they were added to the pool. This guaranteed ordering will be important when I implement the scanner, shortly.

Listing 4-24. *TokenSet.java*

```
1  package com.holub.text;
2
3  import java.util.*;
4  import java.util.regex.*;
5
6  public class TokenSet
```

```
 7  {
 8      private Collection members = new ArrayList();
 9
10      /** Return an iterator across the Token pool. This iterator
11       *  is guaranteed to return the tokens in the order that
12       *  {@link create()} was called.
13       */
14
15      public Iterator iterator()
16      {   return members.iterator();
17      }
18
19      /***********************************************************************
20       * Create a Token based on a specification.
21       * <p>
22       * An appropriate token type is chosen by examining the input
23       * specification. In particular, a {@link RegexToken} is
24       * created unless the input string contains no regular-expression
25       * metacharacters (<em>\\[]{</em>()$^*+?|}) or starts with a single-quote
26       * mark ('). In this case, a
27       * {@link WordToken} is created if the specification ends
28       * in any character that could occur in a Java identifier;
29       * otherwise a {@link SimpleToken} is created.
30       * If a string that starts with a single-quote mark also
31       * ends with a single-quote mark, the end-quote mark
32       * is discarded. The end-quote mark is optional.
33       * <p>
34       * Tokens are always extracted
35       * from the beginning of a String, so the characters that
36       * precede the token are irrelevant.
37       */
38
39      public Token create( String spec )
40      {   Token token;
41          int start = 1;
42
43          if( !spec.startsWith("'") )
44          {   if( containsRegexMetacharacters(spec) )
45              {
46                  token = new RegexToken( spec );
47                  members.add(token);
48                  return token;
49              }
50
51              --start;    // don't compensate for leading quote
52
```

```
53                // fall through to the "quoted-spec" case
54          }
55
56          int end = spec.length();
57
58          if( start==1 &&  spec.endsWith("'") ) // saw leading '
59              --end;
60
61          token = Character.isJavaIdentifierPart(spec.charAt(end-1))
62                  ? (Token) new WordToken   ( spec.substring(start,end) )
63                  : (Token) new SimpleToken( spec.substring(start,end) )
64                  ;
65
66          members.add( token );
67          return token;
68      }
69
70      /** Return true if the string argument contains any of the
71       *  following characters: \\[]$^*+?|()
72       */
73      private static final boolean containsRegexMetacharacters(String s)
74      {   // This method could be implemented more efficiently,
75          // but its not called very often.
76          Matcher m = metacharacters.matcher(s);
77          return m.find();
78      }
79      private static final Pattern metacharacters =
80                          Pattern.compile("[\\\\\\[\\]$\\\\^*+?|()]");
81  }
```

The Scanner: Chain of Responsibility

The Scanner class (Listing 4-25) uses the TokenSet to implement a scanner. You create a scanner for a particular token set like this:

```
TokenSet tokens = new TokenSet();
Token  COMMA      = tokens.create( "','"                      ),
       INPUT      = tokens.create( "INPUT"                    ),
       IN         = tokens.create( "IN"                       ),
       IDENTIFIER = tokens.create( "[a-zA-Z_][a-zA-Z_0-9]*" );

Scanner tokenizer = new Scanner( tokenSet, inputReader );
```

The Scanner looks for tokens in the specified set, reading characters from the specified Reader. The interface to the Scanner is straightforward, but it may be surprising if you've never built a parser. Parsers, in general, are more interested in seeing if the next input token (called the *lookahead* token) is what they expect than they are in actually reading the next token

(removing it from the input). Consequently, the Scanner interface does not have a getToken()
method, simply because such a method wouldn't be used. You use the scanner more or less
like this:

```
TokenSet tokens = new TokenSet();
Token DESIRED_TOKEN   = tokens.create(...);
Token DIFFERENT_TOKEN = tokens.create(...);
//...

Reader inputReader = ...;
Scanner tokenizer = new Scanner( tokens, inputReader );
//...

if( tokenizer.match(DESIRED_TOKEN) )
{   doSomething( t.lexeme(); )  // or use DESIRED_TOKEN.lexeme()
    Token t = tokenizer.advance();
}
else if( tokenizer.match(DIFFERENT_TOKEN) )
{   //...
}
//...
```

The match(...) method just checks to see if the desired token is the next one in the input
stream. The advance() method actually reads (and returns) the next input token. This match/
advance strategy is much more efficient than reading the token because you'd otherwise have
to repetitively push uninteresting tokens back onto the input.

Two convenience methods are provided to simplify scanning: First, matchAdvance(Token)
(Listing 4-25, line 111) combines the match and advance operations. If the token argument
matches the current token, the scanner advances to the next token and returns the current
lexeme. Otherwise, the scanner does nothing and returns null. Second, the required(Token)
method (Listing 4-25, line 127) is a more forceful version of matchAdvance(). It throws a Parse-
Failure exception if the specified token isn't the current token.

The Scanner is implemented in Listing 4-25. From the design-patterns perspective, the
interesting code is the for loop on line 76. I get an iterator across the entire token set and then
ask each token in turn whether its lexeme specification matches the current input sequence.
The work of detecting the match is delegated to the Token objects, each of which checks for a
match in the most efficient way possible.

The design pattern here is **Chain of Responsibility** (sometimes called **Chain of Command**).
The idea is to handle an event (or in this case, an input sequence) by passing it in turn to a set of
Command objects. Those objects that are able to handle the event do so. The object that does
the routing can't predict which handler (some object in the pattern's Handler role) will handle
the event (or input), and usually doesn't care, as long as that event (or input) gets handled. It's
important to note that the list of handlers is put together at runtime. The Client has no way to
know at compile time which handlers will be invoked in which sequence.

This characteristic is important in the current context because the order in which Token
objects attempt to match themselves against the input is important. In the SQL engine, for
example, you have an IN and also an INPUT token. It's important that the Scanner looks for a

match of IN before it looks for INPUT; otherwise it will never find the latter. Similarly, it's important that the IDENTIFIER token, which is declared like this:

```
IDENTIFIER = tokens.create( "[a-zA-Z_0-9/\\\\:~]+" );
```

be at the end of the list of tokens, because the specified regular expression will also match all the keywords. Were IDENTIFIER not declared last, keywords would be incorrectly recognized as identifiers.

The Scanner stops routing the input to Token objects once a Handler (a Token) recognizes an input sequence. The design pattern doesn't require this behavior, however. Several Handlers could all process all or part of the same event. Similarly, Chain of Responsibility doesn't require a separate "router" object that controls who gets a crack at the input. A Handler may keep around a pointer to its own successor, for example, and handle the routing locally.

Listing 4-25. *Scanner.java*

```
1   package com.holub.text;
2
3   import java.util.Iterator;
4   import java.io.*;
5   import com.holub.text.ParseFailure;
6
7   public class Scanner
8   {
9       private Token            currentToken    = new BeginToken();
10      private BufferedReader   inputReader     = null;
11      private int              inputLineNumber = 0;
12      private String           inputLine       = null;
13      private int              inputPosition   = 0;
14
15      private TokenSet tokens;
16
17      public Scanner( TokenSet tokens, String input )
18      {   this( tokens, new StringReader(input) );
19      }
20
21      public Scanner( TokenSet tokens, Reader inputReader )
22      {   this.tokens      = tokens;
23          this.inputReader =
24              (inputReader instanceof BufferedReader)
25                  ? (BufferedReader) inputReader
26                  : new BufferedReader( inputReader )
27                  ;
28          loadLine();
29      }
30
31      /** Load the next input line and adjust the line number
32       *  and inputPosition offset.
```

```
33        */
34        private boolean loadLine()
35        {   try
36            {   inputLine = inputReader.readLine();
37                if( inputLine != null )
38                {   ++inputLineNumber;
39                    inputPosition = 0;
40                }
41                return inputLine != null;
42            }
43            catch( IOException e )
44            {   return false;
45            }
46        }
47
48        /** Return true if the current token matches the
49         *  candidate token.
50         */
51        public boolean match( Token candidate )
52        {   return currentToken == candidate;
53        }
54
55        /** Advance the input to the next token and return it.
56         *  This token is valid only until the next advance() call.
57         */
58        public Token advance() throws ParseFailure
59        {   try
60            {
61                if( currentToken != null )  // not at end of file
62                {
63                    inputPosition += currentToken.lexeme().length();
64                    currentToken  = null;
65
66                    if( inputPosition == inputLine.length() )
67                        if( !loadLine() )
68                            return null;
69
70                    while( Character.isWhitespace(
71                                    inputLine.charAt(inputPosition)) )
72                        if( ++inputPosition == inputLine.length() )
73                            if( !loadLine() )
74                                return null;
75
76                    for( Iterator i = tokens.iterator(); i.hasNext(); )
77                    {   Token t = (Token)(i.next());
78                        if( t.match(inputLine, inputPosition) )
79                        {   currentToken = t;
```

```
 80                        break;
 81                    }
 82                }
 83
 84                if( currentToken == null )
 85                    throw failure("Unrecognized Input");
 86            }
 87        }
 88        catch( IndexOutOfBoundsException e ){ /* nothing to do */ }
 89        return currentToken;
 90    }
 91
 92    /* Throws a ParseException object initialized for the current
 93     * input position. This method lets a parser that's using the
 94     * current scanner report an error in a way that identifies
 95     * where in the input the error occurred.
 96     * @param message the "message" (as returned by
 97     *         {@link java.lang.Throwable.getMessage}) to attach
 98     *         to the thrown <code>RuntimeException</code> object.
 99     * @throws  ParseFailure always.
100     */
101    public ParseFailure failure( String message )
102    {   return new ParseFailure(message,
103                        inputLine, inputPosition, inputLineNumber);
104    }
105
106    /** Combines the match and advance operations. Advance automatically
107     *  if the match occurs.
108     *  @return the lexeme if there was a match and the input was advanced,
109     *       null if there was no match (the input is not advanced).
110     */
111    public String matchAdvance( Token candidate ) throws ParseFailure
112    {   if( match(candidate) )
113        {   String lexeme = currentToken.lexeme();
114            advance();
115            return lexeme;
116        }
117        return null;
118    }
119
120    /**  If the specified candidate is the current token,
121     *    advance past it and return the lexeme; otherwise,
122     *    throw an exception with the error message
123     *    "XXX Expected".
124     *    @throws ParseFailure if the required token isn't the
125     *            current token.
126     */
```

```
127    public final String required( Token candidate ) throws ParseFailure
128    {    String lexeme = matchAdvance(candidate);
129        if( lexeme == null )
130            throw failure(
131                    "\"" + candidate.toString() + "\" expected.");
132        return lexeme;
133    }
134
135    /*------------------------------------------------------------*/
136    public static class Test
137    {
138        private static TokenSet tokens = new TokenSet();
139
140        private static final Token
141            COMMA      = tokens.create( "','"            ),
142            IN         = tokens.create( "'IN'"           ),
143            INPUT      = tokens.create( "INPUT"          ),
144            IDENTIFIER = tokens.create( "[a-z_][a-z_0-9]*" );
145
146        public static void main(String[] args) throws ParseFailure
147        {
148            assert COMMA      instanceof SimpleToken: "Factory Failure 1";
149            assert IN         instanceof WordToken  : "Factory Failure 2";
150            assert INPUT      instanceof WordToken  : "Factory Failure 3";
151            assert IDENTIFIER instanceof RegexToken : "Factory Failure 4";
152
153            Scanner analyzer=new Scanner(tokens, ",aBc In input inputted" );
154
155            assert analyzer.advance() == COMMA      : "COMMA unrecognized";
156            assert analyzer.advance() == IDENTIFIER : "ID unrecognized";
157            assert analyzer.advance() == IN         : "IN unrecognized";
158            assert analyzer.advance() == INPUT      : "INPUT unrecognized";
159            assert analyzer.advance() == IDENTIFIER : "ID unrecognized 1";
160
161            analyzer = new Scanner(tokens, "Abc IN\nCde");
162            analyzer.advance(); // advance to first token.
163
164            assert( analyzer.matchAdvance(IDENTIFIER).equals("Abc") );
165            assert( analyzer.matchAdvance(IN).equals("in")   );
166            assert( analyzer.matchAdvance(IDENTIFIER).equals("Cde") );
167
168            // Deliberately force an exception toss
169            analyzer = new Scanner(tokens, "xyz\nabc + def");
170            analyzer.advance();
171            analyzer.advance();
172            try
173            {    analyzer.advance(); // should throw an exception
```

```
174                     assert false : "Error Detection Failure";
175                 }
176             catch( ParseFailure e )
177             {   assert e.getErrorReport().equals(
178                                     "Line 2:\n"
179                                   + "abc + def\n"
180                                   + "____^\n" );
181             }
182
183             System.out.println("Scanner PASSED");
184
185             System.exit(0);
186         }
187     }
188 }
```

One anti-example of the Chain-of-Responsibility pattern (that is, an example that demonstrates the pattern's shortcomings) is the Windows event model. A Windows UI is a runtime hierarchy of objects. Consider a typical dialog box with a text field on it. Figure 4-13 shows the associated runtime object hierarchy. Now imagine you're typing in the text field and accidentally hit a typically easy-to-remember "hot key" such as Ctrl+Alt+Shift+F12. As you can see by following the sequence of arrows, the key-pressed event can go to many potential handlers (from the text control to its parent window (the Dialog Frame) to its parent (the MDI Child) to its parent (the Main Frame) to the menu bar, to each menu on the menu bar to menu item on that menu bar. Finally, when the key-pressed event gets to the last menu item on the last menu on the menu bar, it's discarded. The same sequence will happen every time the mouse moves one pixel. That's a lot of motion, but no action. This is one reason why Java abandoned this message-routing mechanism with Java 1.1 in favor of its Observer-based system.

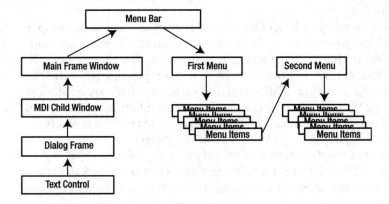

Figure 4-13. *Chain of Command in a Windows UI*

Java has lots of good examples of Chain of Responsibility. One of the better ones is the servlet filter. A *servlet* is a small program that's invoked automatically by the web server in response to an HTTP Post or Get request. Typical servlets are passed data that's specified in an HTML form, and they create a HTML page that's displayed on the client-side browser in response to that form submission. Once you've written a few servlets, you come to realize that they often duplicate the code of other servlets. For example, authentication is a commonplace activity in a servlet. The servlet may read a username and password from the submitted form data, for example, and refuse to proceed with a transaction if the password isn't correct. Alternatively, a servlet may check the *session data* (a packet of information that's associated with the user) to assure that a given user is indeed logged in. Duplicating this authentication code in every servlet increases the complexity of the system as a whole and also tends to create lack-of-consistency problems in the user interface. (Different servlets may handle the same problem in different ways.) Other common problems include things such as database lookup. That is, the session data may contain a key that you need to use to get additional information out of a server-side database. This lookup may occur in several servlets, which can cause serious maintenance problems if the data dictionary needs to change, for example. By the same token, information in the session data may have to be stored persistently in a database.

Chain of Responsibility, as reified in the servlet filter, solves all these problems. Figure 4-14 shows the general flow of data through a system of servlets and filters as some form is being processed. The first filter does authentication. If the user has logged in, this filter is just a *pass through*, doing nothing but passing its input to the next filter in the chain. The second filter handles persistent session information—information that resides in a database rather than information that is created during the course of the session—performing all the required database lookup.

You should note two important points: First, the filters are put into place by the web server, not the servlet. As far as the servlet is concerted, the user is authenticated, and the database information is fetched and stored by magic. Second, each filter handles its part of the current operation and then either allows the next object in the chain of responsibility (the next Filter or the servlet itself) to do additional work or short-circuits the process. Runtime configuration and the relative autonomy of the Handlers are both defining characteristics of the Chain of Responsibility.

One other problem I've solved with Chain of Responsibility deserves mention: user-input processing. You saw earlier how you can use the Builder pattern to isolate UI generation from the underlying "business object," but it's sometimes awkward to use Builder on the input side. For example, you can use Builder to ask an object to build an HTML representation of itself for insertion into a generated page (or build an XML representation of itself that's passed through a XSLT translator to build the HTML). In fact, several objects may contribute user interfaces to the page in this way. (A UI could be built, in fact, by a series of servlet filters, each of which augments a generated HTML page by adding a UI for a particular object.)

The page is served, the user hits the submit button, and the form data comes back to another servlet, but then what? You don't really want the servlet to know how to talk to all the objects that contributed to the original page because it's too much of a maintenance problem. If those objects change their user interfaces in some way, you need to change the servlet as well. These coupling relationships are too tight.

Chain of Responsibility solves the coupling problem. All that the servlet (or some filter) needs to do is keep a list of the objects that contributed to the UI. The servlet passes those objects the complete set of form-input data, and the objects parse out of that list whatever is interesting to them. Since the objects built the form to begin with, the object can generate unique field names on the output side, and the object can search for these same names on the input side. The actual servlet is completely generic with respect to the UI: It just keeps a list of contributing objects, gets HTML from the objects, and routes the form data back to the objects on the list. It has no idea what the objects actually do, and the interface is extremely simple. More important, you can make massive changes to the objects without impacting the code that comprises the servlet at all.

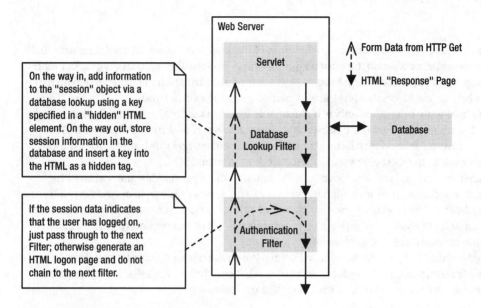

Figure 4-14. *Chain of Command in a Windows UI*

The *ParseFailure* Class

Finishing up loose ends before moving onto the SQL interpreter itself, the one class you haven't looked at yet is the ParseFailure class in Listing 4-26. (I was going to call this class ParserException, but that name was too much like java.text.ParseException.)

Other than the obvious use of having something to throw when a parse error occurs, the ParseFailure object is interesting in the way that I use it to eliminate getter functions from the Scanner class in order to reduce coupling relationships between the Scanner and the rest of the program. Rather than using a getter to find out where on the line that an error occurs, that information is carried around by the exception object itself. This way, you can catch a parse error and print a reasonable error message without having to talk to the Scanner that detected the error at all. The ParseFailure object carries around the input line, line number, and position-on-the-line information, and you can generate a contextual error message that looks like this:

```
Context-specific message
Line 17:
a = b + @ c;
        ^
```

as follows:

```
try
{   // ...
}
catch( ParseFailure e )
{   System.err.println( e.getMessage() );
    System.err.println( e.getErrorReport() );
}
```

I've provided no getter methods (in the sense of methods that access internal state data such as the line number or offset to the error position), simply because they aren't required. Remember the golden rule of implementation hiding: don't ask for the information that you need to do the work; rather, ask the object that has the information to do the work for you.

One final issue exists: Not only is it reasonable for a Scanner to throw ParseFailure objects, but it's reasonable for the parser that uses the scanner to throw them as well. The scanner throws a ParseFailure if the input sequence matches no known token, for example. The parser needs to throw aParseFailure if it finds malformed SQL.

Since the ParseFailure object contains information that's provided by the scanner (the line number and input position), then it makes sense for Scanner objects to act as ParseFailure factories. Rather than having the parser extract line number and position information from the Scanner in order to create a parser-related error message, the parser requests a ParseFailure object that encapsulates that information.

The Scanner, then, is a ParseFailure Factory. When the parser encounters an error at the language (as compared to the lexical-analysis) level, it can throw a ParseFailure object that indicates where the error occurred with code like the following:

```
Scanner lexicalAnalyzer = new Scanner( ... );
//...
if( some_parser_error_occurs() )
{   throw lexicalAnalyzer.failure("Parser-related error message");
}
```

Listing 4-26. *ParseFailure.java*

```
1   package com.holub.text;
2
3   /** Thrown in the event of a Scanner (or parser) failure
4    */
5
6   public class ParseFailure extends Exception
7   {
8       private final String inputLine;
9       private final int    inputPosition;
10      private final int    inputLineNumber;
11
12      public ParseFailure( String message,
13                           String inputLine,
```

```
14                         int inputPosition,
15                         int inputLineNumber )
16      {
17          super( message );
18          this.inputPosition   = inputPosition;
19          this.inputLine       = inputLine;
20          this.inputLineNumber = inputLineNumber;
21      }
22
23      /** Returns a String that shows the current input line and a
24       *  pointer indicating the current input position.
25       *  In the following sample, the input is positioned at the
26       *  @ sign on input line 17:
27       *  <PRE>
28       *  Line 17:
29       *  a = b + @ c;
30       *  _____    ^
31       *  </PRE>
32       *
33       *  Note that the official "message"  [returned from
34       *  {@link Throwable#getMessage()}] is not included in the
35       *  error report.
36       */
37
38      public String getErrorReport()
39      {
40          StringBuffer b = new StringBuffer();
41          b.append("Line ");
42          b.append(inputLineNumber + ":\n");
43          b.append(inputLine);
44          b.append("\n");
45          for( int i = 0; i < inputPosition; ++i)
46              b.append("_");
47          b.append("^\n");
48          return b.toString();
49      }
50  }
```

The *Database* Class

The Database encapsulates the SQL interpreter. Its main job is to transform a set of SQL statements into calls that a Table understands. By introducing SQL into the mix, however, you free the program from needing to know anything about Table objects.

Using the *Database*

You can use a `Database` in one of two ways: as a stand-alone class that represents a SQL database or as a Decorator that wraps a `com.holub.database.Table` temporarily so that you can access the table using SQL. The only difference between these two uses is the constructor you use. Open a stand-alone database like this:

```
Database standalone = new Database("/src/com/holub/database/test");
```

The (optional) argument specifies the path to a directory that represents the database itself. (Tables are stored as individual files.) Convenience constructors let you specify the path with a `File` or `URI` object instead of a `String`. Also, you do not have a no-arg constructor that just puts tables into the current directory. A SQL `USE DATABASE` *directoryName* request causes the `Database` to use the named directory instead of the one specified in the constructor.

To use the `Database` as a Decorator of an existing table (or set of tables), use the following alternative constructor:

```
Table table1 = TableFactory.create( "table1", ... );
Table table2 = TableFactory.create( "table2", ... );
//...

Database wrapped = new Database( "/src/com/holub/database/test",
                                 new Table[]{ table1, table2 } );
```

This isn't a full-blown Gang-of-Four Decorator since `Database` doesn't implement the `Table` interface. It does satisfy the intent of the pattern, however, in that it allows you to augment the `Table` interface by adding SQL support.

Once you've created the database, you talk to it using a single method that takes a `String` argument that specifies a single SQL command. For example, the following code (taken from the `Database` class's unit test) reads a series of SQL statements from a file and executes them:

```
Database d = new Database();
BufferedReader sqlScript = new BufferedReader(
                    new FileReader( "Database.test.sql" ));
String test;
while( (test = sqlScript.readLine()) != null )
{   test = test.trim();
    if( test.length() == 0 )     // ignore blank lines
        continue;

    System.out.println("Parsing: " + test);
    Table result = d.execute( test );        // Result sets come back in a Table

    if( result != null )    // it was a SELECT of some sort
        System.out.println( result.toString() );
}
```

Listing 4-27 shows the SQL that the test-script uses, but it's pretty standard stuff.

Though you can do everything through the execute(...) method, Database provides a few additional methods that let you create, load, and drop tables; dump tables to disk; and manage transactions. I've listed these methods in Table 4-1. An exception toss that occurs when processing a SQL expression submitted to execute() causes an automatic rollback as a side effect. This automatic-rollback behavior *is not implemented* by the methods in Table 4-1, however. If you use these methods, you'll have to catch any exceptions manually and call rollback(...) or commit(...) explicitly.

Table 4-1. *Methods of the* Database *Class*

Method	Description
int affectedRows()	Returns the number of rows that were affected by the most recent execute(java.lang.String) call.
void begin()	Begins a transaction.
void commit(boolean checkForMatchingBegin)	Commits a transaction.
void createDatabase(String name)	Creates a database by opening the indicated directory.
void createTable(String name, List columns)	Creates a new table.
void dropTable(String name)	Destroys both internal and external (on the disk) versions of the specified table.
void dump()	Flushes to the persistent store (for example, disk) all tables that are "dirty" (which have been modified since the database was last committed).
Table execute(String expression)	Executes a SQL statement.
void rollback(boolean checkForMatchingBegin)	Rolls back a transaction.
void useDatabase(File path)	Uses an existing "database."

Listing 4-27. *Database.Test.sql*

```
1   create database Dbase
2
3   create table address \
4       (addrId int, street varchar, city varchar, \
5       state char(2), zip int, primary key(addrId))
6
7   create table name(first varchar(10), last varchar(10), addrId integer)
8
9   insert into address values( 0,'12 MyStreet','Berkeley','CA','99999')
10  insert into address values( 1, '34 Quarry Ln.', 'Bedrock' , 'XX', '00000')
11
12  insert into name VALUES ('Fred',  'Flintstone', '1')
13  insert into name VALUES ('Wilma', 'Flintstone', '1')
14  insert into name (last,first,addrId) VALUES('Holub','Allen',(10-10*1))
15
16  update address set state = "AZ"  where state = "XX"
```

```
17  update address set zip = zip-1 where zip = (99999*1 + (10-10)/1)
18
19  insert into name (last,first) VALUES( 'Please', 'Delete' )
20  delete from name where last like '%eas%'
21
22  select * from address
23  select * from name
24
25  select first, last from name where last = 'Flintstone'
26  select first, last, street, city, zip \
27      from name, address where name.addrId = address.addrId
28
29  create table id (addrId, description)
30  insert into id VALUES (0, 'AddressID=0')
31  insert into id VALUES (1, 'AddressID=1')
32  select first, last, street, city, zip, description \
33      from name, address, id \
34      WHERE name.addrId = address.addrId AND name.addrId = id.addrId
35
36  drop table id
37
38  select first, last from name where last='Flintstone' \
39      AND first='Fred' OR first like '%lle%'
40
41  create table foo (first, second, third, fourth)
42  insert into foo (first,third,fourth) values(1,3,4)
43  update foo set fourth=null where fourth=4
44  select  * from foo
45  select  * from foo where second=NULL AND third<>NULL
46  drop table foo
47
48  select * into existing_copy from existing
49  select * from existing_copy
50
51  create table foo (only)
52  insert into foo values('xxx')
53  begin
54  insert into foo values('should not see this')
55  rollback
56  select * from foo
57
58  begin
59  insert into foo values('yyy')
60  select * from foo
61  begin
62  insert into foo values('should not see this')
63  rollback
```

```
64  begin
65  insert into foo values('zzz')
66  select * from foo
67  commit
68  select * from foo
69  commit
70  select * from foo
71  insert into foo values('end')
72  select * from foo
73  drop table foo
74
75  create table foo (only)
76  begin
77  insert into foo values('a')
78  insert into foo values('b')
79  begin
80  insert into foo values('c')
81  insert into foo values('d')
82  select * from foo
83  commit
84  rollback
85  select * from foo
86
87  drop table foo
```

The Proxy Pattern

The first part of the Database class is in Listing 4-28. Of the fields at the top of the listing, the tables Map (line 41) holds the tables that comprise the database. They're indexed by table name. tables is declared as a Map, but it actually holds a specialization of HashMap (TableMap, declared on line 52).

This specialization adds table-specific behavior to a standard HashMap. First, the get() override uses *lazy instantiation*: When a specific table is first requested, it's loaded from the disk using the CSV Builder. Database methods can act as if all the tables were preloaded into a standard Map , but the tables are actually loaded when they're requested for the first time.

The other modification to the standard HashMap is a put() override, which handles a transaction-related problem that's a side effect of lazy instantiation. The current transaction-nesting level is stored in transactionLevel field declared on line 46. It's incremented by a BEGIN operation and decremented by a COMMIT or ROLLBACK. The code that does the commit/rollback assumes that all the tables in the Map are at the same transaction level. That is, it just commits or rolls back all of them, all at once. If you begin a transaction and then use a table that you haven't used before, that table will not have had a begin() issued against it, yet. The loop in put() solves the problem by issuing begin() requests against the newly loaded table.

Since I don't use it and didn't want to rewrite it, I also overloaded putAll() to throw an UnsupportedOperationException(). I'm playing pretty fast and loose with the class contract here. I wouldn't argue if someone flagged this change as a defect in a code review and forced me to provide a putAll(), but the TableMap is a private inner class—so it can't be extended or used from outside the class definition—I decided that the deviation from the contract was acceptable. I would not make a change of this magnitude if the class were globally accessible.

The remainder of the methods in the Map interface just map through to the contained Map object.

Listing 4-28. *Database.java: Private Data and the* TableMap

```
 1  package com.holub.database;
 2
 3  import java.util.*;
 4  import java.io.*;
 5  import java.text.NumberFormat;
 6  import java.net.URI;
 7
 8  import com.holub.text.Token;
 9  import com.holub.text.TokenSet;
10  import com.holub.text.Scanner;
11  import com.holub.text.ParseFailure;
12  import com.holub.tools.ThrowableContainer;
13
14  /**...*/
15
16  public final class Database
17  {   /* The directory that represents the database.
18       */
19      private File     location     = new File(".");
20
21      /** The number of rows modified by the last
22       *  INSERT, DELETE, or UPDATE request.
23       */
24      private int      affectedRows = 0;
25
26      /** This Map holds the tables that are currently active. I
27       *  have to use be a Map (as compared to a Set), because
28       *  HashSet uses the equals() function to resolve ambiguity.
29       *  This requirement would force me to define "equals" on
30       *  a Table as "having the same name as another table," which
31       *  I believe is semantically incorrect. Equals should match
32       *  both name and contents. I avoid the problem entirely by
33       *  using an external key, even if that key is also an
34       *  accessible attribute of the Table.
35       *
36       *  <p>The table is actually a specialization of Map
37       *  that requires a Table value argument, and interacts
38       *  with the transaction-processing system.
39       */
40
41      private final Map tables = new TableMap( new HashMap() );
```

```
42
43      /** The current transaction-nesting level, incremented for
44       *  a BEGIN and decremented for a COMMIT or ROLLBACK.
45       */
46      private int transactionLevel = 0;
47
48      /** A Map proxy that handles lazy instantiation of tables
49       *  from the disk.
50       */
51
52      private final class TableMap implements Map
53      {
54          private final Map realMap;
55          public TableMap( Map realMap ){ this.realMap = realMap; }
56
57          public Object get( Object key )
58          {   String tableName = (String)key;
59              try
60              {   Table desiredTable = (Table) realMap.get(tableName);
61                  if( desiredTable == null )
62                  {   desiredTable = TableFactory.load(
63                                      tableName + ".csv",location);
64                      put(tableName, desiredTable);
65                  }
66                  return desiredTable;
67              }
68              catch( IOException e )
69              {   // Can't use verify(...) or error(...) here because the
70                  // base-class "get" method doesn't throw any exceptions.
71                  // Kludge a runtime-exception toss. Call in.failure()
72                  // to get an exception object that calls out the
73                  // input filename and line number, then transmogrify
74                  // the ParseFailure to a RuntimeException.
75
76                  String message =
77                      "Table not created internally and couldn't be loaded."
78                                          +"("+ e.getMessage() +")\n";
79                  throw new RuntimeException(
80                                      in.failure( message ).getMessage() );
81              }
82          }
83
84          public Object put(Object key, Object value)
85          {   // If transactions are active, put the new
86              // table into the same transaction state
87              // as the other tables.
88
89              for( int i = 0; i < transactionLevel; ++i )
```

```
90                      ((Table)value).begin();
91
92              return realMap.put(key,value);
93          }
94
95      public void putAll(Map m)
96      {   throw new UnsupportedOperationException();
97      }
98
99      public int       size()              { return realMap.size();        }
100     public boolean   isEmpty()           { return realMap.isEmpty();     }
101     public Object    remove(Object k)    { return realMap.remove(k);     }
102     public void      clear()             {        realMap.clear();       }
103     public Set       keySet()            { return realMap.keySet();      }
104     public Collection values()           { return realMap.values();      }
105     public Set       entrySet()          { return realMap.entrySet();    }
106     public boolean   equals(Object o)    { return realMap.equals(o);     }
107     public int       hashCode()          { return realMap.hashCode();    }
108
109     public boolean   containsKey(Object k)
110     {    return realMap.containsKey(k);
111     }
112     public boolean   containsValue(Object v)
113     {    return realMap.containsValue(v);
114     }
115     }
116
```

The code at which we've been looking—which creates expensive objects on demand—is an example of the **Proxy** design pattern. (The earlier design-patterns diagram (Figure 4-11) had no space for these classes, so I've sketched it out in Figure 4-15.) A proxy is a *surrogate* or *placeholder* for another object, a reference to which is typically contained in the proxy. The TableMap serves as a proxy for the realMap object that it contains. The main idea is that it's convenient, sometimes, to talk to some object (called the Real Subject) through an intermediary (called a Proxy) that implements the same interface as the Real Subject. This intermediary can do things such as lazy instantiation (loading expensive fields on demand).

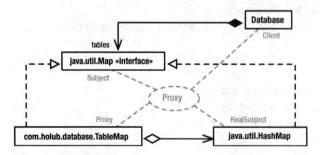

Figure 4-15. *The Proxy pattern*

The Gang-of-Four book mentions the following types of proxies:

- A *remote proxy* exists on one side of a network connection and implements the same interface as does another object on the other side of the network connection. You talk to the proxy, and it talks across the network to the real object. For all practical purposes, the client thinks that the proxy is the remote object because all communication with the remote object is transparent. Java RMI, CORBA, and XML/SOAP are remote-proxy architectures.

- The `TableMap` is an example of a *virtual proxy*, a proxy that creates expensive objects on demand. This particular implementation is not "pure" in the sense that the underlying `HashMap` is not created on demand, but rather the `HashMap` is populated on demand. A "purer" example of a virtual proxy is the `java.awt.Image` class, which serves as a proxy for the real image as it's being loaded. That is, `Runtime.getImage()` immediately returns a proxy for the real image, which is being downloaded across the network by a background thread. You can use the proxy (the `Image` returned by `getImage()`) before the real image arrives, however `getImage()` returns the real image, not the proxy, if it has already downloaded the image.

- A *protection proxy* controls access to an underlying object. For example, the `Collection` implementations returned from `Collections.synchronizedCollection(...)` and `Collections.unmodifiableCollection(...)` are protection proxies.

- A *smart reference* replaces a bare reference in a way that adds additional functionality. Java's "weak reference" mechanism, as is used by a `java.util.WeakHashMap`, is one example of this kind of proxy; the C++ `SmartPointer` is another.

Virtual proxies are particularly useful in database applications because you can delay a query until you actually need the data. Consider an application where you needed to choose one of 10,000 `Employee` objects and then do something with that object. You could go out to the database and fully create all 10,000 `Employee` objects, but that's really a waste of time. It would be better to put the employee names into a single table and then create proxies for the real `Employee` objects. (The proxies would hold the name, but nothing else.) When you called some method of the proxy that used some field other than the name, the proxy would go out to the database and get the required data for that `Employee` only (or perhaps fully populate a full-blown `Employee` from the database).

One significant source of confusion amongst people learning the Proxy pattern is the difference between Proxies and Decorators. The point of a Decorator is to add or modify the behavior of an object. The point of Proxy is to control access to another object. They're structurally identical; thus, confusion exists.

The Token Set and Other Constants

The `Database` definition continues in Listing 4-29 with the token-set definition (lines 128 to 172) As I mentioned earlier, tokens are created in search order, so it's important that the keyword tokens are created before the `IDENTIFIER` token. Listing 4-29 finishes up with two enumerated-type declarations. I've used Bloch's typesafe-enum idiom, discussed in Chapter 1, to define two enumerations. (This idiom gives me both type safety and also a guaranteed constraint on the possible values—a `static final int` does neither.) The `RelationalOperator`

objects are used to identify which relational operator is being processed. MathOperator is the
same but for arithmetic operators.

Listing 4-29. *Database.java continued: Tokens and Enumerations*

```
117        //------------------------------------------------------------
118        // The token set used by the parser. Tokens automatically
119        // The Scanner object matches the specification against the
120        // input in the order of creation. For example, it's important
121        // that the NUMBER token is declared before the IDENTIFIER token
122        // since the regular expression associated with IDENTIFIERS
123        // will also recognize some legitimate numbers.
124
125        private static final TokenSet tokens = new TokenSet();
126
127        private static final Token
128            COMMA       = tokens.create( "','"       ),
129            EQUAL       = tokens.create( "'='"       ),
130            LP          = tokens.create( "'('"       ),
131            RP          = tokens.create( "')'"       ),
132            DOT         = tokens.create( "'.'"       ),
133            STAR        = tokens.create( "'*'"       ),
134            SLASH       = tokens.create( "'/'"       ),
135            AND         = tokens.create( "'AND"      ),
136            BEGIN       = tokens.create( "'BEGIN"    ),
137            COMMIT      = tokens.create( "'COMMIT"   ),
138            CREATE      = tokens.create( "'CREATE"   ),
139            DATABASE    = tokens.create( "'DATABASE"),
140            DELETE      = tokens.create( "'DELETE"   ),
141            DROP        = tokens.create( "'DROP"     ),
142            DUMP        = tokens.create( "'DUMP"     ),
143            FROM        = tokens.create( "'FROM"     ),
144            INSERT      = tokens.create( "'INSERT"   ),
145            INTO        = tokens.create( "'INTO"     ),
146            KEY         = tokens.create( "'KEY"      ),
147            LIKE        = tokens.create( "'LIKE"     ),
148            NOT         = tokens.create( "'NOT"      ),
149            NULL        = tokens.create( "'NULL"     ),
150            OR          = tokens.create( "'OR"       ),
151            PRIMARY     = tokens.create( "'PRIMARY"  ),
152            ROLLBACK    = tokens.create( "'ROLLBACK"),
153            SELECT      = tokens.create( "'SELECT"   ),
154            SET         = tokens.create( "'SET"      ),
155            TABLE       = tokens.create( "'TABLE"    ),
156            UPDATE      = tokens.create( "'UPDATE"   ),
157            USE         = tokens.create( "'USE"      ),
158            VALUES      = tokens.create( "'VALUES"   ),
```

```
159        WHERE        = tokens.create( "'WHERE"    ),
160
161        WORK         = tokens.create( "WORK|TRAN(SACTION)?"      ),
162        ADDITIVE     = tokens.create( "\\+|-"                   ),
163        STRING       = tokens.create( "(\".*?\")|('.*?')"       ),
164        RELOP        = tokens.create( "[<>][=>]?"               ),
165        NUMBER       = tokens.create( "[0-9]+(\\.[0-9]+)?"      ),
166
167        INTEGER      = tokens.create( "(small|tiny|big)?int(eger)?"),
168        NUMERIC      = tokens.create( "decimal|numeric|real|double"),
169        CHAR         = tokens.create( "(var)?char"              ),
170        DATE         = tokens.create( "date(\\s*\\(.*?\\))?"    ),
171
172        IDENTIFIER = tokens.create( "[a-zA-Z_0-9/\\\\:~]+"      );
173
174    private String  expression; // SQL expression being parsed
175    private Scanner in;          // The current scanner.
176
177    // Enums to identify operators not recognized at the token level
178    // These are used by various inner classes, but must be declared
179    // at the outer-class level because they're static.
180
181    private static class  RelationalOperator{ private RelationalOperator() }
182    private static final  RelationalOperator EQ = new RelationalOperator();
183    private static final  RelationalOperator LT = new RelationalOperator();
184    private static final  RelationalOperator GT = new RelationalOperator();
185    private static final  RelationalOperator LE = new RelationalOperator();
186    private static final  RelationalOperator GE = new RelationalOperator();
187    private static final  RelationalOperator NE = new RelationalOperator();
188
189    private static class MathOperator{ private MathOperator() }
190    private static final MathOperator PLUS   = new MathOperator();
191    private static final MathOperator MINUS  = new MathOperator();
192    private static final MathOperator TIMES  = new MathOperator();
193    private static final MathOperator DIVIDE = new MathOperator();
194
```

The next chunk of the Database definition is in Listing 4-30. The constructors—which are pretty self-explanatory—come first, followed by a few private workhorse functions that are used elsewhere in the class. The error(...) method (line 247) is called when a parse error occurs. It's interesting to see how I've used delegation to avoid accessor methods. Since the Scanner already knows how to create a ParseError object that contains a context-sensitive error message, I delegate the creation of the error object to the Scanner object. This way I don't have to extract anything from the scanner to create a sensible error message.

The rest of Listing 4-30 defines most of the convenience methods discussed in Table 4-1. The only interesting method is dump() on line 327, which flushes to disk those tables in the tables Map that have been modified (isDirty() returns true). The design issue here is whether the isDirty() method is needed at all—it is exposing an implementation detail. I could, for example, add an exportIfDirty() method to the Table and dispense with isDirty() altogether. You can see why I opted for the isDirty() solution by looking at the code. I just didn't want to create (and open) a FileWriter if I wasn't going to use it.

Another alternative that I also rejected was adding a writeAsCsvIfDirty() method to the Table. The whole point of using the Builder pattern to export data was to avoid exactly that sort of method.

One solution has none of these problems, but it does introduce a bit of extra complexity. You could introduce a Proxy for the Writer called a DelayedWriter. The DelayedWriter would work exactly like a FileWriter from the outside. Inside, it would create a FileWriter to actually do the output as a side effect of requesting the first write operation. This way, the file wouldn't be opened unless you actually wrote to it. If you implement an exportIfDirty(Exporter builder) method in the Table, and pass it a CSVExporter that uses a DelayedWriter, the file would never be opened if the Table wasn't dirty because the exporter would never write to it. Though the DelayedWriter Proxy would eliminate the need for isDirty(), I eventually decided that it wasn't worth adding the extra complexity, so I didn't implement it.

Listing 4-30. *Database.java continued: Convenience Methods That Mimic SQL*

```
195      //-----------------------------------------------------------------
196      /** Create a database object attached to the current directory.
197       *  You can specify a different directory after the object
198       *  is created by calling {@link #useDatabase}.
199       */
200      public Database() { }
201
202      /** Use the indicated directory for the database */
203      public Database( URI directory ) throws IOException
204      {   useDatabase( new File(directory) );
205      }
206
207      /**  Use the indicated directory for the database */
208      public Database( File path ) throws IOException
209      {   useDatabase( path );
210      }
211
212      /**  Use the indicated directory for the database */
213      public Database( String path ) throws IOException
214      {   useDatabase( new File(path)  );
215      }
216
217      /** Use this constructor to wrap one or more Table
218       *  objects so that you can access them using
219       *  SQL. You may add tables to this database using
220       *  SQL "CREATE TABLE" statements, and you may safely
221       *  extract a snapshot of a table that you create
222       *  in this way using:
```

```
223        *   <PRE>
224        *   Table t = execute( "SELECT * from " + tableName );
225        *   </PRE>
226        *   @param database an array of tables to use as
227        *                   the database.
228        *   @param path    The default directory to search for
229        *                   tables, and the directory to which
230        *                   tables are dumped. Tables specified
231        *                   in the <code>database</code> argument
232        *                   are used in place of any table
233        *                   on the disk that has the same name.
234        */
235       public Database( File path, Table[] database ) throws IOException
236       {   useDatabase( path );
237           for( int i = 0; i < database.length; ++i )
238               tables.put( database[i].name(), database[i] );
239       }
240
241       //----------------------------------------------------------------
242       // Private parse-related workhorse functions.
243
244       /** Asks the scanner to throw a {@link ParseFailure} object
245        *  that highlights the current input position.
246        */
247       private void error( String message ) throws ParseFailure
248       {   throw in.failure( message.toString() );
249       }
250
251       /** Like {@link #error}, but throws the exception only if the
252        *  test fails.
253        */
254       private void verify( boolean test, String message ) throws ParseFailure
255       {   if( !test )
256               throw in.failure( message );
257       }
258
259
260       //----------------------------------------------------------------
261       // Public methods that duplicate some SQL statements.
262       // The SQL interpreter calls these methods to
263       // do the actual work.
264
265       /** Use an existing "database." In the current implementation,
266        *  a "database" is a directory and tables are files within
267        *  the directory. An active database (opened by a constructor,
268        *  a USE DATABASE directive, or a prior call to the current
269        *  method) is closed and committed before the new database is
```

```
270          *   opened.
271          *   @param path A {@link File} object that specifies directory
272          *           that represents the database.
273          *   @throws IOException if the directory that represents the
274          *           database can't be found.
275          */
276         public void useDatabase( File path ) throws IOException
277         {   dump();
278             tables.clear(); // close old database if there is one
279             this.location = path;
280         }
281
282         /** Create a database by opening the indicated directory. All
283          *   tables must be files in that directory. If you don't call
284          *   this method (or issue a SQL CREATE DATABASE directive), then
285          *   the current directory is used.
286          *   @throws IOException if the named directory can't be opened.
287          */
288         public void createDatabase( String name ) throws IOException
289         {   File location = new File( name );
290             location.mkdir();
291             this.location = location;
292         }
293
294         /** Create a new table. If a table by this name exists, it's
295          *   overwritten.
296          */
297         public void createTable( String name, List columns )
298         {   String[] columnNames = new String[ columns.size() ];
299             int i = 0;
300             for( Iterator names = columns.iterator(); names.hasNext(); )
301                 columnNames[i++] = (String) names.next();
302
303             Table newTable = TableFactory.create(name, columnNames);
304             tables.put( name, newTable );
305         }
306
307         /** Destroy both internal and external (on the disk) versions
308          *   of the specified table.
309          */
310         public void dropTable( String name )
311         {   tables.remove( name );  // ignore the error if there is one.
312
313             File tableFile = new File(location,name);
314             if( tableFile.exists() )
315                 tableFile.delete();
316         }
```

```
317
318     /** Flush to the persistent store (e.g. disk) all tables that
319      *  are "dirty" (which have been modified since the database
320      *  was last committed). These tables will not be flushed
321      *  again unless they are modified after the current dump()
322      *  call. Nothing happens if no tables are dirty.
323      *  <p>
324      *  The present implemenation flushes to a .csv file whose name
325      *  is the table name with a ".csv" extension added.
326      */
327     public void dump() throws IOException
328     {   Collection values = tables.values();
329         if( values != null )
330         {   for( Iterator i = values.iterator(); i.hasNext(); )
331             {   Table current = (Table ) i.next();
332                 if( current.isDirty() )
333                 {   Writer out =
334                         new FileWriter(
335                             new File(location, current.name() + ".csv"));
336                     current.export( new CSVExporter(out) );
337                     out.close();
338                 }
339             }
340         }
341     }
342
343     /** Return the number of rows that were affected by the most recent
344      *  {@link #execute} call. Zero is returned for all operations except
345      *  for INSERT, DELETE, or UPDATE.
346      */
347
348     public int affectedRows()
349     {   return affectedRows;
350     }
```

Transaction processing (Listing 4-31) comes next. Most of the work is done in the Table class, which manages undo operations on a specific table, and the TableMap class you just saw. The methods in Listing 4-31 do little more than delegate the begin, commit, and rollback requests to the various Table objects in the tables Map.

From a design point of view, it's difficult to decide where these three methods actually belong. Since the TableMap is doing a lot of the work surrounding transactions, it makes sense to do the rest of the transaction-related work there. On the other hand, it's nice to make the TableMap a "pure" proxy that is just a Map implementation. It's just cleaner not to add additional methods to the Map methods. (Doing so, of course, would make the TableMap both a Decorator and a Proxy.) I decided to leave the methods where they are, primarily because I consider transactions to be operations on a database, not a Map.

Listing 4-31. *Database.java continued: Transaction Processing*

```
351        //-------------------------------------------------------------------------
352        // Transaction processing.
353
354        /** Begin a transaction
355         */
356        public void begin()
357        {   ++transactionLevel;
358
359            Collection currentTables = tables.values();
360            for( Iterator i = currentTables.iterator(); i.hasNext(); )
361                ((Table) i.next()).begin();
362        }
363
364        /** Commit transactions at the current level.
365         *  @throw NoSuchElementException if no <code>begin()</code> was issued.
366         */
367        public void commit() throws ParseFailure
368        {
369            assert transactionLevel > 0 : "No begin() for commit()";
370            --transactionLevel;
371
372            try
373            {   Collection currentTables = tables.values();
374                for( Iterator i = currentTables.iterator(); i.hasNext() ;)
375                    ((Table) i.next()).commit( Table.THIS_LEVEL );
376            }
377            catch(NoSuchElementException e)
378            {   verify( false, "No BEGIN to match COMMIT" );
379            }
380        }
381
382        /** Roll back transactions at the current level
383         *  @throw NoSuchElementException if no <code>begin()</code> was issued.
384         */
385        public void rollback() throws ParseFailure
386        {   assert transactionLevel > 0 : "No begin() for commit()";
387            --transactionLevel;
388            try
389            {   Collection currentTables = tables.values();
390
391                for( Iterator i = currentTables.iterator(); i.hasNext() ;)
392                    ((Table) i.next()).rollback( Table.THIS_LEVEL );
393            }
394            catch(NoSuchElementException e)
395            {   verify( false, "No BEGIN to match ROLLBACK" );
396            }
397        }
```

The Interpreter Pattern

Okay, you've arrived at the dreaded SQL-engine section. This section discusses only one design pattern: **Interpreter**. Interpreter is one of the more complicated patterns and assumes that you know a lot about how compilers work. The odds of your needing to use Interpreter are not high (unless you're building a compiler or interpreter), so feel free to skip forward to "The JDBC Layer" section on page 325.

Supported SQL

The Database class implements a small SQL-subset database that provides a SQL front end to the Table classes. My intent is to do simple things, only. But you can do everything you need to do in most small database applications. SELECT statements, for example, support FROM and WHERE clauses, but nothing else. (DISTINCT, ORDEREDBY, and so on, aren't supported; neither are subqueries, outer joins, and so on.) You can join an arbitrary number of tables in a SELECT, however. A few operators (BETWEEN, IN) aren't supported. Any Java/Perl regular expression can be used as an argument to LIKE, and for SQL compatibility, a % wildcard is automatically mapped to "." The main issue is that you'll have to escape characters that are used as regular-expression metacharacters. All the usual relational and arithmetic operators are supported in a SELECT, and you can SELECT on a formula (SELECT columns WHERE (foo*2) < (bar+1)), but functions are not supported.

Selecting "into" another table works, but bear in mind that the actual data is shared between tables. Since everything in the table is a String, this strategy works fine unless you use the Table object that's returned from execute(...) to add non-String objects directly to the Table. Don't do that.

The Database class uses the file system to store the database itself. A database is effectively a directory, and a table is effectively a file in the directory. The argument to USE DATABASE specifies the path to that directory. The modified database is not stored to disk until a DUMP is issued. (In the JDBC wrapper, an automatic DUMP occurs when you close the connection.)

The SQL parser recognizes types (so you can use them in the SQL), but they are ignored. That is, everything is stored in the underlying database as a String. You can't store a boolean value as such, but if you decide on some string such as "true" and "false" as meaningful, and use it consistently, then comparisons and assignments of boolean values will work fine. Null is supported. Strings that represent numbers (that can be parsed successfully by java.text.NumberFormat in the default Locale) can be used in arithmetic expressions, however. You can use the types in Table 4-2 in your table definitions.

Reasonable defaults are used if an argument is missing. You can also specify a PRIMARY KEY(identifier) in the table definition, but it's ignored, too.

Identifiers follow slightly nonstandard rules. Because the database name is the same as a directory name, I've allowed database names to contain characters that would normally go in a path (/, \, :, ~, and _), but I haven't allowed them to contain a dot or dash. Identifiers can't contain spaces, and they cannot start with digits.

Numbers, on the other hand, must begin with a digit (.10 doesn't work, but 0.10 does), and decimal fractions less than 1.0E-20 are assumed to be 0. (That is, 1.00000000000000000000001 is rounded down to 1.0 and will be put into the table as the integer 1.)

Table 4-2. *SQL Types Recognized (But Ignored) by the Parser*

Types	Description
integer(maxDigits) int(maxDigits) smallint(maxDigits) bigint(maxDigits) tinyint(size)	Integers.
decimal(l,r) real(l,r) double(l,r) numeric(l,r)	Floating point. l and r specify the maximum number of digits to the left and right of the decimal.
char(length)	Fixed-length string.
varchar(maximum_length)	Variable-length string.
date(format)	Date in the Gregorian calendar with optional format.

Transactions are supported, and transactions nest properly, but the transaction model is very simple. (For you database folks, the only part of the ACID test that I've supported is the A—Atomicity. Consistency checks are not made [everything's stored as a String]. The database is not thread safe, so multiple transactions won't work, and there's no Isolation. The database is flushed to disk only when you execute a flush() or close the connection, so there's no Durability at the transaction level. You could fix the latter by flushing after every transaction, but I opted not to do so.)

Initially, no transaction is active, and all SQL requests are effectively committed immediately on execution. This auto-commit mode is superseded once you issue a BEGIN but is reinstated as soon as the matching COMMIT or ROLLBACK is encountered. All requests that occur between the BEGIN and COMMIT are treated as a single unit. The begin(...), commit(...), and rollback(...) methods of the Database class have the same effect as issuing the equivalent SQL requests and are sometimes more convenient to use.

The SQL-subset grammar I've implemented is as follows. Since the Database uses a recursive-descent parser, I've used a strict LL(1) grammar, with the following abbreviations in the terminal-symbol names: "expr"=expression, "id"=identifier, "opt"=optional. I've also used brackets to identify an optional subproduction.

statement	::=	**INSERT INTO IDENTIFIER [LP idList RP] VALUES LP exprList RP**
	|	**CREATE DATABASE IDENTIFIER**
	|	**CREATE TABLE IDENTIFIER LP declarations RP**
	|	**DROP TABLE IDENTIFIER**
	|	**BEGIN [WORK	TRAN[SACTION]]**
	|	**COMMIT [WORK	TRAN[SACTION]]**
	|	**ROLLBACK [WORK	TRAN[SACTION]]**
	|	**DUMP**
	|	**USE DATABASE IDENTIFIER**
	|	**UPDATE IDENTIFIER SET IDENTIFIER EQUAL expr WHERE expr**
	|	**DELETE FROM IDENTIFIER WHERE expr**

	|	**SELECT** [**INTO** identifier] idList **FROM** idList [**WHERE** expr]
idList	::=	**IDENTIFIER** idList' | **STAR**
idList'	::=	**COMMA IDENTIFIER** idList'
	|	ε
declarations	::=	**IDENTIFIER** [type] [**NOT** [**NULL**]] declaration'
declarations'	::=	**COMMA IDENTIFIER** [type] declarations'
	|	**COMMA PRIMARY KEY LP IDENTIFIER RP**
	|	ε
type	::=	**INTEGER** [**LP** expr **RP**]
	|	**CHAR** [**LP** expr **RP**]
	|	**NUMERIC** [**LP** expr **COMMA** expr **RP**]
	|	**DATE**
exprList	::=	expr exprList'
exprList'	::=	**COMMA** expr exprList'
	|	ε
expr	::=	andExpr expr'
expr'	::=	**OR** andExpr expr'
	|	ε
andExpr	::=	relationalExpr andExpr'
andExpr'	::=	**AND** relationalExpr andExpr'
	|	ε
relationalExpr	::=	additiveExpr relationalExpr'
relationalExpr'	::=	**RELOP** additiveExpr relationalExpr'
	|	**EQUAL** additiveExpr relationalExpr'
	|	**LIKE** additiveExpr relationalExpr'
	|	ε
additiveExpr	::=	multiplicativeExpr additiveExpr'
additiveExpr'	::=	**ADDITIVE** multiplicativeExpr additiveExpr'
	|	ε
multiplicativeExpr	::=	term multiplicativeExpr'
multiplicativeExpr'	::=	**STAR** term multiplicativeExpr'
	|	**SLASH** term multiplicativeExpr'
	|	ε
term	::=	**NOT** factor
	|	**LP** expr **RP**
	|	factor
factor	::=	compoundId | **STRING** | **NUMBER** | **NULL**
compoundId	::=	**IDENTIFIER** compoundId'
compoundId'	::=	**DOT** IDENTIFIER
	|	ε

Finally, we've arrived at the actual interpreter.

Consider the following (deliberately complex) SQL statement:

```
SELECT first, last FROM people, zip
    WHERE people.last='Flintstone'
        AND people.first='Fred'
        OR  people.zip > (94700 + zip.margin)
```

The WHERE clause of this expression can be represented by the abstract-syntax tree in Figure 4-16.

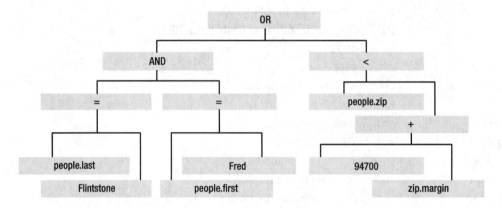

Figure 4-16. *An abstract-syntax tree*

Your first task in implementing a SQL interpreter is to build a parser that creates this abstract-syntax tree as a physical tree in memory. Nodes in the physical tree are all objects of a class that implements the Expression interface. You'll look at all of these subclasses of Expression momentarily, but Figure 4-17 shows which classes are represented in which places in the physical tree that the parser builds from the earlier SQL expression. The main common characteristic of the Expression objects is that they contain references to the objects below them in the tree so can communicate with these descendants. Also note two categories of Expression objects exist: *Terminal* nodes have no children—they're at the ends of the branches. *Nonterminal* nodes are all interior nodes, and all have at least one child. In addition to the children, each object remembers information specific to the input. The RelationalExpression objects remember the operator, for example. AtomicExpression objects contain a Value (more on this in a moment) that represents either a constant value or the table-and-column reference, and so forth. I'll come back to this figure later in this section.

Listing 4-32 shows the actual parser, which interestingly, is not part of the Interpreter pattern itself. This parser is a straightforward recursive-descent parser that directly implements the grammar shown previously. The only deviation from the grammar itself is the elimination of *tail recursion* (situations where the last thing that a recursive method does is call itself) with a loop. For example, these two productions:

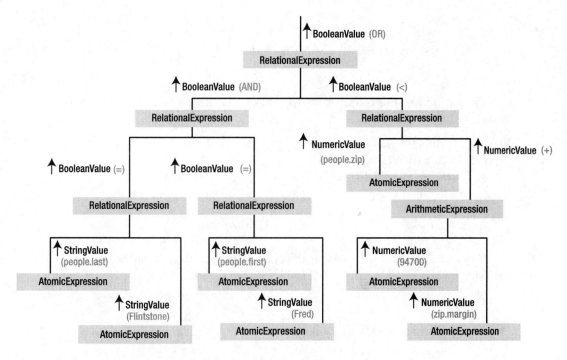

Figure 4-17. *The physical representation of the abstract-syntax tree*

idList	::=	IDENTIFIER idList'
	|	STAR
idList'	::=	COMMA IDENTIFIER idList'
	|	ε

would be implemented naïvely like this (I've stripped out nonessential code):

```
private ... idList()
{
    if( in.matchAdvance(STAR) == null )
        //...
    else
    {   in.required(IDENTIFIER) )
        idListPrime();
    }
}

private ... idListPrime()
{   if( in.matchAdvance( COMMA ) )
    {   in.required( IDENTIFIER );
        //...
```

```
        idListPrime();
    }
    // the "epsilon" is handled by doing nothing
}
```

You can improve this code in two steps. First, eliminate the tail recursion in idList-Prime() as follows:

```
private ... idListPrime()
{   while( in.matchAdvance( COMMA ) )
    {   in.required( IDENTIFIER );
        //...
    }
}
```

Now that idListPrime() is no longer recursive, you can hand-inline the method, replacing the single call to it in idList() with the method body, like so:

```
private ... idList()
{
    if( in.matchAdvance(STAR) == null )
        //...
    else
    {   in.required(IDENTIFIER) )
        while( in.matchAdvance( COMMA ) )
        {   in.required( IDENTIFIER );
            //...
        }
    }
}
```

If you look at the real implementation of idList() (Listing 4-32, line 579), you'll see that it follows the foregoing structure. The only addition I've added in the real code is that idList() assembles (and returns) a List of the identifiers that it recognizes.

I've deliberately not cluttered up the parser with code that manipulates the underlying Table objects—all that code is relegated to private methods I'll discuss shortly. The only real work that the parser does is build a tree of Expression objects (objects whose classes implement Expression) that directly reflects the structure of the abstract-syntax tree. That is, most of the methods that comprise the parser collect Expression objects that are created at levels below the current one and then assemble another Expression object that represents the current operation in the syntax tree (typically passing the constructor to the new Expression references to the objects representing the subexpressions). The method then returns the Expression that represents the current operation.

Taking multiplicativeExpr() (Listing 4-32, line 748, and reproduced next) as characteristic, the calls to term() return an Expression object that represents the subexpression tree. The method creates an ArithmeticExpression to represent itself, passing the ArithmeticExpression constructor the two Expression objects returned from the two term() calls. The method then returns the ArithmeticExpression.

```
private Expression multiplicativeExpr()
{ Expression left = term();
    while( true )
    {   if( in.matchAdvance(STAR) != null)
            left = new ArithmeticExpression( left, term(), TIMES );
        else if( in.matchAdvance(SLASH) != null)
            left = new ArithmeticExpression( left, term(), DIVIDE );
        else
            break;
    }
    return left;
}
```

The balance of the parser is similarly straightforward and should provide no difficulty to
you (provided you've seen a recursive descent parser before).

Listing 4-32. *Database.java: The Parser*

```
398      /**********************************************************************
399       *   Execute a SQL statement. If an exception is tossed and we are in the
400       *   middle of a transaction (a begin has been issued but no matching
401       *   commit has been seen), the transaction is rolled back.
402       *
403       *   @return a {@link Table} holding the result of a SELECT,
404       *       or null for statements other than SELECT.
405       *   @param expression a String holding a single SQL statement. The
406       *       complete statement must be present (you cannot break a long
407       *       statement into multiple calls), and text
408       *       following the SQL statement is ignored.
409       *   @throws com.holub.text.ParseFailure if the SQL is corrupt.
410       *   @throws IOException Database files couldn't be accessed or created.
411       *   @see #affectedRows()
412       */
413
414      public Table execute( String expression ) throws IOException, ParseFailure
415      {   try
416          {   this.expression  = expression;
417              in               = new Scanner(tokens, expression);
418              in.advance();   // advance to the first token.
419              return statement();
420          }
421          catch( ParseFailure e )
422          {   if( transactionLevel > 0 )
423                  rollback();
424              throw e;
425          }
426          catch( IOException e )
```

```
427              {   if( transactionLevel > 0 )
428                      rollback();
429                  throw e;
430              }
431          }
432
433          /**
434           * <PRE>
435           * statement
436           *        ::= CREATE  DATABASE IDENTIFIER
437           *         |   CREATE  TABLE     IDENTIFIER LP idList RP
438           *         |   DROP    TABLE     IDENTIFIER
439           *         |   USE     DATABASE IDENTIFIER
440           *         |   BEGIN    [WORK|TRAN[SACTION]]
441           *         |   COMMIT   [WORK|TRAN[SACTION]]
442           *         |   ROLLBACK [WORK|TRAN[SACTION]]
443           *         |   DUMP
444           *
445           *         |   INSERT  INTO IDENTIFIER [LP idList RP]
446           *                                  VALUES LP exprList RP
447           *         |   UPDATE  IDENTIFIER SET IDENTIFIER
448           *                                  EQUAL expr [WHERE expr]
449           *         |   DELETE  FROM IDENTIFIER WHERE expr
450           *         |   SELECT  idList [INTO table] FROM idList [WHERE expr]
451           * </PRE>
452           * <p>
453           *
454           * @return a Table holding the result of a SELECT, or null for
455           *       other SQL requests. The result table is treated like
456           *       a normal database table if the SELECT contains an INTO
457           *       clause; otherwise it's a temporary table that's not
458           *       put into the database.
459           *
460           * @throws ParseFailure something's wrong with the SQL
461           * @throws IOException a database or table couldn't be opened
462           *       or accessed.
463           * @see #createDatabase
464           * @see #createTable
465           * @see #dropTable
466           * @see #useDatabase
467           */
468          private Table statement() throws ParseFailure, IOException
469          {
470              affectedRows = 0;   // is modified by UPDATE, INSERT, DELETE
471
472              // These productions map to public method calls:
473
```

```
474        if( in.matchAdvance(CREATE) != null )
475        {   if( in.match( DATABASE ) )
476            {   in.advance();
477                createDatabase( in.required( IDENTIFIER ) );
478            }
479            else // must be CREATE TABLE
480            {   in.required( TABLE );
481                String tableName = in.required( IDENTIFIER );
482                in.required( LP );
483                createTable( tableName, declarations() );
484                in.required( RP );
485            }
486        }
487        else if( in.matchAdvance(DROP) != null )
488        {   in.required( TABLE );
489            dropTable( in.required(IDENTIFIER) );
490        }
491        else if( in.matchAdvance(USE) != null )
492        {   in.required( DATABASE   );
493            useDatabase( new File( in.required(IDENTIFIER) ));
494        }
495
496        else if( in.matchAdvance(BEGIN) != null )
497        {   in.matchAdvance(WORK);  // ignore it if it's there
498            begin();
499        }
500        else if( in.matchAdvance(ROLLBACK) != null )
501        {   in.matchAdvance(WORK);  // ignore it if it's there
502            rollback();
503        }
504        else if( in.matchAdvance(COMMIT) != null )
505        {   in.matchAdvance(WORK);  // ignore it if it's there
506            commit();
507        }
508        else if( in.matchAdvance(DUMP) != null )
509        {   dump();
510        }
511
512        // These productions must be handled via an
513        // interpreter:
514
515        else if( in.matchAdvance(INSERT) != null )
516        {   in.required( INTO );
517            String tableName = in.required( IDENTIFIER );
518
519            List columns = null, values = null;
520
```

```
521                 if( in.matchAdvance(LP) != null )
522                 {   columns = idList();
523                     in.required(RP);
524                 }
525                 if( in.required(VALUES) != null )
526                 {   in.required( LP );
527                     values = exprList();
528                     in.required( RP );
529                 }
530                 affectedRows = doInsert( tableName, columns, values );
531             }
532             else if( in.matchAdvance(UPDATE) != null )
533             {   // First parse the expression
534                 String tableName = in.required( IDENTIFIER );
535                 in.required( SET );
536                 final String columnName = in.required( IDENTIFIER );
537                 in.required( EQUAL );
538                 final Expression value = expr();
539                 in.required(WHERE);
540                 affectedRows =
541                     doUpdate( tableName, columnName, value, expr() );
542             }
543             else if( in.matchAdvance(DELETE) != null )
544             {   in.required( FROM );
545                 String tableName = in.required( IDENTIFIER );
546                 in.required( WHERE );
547                 affectedRows = doDelete( tableName, expr() );
548             }
549             else if( in.matchAdvance(SELECT) != null )
550             {   List columns = idList();
551
552                 String into = null;
553                 if( in.matchAdvance(INTO) != null )
554                     into = in.required(IDENTIFIER);
555
556                 in.required( FROM );
557                 List requestedTableNames = idList();
558
559                 Expression where = (in.matchAdvance(WHERE) == null)
560                                 ? null : expr();
561                 Table result = doSelect(columns, into,
562                                 requestedTableNames, where );
563                 return result;
564             }
565             else
566             {   error("Expected insert, create, drop, use, "
567                                 +"update, delete or select");
```

```
568            }
569
570        return null;
571    }
572    //-----------------------------------------------------------------
573    // idList            ::= IDENTIFIER idList' | STAR
574    // idList'           ::= COMMA IDENTIFIER idList'
575    //                   |   e
576    // Return a Collection holding the list of columns
577    // or null if a * was found.
578
579    private List idList()            throws ParseFailure
580    {   List identifiers = null;
581        if( in.matchAdvance(STAR) == null )
582        {   identifiers = new ArrayList();
583            String id;
584            while( (id = in.required(IDENTIFIER)) != null )
585            {   identifiers.add(id);
586                if( in.matchAdvance(COMMA) == null )
587                    break;
588            }
589        }
590        return identifiers;
591    }
592
593    //-----------------------------------------------------------------
594    // declarations  ::= IDENTIFIER [type] declaration'
595    // declarations' ::= COMMA IDENTIFIER [type] [NOT [NULL]] declarations'
596    //                |   e
597    //
598    // type          ::= INTEGER [ LP expr RP            ]
599    //                |    CHAR   [ LP expr RP            ]
600    //                |    NUMERIC [ LP expr COMMA expr RP  ]
601    //                |    DATE            // format spec is part of token
602
603    private List declarations()          throws ParseFailure
604    {   List identifiers = new ArrayList();
605
606        String id;
607        while( true )
608        {   if( in.matchAdvance(PRIMARY) != null )
609            {   in.required(KEY);
610                in.required(LP);
611                in.required(IDENTIFIER);
612                in.required(RP);
613            }
614            else
```

```
615              {    id = in.required(IDENTIFIER);
616
617                   identifiers.add(id);      // get the identifier
618
619                   // Skip past a type declaration if one's there
620
621                   if( (in.matchAdvance(INTEGER) != null)
622                   || (in.matchAdvance(CHAR)     != null)  )
623                   {
624                       if( in.matchAdvance(LP) != null )
625                       {   expr();
626                           in.required(RP);
627                       }
628                   }
629                   else if( in.matchAdvance(NUMERIC) != null )
630                   {   if( in.matchAdvance(LP) != null )
631                       {   expr();
632                           in.required(COMMA);
633                           expr();
634                           in.required(RP);
635                       }
636                   }
637                   else if( in.matchAdvance(DATE)  != null )
638                   {   ; // do nothing
639                   }
640
641                   in.matchAdvance( NOT );
642                   in.matchAdvance( NULL );
643              }
644
645              if( in.matchAdvance(COMMA) == null ) // no more columns
646                  break;
647          }
648
649      return identifiers;
650  }
651
652  // exprList           ::=        expr exprList'
653  // exprList'          ::= COMMA expr exprList'
654  //                      |   e
655
656  private List exprList()          throws ParseFailure
657  {   List expressions = new LinkedList();
658
659      expressions.add( expr() );
660      while( in.matchAdvance(COMMA) != null )
661      {   expressions.add( expr() );
```

```
662            }
663            return expressions;
664        }
665
666        /** Top-level expression production. Returns an Expression
667         *  object which will interpret the expression at runtime
668         *  when you call it's evaluate() method.
669         *  <PRE>
670         *  expr    ::=     andExpr expr'
671         *  expr'   ::= OR  andExpr expr'
672         *          |  e
673         *  </PRE>
674         */
675
676        private Expression expr()              throws ParseFailure
677        {   Expression left = andExpr();
678            while( in.matchAdvance(OR) != null )
679                left = new LogicalExpression( left, OR, andExpr());
680            return left;
681        }
682
683        // andExpr           ::=     relationalExpr andExpr'
684        // andExpr'          ::= AND relationalExpr andExpr'
685        //                   |  e
686
687        private Expression andExpr()            throws ParseFailure
688        {   Expression left = relationalExpr();
689            while( in.matchAdvance(AND) != null )
690                left = new LogicalExpression( left, AND, relationalExpr() );
691            return left;
692        }
693
694        // relationalExpr ::=         additiveExpr relationalExpr'
695        // relationalExpr'::=    RELOP additiveExpr relationalExpr'
696        //                    | EQUAL additiveExpr relationalExpr'
697        //                    | LIKE  additiveExpr relationalExpr'
698        //                    | e
699
700        private Expression relationalExpr()        throws ParseFailure
701        {   Expression left = additiveExpr();
702            while( true )
703            {   String lexeme;
704                if( (lexeme = in.matchAdvance(RELOP)) != null )
705                {   RelationalOperator op;
706                    if( lexeme.length() == 1 )
707                        op = lexeme.charAt(0)=='<' ? LT : GT ;
708                    else
```

```
709                 {   if( lexeme.charAt(0)=='<' && lexeme.charAt(1)=='>')
710                         op = NE;
711                     else
712                         op = lexeme.charAt(0)=='<' ? LE : GE ;
713                 }
714                 left = new RelationalExpression(left, op, additiveExpr());
715             }
716             else if( in.matchAdvance(EQUAL) != null )
717             {   left = new RelationalExpression(left, EQ, additiveExpr());
718             }
719             else if( in.matchAdvance(LIKE) != null )
720             {   left = new LikeExpression(left, additiveExpr());
721             }
722             else
723                 break;
724         }
725         return left;
726     }
727
728     // additiveExpr ::=            multiplicativeExpr additiveExpr'
729     // additiveExpr'    ::= ADDITIVE multiplicativeExpr additiveExpr'
730     //                  |   e
731
732     private Expression additiveExpr()           throws ParseFailure
733     {   String lexeme;
734         Expression left = multiplicativeExpr();
735         while( (lexeme = in.matchAdvance(ADDITIVE)) != null )
736         {   MathOperator op = lexeme.charAt(0)=='+' ? PLUS : MINUS;
737             left = new ArithmeticExpression(
738                         left, multiplicativeExpr(), op );
739         }
740         return left;
741     }
742
743     // multiplicativeExpr    ::=       term multiplicativeExpr'
744     // multiplicativeExpr'  ::= STAR   term multiplicativeExpr'
745     //                      |   SLASH term multiplicativeExpr'
746     //                      |   e
747
748     private Expression multiplicativeExpr()         throws ParseFailure
749     { Expression left = term();
750         while( true )
751         {   if( in.matchAdvance(STAR) != null)
752                 left = new ArithmeticExpression( left, term(), TIMES );
753             else if( in.matchAdvance(SLASH) != null)
754                 left = new ArithmeticExpression( left, term(), DIVIDE );
755             else
```

```
756              break;
757         }
758        return left;
759    }
760
761    // term              ::= NOT expr
762    //                     |   LP expr RP
763    //                     |   factor
764
765    private Expression term()           throws ParseFailure
766    {   if( in.matchAdvance(NOT) != null )
767        {   return new NotExpression( expr() );
768        }
769        else if( in.matchAdvance(LP) != null )
770        {   Expression toReturn = expr();
771            in.required(RP);
772            return toReturn;
773        }
774        else
775            return factor();
776    }
777
778    // factor             ::= compoundId | STRING | NUMBER | NULL
779    // compoundId         ::= IDENTIFIER compoundId'
780    // compoundId'        ::= DOT IDENTIFIER
781    //                     |   e
782
783    private Expression factor() throws ParseFailure
784    {   try
785        {   String  lexeme;
786            Value   result;
787
788            if( (lexeme = in.matchAdvance(STRING)) != null )
789                result = new StringValue( lexeme );
790
791            else if( (lexeme = in.matchAdvance(NUMBER)) != null )
792                result = new NumericValue( lexeme );
793
794            else if( (lexeme = in.matchAdvance(NULL)) != null )
795                result = new NullValue();
796
797            else
798            {   String columnName  = in.required(IDENTIFIER);
799                String tableName   = null;
800
801                if( in.matchAdvance(DOT) != null )
802                {   tableName  = columnName;
```

```
803                    columnName = in.required(IDENTIFIER);
804                }
805
806                result = new IdValue( tableName, columnName );
807            }
808
809            return new AtomicExpression(result);
810        }
811        catch( java.text.ParseException e) { /* fall through */ }
812
813        error("Couldn't parse Number"); // Always throws a ParseFailure
814        return null;
815    }
```

Now that you've looked at how the tree is built, you can look at the **Interpreter** design pattern—the pattern actually has nothing to say about how you could bring an expression tree into existence. You could use a parser, but you could also hand-code the tree.

The basic notion of the Interpreter pattern is to implement an interpreter by traversing a physical tree is a Command object that represents the abstract-syntax tree for an expression in some grammar. Each node in the tree performs the operation that it represents syntacti-cally. For example, the execute() method of the ArithmeticExpression node that was created in the parser's multiplicativeExpression() method performs a single arithmetic operation and returns an object (of class Value) that represents the result of the operation. The tree is traversed in a depth-first fashion. The first thing that a parent-node execute() method does is call the execute() methods of the children, all of which return Value objects to their parents.

The Expression interface and its implementations are all in Listing 4-33. The Expression interface defines only one method: evaluate(...), which causes the Expression object to do whatever it does to evaluate itself and to return a Value that represents the result.

Taking ArithmeticExpression (on line 833) as characteristic, the constructor stores away Expression objects representing the two subexpressions and the operation to perform (oper-ator). The evaluate method gets the values associated with the left and right subexpressions (and stores them in leftValue and rightValue). It then checks that the subexpressions returned values of the correct type. As you can see from the class diagram in Figure 4-12, on page 261, Value is itself an interface, and several implementations represent particular types. A NumericValue represents a number, a StringValue represents a string, and so on. Arith-meticExpression's evaluate() method requires the Values returned from the subexpressions to be NumericValue objects. Finally, evaluate() extracts the actual values (as doubles), performs the arithmetic, and creates a NumericValue to hold the result.

Listing 4-33. *Database.java: Expressions*

```
816
//=======================================================================
817        // The methods that parse the productions rooted in expr work in
818        // concert to build an Expression object that evaluates the expression.
819        // This is an example of both the Interpreter and Composite patterns.
```

```
820     // An expression is represented in memory as an abstract-syntax tree
821     // made up of instances of the following classes, each of which
822     // references its subexpressions.
823
824     private interface Expression
825     {   /* Evaluate an expression using rows identified by the
826          * two iterators passed as arguments. <code>j</code>
827          * is null unless a join is being processed.
828          */
829
830         Value evaluate(Cursor[] tables) throws ParseFailure;
831     }
832     //- - - - - - - - - - - - - - - - - - - - - - - - - - - - - - - - - - - -
833     private class ArithmeticExpression implements Expression
834     {   private final MathOperator   operator;
835         private final Expression     left, right;
836
837         public ArithmeticExpression( Expression left, Expression right,
838                                                   MathOperator operator )
839         {   this.operator = operator;
840             this.left     = left;
841             this.right    = right;
842         }
843
844         public Value evaluate(Cursor[] tables) throws ParseFailure
845         {
846             Value leftValue  = left.evaluate ( tables );
847             Value rightValue = right.evaluate( tables );
848
849             verify
850             (   leftValue  instanceof NumericValue
851              && rightValue instanceof NumericValue,
852               "Operands to < > <= >= = must be Boolean"
853             );
854
855             double l = ((NumericValue)leftValue).value();
856             double r = ((NumericValue)rightValue).value();
857
858             return new NumericValue
859             (   ( operator == PLUS    ) ? ( l + r ) :
860                 ( operator == MINUS   ) ? ( l - r ) :
861                 ( operator == TIMES   ) ? ( l * r ) :
862                 /* operator == DIVIDE */  ( l / r )
863             );
864         }
865     }
866     //- - - - - - - - - - - - - - - - - - - - - - - - - - - - - - - - - - - -
```

```
867    private class LogicalExpression implements Expression
868    {    private final boolean     isAnd;
869         private final Expression left, right;
870
871         public LogicalExpression( Expression left,   Token op,
872                                                       Expression right )
873         {   assert op==AND || op==OR;
874             this.isAnd  = (op == AND);
875             this.left   = left;
876             this.right  = right;
877         }
878
879         public Value evaluate( Cursor[] tables ) throws ParseFailure
880         {   Value leftValue  = left. evaluate(tables);
881             Value rightValue = right.evaluate(tables);
882             verify
883             (    leftValue  instanceof BooleanValue
884               && rightValue instanceof BooleanValue,
885               "operands to AND and OR must be logical/relational"
886             );
887
888             boolean l = ((BooleanValue)leftValue).value();
889             boolean r = ((BooleanValue)rightValue).value();
890
891             return new BooleanValue( isAnd ? (l && r) : (l || r) );
892         }
893    }
894    //- - - - - - - - - - - - - - - - - - - - - - - - - - - - - - - - - -
895    private class NotExpression implements Expression
896    {    private final Expression operand;
897
898         public NotExpression( Expression operand )
899         {   this.operand = operand;
900         }
901         public Value evaluate( Cursor[] tables ) throws ParseFailure
902         {   Value value = operand.evaluate( tables );
903             verify( value instanceof BooleanValue,
904                      "operands to NOT must be logical/relational");
905             return new BooleanValue( !((BooleanValue)value).value() );
906         }
907    }
908    //- - - - - - - - - - - - - - - - - - - - - - - - - - - - - - - - - -
909    private class RelationalExpression implements Expression
910    {
911         private final RelationalOperator    operator;
912         private final Expression             left, right;
913
```

```
914         public RelationalExpression(Expression left,
915                                     RelationalOperator operator,
916                                     Expression right )
917         {   this.operator = operator;
918             this.left     = left;
919             this.right    = right;
920         }
921
922         public Value evaluate( Cursor[] tables ) throws ParseFailure
923         {
924             Value leftValue  = left.evaluate ( tables );
925             Value rightValue = right.evaluate( tables );
926
927             if(     (leftValue  instanceof StringValue)
928                 || (rightValue instanceof StringValue) )
929             {   verify(operator==EQ || operator==NE,
930                             "Can't use < <= > or >= with string");
931
932                 boolean isEqual =
933                     leftValue.toString().equals(rightValue.toString());
934
935                 return new BooleanValue(operator==EQ ? isEqual:!isEqual);
936             }
937
938             if( rightValue instanceof NullValue
939             || leftValue  instanceof NullValue )
940             {
941                 verify(operator==EQ || operator==NE,
942                             "Can't use < <= > or >= with NULL");
943
944                 // Return true if both the left and right sides are instances
945                 // of NullValue.
946                 boolean isEqual =
947                         leftValue.getClass() == rightValue.getClass();
948
949                 return new BooleanValue(operator==EQ ? isEqual : !isEqual);
950             }
951
952             // Convert Boolean values to numbers so we can compare them.
953             //
954             if( leftValue instanceof BooleanValue )
955                 leftValue = new NumericValue(
956                             ((BooleanValue)leftValue).value() ? 1 : 0 );
957             if( rightValue instanceof BooleanValue )
958                 rightValue = new NumericValue(
959                             ((BooleanValue)rightValue).value() ? 1 : 0 );
960
```

```
961             verify(    leftValue   instanceof NumericValue
962                    && rightValue instanceof NumericValue,
963                                  "Operands must be numbers" );
964
965             double l = ((NumericValue)leftValue).value();
966             double r = ((NumericValue)rightValue).value();
967
968             return new BooleanValue
969             (   ( operator == EQ    ) ? ( l == r ) :
970                 ( operator == NE    ) ? ( l != r ) :
971                 ( operator == LT    ) ? ( l >  r ) :
972                 ( operator == GT    ) ? ( l <  r ) :
973                 ( operator == LE    ) ? ( l <= r ) :
974                 /* operator == GE   */  ( l >= r )
975             );
976         }
977     }
978     //- - - - - - - - - - - - - - - - - - - - - - - - - - - - - - - - - - - -
979     private class LikeExpression implements Expression
980     {   private final Expression left, right;
981         public LikeExpression( Expression left, Expression right )
982         {   this.left   = left;
983             this.right  = right;
984         }
985
986         public Value evaluate(Cursor[] tables) throws ParseFailure
987         {   Value leftValue  = left.evaluate(tables);
988             Value rightValue = right.evaluate(tables);
989             verify
990             (   leftValue   instanceof StringValue
991              && rightValue instanceof StringValue,
992                 "Both operands to LIKE must be strings"
993             );
994
995             String  compareTo = ((StringValue) leftValue).value();
996             String  regex     = ((StringValue) rightValue).value();
997                     regex     = regex.replaceAll("%",".*");
998
999             return new BooleanValue( compareTo.matches(regex) );
1000        }
1001    }
1002    //- - - - - - - - - - - - - - - - - - - - - - - - - - - - - - - - - - - -
1003    private class AtomicExpression implements Expression
1004    {   private final Value atom;
1005        public AtomicExpression( Value atom )
1006        {   this.atom = atom;
1007        }
```

```
1008        public Value evaluate( Cursor[] tables )
1009        {   return atom instanceof IdValue
1010                ? ((IdValue)atom).value(tables) // lookup cell in table and
1011                : atom                          // convert to appropriate type
1012                ;
1013        }
1014    }
```

The Value interface and its implementations are in Listing 4-34, and NumericValue is defined on line 1048. This class is little more than a container for a double. In fact, I could have used the introspection classes such as java.lang.Double for values, were it not for the fact that I needed a few operations that the introspection classes don't support and I needed the objects that represent return values to implement a common interface. (Double implements Number, but String does not. NumericValue and StringValue both implement Value, however.)

So far, you've just looked at the Expression objects in the Nonterminal-Expression role (Expression objects that represent interior nodes in the syntax tree). One other sort of Expression exists: an AtomicExpression that is used in the Terminal-Expression role—it represents a leaf of the tree, an object that has no subexpressions (a numeric constant, a string constant, a reference to a cell in a table, or a SQL null). AtomicExpression is at the end of Listing 4-33 (page 314) on line 1003. The only real difference between this Terminal Expression and the Nonterminal Expressions is the absence of subexpressions and their associated evaluate() calls. The AtomicExpression contains a Value, not a pair of Expression objects representing the subexpressions. AtomicExpression objects are created in only one place: in factor(...) (Listing 4-32, line 783). The factor(...) method creates a Value object, the type of which is determined by the input, and then returns an AtomicExpression that wraps that Value.

Returning back to the values in Listing 4-34, with one exception, these classes all just act as containers for the actual value. NumericValue contains a double, StringValue contains a String, BooleanValue contains a boolean, and so forth.

The only interesting Value class is the IdValue (Listing 4-34, line 1068), which represents a reference to a row/column intersection (a *cell*) in a Table. The IdValue's fields are the table and column names. The work of fetching the value for a particular row in that table happens in the toString() method on line 1082, which is passed an array of Cursor objects. (Typically, this array has only one element in it, but in the case of a join, it will have as many elements as there are tables in the join.) The toString() method finds the cursor that's traversing the table whose name it has stored (in tableName) and then extracts the required column from the table using that Cursor. It returns the cell's contents as a String. The value() method in the IdValue (on line 1119) examines the String returned from the toString() override and does a type conversion by creating an appropriate Value type, based on the String's contents.

The important fact to note here is that the value of a cell is not fetched when the interpreter tree is built; rather, it's fetched when the tree is evaluated. At build time, the AtomicExpression stores away the information it needs to access the proper cell at evaluation time. The toString() call, which actually fetches the value of the cell, is made by some Expression object's evaluate() method. The Terminal Expression (the IdValue) accesses the Context (one of the Tables) at expression-evaluation time.

The Table class has the roll of Context in the design pattern. The Context is any data structure that holds the values of variables that are accessed from the interpreted expressions.

Listing 4-34. *Database.java: Values*

```
1015        //-----------------------------------------------------------
1016        // The expression classes pass values around as they evaluate
1017        // the expression.  // There  are four value subtypes that represent
1018        // the possible/ operands to an expression (null, numbers,
1019        // strings, table.column). The implementers of Value provide
1020        // convenience methods for using those operands.
1021        //
1022        private interface Value // tagging interface
1023        {
1024        }
1025        //- - - - - - - - - - - - - - - - - - - - - - - - - - - - - - - -
1026        private static class NullValue implements Value
1027        {   public String toString(){ return null; }
1028        }
1029        //- - - - - - - - - - - - - - - - - - - - - - - - - - - - - - - -
1030        private static final class BooleanValue implements Value
1031        {   boolean value;
1032            public BooleanValue( boolean value )
1033            {   this.value = value;
1034            }
1035            public boolean  value()   { return value; }
1036            public String   toString(){ return String.valueOf(value); };
1037        }
1038        //- - - - - - - - - - - - - - - - - - - - - - - - - - - - - - - -
1039        private static class StringValue implements Value
1040        {   private String value;
1041            public StringValue(String lexeme)
1042            {   value = lexeme.replaceAll("['\"](.*?)['\"]", "$1" );
1043            }
1044            public String value()   { return value; }
1045            public String toString(){ return value; }
1046        }
1047        //- - - - - - - - - - - - - - - - - - - - - - - - - - - - - - - -
1048        private final class NumericValue implements Value
1049        {   private double value;
1050            public NumericValue(double value)   // initialize from a double.
1051            {   this.value = value;
1052            }
1053            public NumericValue(String s) throws java.text.ParseException
1054            {   this.value = NumberFormat.getInstance().parse(s).doubleValue();
1055            }
1056            public double value()
1057            {   return value;
1058            }
1059            public String toString() // round down if the fraction is very small
1060            {
1061                if( Math.abs(value - Math.floor(value)) < 1.0E-20 )
```

```
1062                    return String.valueOf( (long)value );
1063              else
1064                    return String.valueOf( value );
1065        }
1066    }
1067    //- - - - - - - - - - - - - - - - - - - - - - - - - - - - - - - - - -
1068    private final class IdValue implements Value
1069    {   String tableName;
1070        String columnName;
1071
1072        public IdValue(String tableName, String columnName)
1073        {   this.tableName  = tableName;
1074            this.columnName = columnName;
1075        }
1076
1077        /** Using the cursor, extract the referenced cell from
1078         *  the current Row and return its contents as a String.
1079         *  @return the value as a String or null if the cell
1080         *          was null.
1081         */
1082        public String toString( Cursor[] participants )
1083        {   Object content = null;
1084
1085            // If no name is to the left of the dot, then use
1086            // the (only) table.
1087
1088            if( tableName == null )
1089                content= participants[0].column( columnName );
1090            else
1091            {   Table container = (Table) tables.get(tableName);
1092
1093                // Search for the table whose name matches
1094                // the one to the left of the dot, then extract
1095                // the desired column from that table.
1096
1097                content = null;
1098                for( int i = 0; i < participants.length; ++i )
1099                {   if( participants[i].isTraversing(container) )
1100                    {   content = participants[i].column(columnName);
1101                        break;
1102                    }
1103                }
1104            }
1105
1106            // All table contents are converted to Strings, whatever
1107            // their original type. This conversion can cause
1108            // problems if the table was created manually.
1109
```

```
1110                       return (content == null) ? null : content.toString();
1111            }
1112
1113            /** Using the cursor, extract the referenced cell from the
1114             *  current row of the appropriate table, convert the
1115             *  contents to a {@link NullValue}, {@link NumericValue},
1116             *  or {@link StringValue}, as appropriate, and return
1117             *  that value object.
1118             */
1119            public Value value( Cursor[] participants )
1120            {   String s = toString( participants );
1121                try
1122                {   return ( s == null )
1123                            ? (Value) new NullValue()
1124                            : (Value) new NumericValue(s)
1125                            ;
1126                }
1127                catch( java.text.ParseException e )
1128                {   // The NumericValue constructor failed, so it must be
1129                    // a string. Fall through to the return-a-string case.
1130                }
1131                return new StringValue( s );
1132            }
1133        }
```

Watching the Interpreter in Action

The final piece of the Database class pulls together everything I've discussed in this chapter. The methods in Listing 4-35 are the workhorse methods that are called from the parser to execute SQL statements.

Let's start with SELECT, at the top of Listing 4-35. I'll demonstrate how the interpreter works by tracing through the code as it traverses the interpreter tree in Figure 4-17, evaluating the following SQL statement:

```
SELECT first, last FROM people, zip
    WHERE people.last='Flintstone'
        AND people.first='Fred'
        OR  people.zip > (94700 + zip.margin)
```

Here's the parser code (from Listing 4-32) that's executed when a SELECT is encountered:

```
else if( in.matchAdvance(SELECT) != null )
{   List columns = idList();

    String into = null;
    if( in.matchAdvance(INTO) != null )
        into = in.required(IDENTIFIER);
```

```
    in.required( FROM );
    List requestedTableNames = idList();

    Expression where = (in.matchAdvance(WHERE) == null)
                        ? null : expr();
    Table result = doSelect(columns, into,
                            requestedTableNames, where );
    return result;
}
```

The first call to idList() parses the list of columns and returns a java.util.List that contains the two strings "first" and "last". (The idList() method is on line 579 of Listing 4-32.) The second call to idList() does the same thing, but with tables listed in the FROM clause. The call to expr() (Listing 4-32, line 676) builds the tree of Expression objects shown in Figure 4-17, previously. The expr() method returns the RelationalExpression object at the root of the tree.

All this information is then passed to doSelect() (Listing 4-35, line 1137). This method first converts the table names to actual tables by looking up the names in the tables map. It then creates a Strategy object that the Table's select() method can use to select rows and passes it into the primary table. Here's the code for the Strategy object (from Listing 4-32, line -1):

```
Selector selector = (where == null) ? Selector.ALL :
    new Selector.Adapter()
    {   public boolean approve(Cursor[] tables)
        {   Value result = where.evaluate(tables);

            verify( result instanceof BooleanValue,
                    "WHERE clause must yield boolean result" );
            return ((BooleanValue)result).value();
        }
    };

Table result = primary.select(selector, columns, participantsInJoin);
```

As the Table processes the select() statement, it calls approve() for every row, which causes the anonymous Selector.Adapter to ask the root node in the expression tree to evaluate itself. (This ConcreteTable code is way back in Listing 4-17, line 384.)

The topmost node in the expression tree is a RelationalExpression, and the first thing that its evaluate(...) method (Listing 4-33, line 922) does is evaluate the subexpressions.

```
Value leftValue  = left.evaluate ( tables );
Value rightValue = right.evaluate( tables );
```

All of the Nonterminal Expressions start this way, in fact. In the current case, the left child of the root node is itself a RelationalExpression, so you'll traverse the tree recursively down to the AtomicExpression at the far left.

The `AtomicExpression`'s `evaluate(...)` method (Listing 4-33, line 1008) just delegates to the contained `Value`, in this case an `IdValue`, so go to its `value(...)` method (Listing 4-34, line 1119). This method looks up the value of the `last` column on the current row of the `people` table and returns its value as a `StringValue` (shown in Figure 4-17 as an upward-pointing error on the edge leading into the `AtomicExpression` node). The `RelationalExpression` object that called the `AtomicExpression`'s `evaluate(...)` method now calls evaluate on its right child and gets back a `StringValue` that holds the `String` "Flintstone". It compares the two strings and creates a `BooleanValue` object that holds the result of the comparison and then returns that `BooleanValue` object. The code looks like this:

```
if(    (leftValue  instanceof StringValue)
    || (rightValue instanceof StringValue) )
{   verify(operator==EQ || operator==NE,
                "Can't use < <= > or >= with string");

    boolean isEqual =
        leftValue.toString().equals(rightValue.toString());

    return new BooleanValue(operator==EQ ? isEqual:!isEqual);
}
```

The remainder of the `RelationalExpression`'s `evaluate()` method doesn't come into play in this scenario, but it handles the evaluation of relational operators that have numeric or null operands.

The remainder of the expression evaluation proceeds in the same fashion. The `evaluate()` call gets `Value` objects from the child nodes, evaluates those values appropriately, and returns a `Value` that holds the result. By the time you finish with the `evaluate()` method of the root node, you will have evaluated the entire expression.

The `select()` method is the most complex of the methods in Listing 4-35. The others work in pretty much the same way, however. They create a `Selector` that invokes the `execute(...)` method of the root node of the `WHERE`-clause expression tree, and the `Selector` approves or rejects rows by running the interpreter. The remainder of Listing 4-35 is a small unit-test class that runs the SQL script in Listing 4-27.

Listing 4-35. *Database.java: Interpreter Invocation*

```
1134
//======================================================================
==
1135        // Workhorse methods called from the parser.
1136        //
1137        private Table doSelect( List columns, String into,
1138                                        List requestedTableNames,
1139                                        final Expression where )
1140                                        throws ParseFailure
1141        {
1142
1143            Iterator tableNames = requestedTableNames.iterator();
```

```
1144
1145            assert tableNames.hasNext() : "No tables to use in select!" ;
1146
1147            // The primary table is the first one listed in the
1148            // FROM clause. The participantsInJoin are the other
1149            // tables listed in the FROM clause. We're passed in the
1150            // table names; use these names to get the actual Table
1151            // objects.
1152
1153            Table primary = (Table) tables.get( (String) tableNames.next() );
1154
1155            List participantsInJoin = new ArrayList();
1156            while( tableNames.hasNext() )
1157            {   String participant = (String) tableNames.next();
1158                participantsInJoin.add( tables.get(participant) );
1159            }
1160
1161            // Now do the select operation. First create a Strategy
1162            // object that picks the correct rows, then pass that
1163            // object through to the primary table's select() method.
1164
1165            Selector selector = (where == null) ? Selector.ALL :
1166                new Selector.Adapter()
1167                {   public boolean approve(Cursor[] tables)
1168                    {   try
1169                        {
1170                            Value result = where.evaluate(tables);
1171
1172                            verify( result instanceof BooleanValue,
1173                                    "WHERE clause must yield boolean result" );
1174                            return ((BooleanValue)result).value();
1175                        }
1176                        catch( ParseFailure e )
1177                        {   throw new ThrowableContainer(e);
1178                        }
1179                    }
1180                };
1181
1182            try
1183            {   Table result = primary.select(selector, columns, participantsInJoin);
1184
1185                // If this is a "SELECT INTO <table>" request, remove the
1186                // returned table from the UnmodifiableTable wrapper, give
1187                // it a name, and put it into the tables Map.
1188
1189                if( into != null )
```

```
1190               {    result = ((UnmodifiableTable)result).extract();
1191                    result.rename(into);
1192                    tables.put( into, result );
1193               }
1194               return result;
1195          }
1196          catch( ThrowableContainer container )
1197          {    throw (ParseFailure) container.contents();
1198          }
1199     }
1200     //- - - - - - - - - - - - - - - - - - - - - - - - - - - - - - - -
1201     private int doInsert(String tableName, List columns, List values)
1202                                                  throws ParseFailure
1203     {
1204          List  processedValues = new LinkedList();
1205          Table t = (Table) tables.get( tableName );
1206
1207          for( Iterator i = values.iterator(); i.hasNext(); )
1208          {    Expression current = (Expression) i.next();
1209               processedValues.add(
1210                       current.evaluate(null).toString() );
1211          }
1212
1213          // finally, put the values into the table.
1214
1215          if( columns == null )
1216               return t.insert( processedValues );
1217
1218          verify( columns.size() == values.size(),
1219                  "There must be a value for every listed column" );
1220          return t.insert( columns, processedValues );
1221     }
1222     //- - - - - - - - - - - - - - - - - - - - - - - - - - - - - - - -
1223     private int doUpdate( String tableName, final String columnName,
1224                      final Expression value, final Expression where)
1225                                                  throws ParseFailure
1226     {
1227          Table t = (Table) tables.get( tableName );
1228          try
1229          {    return t.update
1230               (    new Selector()
1231                    {    public boolean approve( Cursor[] tables )
1232                         {    try
1233                              {    Value result = where.evaluate(tables);
1234
1235                                   verify( result instanceof BooleanValue,
1236                                       "WHERE clause must yield boolean result" );
1237
```

```
1238                            return ((BooleanValue)result).value();
1239                        }
1240                        catch( ParseFailure e )
1241                        {   throw new ThrowableContainer(e);
1242                        }
1243                    }
1244                    public void modify( Cursor current )
1245                    {   try
1246                        {   Value newValue=value.evaluate( new Cursor[]{current} );
1247                            current.update( columnName, newValue.toString() );
1248                        }
1249                        catch( ParseFailure e )
1250                        {   throw new ThrowableContainer(e);
1251                        }
1252                    }
1253                }
1254            );
1255        }
1256        catch( ThrowableContainer container )
1257        {   throw (ParseFailure) container.contents();
1258        }
1259    }
1260    //- - - - - - - - - - - - - - - - - - - - - - - - - - - - - - - - - -
1261    private int doDelete( String tableName, final Expression where )
1262                                            throws ParseFailure
1263    {   Table t = (Table) tables.get( tableName );
1264        try
1265        {   return t.delete
1266            (   new Selector.Adapter()
1267                {   public boolean approve( Cursor[] tables )
1268                    {   try
1269                        {   Value result = where.evaluate(tables);
1270                            verify( result instanceof BooleanValue,
1271                                "WHERE clause must yield boolean result" );
1272                            return ((BooleanValue)result).value();
1273                        }
1274                        catch( ParseFailure e )
1275                        {   throw new ThrowableContainer(e);
1276                        }
1277                    }
1278                }
1279            );
1280        }
1281        catch( ThrowableContainer container )
1282        {   throw (ParseFailure) container.contents();
1283        }
1284    }
```

One other aspect of the doSelect(...) method at the top of Listing 4-35 (p. 316) bears mentioning. Here's a stripped-down version of the call to the Table's select() method with the interesting code in bold:

```
Selector selector = (where == null) ? Selector.ALL :
    new Selector.Adapter()
    {   public boolean approve(Cursor[] tables)
        {   try
            {   Value result = where.evaluate(tables);
                //...
            }
            catch( ParseFailure e )
            {   throw new ThrowableContainer(e);
            }
        }
    };

try
{   Table result = primary.select(selector, columns, participantsInJoin);
    //...
}
catch( ThrowableContainer container )
{   throw (ParseFailure) container.contents();
}
```

What's that ThrowableContainer doing? The interface defined by Table and Selector is very generic by necessity. The approve() method, for example, is not declared as throwing any sort of exception because it's impossible to predict what that exception may be.

The evaluate() method called in approve() throws a ParseFailure object, and Parse-Failure is a checked exception—I have to deal with it. I want that exception toss to propagate out of approve(...), but to do that, I'd have to add a throws ParseFailure to the approve(...) declaration. The compiler will then (quite rightly) complain, because the definition of approve() in the Selector interface is not declared as throwing any sort of exception at all. I don't want to append a throws ParseFailure the approve() definition in the Selector, however. A ParseFailure exception is used by the current parser only; it is irrelevant to all other implementers of Selector, and I don't want to couple the Table/Selector interfaces to the SQL-interpreter layer.

I've solved the problem with the ThrowableContainer class in Listing 4-36. This class is quite simple; it's nothing but a RuntimeException subclass that holds a Throwable object. The approve(...) method packages the ParseFailure exception into the container and then throws the container. The catch clause that surrounds the select(...) call (which calls approve(...)) catches the container, unpacks the contained ParseException object, and then throws the ParseException object.

The ThrowableContainer is effectively performing what I think of as a lateral type conversion—sideways in the class hierarchy—not to a subclass or superclass type, but to a sibling type. It's as if I have converted an ArrayList to a LinkedList.

The obvious downside of this wrapping strategy is that it subverts the type-safety system. For example, if doSelect(...) were behaving badly, it could just let the ThrowableContainer propagate out to the calling method rather than catching the container and throwing the contained object. The calling method wouldn't have a clue what to do with the Throwable-Container, however. Also on the downside is that I've converted a checked-exception object into a RuntimeException that is not checked, which defeats the whole purpose of checked exceptions. It would be a serious problem, in other words, if I didn't convert the exception object back to its original type by unwrapping it.

These negatives are pretty severe. I'm willing to put up with them in the current code because the packaging and unpackaging operations all occur within a few lines of each other in the source code, so the code remains reasonably maintainable.

Listing 4-36. *ThrowableContainer.java*

```
1  package com.holub.tools;
2
3  /** A convenient container for realying a checked Exception
4   *  from a method that can't declare a throws clause to
5   *  a calling method that can.
6   */
7
8  public class ThrowableContainer extends RuntimeException
9  {   private final Throwable contents;
10      public ThrowableContainer( Throwable contents )
11      {   this.contents = contents;
12      }
13      public Throwable contents()
14      {   return contents;
15      }
16  }
```

The JDBC Layer

You'll be happy to hear that the hard part is over (whew!). All that's left is writing a JDBC driver, which turns out to be a trivial enterprise. A few interesting applications of design patterns exist in the JDBC-driver code, however.

Most of the classes in the following discussion are mine. To make the discussion clear, however, I've set off any classes or interfaces that are part of Java by using their fully qualified class name (java.sql.*Xxx*). If you don't see the (java.sql), then the class is one of mine.

Figure 4-18 shows the structure and patterns for the JDBC layer, and I'll explain this diagram in depth over the course of this section.

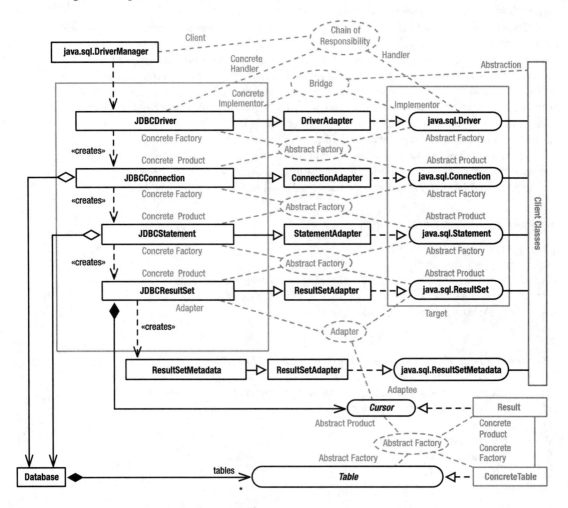

Figure 4-18. *The structure and patterns of the JDBC layer*

If you've never used JDBC, the easiest way to learn it is to look at a simple application. Listing 4-37 is a small test program that's a minor adaptation of the example in Sun's JDBC documentation. I'll explain this listing throughout the rest of this section.

Listing 4-37. *JDBCTest.java*

```
1   package com.holub.database.jdbc;
2
3   import java.sql.*;
4
5   public class JDBCTest
6   {
```

```
 7      static String[] data =
 8      {   "(1,  'John',    'Mon', 1, 'JustJoe')",
 9          "(2,  'JS',      'Mon', 1, 'Cappuccino')",
10          "(3,  'Marie',   'Mon', 2, 'CaffeMocha')",
11      };
12
13      public static void main(String[] args) throws Exception
14      {
15          Class.forName( "com.holub.database.jdbc.JDBCDriver" )
16                                          .newInstance();
17
18          Connection connection = null;
19          Statement  statement  = null;
20          try
21          {   connection = DriverManager.getConnection(
22                          "file:/c:/src/com/holub/database/jdbc/Dbase",
23                          "harpo", "swordfish" );
24
25              statement = connection.createStatement();
26
27              statement.executeUpdate(
28                  "create table test (" +
29                  "  Entry      INTEGER      NOT NULL"  +
30                  ", Customer   VARCHAR (20) NOT NULL"  +
31                  ", DOW        VARCHAR (3)  NOT NULL"  +
32                  ", Cups       INTEGER      NOT NULL"  +
33                  ", Type       VARCHAR (10) NOT NULL"  +
34                  ", PRIMARY KEY( Entry )"              +
35                  ")"
36              );
37
38              for( int i = 0; i < data.length; ++i )
39                  statement.executeUpdate(
40                          "insert into test VALUES "+ data[i] );
41
42              // Test Autocommit stuff. If everything's working
43              // correctly, there James should be in the databse,
44              // but Fred should not.
45
46              connection.setAutoCommit( false );
47              statement.executeUpdate(
48                          "insert into test VALUES "+
49                          "(4, 'James',  'Thu', 1, 'Cappuccino')" );
50              connection.commit();
51
52              statement.executeUpdate(
53                          "insert into test (Customer) VALUES('Fred')");
54              connection.rollback();
```

```
55                    connection.setAutoCommit( true );
56
57                    // Print everything.
58
59                    ResultSet result = statement.executeQuery( "select * from test" );
60                    while( result.next() )
61                    {   System.out.println
62                        (       result.getInt("Entry")        + ", "
63                            + result.getString("Customer")  + ", "
64                            + result.getString("DOW")       + ", "
65                            + result.getInt("Cups")         + ", "
66                            + result.getString("Type")
67                        );
68                    }
69              }
70          finally
71          {
72              try{ if(statement != null) statement.close(); }catch(Exception e)
73              try{ if(connection!= null) connection.close();}catch(Exception e)
74          }
75      }
76  }
```

Probably the most confusing part of using JDBC is the driver-management mechanism. The problem Sun is trying to solve is a single program that needs to talk to a heterogeneous set of databases. That is, you need to talk to Oracle, Sybase, and SQL Server in a single program, and each database has a different driver.

Sun's solution is a little odd, however. The java.sql.DriverManager class is an everything-is-static Singleton whose job is, not surprisingly, to manage a set of JDBC drivers. Before you can use the java.sql.DriverManager, however, you have to bring the vendor-specific drivers into existence. These drivers typically register themselves with the java.sql.DriverManager when they're loaded (code in the driver's static initializer block does the registration). So you have to load the class files for all the JDBC drivers that you need to use before you use the java.sql.DriverManager. That loading is done by the forName() call at the top of main() (Listing 4-37, line 15), which loads the class file and brings an instance into existence, causing the static-initializer block to execute as a side effect.

The JDBC driver for the current implementation is the JDBCDriver class in Listing 4-38. There's not much to it. The static-initializer block that registers the driver object with the java.sql.DriverManager is on line 18. The jdbcCompliant() override (Listing 4-38, line 43) is small but important. By returning false it tells the users of this driver that the driver is not fully JDBC compliant. In other words, it's perfectly okay for a JDBC implementation to be minimal, as long as it announces this to the world. As you'll see in a moment, attempts to call unsupported methods in this minimal implementation result in an exception toss. Unfortunately, there's no standard for "minimal," so every driver has to document operations it supports. No "introspection" mechanism exists that you can use to find this information at runtime.

The other critical method is the acceptsURL(...) method on line 27 of Listing 4-38. To see why, go back to line 21 of Listing 4-37, reproduced here:

```
import java.sql.DriverManager;
//...

connection = DriverManager.getConnection(
            "file:/c:/usr/src/com/holub/database/jdbc/Dbase",
            "Harpo", "swordfish" );
```

All calls to a database start out by getting a java.sql.Connection to that database from the java.sql.DriverManager—you can't talk to the database at all without a connection to it. To get a java.sql.Connection object that represents the connection, you call DriverManager.getConnection() with three arguments: a URL that typically specifies both the database type (MySQL, PostgreSQL, and so on) and the name of the database, along with a username and password. My code just uses a simple "file:" URL with no database-identifying prefix, but a more realistic example may look like this:

```
jdbc:postgresql=//postgresql.holub.com:1234/sales_database
```

Everything between the first colon and the equals sign specifies what sort of driver to use; the remainder of the URL identifies the server and port number on which the database resides and the name of the database itself.

The java.sql.DriverManager chooses the correct driver using the Chain-of-Responsibility pattern. It keeps a list of registered drivers, and when you request a connection, it passes each driver in the list an acceptsURL(...) message. As you can see in the version in Listing 4-38 (line 27), all this method typically does is examine the first part of the URL and report true if the current database is described. The PostgreSQL driver probably implements the method as follows:

```
public boolean acceptsURL(String url) throws SQLException
{   return url.startsWith("jdbc:postgresql");
}
```

Once the java.sql.DriverManager has identified the correct driver, it requests a connection by calling the driver's connect() method. The current implementation is on line 31 of Listing 4-38. As you can see from Figure 4-18 (on p. 326), the JDBCDriver (up at the top of the picture) is both an Abstract java.sql.Connection Factory and a Chain-of-Responsibility Handler.

Listing 4-38. *JDBCDriver.java*

```
1  package com.holub.database.jdbc;
2
3  import java.sql.*;
4  import java.util.*;
5  import java.net.*;
6
7  /** A JDBC driver for a small in-memory database that wraps
8   * the {@link com.holub.database.Database} class. See that
```

```
 9    *    class for a discussion of the supported SQL.
10    *
11    *    @see com.holub.database.Database
12    */
13
14   public class JDBCDriver implements java.sql.Driver
15   {
16
17        private JDBCConnection connection;
18        static
19        {   try
20            {   java.sql.DriverManager.registerDriver( new JDBCDriver() );
21            }
22            catch(SQLException e)
23            {   System.err.println(e);
24            }
25        }
26
27        public boolean acceptsURL(String url) throws SQLException
28        {   return url.startsWith("file:/");
29        }
30
31        public Connection connect(String uri, Properties info)
32                                                  throws SQLException
33        {   try
34            {   return connection = new JDBCConnection(uri);
35            }
36            catch( Exception e )
37            {   throw new SQLException( e.getMessage() );
38            }
39        }
40
41        public int      getMajorVersion() { return 1; }
42        public int      getMinorVersion() { return 0; }
43        public boolean  jdbcCompliant()   { return false; }
44
45        public DriverPropertyInfo[]
46        getPropertyInfo(String url, Properties info) throws SQLException
47        {   return new DriverPropertyInfo[0];
48        }
49   }
```

The next step in the JDBC process is to create a java.sql.Statement object that encapsu-lates the SQL processing. You get a java.sql.Statement from a java.sql.Connection and then use the java.sql.Statement to issue a SQL request like this:

```
java.sql.Statement SQLStatement = connection.createStatement();

SQLStatement.executeUpdate
(   "create table test (" +
    "  Entry       INTEGER      NOT NULL"  +
    ", Customer    VARCHAR (20) NOT NULL"  +
    ", Cups        INTEGER      NOT NULL"  +
    ", Type        VARCHAR (10) NOT NULL"  +
    ", PRIMARY KEY( Entry )"               +
    ")"
);
```

A java.sql.Connection is an Abstract java.sql.Statement Factory, which is interesting because the single class serves in different roles in two separate reifications of Abstract Factory. JDBConnection is a Concrete Product (created by the JDBCDriver factory) in one reification and a Concrete Factory (of java.sql.Statement objects) in the other. Looking at Figure 4-11, you'll see that the same dual participation occurs with several other JDBC classes as well. A JDBCDriver is a factory of JDBCConnection objects, which are, in turn, JDBCStatement factories, which are themselves JDBCResultSet factories.

The JDBCConnection class that I'll describe in the following section (in Listing 4-40) implements the java.sql.Connection interface, but it does so indirectly. JDBCConnection extends com.holub.database.jdbc.adapters.ConnectionAdapter (in Listing 4-39), which implements java.sql.Connection. The ConnectionAdapter class implements all the interface methods with versions that throw exceptions. It provides a way of not cluttering up the real code with methods that aren't implemented. I've used the same strategy to handle unsupported methods in the java.sql.ResultSet, java.sql.ResultSetMetaData, and java.sql.Statement interfaces. The ResultSetAdapter, ResultSetMetaDataAdapter, and StatementAdapter classes implement the matching interface with methods that do nothing but throw an exception. I haven't bothered to provide listings for these classes here, but they're in the source code on the web site.

Listing 4-39. *ConnectionAdapter.java (Partial Listing)*

```
1   package com.holub.database.jdbc.adapters;
2   import java.sql.*;
3   public class ConnectionAdapter implements java.sql.Connection
4   {
5       public ConnectionAdapter()
6       throws SQLException
7
8       public ConnectionAdapter(java.sql.Driver driver, String url,
9                           java.util.Properties info)
10      throws SQLException
11      {throw new SQLException("unsupported"); }
12
13      public void setHoldability(int h)
14      throws SQLException
```

```
15        {throw new SQLException("unsupported"); }
16
17        public int getHoldability()
18        throws SQLException
19        {throw new SQLException("unsupported");  }
20
21        //...
22
23        public void setTypeMap(java.util.Map map)
24        throws SQLException
25        {throw new SQLException("unsupported");  }
26    }
27
```

The State Pattern and *JDBCConnection*

The JDBCConnection class (Listing 4-40) serves as a wrapper for the Database class. It implements that part of the JDBC bridge that represents the database itself. The Database object is created by the JDBCConnection constructors, and the database contents are dumped to disk when the connection is closed.

Most of the methods of JDBCConnection implement JDBC's rather odd (to me) transaction mechanism: When you set auto-commit mode off by calling setAutoCommit(false), the system issues a BEGIN request. Subsequent calls to commit() or rollback() issue the matching SQL and then issue another BEGIN request. No begin() method exists. If you never call setAutoCommit(false), then every SQL request you issue is treated as a transaction and cannot be rolled back. JDBC does not support nested transactions. Nonetheless, you can ignore all the methods I've just been discussing and do transactions using executeUpdate(...) to issue BEGIN, COMMIT, and ROLLBACK requests at the SQL level.

I've implemented the auto-commit behavior using the Gang-of-Four State pattern, pictured in Figure 4-19. The **State** pattern provides a way of organizing a class whose objects change behavior when they change state. In the current example, the behavior of four methods (close(), commit(), rollback(), and setAutoCommit(...)) changes, depending on whether the connection is in the auto-commit-enabled state.

The naïve way to implement behavior that changes with state is to put a field in the class that indicates the current state and then put a switch statement or equivalent in every method, with the state-related behavior put into the case statements. Here's a simplistic example:

```
class ChangesBehaviorWithState
{
    private static int state = 0;

    public void methodOne()
    {   switch( state )
        {
        case 0: /* behavior for state 0 goes here */ break;
        case 1: /* behavior for state 1 goes here */ break;
        case 2: /* behavior for state 2 goes here */ break;
```

```
        }
    }

    public void methodTwo()
    {   switch( state )
        {
        case 0: /* behavior for state 0 goes here */ break;
        case 1: /* behavior for state 1 goes here */ break;
        case 2: /* behavior for state 2 goes here */ break;
        }
    }
    //...
}
```

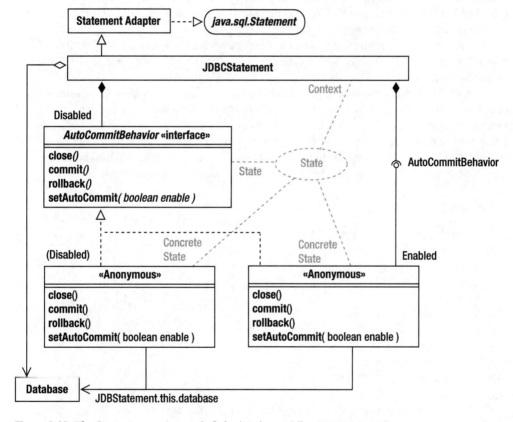

Figure 4-19. *The State pattern in* com.holub.database.jdbc.JDBCConnection

This approach has two problems. First, all those switch statements add a lot of clutter to the code and make it hard to read. Second, the code is inherently difficult to maintain since the behavior associated with a given state is scattered all over the class definition. Changing the underlying state machine (the rules that determine how you get from one state to another and definitions of the behavior associated with each state) is particularly difficult.

The **State** pattern solves both problems. Here's the structure:

First create an interface that contains definitions for those methods whose behavior changes with state. I've done that in Listing 4-40 with the `AutoCommitBehavior` interface on line 104. In the State pattern, this interface has the role of State.

Next, implement that interface as many times as there are states. Each implementation defines the behavior associated with one and only one state. In Listing 4-40, the auto-commit-enabled behavior is defined in the anonymous inner class assigned to `enabled` on line 111; the auto-commit-disabled behavior is defined in the anonymous inner class assigned to `disabled` on line 124. In the State pattern, these implementers of the State has the role of Concrete State.

Next, define a variable that points at an object representing the behavior associated with the current state. I've done that with the `autoCommitState` field declared on line 165 in Listing 4-40.

Finally, in the methods whose behavior changes with state, you delegate to the object that represents the current-state's behavior. For example, `rollback()` (on line 143 of Listing 4-40) just calls `autoCommitState.rollback()`. The class that uses the State objects (the `JDBCConnection`) has the role of Context in the pattern.

In the current implementation, state changes are accomplished by the `setAutoCommit()` calls in the Concrete State objects. The pattern does not require that you change state in this particular way, however.

As a final observation on State, you often find State and Proxy combined. Consider a proxy for a slowly loading object such as Java's `Image` class. (To remind you, the `getImage()` method returns a proxy for the real image that is being downloaded slowly in the background. You can use the `Image` proxy even before the entire actual image has been pulled across the network.) This sort of Proxy can be in two states (Real Subject available and Real Subject unavailable), and you can use the State pattern for the code that handles these states.

Listing 4-40. *JDBCConnection.java*

```
1   package com.holub.database.jdbc;
2
3   import java.io.*;
4   import java.net.*;
5   import java.util.*;
6   import java.sql.*;
7
8   import com.holub.database.*;
9   import com.holub.database.jdbc.adapters.*;
10  import com.holub.text.ParseFailure;
11
12  /** A limited version of the Connection class. All methods
13   *  undocumented base-class overrides throw a
14   *  {@link SQLException} if called.
15   *  <p>
16   *  Note that you can't
17   *  mix non-autocommit behavior with explicit
18   *  SQL begin/commit statements. For example, if you
19   *  turn off autocommit mode (which causes a SQL begin
```

```
20   *   to be issued), and then execute a SQL begin manually,
21   *   a call to <code>commit</code> will commit the inner transaction,
22   *   but not the outer one. In effect, you can't do
23   *   nested transactions using the JDBC {@link commit} or
24   *   {@link rollback}  methods.
25   */
26
27   public class JDBCConnection extends ConnectionAdapter
28   {
29       private Database database;
30
31       // Establish a connection to the indicated database.
32       //
33       public JDBCConnection(String uri) throws SQLException,
34                                                 URISyntaxException,
35                                                 IOException
36       {   this( new URI(uri) );
37       }
38
39       public JDBCConnection(URI uri) throws    SQLException,
40                                                IOException
41       {   database = new Database( uri );
42       }
43
44       /** Close a database connection. A commit is issued
45        *   automatically if auto-commit mode is disabled.
46        *   @see #setAutoCommit
47        */
48       public void close() throws SQLException
49       {   try
50           {
51               autoCommitState.close();
52
53               database.dump();
54               database=null;  // make the memory reclaimable and
55                               // also force a nullPointerException
56                               // if anybody tries to use the
57                               // connection after it's closed.
58           }
59           catch(IOException e)
60           {   throw new SQLException( e.getMessage() );
61           }
62       }
63
64       public Statement createStatement() throws SQLException
65       {   return new JDBCStatement(database);
66       }
```

```
67
68     /** Terminate the current transactions and start a new
69      *  one. Does nothing if auto-commit mode is on.
70      *  @see #setAutoCommit
71      */
72     public void commit() throws SQLException
73     {   autoCommitState.commit();
74     }
75
76     /** Roll back the current transactions and start a new
77      *  one. Does nothing if auto-commit mode is on.
78      *  @see #setAutoCommit
79      */
80     public void rollback() throws SQLException
81     {   autoCommitState.rollback();
82     }
83
84     /**
85      * Once set true, all SQL statements form a stand-alone
86      * transaction. A begin is issued automatically when
87      * auto-commit mode is disabled so that the {@link #commit}
88      * and {@link #rollback} methods will work correctly.
89      * Similarly, a commit is issued automatically when
90      * auto-commit mode is enabled.
91      * <p>
92      * Auto-commit mode is on by default.
93      */
94     public void setAutoCommit( boolean enable ) throws SQLException
95     {   autoCommitState.setAutoCommit(enable);
96     }
97
98     /** Return true if auto-commit mode is enabled */
99     public boolean getAutoCommit() throws SQLException
100    {   return autoCommitState == enabled;
101    }
102
103    //-------------------------------------------------------------------
104    private interface AutoCommitBehavior
105    {   void close() throws SQLException;
106        void commit() throws SQLException;
107        void rollback() throws SQLException;
108        void setAutoCommit( boolean enable ) throws SQLException;
109    }
110
111    private AutoCommitBehavior enabled =
112        new AutoCommitBehavior()
113        {   public void close() throws SQLException {/* nothing to do */}
```

```
114          public void commit()                   {/* nothing to do */}
115          public void rollback()                 {/* nothing to do */}
116          public void setAutoCommit( boolean enable )
117          {   if( enable == false )
118              {   database.begin();
119                  autoCommitState = disabled;
120              }
121          }
122      };
123
124      private AutoCommitBehavior disabled =
125          new AutoCommitBehavior()
126          {   public void close() throws SQLException
127              {   try
128                  {   database.commit();
129                  }
130                  catch( ParseFailure e )
131                  {   throw new SQLException( e.getMessage() );
132                  }
133              }
134              public void commit() throws SQLException
135              {   try
136                  {   database.commit();
137                      database.begin();
138                  }
139                  catch( ParseFailure e )
140                  {   throw new SQLException( e.getMessage() );
141                  }
142              }
143              public void rollback() throws SQLException
144              {   try
145                  {   database.rollback();
146                      database.begin();
147                  }
148                  catch( ParseFailure e )
149                  {   throw new SQLException( e.getMessage() );
150                  }
151              }
152              public void setAutoCommit( boolean enable ) throws SQLException
153              {   try
154                  {   if( enable == true )
155                      {   database.commit();
156                          autoCommitState = enabled;
157                      }
158                  }
159                  catch( ParseFailure e )
160                  {   throw new SQLException( e.getMessage() );
```

```
161                          }
162                      }
163              };
164
165       private AutoCommitBehavior autoCommitState = enabled;
166  }
```

Statements

As you saw earlier, you issue a SQL request through a java.sql.Statement object that is manufactured by the java.sql.Connection's createStatement() call. (The version on line 64 of
Listing 4-41, discussed next, just hides a call to new.)

The JDBCStatment class (my implementation of java.sql.Statement) is laid out in Listing
4-41. There's not much to it. The executeUpdate(...) method is used for all SQL statements
that don't return a value (everything except a SELECT); executeQuery(...) is used for SELECT.
Both methods just delegate to the underlying Database object, though executeQuery(...)
wraps in a java.sql.ResultSet object the Cursor across the rows of the Table object that
holds the query results.

Listing 4-41. *JDBCStatement.java*

```
1    package com.holub.database.jdbc;
2
3    import java.sql.*;
4    import java.io.*;
5
6    import com.holub.database.*;
7    import com.holub.database.jdbc.adapters.*;
8
9    public class JDBCStatement extends StatementAdapter
10   {   Database database;
11
12       public JDBCStatement(Database database)
13       {   this.database = database;
14       }
15
16       public int executeUpdate(String sqlString) throws SQLException
17       {   try
18           {   database.execute( sqlString );
19               return database.affectedRows();
20           }
21           catch( Exception e )
22           {   throw new SQLException( e.getMessage() );
23           }
24       }
25
26       public ResultSet executeQuery(String sqlQuery) throws SQLException
27       {   try
```

```
28              {   Table result = database.execute( sqlQuery );
29                  return new JDBCResultSet( result.rows() );
30              }
31          catch( Exception e )
32              {   throw new SQLException( e.getMessage() );
33              }
34      }
35  }
```

The Adapter Pattern (Result Sets)

The only Gang-of-Four design pattern I haven't yet covered is **Adapter**, and the JDBCResultSet class has an example of it (Listing 4-42). Figure 4-20 shows the generalized form of the pattern.

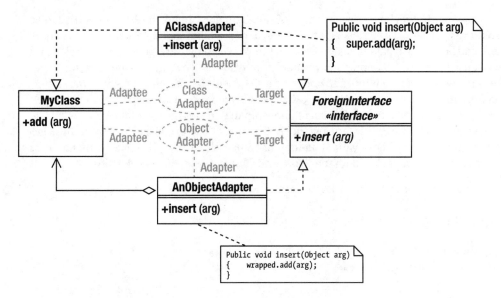

Figure 4-20. *Object and class forms of Adapter*

The term *Adapter* stems from an electrical adapter. You want to plug your 110v-60Hz-3-prong-plug radio into a European 220v-70Hz-2-cylindrical-prong outlet, so you use an adapter. This way, your radio's interface to the power system appears to be the interface that the power system expects. Adapting this notion to software (so to speak), an Adapter makes an existing object of some class appear to implement an interface that it doesn't actually implement (a "foreign" interface).

In the current situation, no difference really exists at all between a Cursor and a java.sql .ResultSet, at least in terms of core functionality. The JDBCResultSet class wraps a Cursor object so that the Cursor object can appear to implement the JDBCResultSet interface. The JDBCResultSet is an Adapter that makes a Cursor (the Adaptee) implement a foreign (or Target) interface (the java.sql.ResultSet).

Another example of Adapter is the ArrayIterator class (in Listing 4-10) you saw earlier. This Adapter lets you access an array as if it implements the Iterator interface.

The flavor of Adapter characterized by JDBCResultSet—which uses a wrapping strategy—is called an **Object Adapter**. Adapter has two other flavors, one identified by the Gang of Four and another that they don't talk about but is worth examining. A **Class Adapter** uses extends relationships rather than wrapping.

If the Results class (the Concrete Class implemented by the Cursor returned from the ConcreteTable) was public, I could implement a Class-Adapter version of JDBCResultSet like this:

```
class ClassAdapterResultSet extends Results implements java.sql.ResultSet
{
    // Implement all methods of ResultSet here, delegating to
    // superclass (Results) methods whenever possible.
}
```

Class Adapters do have the advantage of simultaneously being the Adapter and Adaptee. (I could pass a ClassAdapterResultSet object to a method that took a Result or Cursor argument, and I could also pass it to a method that took a ResultSet argument.) Nonetheless, I haven't used them much in practice, primarily because of the overhead of creating one. That is, if you have a Cursor in hand, and you need a JDBCResultSet, you must copy all the state data from the Cursor object to the JDBCResultSet object if it's a class adapter. This copying also usually mandates a tight coupling relationship that makes me uncomfortable.

A third possibility would work just fine in the current context. I think of it as an **Interface Adapter** (not a Gang-of-Four variant of Adapter). Since the Results object implements Cursor, I could get the advantages of both the Class- and Object-Adapter forms like this:

```
class InterfaceAdapterResultSet implements Cursor, java.sql.ResultSet
{
    private Cursor  adaptee;

    public InterfaceAdapterResultSet( Cursor adaptee )
    {   this.adaptee = adaptee;
    }

    // Implement all methods of both interfaces here. Cursor
    // methods do nothing but delegate to the adaptee.
}
```

This way, I'm still using containment rather than implementation inheritance, so none of the copying and the tight coupling that the copying implies is required. I implement both the Target and Adaptee interfaces, however, so I have the flexibility of the Class Adapter. You obviously can't use this form of Adapter if the Adaptee doesn't implement a well-defined interface.

The only use of Adapter in the Java libraries that comes to mind are the I/O system adapters, some of which were shown in Figure 4-9. A StringBufferInputStream, for example, is adapting StringBuffer so that it appears to implement the InputStream interface. String-BufferInputStream effectively changes the interface to a StringBuffer so that it can be treated as an InputStream.

The Java libraries don't have many other Adapters, primarily because Adapters are usually used to force-fit a library into an existing context. You'll typically find them in the code that uses the library, not in the library itself. Let's say, for example, that you had written an application that used AWT for its user interface and that your boss suddenly announced that AWT was garbage, and you had to reimplement the application in terms of some off-the-wall library written by your boss's brother-in-law. Refactoring 100,000 lines of code is one possibility, but it's easier to write a set of Adapters that make the brother-in-law library appear to be AWT. This way you don't have to rewrite your existing code.

People often confuse Bridge and Adapter. Keep things straight by keeping the intent of the pattern in mind. The point of Bridge is to isolate subsystems. The point of Adapter is to shoehorn a class into a program that was written in terms of an interface that the class doesn't implement. Also, Bridges are big things, and Adapters are little things.

People also confuse Adapters and Decorators since they're both wrappers. The point of a Decorator, however, is to change the behavior of one or more methods of some class without using extends. In terms of structure, a Decorator will always implement the same interface as the object it's decorating. An Adapter probably won't implement the interface of the wrapped object (though it may).

Getting back to the JDBC-layer code, the JDBCResultSet class (in Listing 4-42) is interesting in that it's a true Gang-of-Four Object Adapter. It makes objects that implement Cursor appear to implement the ResultSet interface. For example, it changes the name of the advance() method to next(), and it hides the generic column(...) method (which gets a specified column of the current row) in a set of methods that get the column and do a type conversion as well (getString(), getDouble(), and so on). It also provides a few type-safe updatexxx() methods. These database accessors are useful in that they provide a modicum of type safety when the underlying system provides no type safety at all. (The Table stores everything as an Object, and the Database stores everything as a String.)

One final word on the subject of adapters is in order. My earlier use of the word *Adapter* in the JDBC-interface-implementation-class names (for example, ConnectionAdapter) is somewhat misleading. I've used the word *Adapter* because Java uses a similar default-implementation-that-does-nothing strategy in the AWT event model, and all those classes are called *Adapters*. (For example, MouseAdapter implements MouseListener.) These "Adapter" classes are not Adapters in the design-pattern sense of a class that makes an object appear to implement a foreign interface. This use of "Adapter" is just an unfortunate Java naming convention.

Listing 4-42. *JDBCResultSet.java*

```
1  package com.holub.database.jdbc;
2
3  import java.sql.*;
4  import java.text.*;
5
6  import com.holub.database.*;
7  import com.holub.database.jdbc.adapters.*;
8
9  /** A limited version of the result-set class. All methods
```

```
10    *   not shown throw a {@link SQLException} if called. Note
11    *   the underlying table actually holds nothing but
12    *   strings, so the numeric accessors and mutators
13    *   (e.g. {@link getDouble} and {@link setDouble})
14    *   are doing string-to-number and number-to-string
15    *   conversions. These conversions might fail if the
16    *   underlying String doesn't represent a number.
17    */
18
19   public class JDBCResultSet extends ResultSetAdapter
20   {
21       private         final Cursor cursor;
22       private static final NumberFormat  format =
23                                   NumberFormat.getInstance();
24
25       /** Wrap a result set around a Cursor. The cursor
26        *  should never have been advanced; just pass this constructor
27        *  the return value from {@link Table#rows}.
28        */
29       public JDBCResultSet(Cursor cursor) throws SQLException
30       {   this.cursor = cursor;
31       }
32
33       public boolean next()
34       {   return cursor.advance();
35       }
36
37       public String getString(String columnName) throws SQLException
38       {   try
39           {   Object contents = cursor.column(columnName);
40               return (contents==null) ? null : contents.toString();
41           }
42           catch( IndexOutOfBoundsException e )
43           {   throw new SQLException("column "+columnName+" doesn't exist" );
44           }
45       }
46
47       public double getDouble(String columnName) throws SQLException
48       {   try
49           {   String contents = getString(columnName);
50               return (contents == null)
51                       ? 0.0
52                       : format.parse( contents ).doubleValue()
53                       ;
54           }
55           catch( ParseException e )
56           {   throw new SQLException("field doesn't contain a number");
```

```
57              }
58          }
59
60      public int getInt(String columnName) throws SQLException
61      {   try
62          {   String contents = getString(columnName);
63              return (contents == null)
64                      ? 0
65                      : format.parse( contents ).intValue()
66                      ;
67          }
68          catch( ParseException e )
69          {   throw new SQLException("field doesn't contain a number");
70          }
71      }
72
73      public long getLong(String columnName) throws SQLException
74      {   try
75          {   String contents = getString(columnName);
76              return (contents == null)
77                      ? 0L
78                      : format.parse( contents ).longValue()
79                      ;
80          }
81          catch( ParseException e )
82          {   throw new SQLException("field doesn't contain a number");
83          }
84      }
85
86      public void updateNull(String columnName )
87      {   cursor.update(columnName, null );
88      }
89      public void updateDouble(String columnName, double value)
90      {   cursor.update(columnName, format.format(value) );
91      }
92      public void updateInt(String columnName, long value)
93      {   cursor.update(columnName, format.format(value) );
94      }
95      public ResultSetMetaData getMetaData() throws SQLException
96      {   return new JDBCResultSetMetaData(cursor);
97      }
98  }
```

Finishing Up the Code

The final implementation class is JDBCResultSetMetaData in Listing 4-43, which normally provides metadata information about the columns. Since there is no typing in the current implementation, all columns are treated as a SQL VARCHAR.

Listing 4-43. *JDBCResultSetMetaData.java*

```
1   package com.holub.database.jdbc;
2
3   import java.sql.*;
4   import java.util.*;
5
6   import com.holub.database.*;
7   import com.holub.database.jdbc.adapters.*;
8
9   /** A limited version of the result-set metadata class. All methods
10  *  not shown throw a {@link SQLException} if called.
11  */
12  public class JDBCResultSetMetaData extends ResultSetMetaDataAdapter
13  {
14      private final Cursor cursor;
15
16      public JDBCResultSetMetaData(Cursor cursor)
17      {   this.cursor = cursor;
18      }
19
20      public int getColumnType(int column) throws java.sql.SQLException
21      {   return java.sql.Types.VARCHAR;
22      }
23
24      public String getColumnTypeName(int column)throws java.sql.SQLException
25      {   return "VARCHAR";
26      }
27  }
```

When Bridges Fail

The JDBC layer that you've been looking at is another example of the Bridge pattern discussed earlier (in "The Bridge Pattern" section). You're seeing only the implementation half of the Bridge, however (see Figure 4-4, on p. 199). As a Bridge, it does serve to isolate your code from some of the problems that can emerge when you change databases.

JDBC is also a good example of how the Bridge pattern can fail, however. The problem is the SQL itself. Every database seems to use a different dialect of SQL, which is an enormous problem from a portability perspective. The whole point of Bridge is to replace some subsystem (for example, database) with a completely different implementation (for example, a different database) without impacting your application code. You can certainly replace a SQL Server driver with a PostgreSQL driver with no difficulty. Unfortunately, though your code will still compile just fine, it probably won't work anymore because PostgreSQL won't recognize the SQL Server SQL dialect.

This problem has some solutions, but nobody has implemented them. One solution is to eliminate SQL altogether and provide a set of methods in the Bridge that does everything that you would normally do with SQL. A conforming driver would then have to implement these methods appropriately for its database. The main (significant) downside to this approach is that you can't get a DBA to write SQL for you anymore; everything has to be done in Java.

A second "solution" is to require all drivers to support some defined standard SQL and to map this standard SQL to the native dialect as necessary. To really guarantee portability, the driver would also have to detect an attempt to issue a nonstandard SQL request and refuse to execute the request. The problem with this approach is a practical one. Most databases support a host of useful nonstandard features, and it's often these nonstandard features that drive the decision to adopt a particular database. It's simply not practical or appropriate to prevent a user of JDBC from using the very features that led him or her to select a particular database. It's true that there's a nontrivial common intersection between major SQL dialects, but you have to give up too much if you restrict yourself to that subset.

The same problem exists with the AWT bridge I mentioned earlier in the chapter. In both the JDBC and AWT case, you can even change runtime environments (or databases) on the fly as the program works. You certainly don't have to recompile if you're using a Bridge. However, as with JDBC, the behavior of the UI under AWT will change with the new environment, and things that used to work don't work anymore. People used to jokingly call AWT the Write-Once-Test-Everywhere environment (as a foil to Sun's Write-Once-Run-Everywhere slogan). The fact that Bridge rarely gives you complete isolation between subsystems is not insurmountable. Eclipse's SWT library uses the Bridge pattern more effectively than did AWT, for example, primarily by making the Bridge so powerful that nobody needs to use OS-specific features. It is difficult to achieve true independence between subsystems, however.

Whew!

So, that's all of the Gang-of-Four design patterns, all tangled together in two programs. As I said back in the preface, this is the way the patterns appear in the real world, and I hope you'll develop a better understanding of the patterns by looking at them in a realistic context than you would by looking at a catalog. (Nonetheless, I've provided a catalog as an Appendix so that you can have a quick pattern reference.)

You'll find two things start to happen as you become more familiar with the patterns. First, it will be a lot easier to talk about your code to other pattern-savvy programmers. It's a lot easier to say "this is a Visitor" than it is to describe the structure of the code every time you talk about it.

The second emanation of pattern savvy is more important. As you build a mental catalog of not only the Gang-of-Four patterns but also the myriad other patterns that are documented in the literature, you'll find that you code more effectively. You'll be able to see where a pattern applies before you write the code and then write it "right" from the beginning.

So, go forth and program!

APPENDIX

■■■

A Design-Pattern Quick Reference

This appendix is a reference of the Gang-of-Four design patterns, intended to jog your memory about how the patterns work. Ironically, the original Gang-of-Four presentation was this brief, but they expanded things in the book to make it more accessible. Once you know the patterns, however, brevity is good. This catalog probably won't be of much use if you don't already have some familiarity with the patterns, however. A lot of the material you'd find in an introductory-level discussion is either missing or condensed in this appendix.

Though I've followed the Gang-of-Four organization (alphabetical by category), I have deliberately not followed the Gang-of-Four format for the pattern description itself. In particular, I've restated their "intent" section to make it more understandable. I've also used stripped-down examples, and my examples are not the same as the Gang-of-Four examples. In particular, since most of us aren't doing GUI work, I've tried to eliminate GUI-related example code.

I've tried to make up for some of this brevity by listing places where the design patterns are found in the Java packages so you can see how they're applied in practice. (Some patterns don't appear in Java, in which case the "Usage" example will say so). Also, you can find detailed code similar to my stripped-down examples in one of the volumes of Chan, Lee, and Kramer's *The Java Class Libraries* (Addison-Wesley, various editions) or in the Java documentation or tutorials available on the Sun web site.

I've played fast and loose with the code in the interest of saving space—I've omitted required `import` statements, access privileges, exceptions, and so on. The formatting isn't ideal in places. I'm assuming you know what you're doing in the Java-programming department and are more interested in the clarity of the example than in having cut-and-paste code. The code won't always compile cleanly as it stands.

Finally, I've said a few things in these notes that you may find shocking if you haven't read the rest of the book or some of my other work—things such as "objects must be responsible for building their own user interfaces." I simply have no room to explain this sort of thing in a quick reference; you have to read the rest of the book.

[This page intentionally left blank[1]]

---

1. Rather an odd thing to say, since the page isn't blank at all—it contains the text "This page intention-ally left blank" —but imagine that it's blank.

Creational Patterns

The creational patterns are all concerned with object creation (fancy that!). Most of them provide ways to create objects without knowing exactly what you're creating (beyond the interfaces supported by the created objects). Programming in terms of interfaces rather than concrete-classes is essential if you intend to write flexible, reusable code. My rule of thumb is that as much as 80 percent of my code should be written in terms of interfaces.

Abstract Factory

Create objects knowing only the interfaces they implement (without knowing the actual class). Typically, create one of a "family" of objects (one of several kinds of Iterators, one of several kinds of graphical widgets, and so on).

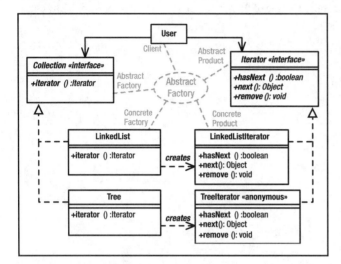

Abstract Factory: Interface to the actual factory.

Concrete Factory: Implements the Abstract Factory interface to create a specific class of object.

Abstract Product: The sort of product that the Abstract Factory creates.

Concrete Product: The actual object (whose class you don't know) created by the factory.

Client: Uses the created objects only through their interfaces.

What Problem Does It Solve?

Abstract Factory makes it easy to create and manipulate objects without knowing exactly what they are. (This example uses an Iterator—it doesn't care what kind.) This way, it's easy to add new sorts of concrete products to the system without changing any of the code that uses those products.

Abstract Factory also makes it easy for your code to operate in diverse environments. The system creates a unique Concrete Factory (which creates unique Concrete Products) for each environment, but since you use the interface, you don't actually know which environment (or which Concrete Product) you're using.

Pros (✔) and Cons (✖)

✔ The anonymity of the Concrete Factory and Product promotes reuse—the code that uses these objects doesn't need to be modified if the Factory produces instantiations of different classes than it used to do.

✖ If the product doesn't do what you want, you may have to change the Abstract Product interface, which is difficult. (You have to change all the Concrete Product definitions.)

Often Confused With

Builder: Builder's Director may use an Abstract Factory to create Builder objects, but the point of Builder is that the Director doesn't know what it's building.

Factory Method: A Factory Method—an unfortunate choice of pattern name on the part of the Gang of Four—is an abstract method that a subclass overrides. The Abstract-Factory method that creates objects is only rarely a Factory Method.

See Also

Singleton, Factory Method, Builder

Implementation Notes and Example

```
interface Collection
{  Iterator iterator();
   //...
}
interface Iterator
{   boolean hasNext();
    Object next();
    //...
}
class Tree implements Collection
{   public Iterator iterator()
    {   return new Iterator()
        {   // Implement Iterator interface
            // here (to traverse a Tree).
            // (See description of Iterator
            // pattern for implemenation.)
        }
    }
}
class User        // uses only interfaces
{
    public void operation( Collection c )
    {   Iterator i = c.iterator();
        while( i.hasNext() )
            doSomethingWith( i.next() );
    }
}
```

Collection is the Abstract Factory, Iterator is the Abstract Product, Tree is the Concrete Factory, and the anonymous-inner-class Iterator implementation is the Concrete Product.

Abstract Factory has many variants, probably the most common of which is a Concrete Factory that comprises its own interface—no "Abstract Factory" interface as such exists. This Concrete Factory is typically a Singleton. The methods of the class effectively comprise the Abstract Factory interface.

```
class SingletonFactory
{  private static instance=newSingletonFactory();
   public static SingletonFactory instance()
   {   return instance;
   }

   void factoryOperation1(){/*...*/}
   void factoryOperation2(){/*...*/};
}
```

A similar, though more abstract, example is described in the entry for Factory Method.

No reason exists why, in the no-Abstract-Factory variant, the Concrete Factory cannot create a user interface that allows the physical user to select which of several possible concrete products to create. Consider a drawing program whose "shape" factory creates a user interface showing a palate of possible shapes. The user can then click a shape to determine which Concrete Product (shape derivative) to create in response to a newShape() request.

Usage

`f(Collection c)`
`{   Iterator i = c.iterator();`
`    //...`
`}`
	Collection and Iterator are the Abstract Factory and Product. Concrete Factories and Products are anonymous.

`ButtonPeer peer =`
`    Toolkit.getDefaultToolkit().`
`                createButton(b);`
	Toolkit is both a Singleton and an Abstract Factory. Most of the methods of Toolkit are abstract, and getDefaultToolkit() returns an unknown derivative of Toolkit. No need exists for an Abstract Factory interface per se.

`URL home = new URL("http://www.holub.com");`
`URLConnection c = home.getConnection();`
`InputStream in = c.getInput();`
	URL is a concrete URLConnection factory, and URLConnection is an abstract InputStream factory, so URLConnection is both an Abstract Product and an Abstract Factory, depending on context. URL, URLConnection, and InputStream are interfaces by use, not by declaration.

Builder

Separate the construction of a complex object from its representation so that the same construction process can create different representations without having to modify the constructing object.

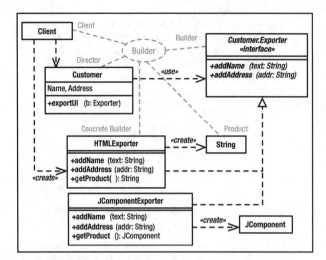

Director: Builds an object without knowing exactly what it's building.

Builder: Interface used by the Director to do the construction.

Concrete Builder: Actually builds the product by following directions given by the Director. Typically created externally (by the Client) or by an Abstract Factory.

Product: The object built by the Builder under the direction of the Director.

What Problem Does It Solve?

It's desirable to separate business logic from UI logic, but in an OO system you cannot expose implementation details. A well-done class definition will not have "get" methods that return state information, so an object must build its own UI. Nonetheless, it's sometimes necessary for an object to build more than one representation of itself, and it's undesirable to clutter up the business-logic code with the details needed to build multiple representations.

Builder solves this problem by putting the representation-specific code into a Builder object that's distinct from a Director ("business") object. Builder also easily lets you add representations later without impacting existing code at all.

Non-UI applications: credit-card processing; for example, every credit-card-payment processor requires a different protocol, with identical information presented in different ways. Builder separates you from the needs of the credit-card processor, letting you build a packet of information without needing to know which processor will receive that information. The organization of the data is hidden from you in the "concrete builder" that you talk to via a public, processor-independent, interface.

Pros (✔) and Cons (✖)

✔ Builder nicely isolates the representation of an object from the associated "business" logic, making it easy to add new (or change) representations of an object without modifying business logic.

✖ A change in the Builder interface mandates changes in all implementing classes.

✖ It's awkward to represent some UI elements cleanly in all representations (for example, HTML vs. Swing).

Often Confused With

Bridge: An application building a UI using AWT is a Director—the actual representation is unknown to the application. In this way, AWT reifies both Builder and Bridge.

Visitor: A visitor could build a UI by visiting every element of a data structure. It is "pulling" information for UI construction from the model rather than having that information "pushed" onto it.

See Also

Bridge, Visitor

Implementation Notes and Example

```
class Customer
{   private Address address;
    Private String  name;
    public void exportUI( Exporter b )
    {   b.addName(name);
        b.addAddress(address.toString());
        //...
    }
    public interface Exporter
    {   void addName(String text);
        void addAddress(String addr);
        //...
    }
}
class HTMLExporter implements Customer.Exporter
{   // Implement Builder methods here. This
    // Implementation creates an HTML
    // representation of the object.
    //...
    public String getProduct()
    {   // Return HTML String.
    }
}
class JComponentExporter implements Customer.Exporter
{   JComponent product;
    // Implement Builder methods here. This
    // Implementation creates a Jcomponent
    // that represents the object.
    //...
    public JComponent getProduct()
    {   return product;
    }
}
class Client
{   Employee director;
    //...
    public void addYourUITo(JPanel someWindow)
    {   Customer.Exporter b =
                    JComponentExporter();
        director.exportUI( b );
        someWindow.add( b.getProduct() );
    }
}
```

The createUI() method is passed a Builder that could be an HTMLExporter (that creates an HTML representation) or a JComponentExporter (that produces a JComponent). The Director object doesn't know which of these products it is building—it just calls interface methods.

The Client object that's driving this process *does* know what it's building since it created the Builder. Consequently, it's reasonable for it to extract the correct product.

You could get better abstraction by using an Abstract Factory to create the Builder objects rather than new. By the same token, if all output was going to a file, you could add a print-YoursefToFile(String name) method to the Builder interface; the Director could call that method at an appropriate time, and the Client wouldn't have to extract anything; it would just supply a filename.

Builder implementations could be public inner classes of the Director. I'd probably do it that way unless I expected that Builders would be defined elsewhere in the code.

The Director is "pushing" information into the Builder. Consequently, you have no need for accessors (get methods) in the Director, and the coupling between the Builder and Director is very light. In general, accessors violate the integrity of the object by exposing implementation detail. Avoid them.

Usage

```
URL url = new URL("http://www.holub.com");
URLConnection connection = url.openConnection();
connection.setDoOutput( true );
connection.connect();
OutputStream out = connection.getOutputStream();
while( c = getCharacterFromSomewhere() )
   out.write( c );
out.close();
```

This code comprises a Director. It uses Abstract Factory (URLConnection) to get a Builder (the OutputStream), which builds an HTTP packet. The Director doesn't know that it's building an HTTP packet, however. (If an ftp:// URL had been specified, it would be building an FTP packet.) The close() call, instead of getting the product, just sends it off.

Factory Method

Let subclasses decide what which objects to instantiate.

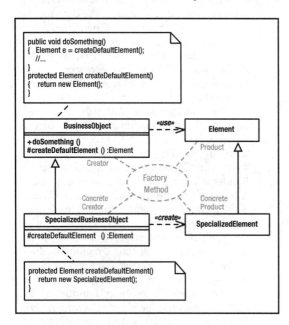

Creator: Defines a method that needs to create an object whose actual type is unknown. Does so using abstract-method call.

Concrete Creator: Subclass that overrides the abstract object-instantiation method to create the Concrete Product.

Product: Interface implemented by the created product. Creator accesses the Concrete Product object through this interface.

Concrete Product: Object used by the Creator (superclass) methods. Implements the Product interface.

What Problem Does It Solve?

This pattern is useful when you can do all (or most) of the work at the superclass level but want to put off deciding exactly which sort of object you'll be working on until runtime. (You'll manipulate objects that a derived-class creates through an interface that you define.)

It is often the case that a superclass object needs to create worker objects of some default type, but the superclass can work equally well using worker objects that are extensions of the original type. This pattern lets you create specialized worker objects in a specialized subclass.

This way of doing things is often useful when you create an implementation-inheritance-based "framework" that you expect users to customize using derivation.

Pros (✔) and Cons (✘)

✔ Easy to implement when a full-blown Abstract Factory is overkill.

✘ This pattern forces you to use implementation inheritance, with all its associated maintenance problems.

✘ Inheritance-based framework architectures, in which Factory Methods are usually found, are not the best way to achieve reuse. Generally, it's best if a framework class can simply be instantiated and used directly, without forcing a programmer to create a subclass to make the superclass useful. Implementation inheritance should be reserved for situations where you need to modify superclass behavior to perform in an unusual way.

Often Confused With

Abstract Factory: The Concrete Factory can use Factory Method to create Concrete Products. The creational method does not have to use this design pattern, though. A method is not a Factory Method simply because it manufactures objects. (I've seen the term misused in the Java documentation, among other places.) In Factory Method, a derived-class override makes the object.

See Also

Abstract Factory, Template Method

Implementation Notes and Example

```
public class BusinessObject
{   public void doSomething()
    {   Element e = createDefaultElement();
        //…
    }
    protected Element createDefaultElement()
    {   return new Element();
    }
}
public class Element
{   public void f(){/*…*/}
}

public class SpecializedBusinessObject
{   protected Element createDefaultElement()
    {   return new SpecializedElement();
    }
    private class SpecializedElement extends Element
    {   public void f(){ /*…*/ }
    }
}
```

You can sometimes customize superclass behavior by providing nonstandard objects for it to work with. In this example, a specialized form of a business object is created by extending the generalized version in such a way that it provides a specialized element rather than the default element.

The negative side to this architecture is that you often must modify the superclass if you add a subclass. The java.awt.Toolkit Abstract Factory overcomes this problem while still using an abstract-superclass architecture by instantiating objects with Class.forname() rather than an abstract-method call. This structure is still Factory Method, since the decision about which class to instantiate is deferred to runtime—it's just not a subclass that's making the decision.

It is often inappropriate to use Factory Method if the only method provided by the subclass is the Factory Method itself. You're adding complexity with little commensurate benefit.

Never leverage the fact that protected grants package access in Java. The create-DefaultElement() method is protected only because I expect it to be overridden by a subclass (otherwise it would be private). This method should not be called from anywhere other than the BusinessObject superclass. The language, unfortunately, grants package access to protected members, but it's best to pretend that package access is not possible.

This pattern is so trivial as to almost not be worth calling it a pattern. It's more interesting in C++, where it's called a *virtual constructor* and is implemented by overriding operator new().

Usage

```
public class MarkupPanel extends JEditorPane
{ public MarkupPanel()
  { setEditorKit(
      new HTMLEditorKit()
      { public ViewFactory getViewFactory()
        {   return new CustomViewFactory();
        }
      }
    );
  }
  private class CustomViewFactory
              extends HTMLEditorKit.HTMLFactory
  { public View create(Element e)
    { return new View()
      { protected Component createComponent()
        {   return new Component(){/*...*/};
        }
      }
    }
  }
}
```

In Swing's JEditorPane, various HTML elements are displayed as "views." When a parser recognizes an HTML element, it requests a "view" that renders the component. You specify a custom representation of an HTML element by providing a derived-class override of a create() method that returns a component of your choice.

Component is the Product. The (anonymous) implementation of Component is the Concrete Product. The MarkupPanel is the Creator, and the CustomViewFactory is the Concrete Creator. createComponent() is the Factory Method. Similarly, getViewFactory() is a Factory Method that produces custom view factories. A subclass specifies alternative view factories by overriding getViewFactory().

Prototype

Create objects by making copies of (*cloning*) a prototypical object. The prototype is usually provided by an external entity or a Factory, and the exact type of the prototype (as compared to the interfaces it implements) may not be known.

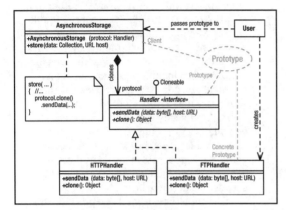

Prototype: Interface of object to copy; must define a mechanism for cloning itself.

ConcretePrototype: Object that's copied; implements cloning mechanism.

Client: Creates a new object by asking the Prototype for a clone.

What Problem Does It Solve?

1. Allows you to create several objects of the same type, even if you don't know exactly what that type is.

2. In Abstract Factory, information needed to initialize the Concrete Product (constructor arguments, for example) must be known at compile time. Most Abstract Factory reifications use the default, no-arg constructor. When you use Abstract Factory to make objects that must be in a nondefault state, you must first create the object and then modify it externally, and this external modification may happen in many places in the code. It would be better to create objects with the desired initial (nondefault) state and simply copy those objects to make additional ones. You may use Abstract Factory to make the prototype object.

3. Sometimes objects will be in only a few possible states, but you have many objects in each state. (The Gang of Four describe a Note class in a music-composition system; many instances of whole-note, half-note, and quarter-note objects exist—all whole notes are in an identical state.

4. Sometimes classes are specified at runtime and are created with *dynamic loading* (for example, `Class.forname("class.name")`) or a similarly expensive process (when initial state is specified in an XML file, for example). Rather than repeatedly going through the expense of creating an object, create a single prototype and copy it multiple times.

Pros (✔) and Cons (✖)

✔ You can install a new concrete product into a Factory simply by giving the Factory a prototype at runtime. Removal is also easy.

✔ Prototype can reduce object-creation time.

✔ Abstract Factory forces you to define classes with marginally different behavior using subclassing. Prototype avoids this problem by using state. When an object's behavior changes radically with state, you can look at the object as a dynamically specifiable class, and Prototype is your instantiation mechanism.

✖ You must explicitly implement `clone()`, which can be quite difficult. Also, think about deep-vs.-shallow copy issues. (Should you copy a reference, or should you clone the referenced object?) Finally, sometimes the clone method should act like a constructor and initialize some fields to default values. A clone of a list member cannot typically be in the list, for example.

See Also

Abstract Factory, State

Implementation Notes and Example

```
class AsynchronousStorage
{   private Handler protocol;
    public AsynchronousStorage( Handler protocol )
    {   this.protocol = protocol;
    }

    void store( Collection data, URL host )
    {   byte[] bytes = new byte[128];
        //...
        Handler handler=(Handler)protocol.clone();
        handler.sendData(bytes, host);
    }
}

interface Handler extends Cloneable
{   void sendData(byte[] data, URL host);
    Object clone();
}

class HTTPHandler implements Handler
{   public void sendData(byte[] data, URL host)
    {   // Send data asynchronously to
        // host using HTTP protocol, creating
        // background thread if necessary
    }
    public Object clone(){ /*...*/ }
}

class FTPHandler implements Handler
{   public void sendData(byte[] data, URL host)
    {   // same as above, but use FTP protocol
    }
    public Object clone(){ /*...*/ }
}

class User
{   private Collection theData;
    private AsynchronousStorage dataStore =
                new AsynchronousStorage(
                         new HTTPHandler() );
    public void flush()
    {   dataStore.store(theData, new URL(/*...*/));
    }
}
```

In this example, HTTPHandler talks asynchronously to a remote host using HTTP, and FTPHandler talks using FTP. One handler exists for each communication; several handlers can be active simultaneously, each talking to their respective hosts. Prototype is used to decouple the protocol from the AsynchronousStorage class. The User class decides which protocol to use and then passes an appropriate handler to the AsynchronousStorage object, which uses clones of the prototype to do the actual work.

You cannot use new to implement a "clone" method. The following code won't work:

```
Class Grandparent
{   public Grandparent(Object args){/*...*/}
    Base myClone(){ return new Base(args);}
}
Class Parent
{   public Parent(){   super("arg");}
    Derived myClone(){return new Parent(args)}
}
Class Child
{   public Child(){ super(); }
    /* inherit the superclass myClone */
}
//...
Grandparent g = new Child();
//...
g.myClone(); // Returns a Parent, not Child!
```

Using Java's clone() solves this problem by getting memory from super.clone().

Usage

(Not used)	Prototype is used in the implementations of several classes but not in the external interfaces to any of the Java classes. You do see it in the Bean Box application that demonstrates GUI-style JavaBeans. When you customize an object and put it on the palate, you're creating a prototype. When you drag the customized object from the palate to the dialog box that you're constructing, you're making a copy of the prototype.

Singleton

A class with a constrained number of instances (typically one). The instance is globally accessible.

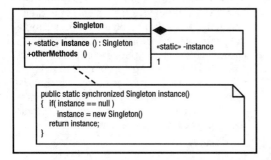

Singleton: The object being created; defines a class-level (`static`) get-instance method that returns the instance. The class-level get-instance method may create the object if necessary.

What Problem Does It Solve?

Programs often have a need for single-instance objects. Objects, for example, may represent a single database, a single company, and so forth.

Pros (✔) and Cons (✘)

✔ Better than a global object in that access is controlled, and the global namespace isn't cluttered with hard-to-find objects.

✔ Singleton guarantees that the object is created (and destroyed) only once—essential when the Singleton manages a global resource such as a database connection.

✘ Easy to abuse. A Singleton called `Globals` that contains nothing but public *variables* is an abomination. (A Singleton containing global *constants* is reasonable if the values of the constants need to be initialized at runtime. If the values are known at compile time, use an interface made up solely of static final fields.)

✘ Another common abuse of Singleton defines a `User` object that contains all the user-interface code. In a properly done OO system, objects must be responsible for building their own user interfaces. Similarly, you should not have a "system" or "main" singleton. The system is the entire program, not a single object. System objects are what Arthur Riel calls *god classes* (in his book *Object-Oriented Design Heuristics*, (Addison-Wesley, 1996). Avoid them.

Often Confused With

Utility: A Utility is a class comprised solely of static methods, the purpose of which is to provide a grab bag of global methods that often compensate for some deficiency in the language or libraries. Examples include Java's `Math` and `Arrays` utilities.

Singleton can be implemented the same way as Utility—as a class made up solely of static methods. That is, when all fields of a class are static, the class is effectively an object: It has state and methods. The main disadvantage to this everything-is-static approach is that you can't change the behavior of a Singleton using derivation.

See Also

Abstract Factory

Implementation Notes and Examples

```
Class Singleton1
{   private static Singleton instance;
    private Singleton1()
    {   Runtime.getRuntime().addShutdownHook
        (   new Thread()
            {   public void run()
                {   /* clean-up code here */
                }
            }
        );
    }
    public static synchronized Singleton instance()
    {   if( instance == null )
            instance = new Singleton();
        return instance;
    }
}
class Singleton2
{   private static final Singleton instance =
                            new Singleton2();
    public  static Singleton instance()
    {   return instance;
    }
    //...
    //Other than creating object in static
    //initializer, is identical to Singleton1
}
class Singleton3
{   static Type allFields;
    static Type allOperations();
    // No instance() method, just use the
    // class name to the left of the dot.
}
```

Use the Singleton1 form when you can't create the object at class-load time (for example, you didn't have information that's determined by program state or is passed to the creation method).

You *must* synchronize the instance() method of Singleton1 as shown. "Clever" ways to eliminate synchronization such as "double-checked locking" don't work. (Period. Don't do it!)

Use the Singleton2 or Singleton3 form when possible; synchronization is not required during access. (The JVM may load the class at any time, but it shouldn't initialize the Class object until first use (Java Language Specification, 12.4.1); static initializers shouldn't execute until first use.

Call addShutdownHook() in the constructor when program-shut-down cleanup activities (such as shutting down database connections in an orderly way) are required. Do not use a finalizer, which may never be called.

A private constructor prevents someone from saying new Singleton(), thereby forcing access through instance().

You have no requirement that only one instance of the Singleton exists, only that the number of instances are constrained and that access to the instances are global. For example, a DatabaseConnection.getInstance() method may return one of a pool of database connections that the Singleton manages.

In UML, the role associated with the Singleton is usually also the class name.

Usage

`Image picture =` `Toolbox.getDefaultToolbox().getImage(url);`	The Toolbox is a classic form of Singleton1 in the "Examples" section. getDefaultToolbox() returns a Toolbox instance appropriate for the operating system detected at runtime.
`Border instance =` `    BorderFactory.createBevelBorder(3);`	Manages several Border instances, but only one instance of a Border object with particular characteristics (in this case, a three-pixel beveled border) will exist, so it's a Singleton. All subsequent requests for a three-pixel beveled border return the same object.
`Class classObject =` `    class.forName("com.holub.tools.MyClass");`	There's only one Class object for a given class, which effectively contains all static members.

[This page intentionally left blank.[2]]

---

2. Here, we have the second reification of the this-page-intentionally-left-blank pattern.

Structural Patterns

The structural patterns concern themselves with the organization of the program. I think of them as static-model patterns. Their intent is always to organize classes so that certain structural ends can be achieved. For example, the purpose of Bridge is to organize two subsystems in such a way that one subsystem can change radically (even be replaced entirely) without affecting the code in the other subsystem. The whole point of this organization is that you can make changes to the program without having to change the dynamic model at all.

Adapter

Make a class appear to support a familiar interface that it doesn't actually support. This way, existing code can leverage new, unfamiliar classes as if they are existing, familiar classes, eliminating the need to refactor the existing code to accommodate the new classes.

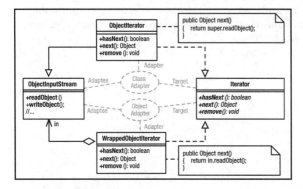

Adaptee: An object that doesn't support the desired interface

Target: The interface you want the Adaptee to support.

Adapter: The class that makes the Adaptee appear to support the Target interface. Class Adapters use derivation. Object Adapters use containment.

What Problem Does It Solve?

1. A library that you're using just isn't working out, and you need either to rewrite it or to buy a replacement from a third party and slot this replacement into your existing code, making as few changes as possible.

2. You may need to refactor a class to have a different interface than the original version (you need to add arguments to a method or change an argument or return-value type). You could have both old-style and new-style versions of the methods in one giant class, but it's better to have a single, simpler class (the new one) and use Adapter to make the new object appear to be one of the old ones to existing code.

3. Use an Adapter to make an old-style object serialized to disk appear to be a new-style object when loaded.

Pros (✔) and Cons (✖)

✔ Makes it easy to add classes without changing code.

✖ Identical looking Object and Class Adapters behave in different ways. For example, new ObjectAdapter(obj) and new ClassAdapter(obj) are both supported; the Object Adapter simply wraps obj, but the Class Adapter copies the fields of obj into its superclass component. Copying is expensive. On the plus side, a Class Adapter *is* an Adaptee, so it can be passed to methods expecting an object of the Adaptee class and also to methods that expect the Target interface. It's difficult to decide whether

an Object or Class Adapter is best. It's a maintenance problem to have both.

✖ Difficult to implement when the library is designed poorly. For example, java.io.InputStream is an abstract class, not an interface, so you can't use the Class-Adapter pattern to create a RandomAccessFile that also supports the InputStream interface (you can't extend both RandomAccessFile and InputStream). You *can* use Object Adapter, or you can refactor the code to make InputStream an interface (as it should have been) and then implement that interface in an AbstractInputStream that has all the functionality now in InputStream. Collections do it correctly.

Often Confused With

Mediator: Mediator is the dynamic-model equivalent of Adaptor. Adapters are passive, passing messages to single Adaptees. Mediators interact with many colleagues in complex ways.

Bridge: Adapters change interfaces. Bridges isolate subsystems. Adapters are little things; Bridges are big.

Decorator: The encapsulated object in Decorator has the same interface as the container. Decorator modifies the behavior of some method or adds methods, but otherwise looks exactly like the wrapped object. Object Adapters have different interfaces than the wrapped object and don't change its behavior.

See Also

Mediator, Bridge, Decorator

Implementation Notes and Example

```
class ObjectIterator extends ObjectInputStream
                implements Iterator
{   private boolean atEndOfFile = false;
    public ObjectIterator(InputStream src)
                    throws IOException
    {   super(src);
    }
    public boolean hasNext()
    {   return atEndOfFile == false;
    }
    public Object next()
    {   try
        {   return readObject();
        }
        catch( Exception e )
        {   atEndOfFile = true;
            return null;
        }
    }
    public void remove()
    {   throw new UnsupportedOperationException();
    }
}
class WrappedObjectIterator  implements Iterator
{   private boolean atEndOfFile = false;
    private final ObjectInputStream in;
    public
    WrappedObjectIterator(ObjectInputStream in)
    {   this.in = in;
    }
    public boolean hasNext()
    {   return atEndOfFile == false;
    }
    public Object next()
    {   try
        {   return in.readObject();
        }
        catch(Exception e){/* as above */}
    }
    public void remove()
    {   throw new UnsupportedOperationException();
    }
}
```

ObjectIterator is a Class Adapter that adapts an ObjectInputStream to implement the Iterator interface. This way, you can use existing methods that examine a set of objects by using an Iterator to examine objects directly from a file. The client doesn't know or care whether it's reading from a file or traversing a Collection of some sort. This flexibility can be useful when you're implementing an Object cache that can overflow to disk, for example. More to the point, you don't need to write two versions of the object-reader method, one for files and one for collections.

WrappedObjectIterator is an Object Adapter version of ObjectIterator that uses containment rather than inheritance.

The Class Adapter, since it *is* an Object-InputStream that implements Iterator, can be used by any method that knows how to use either ObjectInputStream or Iterator. The Object Adapter, since it encapsulates the input stream, cannot be used as an ObjectInput-Stream, but you can use the input stream for a while, temporarily wrap it in a WrappedObject-Iterator to extract a few objects, and then pull the input stream out again.

The two implementations require about the same amount of work so it's a judgment call which one is best. It all depends on what you're using it to do.

Usage

```
InputStream in = new StringInputStream("hello");
```

Adapter lets you access a String as if it were a file (InputStream). Similar adapters include ByteArrayInputStream, CharArrayReader, PipedInput-Stream, PipedReader, and StringReader. Don't confuse these adapters with the Decorators in *java.io* (BufferedInputStream, PushbackInputStream, and so on).

Bridge

To decouple subsystems so that either subsystem can change radically without impacting any code in the other one, put a set of interfaces between two subsystems and code to these interfaces.

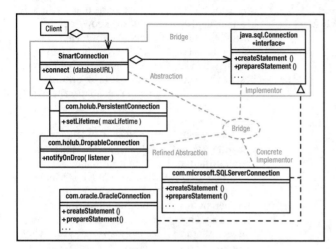

Abstraction: A subsystem-independent portal into subsystem-specific code.

Implementor: An interface used by the Abstraction to talk to a subsystem-specific implementation. Typically is also the Abstract Product of an Abstract Factory.

Refined Abstraction: Often omitted, a version of the Abstraction, customized for a particular application.

Concrete Implementor: A subsystem-specific implementation of the Implementor.

What Problem Does It Solve?

Often used to achieve platform independence. Application-specific code on one side of the bridge uses platform-dependant code on the other side. Reimplement that interface, and the "business" logic doesn't know or care. Change the business logic, and the platform-specific interface implementations don't care. Often, you'll combine Bridge and Abstract Factory so that the Factory can supply the correct set of implementers at runtime, further isolating the two sides of the bridge. Examples of Bridge in Java are AWT and JDBC.

Pros (✔) and Cons (✖)

✔ In a pure inheritance model, you'd have a superclass that implemented some behavior and subclasses that customized this behavior for a specific platform. In Bridge, the superclass is effectively replaced by an interface, so the problems associated with implementation inheritance are minimized, and the total number of classes are reduced.

✖ It's difficult to implement interfaces so that each implementation behaves identically. Java's AWT Bridge implements windowing components for different operating environments, but the Motif implementation behaved differently on the screen than the Windows implementation.

Often Confused With

Bridge is more of an architecture than a design pattern. A Bridge is often a *set* of interfaces and classes (called *abstractions*, unfortunately— they're typically not abstract) that contain references to objects that implement a platform-independent interface in a platform-dependant way (Adapters). The Adapters are typically created by the Abstraction object using a Singleton-based Abstract Factory.

Adapter: Bridges separate subsystems, and Adapters make objects implement foreign interfaces. A one-interface bridge looks like a Class Adapter, however.

Facade: Facade simplifies the interface to a subsystem but may not isolate you from the details of how that subsystem works. Changes made on one side of the facade might mandate changes both to the other side of the facade and to the facade itself.

See Also

Abstract Factory, Singleton, Adapter, Facade, Mediator

Implementation Notes and Example

```
class SmartConnection
{   String username, password;
    java.sql.Connection connection;
    //...
    public void connect(String databaseURL)
                                throws Exception
    {   Class.forName( databaseURL ).newInstance();

        Connection connection = null;
        Statement  statement  = null;
        //...
        connection =
            DriverManager.getConnection(
                databaseURL, username, password );
    }
}

class PersistentConnection extends SmartConnection
{   long maxLifetime;
    public void setLifetime(long maxLifetime)
    {   // Arrange for connection to time
        // out after lifetime expires.
    }
}

class PooledConnection extends SmartConnection
{   public void notifyOnDrop(Runnable dropped)
        {   // Arange to call dropped.run()
            // when connection is dropped.
        }
}

//-----------------------------------------

class SQLServerConnection
            implements java.sql.Connection
{   // Implementation that support SQL Server
    // interface.
}

class OracleConnection implements
java.sql.Connection
{   // Implemenation that supports Oracle's
interface.
}
```

The abstraction classes (SmartConnection, PersistentConnection, and DropableConnection) use the Bridge interface (*java.sql.Connection*) to talk to the implementation classes (OracleConnection, SQLServerConnection).

The two sides of the Bridge can change independently. For example, I can change OracleConnection radically, and the classes on the other side of the Bridge (SmartConnection, for example) are completely unaware of that change. This isolation is possible because Factory is used to create the Concrete Implementers.

I can even support additional databases (by extending java.sql.Connection) without affecting the other side of the Bridge. By the same token, I can modify the SmartConnection class (and its subclasses) and even add additional subclasses, without impacting the other side of the bridge (the java.sql.Connection implementers).

Note that the Bridge completely isolates the subsystems from each other. The Client class knows only about the abstraction classes.

A Bridge is often very large. The JDBC Bridge consists of many Implementor interfaces and associated Concrete Implementations, and some of these interfaces are very large.

Composite

Organize a runtime hierarchy of objects that represent container/content (or whole/part) relationships as a collection of objects that implement a common interface. Some of the implementers of this interface define stand-alone objects, and others define containers that can hold additional objects, including other containers.

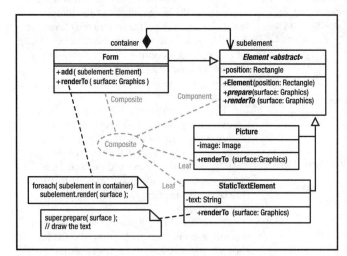

Component: An interface or abstract class that represents all objects in the hierarchy.

Composite: A Component that can hold other Components. It doesn't know whether these subcomponents are other Composites or are Leaves.

Leaf: A Component that stands alone; it cannot contain anything.

What Problem Does It Solve?

Often data structures can be organized into hierarchies in which everything in the hierarchy has a common subset of similar properties. For example, directories are files that can contain other files; a file can be atomic (a simple file not containing anything) or a subdirectory (a file that holds references to other files, including subdirectories). Composite lets you create these sort of containment hierarchies in such a way that a given container doesn't need to know whether its contents are atomic or composite objects. They both implement the same interface, so can be treated identically.

Pros (✔) and Cons (✖)

✔ The container is simple to implement because it treats all contents uniformly.

✔ It's easy to add new Component classes, just derive another class from the Component class (or interface).

✖ The Component tends to specify an unsatisfactory least-common-denominator interface.

✖ It's not always meaningful or appropriate for every Composite or Leaf to implement every method of the Component. It's an awkward runtime error if an unimplementable method throws an exception.

Often Confused With

Chain of Responsibility: Chain of Responsibility is also implemented using a runtime hierarchy of objects, but the point of Chain of Responsibility is to catch messages in appropriate places.

Decorator: Decorator also uses a containment strategy, but Decorators add or modify functionality of a single containee. The point of Composite is to make it easier to manipulate a *set* of contained objects.

See Also

Chain of Responsibility, Decorator, Flyweight

Implementation Notes and Example

```java
abstract class Element
{   private Rectangle position;
    public Element(Rectangle position)
    {   this.position = position;
    }
    protected void prepare(Graphics surface)
    {   // modify the surface's coordinate
        // system so that (0,0) is at the
        // current Element's position.
    }
    public abstract void renderTo(Graphics surface);
}

class Form extends Element
{   private Collection subelements
                    = new ArrayList();
    public Form( Rectangle position )
    {   super(position);
    }
    public void add(Element subelement)
    {   subelements.add( subelement );
    }
    public void renderTo(Graphics surface)
    {   prepare(surface);
        Iterator i = subelements.iterator();
        while( i.hasNext() )
            ((Element)i.next()).render(surface);
    }
}
class StaticText extends Element
{   private String text;
    public StaticText(Rectangle position,
                                String text)
    {   super(position);
        this.text = text;
    }
    public void renderTo(Graphics surface)
    {   prepare(surface);
        surface.drawText(text);
    }
}
```

Element, is an abstract class that defines operations common to all Element objects (for example, the Element's relative position on the form). I've avoided making this information public (thereby damaging the integrity of the object) by providing a prepare() method that modifies the coordinate system of the Graphics object so that the current object can render itself in the upper-left corner of the surface. This way a getPosition() method is unnecessary, and the resulting class system is more robust.

The Form class has the role of Composite in the pattern. It's an Element that holds other Elements, some of which may be Forms and some of may might be StaticText. The point is that the Form class's render() method doesn't know or care about the actual type of the subelement. The subelements may be Elements, or they may be sub-Forms. All subelements are rendered identically (by passing them render() messages).

The StaticText class is a Leaf. It is an Element that doesn't contain other Elements and thus forms a leaf on the runtime-hierarchy tree. It has to know how to render itself, of course. Here, it just delegates to the Surface object.

Usage

```java
Dialog box = new Dialog();
box.add( new Label("Lots of information") );

Panel  subpanel = new Panel();
subpanel.add( new Label("Description") );
subpanel.add( new TextField() );
box.add( subpanel );
```

A Dialog is a Composite that can hold Leaves (such as Label) and other Composites (such as Panel). This example also nicely demonstrates the affinity between Composite and Bridge, since AWT is also a bridge. (A DialogFrame, for example, is simultaneously a Composite in Composite and an Abstraction in Bridge.

Another good example of Composite is the new JDOM classes (http://www.jdom.org). An XML document is a list of Elements.

Decorator

Attach new responsibilities to (or modify the behavior of) an *object* at runtime. Decorators can simplify class hierarchies by replacing subclassing with containment.

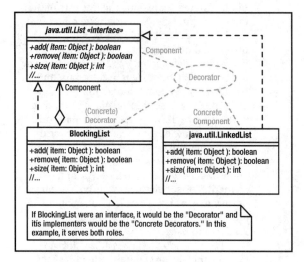

Component: An interface for objects that can have responsibilities added to them (or have behavior modified) at runtime.

Concrete Component: An object to which additional responsibilities or new behavior is attached.

Decorator: Wraps a Component and defines an interface that conforms to the Component's interface but behaves differently.

Concrete Decorator: Extends the Decorator to define the additional behavior.

What Problem Does It Solve?

Using derivation hierarchies to add features is not a great idea. Consider an input stream. To add buffering, you'd derive a class that overrode the input() method to do buffering (doubling the number of classes). To add pushback, you'd have to derive from both classes, providing buffered and nonbuffered versions of input() that pushed characters back. In fact, every feature that you add through subclassing will require you to double the size of the class hierarchy. Decorator, on the other hand, is linear. To add a feature, you add exactly one Decorator class, no matter what the size of the original hierarchy.

Decorator also nicely solves the problem of runtime configuration. Sometimes, you don't know exactly how an object should behave until runtime. Behavior may be specified in a configuration file, for example. Decorator allows you to assemble (at runtime) a composite object that contains exactly the mix of capabilities you need without having to know which of these capabilities will be needed when you write the code.

Decorator helps you break up large complex operations into small simple operations.

Pros (✔) and Cons (✖)

✔ The size and complexity of the class hierarchy is considerably reduced.

✖ A feature introduced in a Decorator (such as pushback) is at best hard (or even dangerous) to access if the decorator is itself decorated. The system is sensitive to the order in which Decorators are applied. Java's PushbackInput-Stream works well at the outermost layer, but a PushbackInputStream wrapped with a BufferedInputStream doesn't work. (It doesn't push back into the buffer.)

Often Confused With

Adapter: Changes an interface; Decorator changes behavior.

Chain of Responsibility: Passes messages to the most appropriate handler. In Decorator, messages are handled by the outermost Concrete Decorator.

Composite: Decorators add responsibilities. Composites never do.

See Also

Strategy

Implementation Notes and Example

```
import java.util.*;

/* I would prefer for this class to be a LinkedList,
 * but LinkedList is not an interface, and
 * useful methods like addFirst() and removeFirst()
 * are not defined in an interface.
 */

public class BlockingList implements List
{   private final List component;

    public BlockingList( List component )
    {   this.component = component;
    }

    private boolean noLongerEmpty()
    {   try
        {   while( component.size() == 0 )
                wait();
            return true;
        }
        catch( InterruptedException e )
        {   return false;
        }
    }

    synchronized public boolean add(Object o)
    {   boolean toReturn = component.add(o);
        notifyAll();
        return toReturn;
    }

    synchronized public boolean remove(Object o)
    {   if( noLongerEmpty() )
            return component.remove(o);
        return false;
    }

    public int size()
    {   return component.size();
    }

    /* Syncrhonized versions of all other methods of
     * the List interface are implemented here ...
     */
}
```

Think fish. Bigger fish are Decorators that implement the same interfaces as the smallest fish (the Component). If a smaller fish has swallowed a hook and line, talk to it by yanking the string.

BlockingList is a Decorator that modifies the behavior of any List imple- mentation so that a thread that tries to remove something from an empty list will block (be suspended) until some other thread adds something to the list—a common interthread communication architecture. Use a BlockingList to add this behavior to any class of objects that implement the List interface. Create a blocking list like this:

```
List blockingList =
    new BlockingList(
        new LinkedList() );
```

Many methods (such as size() and contains()) behave exactly as they do in the List, so they are implemented as simple pass- through methods. Other methods (such as add() and remove()) implement different behavior, so must be implemented at length in the Concrete Decorator.

The behavior of every method in the blocking version at left has changed, however: Everything is now synchronized. If only a hand- ful of methods change behavior (or a Decorator just adds a method), simplify implementation with an abstract Decorator class that does nothing but define simple pass-through methods to the contained object. Extend the abstract class to form a Concrete Decorator, overriding those methods whose behavior changes.

Other Decorators may add other features. A LazyList may add a close() method that allows subsequent removals from the list but disallows additions, for example.

Usage

`JComponent widget = new JtextArea(80,200);`
`widget = new JScrollPane(widget);`
`Jframe frame  = new JFrame();`
`Frame.getContentPane().add( widget );`
	Combines *Decorator* and *Composite: Composite* because everything's a JComponent; *Decorator* because each successive layer adds functionality (and changes appearance).

`InputStream in = new FileInputStream("x.txt");`
`in = new BufferedInputStream( in );`
`in = new PushBackInputStream( in );`
	The data source is wrapped by a Decorator that adds buffering, which is in turn wrapped by a decorator that supports pushback. Could add decompression, and so on, with additional decorators (GzipInputStream, and so on).

Facade

Provide a single interface through which all the classes in a complex subsystem are manipulated. Facade allows you to treat a complex subsystem as if it were a single course-grained object with a simple easy-to-use interface.

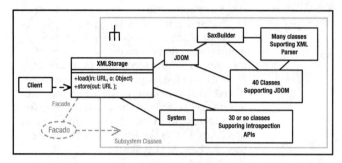

Facade: Provides a simple interface to a complex subsystem.

Subsystem Classes: Classes that comprise one or more complex subsystems.

What Problem Does It Solve?

Facade simplifies complex code, making it easier to use poorly designed, overcomplex subsystems.

Subsystems, especially older ones, are masses of spaghetti code. When two subsystems must interact, they often make calls directly into each other, and these myriad tendrils of connectivity are a maintenance nightmare. The subsystems become very delicate since making seemingly insignificant changes in a single subsystem can affect the entire program. Facade addresses the problem by forcing programmers to use a subsystem indirectly through a well-defined single point of access, thereby shielding the programmers from the complexity of the code on the other side of the facade.

Facade improves the independence of the subsystems, making it easy to change—or even replace—them without impacting outside code.

Facade also provides a manageable way to migrate legacy code to a more object-oriented structure. Start by breaking up the existing code into a small number of independent subsystems, modeled as very heavyweight objects with well-defined, simple interfaces. Eliminate all "end runs" around these interfaces. Then systematically replace each subsystem. This evolutionary approach significantly reduces the risk inherent in an all-at-once rewrite.

Facade hides badly done, overly complex legacy code.

Facade lets you treat an entire legacy system as if it were a single, coarse-grained object.

Pros (✔) and Cons (✖)

✔ Coupling relationships between subsystems are weakened, improving maintenance and flexibility.

✖ It's still possible for programmers to ignore the Facade and use subsystem classes directly.

Often Confused With

Bridge: Both Facade and Bridge help maintenance by isolating subsystems from each other. Facade simplifies access to, but does not hide, a subsystem. Bridge completely isolates you from the subsystem—you don't know that the subsystem exists if you use Bridge. You can use a Facade is to simplify access to a bridge. (For example, a Company class could act as a facade to the JDBC Bridge. You'd say Company.getEmployee() and the Facade takes care of the complex series of JDBC calls needed to create the Employee object.)

Mediator: A Facade's communication with a subsystem is unidirectional, or at least simple. Your program sends a message to the Facade, which causes it to send several messages to a subsystem. The subsystem does not talk to, or even know about, the Facade object. Mediators have complex bidirectional conversations with their Colleagues.

See Also

Bridge, Mediator, Observer

Implementation Notes and Example

```
class XMLStorage
{   public store(URL out, Object toStore)
    {  /* Code goes here that uses the
       *  introspection APIs in the System
       *  class to get the class name and the
       *  values of all the public fields in
       *  the class. The name and the values of
       *  those fields are then used to build a
       *  JDOM tree, which is passed to an
       *  "outputter" to send an XML
       *  representation of the tree to the
       *  OutputStream.
       */
    }

    public Object load(URL in);
    {  /* Code goes here that creates a
       *  JDOM SaxBuilder for the InputStream,
       *  uses it to build a JDOM, instantiates
       *  a class named in the XML file,
       *  then initializes that class using
       *  one of the constructors or a series
       *  of get/set methods.
       */
    }
}
```

The problem with providing a full-blown example of a Facade is that there's entirely too much code to represent in 40 or so lines—that's the whole point of the pattern.

I'm imagining that the storage method uses Java's introspection APIs to analyze the document and discover the fields to save. (It could just save everything that's public, or it could look for JavaBean-style get/set methods.) I would use the JDOM XML APIs to build a tree representation of an XML output file and then send the tree to a JDOM "outputter" class that would write the appropriate XML to a file. The loading function reverses this process. By using the facade, you isolate yourself from all the mechanics of introspection, XML parsing, and JDOM.

Messaging is one way; there is no complex back-and-forth interaction between the XMLStorage facade and the subsystems that it uses. The Facade object simply builds a tree and then outputs the tree.

We have a facade within a facade here. The SAXBuilder class itself comprises a facade that isolates you from the mechanics of the SAX-parser subsystem.

The program can access the JDOM, XML, and Introspection APIs directly. Ease of maintenance is compromised if you do so and any of these subsystems change. You could avoid this problem by putting the subsystems in an inaccessible package (such as the *com.sun.xxx* packages in Java). A Singleton can then be used to get a Facade, through which all access occurs.

Usage

`SomeString.matches("^[a-zA-Z]{1,3}$");`	String acts as a Facade for the regular-expression-matching package, isolating the user from things such as Pattern objects.
`Socket s = new Socket("holub.com",7);` `InputStream in = s.getInputStream();`	These two lines hide several pages of C code and all the enormous complexity needed to get a socket to work in a cross-platform way.
`AppletContext a = getAppletContext();` `a.showDocument("http://www.holub.com/index.html")`	AppletContext is a Facade for the browser subsystem. Note that this architecture prohibits "end runs" around the facade because subsystem classes are accessible only through the Facade. You can't get at them directly.

Flyweight

To minimize memory usage, make objects smaller by using *extrinsic* state (for example, putting state information into a container or computing it on each access) and *sharing* (using multiple references to single objects rather than multiple copies of objects).

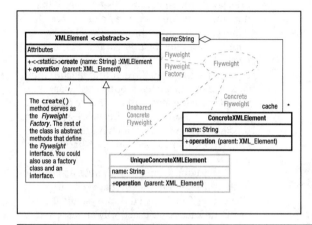

Flyweight: Defines an interface for messages that use extrinsic state.

Concrete Flyweight: Implements Flyweight with methods that compute state information or get it from an external source (extrinsic state).

Unshared Concrete Flyweight: Not used here, but if present, implements Flyweight using internal state variables rather than extrinsic state.

Flyweight Factory: Creates and manages flyweights. Supplies an existing Concrete Flyweight if one exists; otherwise creates one.

What Problem Does It Solve?

An object is defined by *what* it does, not how it does it. Objects are defined by their methods; state information can be inside or outside the object.

Sometimes, programs with large numbers of objects require more memory for those objects than is available. In a document editor, every character of a naïve implementation might hold its value, font, color, size, encoding, position on the page, and so on. This information, duplicated in most characters, can be moved to a containing paragraph. If characters take up more space than references, keep multiple references to a single "character" object rather than many identical characters.

A naïve implementation of the Game of Life "cell" may carry a Boolean "is-alive" state and references to eight neighbors. A small 1024×1024 grid requires about 40MB just to hold the cells. In a Flyweight version, the cell's container knows who the cell's neighbors are and passes that information to the cell. The cell needs to remember its is-alive state only. By making the neighbor references *extrinsic*, you reduce the memory requirement for the basic grid to a single megabyte.

In a "flyweight pool," all objects with the same state are represented by a single object. You request objects from the pool, which returns an existing object if possible; otherwise, the pool creates a new object.

Pros (✔) and Cons (✘)

✔ Some programs simply cannot be written in an object-oriented way without using Flyweight.

✔ When you use flyweight pools, you can determine equality using Java's == operator.

✘ If extrinsic state is stored in a container, then you must access the object through the container. If extrinsic state is computed (for example, goes to a database every time a particular attribute is used), then access is slow.

✘ Flyweights add complexity to the code, impacting maintenance and increasing code size.

Often Confused With

Composite: Flyweights are often combined with Composite. Both Leaf and Component nodes can export extrinsic state to their containers.

See Also

Composite, Prototype, Singleton

Implementation Notes and Example

```
abstract class XMLElement
{   static Map cache = new HashMap();
    public static
    XMLElement create(String name)
    {   name = name.intern();
        XMLElement exists =
                (XMLElement)(cache.get(name));
        if( exists == null )
        {   exists =
                new ConcreteXMLElement(name);
            cache.put(name,exists);
        }
        return exists;
    }
    private XMLElement(){}

    abstract void operation( XMLElement parent );

    private static class ConcreteXMLElement
                            extends XMLElement
    {   private String name;
        ConcreteXMLElement(String name)
        {   this.name = name.intern();
        }
        void operation(XMLElement parent)
        {   //...
        }
        public int hashCode()
        {   return name.hashCode();
        }
        public boolean equals( Object o )
        {   return name ==
                ((ConcreteXMLElement)o).name ;
        }
    }
}
```

XMLElement is a Flyweight that represents an Element in an XML Document (effectively a node in a tree). The element is identified only by name, though a more realistic implementation would identify it both by name and attribute values.

Sharing is used to guarantee that only one instance of a given element exists. (You could argue reasonably that XMLElement is a Singleton; that is, sharing is implemented using Singleton.) The private constructor (and the fact that it's abstract) force users to use create() rather than new XMLElement(). The create() method keeps a cache of XMLElement objects, keyed by name. If an object with the requested name exists, it is just returned. The create() method adds an element to the cache only if an element with that name does not already exist. If the Element doesn't need to know its own name, its name field can be eliminated to save space.

Don't be confused by the fact that XMLElement fills two roles in the pattern: Flyweight Factory and Flyweight. Putting the abstract methods of XMLElement into an interface to separating them from the "factory" functionality makes sense in many situations. Here, it just adds an unnecessary class.

The intern() method of the String class enforces sharing in a similar way (see "Usage").

XMLElement also has one extrinsic attribute: its parent. A heavyweight implementation may keep a parent reference as a field, but here the parent reference is passed as an argument to operation(). This organization saves space, but means that operations on elements that need to know their parent must be started at the root node so that the parent reference can be passed down to them.

Usage

`JPanel p = new JPanel();`
`p.setBorder(`
`   BorderFactory.createEmptyBorder(5,5,5,5) );`
	The border size is extrinsic—it's fetched at runtime from the Component that it borders. The BorderFactory makes sure that two borders with the same internal state don't exist (when you ask for the second one, you get back a reference to the first one).

`StringBuffer b = new StringBuffer();`
`//...    assemble string here.`
`String s = b.toString().intern();`
	If an existing String literal has the same value as the assembled StringBuffer, then use the existing literal; otherwise, add the new value to the JVM's internal table of String literals and use the new one.

Proxy

Access an object through a "surrogate or placeholder" object.

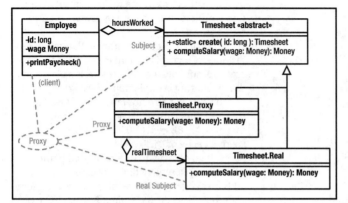

Proxy: Maintains a reference, and controls access, to the Real Subject. Implements the same interface as the Real Subject so it can be used in place of the Real Subject.

Subject: An interface implemented by both the Proxy and the Real Subject; allows them to be used interchangeably.

Real Subject: The real object that the Proxy represents.

What Problem Does It Solve?

A *virtual proxy* creates expensive objects on demand. For example, database access may be deferred by a proxy until the data is actually used. A large image may be fetched across the network in the background while the user of the image thinks it's already there. This process is often called *lazy instantiation*. Virtual proxies are also useful in implementing a *copy-on-write* strategy. When you request a copy of an object, you get back a proxy that simply references the original object. Only when you modify the so-called copy does the proxy actually copy the state from the original object into itself.

A *remote proxy* is a client-side representation of a server-side object. The proxy relays requests across the network to be handled by a sever-side object. CORBA and RMI stubs are proxies for server-side skeleton objects.

A *protection proxy* controls access to certain methods of a second object that implements the same interface. The proxy method may be passed an authentication token and throw an exception if the token didn't authorize the requested operation. For example: the `Collection` implementation returned from `Collections.unmodifiableCollection(…)` is a protection proxy.

A *smart reference* automatically handles annoying background tasks such as deletion. Java's `WeakReference` is an example.

Pros (✔) and Cons (✖)

✔ Proxies hide many optimizations from their users, simplifying the code considerably.

✖ Once the real object has been created, access through the proxy adds overhead. The whole point of the pattern is to be able to treat the proxy as if it were the real object, so a method such as `getRealObject()` violates the spirit of the pattern.

✖ You may need to use many remote proxies to talk to a large subsystem. It's better to create a single remote proxy for a Facade than it is to create proxies for every class in the subsystem.

Often Confused With

Decorator: A protection proxy in particular could be looked at as a Decorator. There's no difference in structure, but the intent is different—Decorator allows undecorated objects to be accessed indiscriminately.

See Also

Decorator, Flyweight

Implementation Notes and Example

```
class Employee
{   private long      id;
    private Money     wage; // hourly wage
    private Timesheet hoursWorked;
    public Employee(long id)
    {   this.id     = id;
        hoursWorked = Timesheet.create(id);
        wage        = Database.getHourlyWage(id);
    }
    void printPaycheck()
    {   Money weeklyWage =
              hoursWorked.computeSalary(wage);
        //...
    }
}
abstract class Timesheet
{   //...
    public static Timesheet create(long id)
    {   return ( dataAlreadyInMemory )
                    ? new Real(id)
                    : new Proxy(id);
    }
    public abstract Money computeSalary(Money wage);
    //---------------------------------------
    private static class Proxy extends Timesheet
    {   Timesheet realTimesheet = null;
        long      id;
        Proxy(long id){this.id = id;}
        public Money computeSalary(Money wage)
        {   if( realTimesheet == null )
                realTimesheet = new Real(id);
            return realTimesheet.
                        computeSalary(wage);
        }
    }
    //---------------------------------------
    private static class Real extends Timesheet
    {   Real(long employeeId)
        {   // load data from the database.
        }
        public Money computeSalary(Money wage)
        {   // Compute weekly salary.
            return null;
        }
    }
}
```

Assume that hourly wage is used heavily enough to justify a database access when the object is created but that the total hours worked is used only rarely and the Timesheet is needed by only a few methods.

I've made the employee identifier a long to simplify the example. In real code, it would be an instance of class Identity.

You could reasonably argue that that the Employee should just use lazy loading for the Timesheet and dispense with the Proxy object, but the more that Timesheet was used, the less weight this argument would hold.

I've made Timesheet an abstract class rather than an interface so that I can use it as a factory; otherwise, I'd need a separate TimesheetFactory class.

Accessor methods (get and set functions) are evil because they expose implementation detail and impact maintenance. Though it's tempting to use them in this pattern, you'll note that no getSalary() or getHoursWorked() method is needed because of the way I've structured the messaging system. Don't ask for information you need to do the work; ask the object that has the information to do the work for you. One exception to the get/set-is-evil rule is Database.getHourlyWage(). A database is fundamentally non-object-oriented; it's just a bag of data with no operations at all. Consequently, it must be accessed procedurally.

If the Timesheet.Proxy threw away the data after computing the salary, it would be a Flyweight, not a Proxy.

Usage

```
public void paint(Graphics g)
{   Image img=Toolkit.getDefaulToolkit().getImage(
        new URL("http://www.holub.com/image.jpg"));
    g.drawImage(img,...);
}
```

The object returned from getImage() is a proxy for the real image, which is loaded on a background thread. (getImage() is *asynchronous*; it returns immediately, before completing the requested work.) You can use the image as if all bits had been loaded, even when they haven't.

[This page intentionally left blank]

Behavioral Patterns

The behavioral patterns concern themselves with the runtime behavior of the program. I think of them as dynamic-model patterns. They define the roles that *objects* take on and the way that these objects interact with each other. For example, Chain of Responsibly defines the way that a set of objects routes messages to each other at runtime (so that the object best suited to field a message actually handles the message). All these objects are instances of the same class (or at least implement the same interface), so there's not much in the way of structure in Chain of Responsibility. It's the dynamic behavior of the objects that are important.

Chain of Responsibility

A set of objects relay a message from one to another along a well-defined route, giving more than one object a chance to handle the message. The object that's best suited to field a given message actually does the handling. It's possible for more than one object on the route to act on the message.

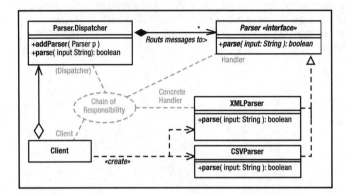

Handler: Defines event-handling interface and optional successor link.

Concrete Handler: Handles request or, by doing nothing, causes event to be forwarded to successor.

Dispatcher (not a Gang-of-Four role): Routes the event to each handler in turn. Not required if Handlers are organized as a linked list.

What Problem Does It Solve?

Makes it easy to add new customized message handling at runtime. An "event" or a message can be passed to a sequence of handlers, and the one that is best suited to handle the message actually does so.

In Microsoft Windows, every button, frame, and so on, is a Window object, arranged using the Composite pattern. *Events* (messages created by a user action) are passed to the window that has the focus (typically a button or other *widget*), and if that window can't handle the message, it passes it to its parent window (typically a frame window or a menu bar). The Window that understands the message actually handles it.

Servlet "filters" are another use of the pattern. An incoming HTTP packet is passed through a sequence of filters, which can process the packet directly or pass the packet to the next filter in the chain (or both).

Also consider a system of subclasses in which each constructor parses from a String the information of interest to it, and then it passes the String to the superclass constructor.

Pros (✔) and Cons (✖)

✔ The dynamic behavior of the program can be easily changed at runtime by adding new handlers to the chain or changing the ordering of handlers.

✔ The coupling between objects in the program is loosened if an implementation permits Handler classes not to know about each other.

✖ In Windows, when a mouse moves one pixel, the WM_MOUSEMOVE message is first received by the window that has focus, perhaps a text control. This control doesn't know how to handle it, so it passes the message to the containing panel, which passes it to the MDI child window, which passes it to the main frame, which passes it to the menu bar, which passes it to each menu item. None of these objects can handle the message, so it's discarded. This is a lot of work to do nothing.

✖ Many reifications force you to use implementation inheritance to specify a message handler, inappropriately forcing strong coupling between Handler classes and introducing fragile base classes into the model.

Often Confused With

Composite: Composite specifies one way that a Chain of Responsibility may be ordered (from contained object to container, recursively). This is not the only way to order the chain, however.

See Also

Composite, Observer

Implementation Notes and Example

```
interface Parser
{   boolean parse( String input );
    static class Dispatcher
    {   private List parsers = new LinkedList();
        public void addParser( Parser p )
        {   parsers.add( p );
        }
        public boolean parse( String input )
        {   for( Iterator i=parsers.Iterator();
                            i.hasNext(); )
            { Parser p = (Parser)( i.next() );
                    if( p.parse( input ) )
                        return true;
            }
            return false;
        }
    }
}
class XMLParser implements Parser
{   private static Pattern scanner =
                Pattern.compile("^\\s*<");
    public boolean parse( String input )
    {   Matcher regex = scanner.matcher(input);
        if( !regex.lookingAt() )
            return false;
        // Parse the XML file here.
        return true;
    }
}
class CSVParser implements Parser
{   private static Pattern scanner =
            Pattern.compile(
            "([a-zA-Z0-9]*,)*[a-zA-Z0-9]+");
    public boolean parse( String input )
    {   Matcher regex = scanner.matcher(input);
        if( !regex.matches() )
            return false;
        // Parse a comma-separated-value string
        return true;
    }
}
```

Create a parser for a particular input format by implementing the Parser interface. The two versions at left (XMLParser and CVSParser) handle XML and comma-separated-value formats. The parse(…) method examines the input, and if it recognizes the input format, it parsers it and returns true; otherwise, parse(…) returns false. The Parser.Dispatcher() object just keeps a list of Parser implementations and passes the messages to them one at a time until it finds one that can handle the input string.

Parse an input string like this:

```
Parser.Dispatcher dispatcher =
            new Parser.Dispatcher();
dispatcher.addParser( new XMLParser() );
dispatcher.addParser( new CSVParser() );
//…
if( !dispatcher.parse( inputString ) )
    System.err.println("Can't parse input");
```

The Gang-of-Four reification does not have an object in the Dispatcher role. (The term dispatcher is mine.) In the Gang-of-Four reification, the Concrete Handler objects form a simple linked list, the input is passed to the first handler in the list, and any handler that can't process the input just delegates to the next handler in the list.

Usage

```
public class MyFilter
        implements javax.servlet.Filter
{ //...
    public void doFilter(ServletRequest req,
                    ServletResponse rsp,
                    FilterChain chain)
    { //...
        chain.doFilter(request, response );
        //...
    }
}
```

Each object on the route typically keeps a reference to its successor, but the pattern doesn't mandate this organization. For example, a centralized dispatcher may pass a message to several objects in turn. What's important is that the object, not the dispatcher, decides whether to handle the message. Servlet filters are dispatched by the web server. Tomcat, for example, uses information that you put into a configuration file to determine the dispatch sequence.

```
class MyWindow extends Component
{ public boolean keyDown(Event e, int key)
    { // code to handle key press goes here.
    }
}
```

Chain-of-Command GUI handling was abandoned as unworkable in version 1.1 of Java (in favor of the better Observer pattern). This deprecated method is a holdover from then.

Command

Encapsulate a request or unit of work into an object. Command provides a more capable alternative to a function pointer because the object can hold state information, can be queued or logged, and so forth.

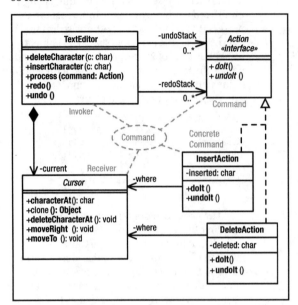

Command: Defines an interface for executing an operation or set of operations.

Concrete Command: Implements the Command interface to perform the operation. Typically acts as an intermediary to a Receiver object.

Invoker: Asks the command to carry out a request.

Receiver: Knows how to carry out the request. This functionality is often built in to the Command object itself.

What Problem Does It Solve?

You can't have a function pointer in an OO system simply because you have no functions, only objects and messages. Instead of passing a pointer to a function that does work, pass a reference to an object that knows how to do that work.

A Command object is effectively a transaction encapsulated in an object. Command objects can be stored for later execution, can be stored as-is to have a transaction record, can be sent to other objects for execution, and so on.

Command is useful for tasks such as "undo" operations. It's not possible to undo an operation simply by rolling the program back to a previous state; the program may have had an effect on the outside world while transitioning from the earlier state to the current one. Command gives you a mechanism for actively rolling back state by actively reversing side effects such as database updates.

By encapsulating the work in an object, you also define several methods, and even state information, that work in concert to do the work. For example, a single object can encapsulate both "undo" and "redo" operations and the state information necessary to perform these operations.

Command also nicely solves "callback" problems in multithreaded systems. A "client" thread creates a Command object that performs some operation and then notifies that client when the operation completes. The client then gives the Command object to a second thread on which the operation is actually performed.

Pros (✔) and Cons (✘)

✔ Command decouples operations from the object that actually performs the operation.

Often Confused With

Strategy: The invoker of a Command doesn't know what the Command object will do. A Strategy object encapsulates a method for doing a specific task for the invoker.

See Also

Memento, Strategy

Implementation Notes and Example

```
abstract class Cursor extends Cloneable
{   public Object clone();
    public char   characterAt();
    public void   deleteCharacterAt();
    public void   insertCharacterAt(
                        char newCharacter);
    public void   moveTo(Cursor newPosition);
    public void   moveRight();
    //...
}
class TextEditor
{   private Cursor current = new Cursor();
    private LinkedList undoStack =
                        new LinkedList();
    private LinkedList redoStack =
                        new LinkedList();
    public void insertCharacter(char c)
    {   process( new Inserter(c) );
    }
    public void deleteCharacter()
    {   process( new Deleter() );
    }
    private void process( Action command )
    {   command.doIt();
        undoStack.addFirst(command);
    }
    public void undo()
    {   Action action =
            (Action) undoStack.removeFirst();
        action.undoIt();
        redoStack.addFirst( action );
    }
    public void redo()
    {   Action action =
            (Action) redoStack.removeFirst();
        action.doIt();
        undoStack.addFirst( action );
    }
    private interface Action
    {   void doIt  ();
        void undoIt();
    }
    private class InsertAction implements Action
    {   Cursor where = (Cursor) current.clone();
        char   inserted;
```

```
        public InsertAction(char newCharacter)
        {   inserted = newCharacter;
        }
        public void doIt()
        {   current.moveTo( where );
            current.
                insertCharacterAt(inserted);
            current.moveRight();
        }
        public void undoIt()
        {   current.moveTo( where );
            current.deleteCharacterAt();
        }
    }
    private class DeleteAction implements Action
    {   Cursor where = (Cursor) current.clone();
        char   deleted;
        public void doIt()
        {   current.moveTo( where );
            deleted = current.characterAt();
            current.deleteCharacterAt();
        }
        public void undoIt()
        {   current.moveTo( where );
            current.insertCharacterAt( deleted );
            current.moveRight();
        }
    }
    //...
}
```

Most of the work is done by the Cursor, which reifies Iterator. The TextEditor is driven by a Client class (not shown) that interprets user input and tells the editor to perform tasks such as inserting or deleting characters. The TextEditor performs these request by creating Command objects that implement the Action interface. Each Action can both do something and also undo whatever it did. The editor tells the Action to do whatever it does and then stacks the object. When asked to undo something, the editor pops the Action off the undo stack, asks it to undo whatever it did, and then puts it on a redo stack. Redo works in a similar way, but in reverse.

Usage

```new Thread()```
 ```{   public void run(){ /*...*/ }```
 ```}.start();```
	Thread is passed a Runnable *Command* object that defines what to do on the thread.

```java.util.Timer t = new java.util.Timer();```
 ```t.schedule(new java.util.TimerTask()```
 ```   { public void run()```
 ```   {System.out.println("hello world");}```
 ```   }, 1000);```
	Print *hello world* one second from now. The TimerTask is a Command object. Several TimerTask objects may be queued for future execution.

Interpreter

Implement an interpreter for a language, first defining a formal *grammar* for that language and then implementing that grammar with a hierarchy of classes (one subclass per *production* or *nonterminal*).

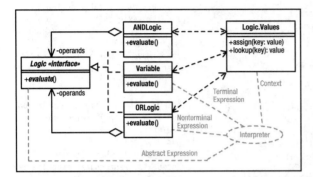

Abstract Expression: Defines an "interpret" operation (or operations). A node in the abstract-syntax tree.

Terminal Expression: Implements an operation for a terminal symbol (which appears in the input).

Nonterminal Expression: Implements an operation for a nonterminal symbol (a grammatical rule).

Context: Global information (for example, variable values).

What Problem Does It Solve?

You sometimes cannot define all the required behavior of a program when you write it. For example, there's no way for the browser writer to predict the way a site designer may want a web page to behave. An interpretive language such as JavaScript can add behavior to the program that wasn't contemplated by the author.

The interpreter pattern defines one way to build an interpreter. You first define a formal *grammar* that lists rules (called *productions*) that describe the syntax of the language. You then implement a class for each production. These classes share a Context object from which they get input, store variable values, and so forth. An interpreter may (or may not) create an efficient output processor (such as a state machine) that does the actual work.

Pros (✔) and Cons (✖)

✖ The pattern says nothing about how to create the graph of objects that comprise the interpreter (the Abstract Syntax Tree). Interpreter often requires a nontrivial parser to construct this graph, and often this parser can just do the interpretation.

✔ Modifying the grammar is relatively straightforward; you just create new classes that represent the new productions.

✖ Interpreter doesn't work well if the grammar has more than a few productions. You need too many classes. Use traditional compiler tools (such as JYACC, CUP, and so on) or a hand-coded recursive-decent parser for nontrivial languages.

✖ Why provide an interpreter when you have a perfectly good one already in memory:

the JVM? Your users write scripts in Java and provide you with a string holding the class name. Use Java's introspection APIs to load and execute the user-supplied code, or, if the user code implements a well-defined interface, then execute directly. Given the following:

```
public interface UserExtension
    {   void doSomething();
    }
```

instantiate and execute a user object like this:

```
String name =
    System.getProperty("user.extension");
class userMods = Class.forname(name);
UserExtension userExtentionObject =
    (UserExtension) userMods.newInstance();
userExtensionObject.doSomething();
```

Write your own class loader and/or security manager to create a sandbox.

Applets demonstrate this technique. Rather than interpret code (à la JavaScript), you provide a class to the browser, which it executes. Applets communicate with the browser via the AppletContext Facade.

Often Confused With

Chain of Responsibility: Chain of Responsibility is used in interpreter to evaluate the input *sentence*. It's Interpreter *only* when the objects implement grammatical rules.

Composite: Interpreter is implemented as a Composite.

See Also

Strategy, Visitor

Implementation Notes and Example

```
interface Logic
{   public static class Values
    {   static Map vars = new HashMap();
        static void assign( String  key,
                                boolean value )
        {   if(key==null || key.length() <= 0)
                throw new Exception("Logic");
            vars.put(key, value? Boolean.TRUE
                            : Boolean.FALSE);
        }
        static boolean lookup( String key )
        {   Object got = vars.get(key);
            return ((Boolean)got).booleanValue();
        }
    }
    boolean evaluate();
}


class ANDLogic implements Logic
{   Logic left, right;
    public ANDLogic(Logic left, Logic right)
    {   this.left  = left;
        this.right = right;
    }
    public boolean evaluate()
    {   return left.evaluate()
                && right.evaluate();
    }
}


class ORLogic  implements Logic{/*...*/}
class NOTLogic implements Logic{/*...*/}


class AssignmentLogic implements Logic
{   Logic left, right;
    public AssignmentLogic(Logic l, Logic r)
    {   this.left  = l;
        this.right = r;
    }
    public boolean evaluate()
    {   boolean r = right.evaluate();
        Logic.Values.assign(left.toString(),r);
        return r;
    }
}
class Variable implements Logic
{   private String name;
    public Variable(String s){name = s;}
    public String toString(){ return name; }
    public boolean evaluate()
    { return Logic.Values.lookup(name);
    }
}
```

Consider the following Boolean-expression grammar:

```
e ::=  e  '&'  e
    |  e  '|'  e
    |  '!'  e
    |  '('  e  ')'
    |  var  '='  e
    |  var
```

The code at the left comprises an interpreter for that grammar. (I haven't shown ORLogic and NOTLogic classes, since they're trivial variants on ANDLogic.) Variable values are held in the Values Singleton. Create an interpreter for X=(A & B) | !C as follows:

```
Logic term = new ANDLogic(
                new Variable("A"),
                new Variable("B")
            );
term = new ORLogic(
            term,
            new NOTLogic( new Variable("C") )
        );
term = new AssignmentLogic(
                new Variable("X"), term );
```

Assign values in the code (or by reading user input) like this:

```
Logic.Values.assign("A", true);
Logic.Values.assign("B", true);
Logic.Values.assign("C", false);
boolean result = term.evaluate();
```

The Interpreter pattern makes no suggestions as to *how* you may construct the abstract-syntax tree that represents the expression (the tree of Logic objects), but some sort of parser is implied.

Alternatively, you could use Visitor to traverse the syntax tree: Visit the notes in depth-first order; code in the visitor object determines what happens as it visits each node. You could traverse once to test internal integrity, traverse again to optimize the tree, traverse a third time to evaluate the expression, and so on. Separating the structure of the abstract syntax tree from the logic of code generation and optimization can clean up the code substantially, but the visitor can end up as a quite-large class and will be hard to maintain as a consequence.

Usage

```
java.util.regex.Pattern p=Pattern.compile("a*b");
java.util.regex.Matcher m = p.matcher("aaaaab");
boolean b = m.matches();
```

Uses *Interpreter* internally. (See the source code shipped with the JDK.)

Iterator

Access the elements of an aggregate object sequentially without exposing how the aggregation is implemented.

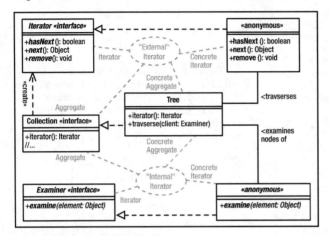

Iterator: Interface for accessing and traversing elements.

Concrete Iterator: Implements Iterator and keeps track of current position.

Aggregate: Defines an interface for creating an iterator. (Omit if no Abstract Factory required.)

Concrete Aggregate: Holds the data. Implements the creation interface to manufacture an iterator.

What Problem Does It Solve?

Iterators isolate a data set from the means that's used to store the set. For example, Java `Collection` and `Map` classes don't implement a common interface. You can, however, extract an iterator from a `Collection` (using `iterator()`) and from a `Map` (using `values().iterator()`). Pass the iterator to a method for processing, thereby isolating that method from knowledge of how the objects are stored.

The set of objects need not be stored internally at all—an iterator across a *Flyweight* may read objects from disk or even synthesize them.

Iterators make it easy to have multiple simultaneous iterators across an aggregation.

Iterators can manipulate the aggregation. The `Cursor` class in the Command example is an iterator. Java's `ListIterator` can modify the list.

External or *active* iterators are controlled by the client (for example, Java's `Iterator` class). *Internal* or *passive* iterators are controlled by the aggregate object. A tree may have a `traverse-PostOrder()` method that's passed a `Command` object that is, in turn, passed each node in the tree. External iterators are often harder to implement than internal ones.

Pros (✔) and Cons (✘)

✔ Promotes reuse by hiding implementation.

✘ A client may modify the elements of the aggregation, damaging the aggregate (for example, change the key in sorted aggregate).

✘ The aggregate may store references to its iterators; memory leaks are possible if you discard an iterator without notifying the aggregate.

✘ It's difficult to control the traversal algorithm and retain the generic quality of an iterator. For example, there's no way to specify a post-order traversal from the iterator returned from a `TreeSet`. This problem extends to most Composite reifications.

✘ It's difficult to implement Iterator in an environment that supports simultaneous iteration and modification. (If you add an item to an aggregate while iterations are in progress, should the iterator visit the newly added item? What if the list is ordered and you've already passed the place where the new item is inserted? Should attempts to modify the aggregation fail if iterators are active? There are no "correct" answers to these questions.)

Often Confused With

Visitor: Visitor can be implemented with a passive iterator. Iterators should examine data, not modify it. Visitors are passed from node to node; Iterators are passed the node to visit.

See Also

Composite, Visitor

Implementation Notes and Example

```
class Tree implements Collection
{   private Node root = null;
    private static class Node
    {   public Node left, right;
        public Object item;
        public Node( Object item )
        {   this.item = item;      }
    }
    Iterator iterator()
    {   return new Iterator()
        {   private Node current = root;
            private LinkedList stack =
                    new LinkedList();
            public Object next()
            {   while( current != null )
                {   stack.addFirst( current );
                    current = current.left;
                }
                if( stack.size() != 0 )
                {   current = (Node)
                        ( stack.removeFirst() );
                    Object toReturn=current.item;
                    current = current.right;
                    return toReturn;
                }
                throw new NoSuchElementException();
            }
            public boolean hasNext()
            {   return !(current==null
                        && stack.size()==0);
            }
            public void remove(){ /*...*/ }
        };
    }
    public interface Examiner
    {   public void examine( Object o );   }
    void traverse( Examiner client )
    {   traverseInorder( root, client );
    }
    private void traverseInorder(Node current,
                        Examiner client )
    {   if( current == null )
            return;
        traverseInorder(current.left,  client);
        client.examine  (current.item );
        traverseInorder(current.right, client);
    } // ...
}
```

The previous code implements a simple binary tree. (I've omitted the methods of Collection that aren't relevant to Iterator.) The iterator() method returns an external iterator that implements the java.util.Iterator interface. Use it like this:

```
Iterator i = t.iterator();
while( i.hasNext() )
    System.out.print(i.next().toString() );
```

You can't use recursive traversal in an external iterator because next() must return after getting each element, and you can't stop the recursion in midstream. My implemenation uses a stack to remember the next parent to visit in the traversal (the same information that would be on the runtime stack in a recursive traversal). You can easily see the extra complexity mandated by this approach, but other nonrecursive traversal algorithms are, if anything, messier.

The traverse() method demonstrates an internal iterator. You pass traverse() a Command object that implements the Examiner interface. Traverse does a simple recursive traversal, passing each node to the Examiner's examine() method in order. Here's an example:

```
t.traverse(
    new Tree.Examiner()
    {   public void examine(Object o)
        {   System.out.print(o.toString());
        }
    }          );
```

As you can see, the code is much simpler, but you lose the flexibility of an external iterator (which you could keep positioned in the middle of the tree, for example; an internal iterator doesn't give you the option of not advancing).

Both iterators access private fields of Tree. Think of an external iterator as an extension of the object that creates it. Private access is okay if it doesn't expose implementation information. Nonetheless, iterators are tightly coupled to the aggregate by necessity.

Usage

```
f( Collection c )
{   Iterator i = c.iterator();
    while( i.hasNext() )
        doSomething( i.next() );
}
```

Iterators are used heavily in all the Java Collection classes.

```
String query = "SELECT ID FROM TAB";
ResultSet results = stmt.executeQuery(query);
while( results.next() )
    String s = results.getString("ID");
```

A database cursor iterates across rows in a table.

Mediator

Define a single object that encapsulates a set of complex operations. Mediator simplifies your code by hiding complexity; it loosens coupling between the objects that use the mediator and the objects the mediator uses.

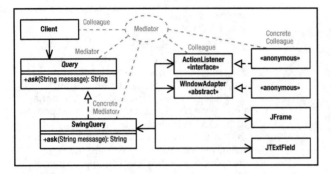

Mediator: (Often omitted.) Defines an interface to Colleagues.

Concrete Mediator: Implements the Mediator interface to interact with Colleagues and manage communication between them.

Colleagues: A system of interfaces and classes that communicate bidirectionally through the mediator rather than directly. Note that the client is a Colleague.

What Problem Does It Solve?

Mediator makes complex operations simple.

Too-complex code is damaging to any program. Mediator solves this problem by taking complex code that would otherwise appear all over the program and encapsulating it into a single object with a simple interface that's used all over the program. Mediators hide complex protocols.

Pros (✔) and Cons (✖)

✔ Mediators improve code organization in many ways: reducing subclassing, decoupling subsystems, and simplifying messaging systems and protocols.

✖ Complexity can creep into a Mediator over time as you customize it for new applications. You've missed the point if you allow a Mediator to become too complex. Several Mediators tailored for specific applications can help. Be careful not to add back the complexity you're trying to eliminate.

✖ A mediator can turn into a "god" class if you're not careful. A good OO program is a network of cooperating agents. There is no spider in the middle of the web pulling the strands. Focus your mediators on doing one thing only.

Often Confused With

Facade: Facade eases simple one-way communication with a subsystem helps isolate the subsystem from the rest of the program. Mediators encapsulate complex interactions, but communication is bidirectional and they do not isolate anything from anything. It's possible, however, for a set of classes to participate simultaneously in both patterns.

Bridge: Bridge and Mediator both reduce coupling between subsystems. Bridge defines a standard (often complicated) interface and then implements it in various ways. Bridges are systems of *classes*. Mediators are *objects* that have simple interfaces but do complex work at runtime. Mediator does promote decoupling, though. If a protocol changes, for example, the scope of that change is typically limited to the Mediator itself.

See Also

Facade, Bridge

Implementation Notes and Example

```
interface Query
{   String ask( String question );
}
class SwingQuery implemnts Query
{ public String ask( String question )
  { final Object done  = new Object();
    final Object init  = new Object();
    final JFrame frame = new JFrame("Query");
    final JTextField answer= new JTextField();
    answer.setPreferredSize(
      new Dimension(200,20));
    frame.getContentPane().setLayout(
      new FlowLayout() );
    frame.getContentPane().add( answer );
    frame.getContentPane().add(
                     new JLabel(question) );
    answer.addActionListener  // submit
    ( new ActionListener()
      { public void actionPerformed(ActionEvent e)
        { synchronized( init )
          { synchronized( done )
            { frame.dispose();
              done.notify();
    }}}});
    frame.addWindowListener  // cancel
    ( new WindowAdapter()
      { public void windowClosing(WindowEvent e)
        { synchronized( init )
          { synchronized( done )
            { frame.dispose();
              answer.setText("");
              done.notify();
    }}}});
    synchronized( done )
    { synchronized( init )
      { frame.pack();
        frame.show();
      }
      try{ done.wait(); }
      catch( InterruptedException e ){}
    }
    return answer.getText();
  }
}
```

The previous code lets you ask the user a simple question. When you make this call:

```
Query user = new SwingQuery();
String answer = user.ask("How are you");
```

The method displays the small window shown previously. You type your answer and hit Enter, the window shuts down, and ask(...) returns what you typed (in this case, the string "Fine"). If you click the *X* box in the upper-right corner of the control, the window shuts down and ask(...) returns an empty string.

The details of the code are actually not relevant to the current discussion. The main issue is that the code encapsulates a complex interaction with the GUI subsystem (and would be even more complex if you were working in the raw OS rather than Java), but the user exercises all this complexity by doing a simple thing. The details are all hidden. Moreover, code that *uses* Query is now considerably simplified, and a lot of complicated junk isn't duplicated all over the program.

It would be better if the Concrete Mediator (the SwingQuery) were created by an Abstract Factory rather than by invoking new.

Note that Mediator does not isolate the program from the entire Swing subsystem (unlike Bridge). Mediator does not prohibit other parts of your program from talking directly to Swing. Also note that the communication between the Mediator (Query) and its colleagues (everything else) is bidirectional, and that all communication (at least in the context of asking the user a question) happens through the mediator.

Usage

`URL home = new URL("http://www.holub.com");`
`URLConnection c = home.getConnection();`
`    //...`
`OnputStream out = c.getOutput();`
`c.write( someData );`
	The output stream returned from the URLConnection is a Mediator. You just write data to it. It encapsulates the complex interaction needed to establish a connection and implement whatever protocol was specified in the original URL.

`JButton b = new JButton("Hello");` `//...`	The JButton deals with all the complexity of fielding mouse clicks, changing the image the user sees when the button should be "down," and so on.
`JOptionPane.showMessageDialog("Error... ");`	Hides the complexity of creating and showing a dialog box.

Memento

Encapsulate an object's state in such a way that no external entity can know how the object is structured. An external object (called a *caretaker*) can store or restore an object's state without violating the integrity of the object.

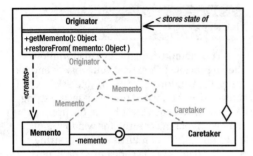

Originator: Creates a memento that holds a "snapshot" of its current state.

Memento: Stores the internal state of the Originator in a way that does not expose the structure of the Originator. Supports a "wide" interface used by the originator and a "narrow" interface used by everyone else.

Caretaker: Stores the mementos but never operates on them.

What Problem Does It Solve?

The ubiquitous get/set (*accessor*) function is evil. Allowing access to internal fields—either directly by making them `public` or indirectly through an accessor method—flies in the face of the basic object-oriented principle of implementation hiding. The whole point of an OO structure is that you can make radical changes to an object's implementation without impacting the code that uses those objects. An object should not get the data that it needs to do work—it should ask the object that has the data to do the work for it (delegation). The only exception to this rule is an accessor that returns an object that opaquely encapsulates the data. The point is not to expose implementation details.

If you use simplistic accessors, even small changes, such as changing a field's type, impact every part of the program that uses that accessor. Programs that use accessors are difficult to maintain and simply aren't object oriented. (A program isn't OO just because it uses classes, derivation, and so on, or is written in Java or C++.)

But what if an external entity needs to remember the state of some object, perhaps to restore that state in an undo operation or equivalent? Memento solves this problem by having the original object return a black box, an impenetrable container that the caretaker can store but not manipulate. The object that manufactures the black box *does* know what's in it, though, so it can use this information at will (to restore state, for example).

Pros (✔) and Cons (✖)

✔ Allows an object's state to be stored externally in such a way that the maintainability of the program is not compromised.

✔ Allows a "caretaker" object to store states of classes that it knows nothing about.

✖ Versioning can be difficult if the memento is stored persistently. The Originator must be able to decipher mementos created by previous versions of itself.

✖ It's often unclear whether a memento should be a "deep" copy of the Originator. (in other words, should recursively copy not just references but the objects that are referenced as well). Deep copies are expensive to manufacture. Shallow copies can cause memory leaks, and referenced objects may change values.

✖ Caretakers don't know how much state is in the memento, so they cannot perform efficient memory management.

Often Confused With

Command: Command objects encapsulate operations that are known to the invoker. Mementos encapsulate state—operations are unknown to the caretaker.

Implementation Notes and Example

```
class Originator
{   private String    state;
    private int       more;

    private class Memento
    {   private String state =
           Originator.this.state;
        private int more =Originator.this.more;
        public toString()
        {   return state + ", " + more ;
        }
    }

    public Object getMemento()
    {   return new Memento();
    }

    public Object restore(Object o)
    {   Memento m = (Memento) o;
        state = o.state;
        more  = o.more;
    }
}

class Caretaker
{   Object memento;
    Originator originator;
    public void captureState()
    {   memento = originator.getMemento();
    }
    public void restoreYourself()
    {   originator.restore( memento );
    }
}
```

Making Memento private with nothing but private fields guarantees that unsafe access is impossible. (Some idiot may try to circumvent encapsulation using the introspection APIs,

but "against stupidity, even the gods themselves contend in vain.") The Caretaker treats the Memento as a simple Object. Memento defines a "narrow" interface (toString()) that doesn't expose structure. A much more complicated memento is presented in Chapter 3 in the Game-of-Life example.

One great example of Memento is an "embedded" object in Microsoft's Object Linking and Embedding (OLE) framework. Consider an Excel spreadsheet that you've embedded as a table in a Word document. When you create the table, Excel is running. It negotiates with Word to take over some of its UI (Excel adds menus to Word's menu bar and is in control of the subwindow that holds the table, for example). When you click outside the table, Excel shuts down and produces a memento—a blob of bytes that holds its state— and an image that Word displays in place of the original Excel UI. All that Word can do with this image is display it. All that Word can do with the data "blob" is hold onto it. The next time the user wants to edit the table, Word passes the blob back to Excel, but Excel has to figure out what to do with it. Since Excel's data representation is completely hidden from Word, it can change the representation without impacting any of the code in Word itself.

A memento can have a "narrow" interface that does something such as display its state on a screen or store its state as an XML file. Just make sure that this interface doesn't expose any structure to the caretaker.

"Undo" is hardly ever implementable solely with a memento (see "Command").

Usage

```
class Originator implements Serializable{ int x; }

ByteArrayOutputStream bytes = new ByteArrayOutputStream();
ObjectOutputStream out= new ObjectOutputStream( bytes );

Originator instance = new Originator();   // create
out.writeObject( instance );              // memento
byte[] memento = bytes.toByteArray();

ObjectInputStream in =              // restore object
    new ObjectInputStream(          // from memento
        new ByteArrayInputStream(memento));
instance= (Originator) in.readObject();
```

A byte array is about as black as a box can be. Decorator is used here to produce a system of streams that manufacture the memento. This example also nicely illustrates a flaw in Decorator—that you sometimes have to access an encapsulated decorator to do work.

Observer (Publish/Subscribe)

When an object changes states, it notifies other objects that have registered their interest at runtime. The notifying object (publisher) sends an event (publication) to all its observers (subscribers).

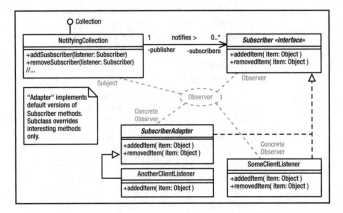

Subject (The *publisher*). Notifies Observers that some event has occurred. Keeps a *subscription* list and a means for modifying the list. Sometimes Subject is an interface implemented by a Concrete Subject.

Observer (The *subscriber*). Defines an interface for notifying Observers.

Participant: Implements the Observer interface to do something when notified.

What Problem Does It Solve?

In Chain of Responsibility, a button notifies a parent of a press event like this:

```
class Window
{   void buttonPressed() {/*...*/}
    //...
}

class Button implements Window
{   private Window parent;
    public Button(Window parent)
    {   this.parent = parent;   }
    public void onMouseClick()
    {   parent.buttonPressed(); }
}
```

An abstraction-layer (business) object must learn about presses through a Mediator called a *controller*—a Window derivative that overrides buttonPressed() to send a message to the business object. The coupling relationships between the controllers, the abstraction layer, and the presentation (the button) are too tight. Too much code is affected if anything changes.

The Observer pattern addresses the problem by adding an interface between the *publisher* of an event (the button) and a *subscriber* (the business object that's actually interested in the button press). This interface decouples the publisher and makes it reusable in the sense that it's a stand-alone component, with no dependencies on the rest of the system. A Subject can notify any class that implements the Observer interface, as compared to the earlier example, where a Button could notify only a Window.

Pros (✔) and Cons (✘)

✔ Observer nicely isolates subsystems, since the classes in the subsystems don't need to know anything about each other except that they implement certain "listener" interfaces. This isolation makes the code much more reusable.

✘ You have no guarantee that a subscriber won't be notified of an event after the subscriber cancels its subscription—a side effect of a thread-safe implementation. (AWT and Swing both have this problem.)

✘ Publication events can propagate alarmingly when observers are themselves publishers. It's difficult to predict that this will happen.

✘ Memory leaks are easily created by "dangling" references to subscribers. (When the only reference to an Observer is the one held by a Subject, a dangling Concrete Observer may not be garbage collected.) It's difficult in Java, where there are no "destructor" methods, to guarantee that publishers are notified when a subscriber becomes irrelevant, and it's easy to forget to explicitly cancel the subscription.

Often Confused With

Command: Command objects are very generic. Observers are used solely for notification.

Strategy: Strategy objects define a strategy for performing some work. Observers do implement a notification strategy but, unlike Strategy objects, are not called from within methods to do work.

See Also

Chain of Responsibility

Implementation Notes and Example

```
public final class NotifyingCollection
                    implements Collection
{ private final Collection c;
  public NotifyingCollection(Collection wrap)
  { c = wrap;   }
  private final Collection subscribers
                    = new LinkedList();
  public interface Subscriber
  { void addedItem   ( Object item );
    void removedItem ( Object item );
  }
  synchronized public void addSubscriber(
                    Subscriber subscriber)
  { subscribers.add( subscriber ); }
  synchronized public void removeSubscriber(
                    Subscriber subscriber)
  { subscribers.remove( subscriber );
  }

  private void notify(boolean add, Object o)
  { Object[] copy;
    synchronized(this)
    { copy = subscribers.toArray();
    }
    for( int i = 0; i < copy.length; ++i )
    { if( add )
        ((Subscriber)copy[i]]).addItem(o);
      else
        ((Subscriber)copy[i]).removeItem(o);
    }
  }

  public boolean add(Object o)
  { notify(true,o);   return c.add(o);      }
  public boolean remove(Object o)
  { notify(false,o); return c.remove(o);  }
  public boolean addAll(Collection items)
  {   Iterator i = items.iterator()
      while( i.hasNext() )
        notify( true, i.next() );
      return c.addAll(items);
  }
  // pass-through implementations of other
  // Collection methods go here...
}
```

The example at left is a Decorator that wraps a collection to add a notification feature. Objects that are interested in finding out when the collection is modified register themselves with the collection.

In the following example, I create an "adapter" (in the Java/AWT sense, this is *not* the Adapter pattern) that simplifies subscriber creation. By extending the adapter rather than implementing the interface, I'm saved from having to implement uninteresting methods. I then add a subscriber, like so:

```
class SubscriberAdapter implements
            NotifyingCollection.Subscriber
{   public void addedItem(Object item){}
    public void removedItem(Object item){}
}

NotifyingCollection c =
    new NotifyingCollection(new LinkedList());
c.addSubscriber
( new SubscriberAdapter()
    { public void added( Object item )
        { System.out.println("Added " + item);
        }
    }
}
```

This implemenation of Observer is simplistic—copy is a very inefficient strategy for solving the problem of one thread adding or removing a subscriber while notifications are in progress. A more realistic implementation was presented in Chapter 3.

Observer encompasses both one-to-many and many-to-one implementations. For example, one button could notify several observers when it's pressed, but by the same token, several buttons could all notify the same subscriber, which would use some mechanism (perhaps an event object passed as an argument) to determine the publisher.

Usage

```
JButton b = new JButton("Hello");
b.addActionListener(
    new ActionListener()
    { public void actionPerformed(ActionEvent e)
      {   System.out.println("World");
      }
    } );
```

Print *World* when the button is pressed. The entire AWT event model is based on Observer. This model supersedes a Chain-of-Responsibility-based design that proved unworkable in an OO environment.

```
Timer t = new java.util.Timer();
t.scheduleAtFixedRate( new TimerTask()
    { public void run()
      { System.out.println(new Date().toString());
      }
    }, 0, 1000 );
```

Print the time once a second. The Timer object notifies all its observers when the time interval requested in the schedule method elapses.

State

Objects often need to change behavior when they are in certain states. Define an interface comprising all methods that change behavior; interface implementations define behavior for each state.

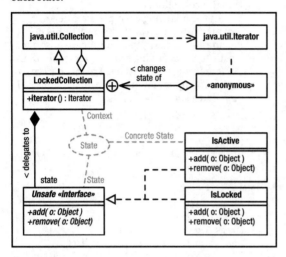

Context: Defines a public interface to the outside world, methods of which change behavior with object state. Maintains an instance of a Concrete State class.

State: Defines an interface that comprises all the behavior that changes with state.

Concrete State: Implements State to define behavior for a particular state.

What Problem Does It Solve?

Objects often need to change behavior with state. The "obvious" way to implement this change is for each method to contain a large switch statement or equivalent, with a case for each possible state, and the selector is an instance variable. This structure is difficult to maintain at best, and changing the state table or introducing new states is difficult, requiring many changes to many methods.

In the State pattern, each state is represented by a State object that implements the behavior of the Context object when the Context is in a given state. An instance variable references an object that implements the current state's behavior. A public method that changes behavior with state just delegates to the current state object. To change state, modify the current state reference to reference an object that implements behavior for the new state.

Pros (✔) and Cons (✖)

✔ State machines are easier to maintain since all the behavior for a given state is in one place.

✔ Eliminates long, hard-to-maintain switch statements in the methods.

✖ State tables (indexed by current state and stimulus, holding the next state) are difficult to implement.

✖ Increases the number of classes in the system along with concomitant maintenance problems.

✖ If only a few methods change behavior with state, this solution may be unnecessarily complex.

Often Confused With

Strategy: The state objects do implement a strategy for implementing a single state, but that strategy is not provided by an outside entity.

See Also

Singleton

Implementation Notes and Example

```java
public final class LockedCollection
                    implements Collection
{ private final Collection c;
  private int activeIterators = 0;

  private Unsafe active = new IsActive();
  private Unsafe locked = new IsLocked();
  private Unsafe state  = active;

  public LockedCollection(Collection c)
  { this.c = c;
  }
  public Iterator iterator()
  { final Iterator wrapped = c.iterator();
    ++activeIterators;
    state = locked;

    return new Iterator()
    { private boolean  valid = true;
      //...
      public boolean hasNext()
      { return wrapped.hasNext();
      }
      public Object next()
      { Object next = wrapped.next();
        if( !hasNext() )
        { if( --activeIterators == 0 )
            state = active;
          valid = false;
        }
        return next;
      }
    };
  }
  public int size()
        { return c.size();   }
  public boolean isEmpty()
        { return c.isEmpty(); }
  // ...
  // Collection methods that don't
  // change behavior are defined here.

  public boolean add(Object o)
       {return state.add(o);}
  public boolean remove(Object o)
       {return state.remove(o);}

  private interface Unsafe
  { public boolean add(Object o);
    public boolean remove(Object o);
    //...
  }
  private final class IsActive
            implements Unsafe
  { public boolean add(Object o)
        {return c.add(o);}
    public boolean remove(Object o)
        {return c.remove(o);}
```

```java
    //...
  }
  private final class IsLocked
            implements Unsafe
  { public boolean add(Object o)
        { throw new Exception("locked"); }
    public boolean remove(Object o)
        { throw new Exception("locked"); }
    //...
  }
}
```

This code combines Decorator, Abstract Factory, and State. It implements a Collection that changes behavior when iterators are active. *Active* means that an iterator has been created, but the last element of the Collection has not been examined through that iterator. (Java's Collection implementations do just that, but it makes a good example.) The class tosses an exception if you attempt to modify a collection while iterators are active.

The Unsafe interface defines those Collection methods that are unsafe to call during iteration. This interface is implemented by two classes: IsActive implements normal collection behavior. IsLocked implements the iterators-are-active behavior. The classes are Singletons whose instances are referenced by active and locked. The variable state defines the current state and points to one or the other of the Singletons.

Public methods that don't change state with behavior (such as size()) delegate to the contained Collection, c. Public methods that do change state (such as add(Object)) delegate to whichever state object is referenced by state. The iterator() method forces a change of state to locked when it issues an iterator. It also increments an active-iterator count. This count is decremented by the Iterator's next() method when it reaches the last element, and when the count goes to zero, the active state is activated.

The iterator also changes behavior with state, but only one method is affected, so the State pattern isn't used.

No reason exists why you can't create new objects each time a state transition is made. This way the individual state object can itself keep local state information.

Strategy

Define an interface that defines a strategy for executing some algorithm. A family of interchangeable classes, one for each algorithm, implements the interface.

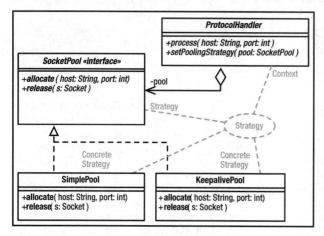

Strategy: An interface that allows access to an algorithm.

Concrete Strategy: Implements a particular algorithm to conform to the Strategy interface.

Context: Uses the algorithm through the Strategy interface.

What Problem Does It Solve?

Sometimes, the only difference between subclasses is the strategy that's used to perform some common operation. For example, a frame window may lay out its components in various ways, or a protocol handler may manage sockets in various ways. You can solve this problem with derivation—several frame derivatives would each lay out subcomponents in different ways, for example. This derivation-based solution creates a proliferation of classes, however. In Strategy, you define an interface that encapsulates the strategy for performing some operation (such as layout). Rather than deriving classes, you pass the Context class the strategy it uses to perform that operation.

Pros (✔) and Cons (✖)

✔ Strategy is a good alternative to subclassing. Rather than deriving a class and overriding a method called from the superclass, you implement a simple interface.

✔ The Strategy object concentrates algorithm-specific data that's not needed by the *Context* class in a class of its own.

✔ It's easy to add new strategies to a system, with no need to recompile existing classes.

✖ Communication overhead is small. Some of the arguments passed to the Strategy objects may not be used.

Often Confused With

Command: Command objects are very generic. The invoker of the command doesn't have a clue what the Command object does. A Strategy object performs a specific action.

See Also

Command

Implementation Notes and Example

```
interface SocketPool
{ Socket  allocate( String host, int port )
  void    release ( Socket s )
}
class SimplePool implements SocketPool
{ public Socket allocate(String host,int port)
  { return new Socket(host, port);
  }
  public void release(Socket s)
  { s.close();
  }
};
class KeepalivePool implements SocketPool
{ private Map connections = new HashMap();
  public Socket allocate(String host,int port)
  { Socket connection =
      (Socket)connections.get(host+":"+port);
    if(connection == null)
      connection = new Socket(host,port);
    return connection;
  }
  public void release(Socket s)
  { String host =
          s.getInetAddress().getHostName();
    connections.put( host+":"+s.getPort(),s );
  }
  //...
}
class ProtocolHandler
{ SocketPool pool = new SimplePool();
  public void process( String host, int port )
  { Socket in = pool.allocate(host,port);
    //...
    pool.release(in);
  }
  public void setPoolingStrategy( SocketPool p )
  { pool = p;
  }
}
```

The previous code implements a skeleton protocol handler. Some of the hosts that the handler talks to require that sockets used for communication are closed after every message is processed. Other hosts require that the same socket be used repeatedly. Other hosts may have other requirements. Because these requirements are hard to predict, the handler is passed a socket-pooling strategy.

The default strategy (SimplePool) simply opens a socket when asked and closes the socket when the ProtocolHandler releases it.

The KeepalivePool implements a different management strategy. If a socket has never been requested, this second strategy object creates it. When this new socket is released, instead of closing it, the strategy object stores it in a Map keyed by combined host name and port number. The next time a socket is requested with the same port name and host, the previously created socket is used. A more realistic example of this second strategy would probably implement notions such as *aging*, where a socket would be closed if it hadn't been used within a certain time frame.

In the interest of clarity, I've left out the exception handling.

Usage

```
JFrame frame = new JFrame();
frame.getContentPane().setLayout( new FlowLayout() );
frame.add( new JLabel("Hello World");
```

The LayoutManger (FlowLayout) defines a strategy for laying out the components in a container (JFrame, the Context)

```
String[] array = new String[]{ ... };
Arrays.sort
( array,
  new Comparator
  { int Compare( Object o1, Object o2 )
    { return ((String)o1).compareTo((String)o2);
    }
  }
);
```

The Arrays.sort(...) method is passed an array to sort and a Comparator that defines a strategy for comparing two array elements. This use of Strategy makes sort(...) completely generic— it can sort arrays of anything.

Template Method

Define an algorithm at the superclass level. Within the algorithm, call an abstract method to perform operations that can't be generalized in the superclass. This way you can change the behavior of an algorithm without changing its structure.

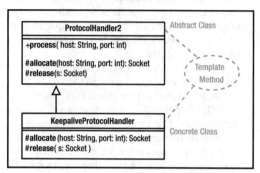

Abstract Class: Defines an algorithm that uses "primitive" operations that are supplied by a subclass.

Concrete Class: Implements the "primitive" operations.

What Problem Does It Solve?

Template Method is typically used in derivation-based application frameworks. The framework provides a set of superclasses that do 90 percent of the work, deferring application-specific operations to abstract methods. That is, superclass methods call abstract template methods. You use the framework by deriving classes that implement this application-specific behavior by providing template-method overrides.

Pros (✔) and Cons (✖)

✖ Template method has little to recommend it in most situations. Strategy, for example, typically provides a better alternative. Well-done class libraries work "out of the box." You should be able to instantiate a framework class, and it should do something useful. Generally, the 90/10 rule applies (10 percent of the functionality is used 90 percent of the time, so the 10 percent should define the default behavior of the class). In template method, however, the framework often defines *no* default behavior, but rather you are required to provided subclasses for the superclass to do anything useful. Given the 90/10 rule, this means you have to do unnecessary work 90 percent of the time.

Template method does not prohibit the class designer from providing useful default functionality at the superclass level, expecting that the programmer will modify the behavior of the superclass through derived-class overrides if necessary. In an OO system, though, using derivation to modify superclass behavior is just run-of-the-mill programming that's hardly worth glorifying as an official pattern.

✔ One reasonable application of Template Method is to provide empty "hooks" at the superclass level solely so that a programmer can insert functionality into the superclass via derivation.

Often Confused With

Factory Method: Factory Method is nothing but a Template Method that creates objects. To be a template method, you must intend for a subclass to override the template method in order to change the behavior of a superclass method that calls the template method.

See Also

Factory Method

Implementation Notes and Example

```
class ProtocolHhandler2
{ protected Socket allocate(String host,int port)
  { return new Socket(host, port);
  }
  protected void release(Socket s)
  { s.close();
  }

  public void process( String host, int port )
  { Socket in =
            socketPool.allocate(host,port);
    //...
    socketPool.release(in);
  }
}

class KeepaliveProtocolHandler
{
  private Map connections = new HashMap();

  public Socket allocate(String host,int port)
  { Socket connection =

(Socket)connections.get(host+":"+port);
    if(connection == null)
      connection = new Socket(host,port);
    return connection;
  }
  public void release(Socket s)
  { String host=
            s.getInetAddress().getHostName();
    connections.put( host+":"+s.getPort(),s);
  }
}
```

This example comes from the reference page for Strategy, rewritten to use Template Method. Rather than provide a Strategy object, you derive a class that modifies the superclass behavior. Put differently, you modify the behavior of the protocol-processing algorithm with respect to socket management by over-riding a method that implements that algorithm.

Note that the class in the Abstract Class role (ProtocolHandler) is not actually abstract. In this reification, the superclass provides reasonable default behavior that a subclass can modify. Also note that the template methods are protected, almost always the case for template methods because they are not intended for outside access. (Ignore the fact that Java grants package access to protected fields—that is really a design flaw in the language.)

Usage

```
class MyPanel extens JPanel
{   public void paint( Graphics g )
    { g.drawString("Hello World", 10, 10);
    }
}
```

Define painting behavior by overriding the paint(...) method. You could easily do the same thing by passing a Panel a "paint" strategy.

Visitor

Add operations to a "host" object by providing a way for a visitor—an object that encapsulates an algorithm—to access the interior state of the host object. Typically, this pattern is used to interact with elements of an aggregate structure. The visitor moves from object to object within the aggregate.

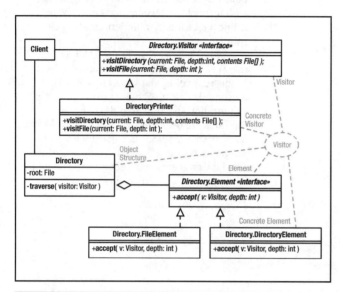

Visitor: Defines an interface that allows access to a Concrete Element of an Object Structure. Various methods can access elements of different types.

Concrete Visitor: Implements an operation to be performed on the Elements. This object can store an algorithm's local state.

Element: Defines an "accept" operation that permits a Visitor to access it.

Concrete Element: Implements the "accept" operation.

Object Structure: A composite object that can enumerate its elements.

What Problem Does It Solve?

Visitor's primary use is to effectively add methods to a class without needing to derive classes. Visitors can also collect information or perform operations on all the elements of some aggregation. For example, a Visitor could test all the elements of an aggregation for consistency.

Pros (✔) and Cons (✖)

✔ It's easy to add operations that haven't thought of yet.

✔ Allows the class to be smaller since rarely used operations can be defined externally.

✔ Visitors can accumulate state as the visit elements. A "mobile agent" can visit remote objects (database servers, for example) and accumulate a composite result from a distributed database.

✖ The internal structure of the composite object is sometimes opened to the visitor, violating encapsulation. For example, an evil visitor could be passed elements of a tree and change their "key" values, thereby turning the tree to garbage. The visitors are tightly coupled to the object they are visiting.

Often Confused With

Iterator: A Visitor is a lot like an internal (passive) iterator. The main difference is that the visitor object is passed from node to node. In Iterator, the nodes are passed, one at a time, to the iterator. The Visitor structure is different than the Iterator structure in that it gives the element control over whether to accept the visitor.

Strategy: A Visitor is, in a way, a "visiting strategy." The focus of visitor is to visit every node of a data structure and do something. Strategy is much more general and has no connection to a data structure.

See Also

Strategy, Iterator

Implementation Notes and Example

```
class Directory
{
  public interface Visitor
  { void visitFile(File current, int depth);
    void visitDirectory( File current,
                int depth, File[] contents );
  }
  public interface Element
  { void accept( Visitor v, int depth );
  }
  public class DirectoryElement
                implements Element
  { private File f;
    public DirectoryElement(File f){this.f=f;}
    public void accept( Visitor v, int depth )
    { v.visitDirectory(f,depth,f.listFiles());
    }
  }
  public class FileElement implements Element
  { private File f;
    public FileElement(File f){this.f = f;}
    public void accept( Visitor v, int depth )
    {   v.visitFile( f, depth );
    }
  }
  //=============================
  private File root;
  public Directory(String root)
  { this.root = new File(root);
  }

  public void traverse( Visitor visitor )
  { topDown( root, visitor, 0 );
  }

  private void topDown( File root,
                Visitor visitor, int depth )
  { Element e =
      root.isFile()
      ? (Element)(new FileElement(root))
      : (Element)(new DirectoryElement(root))
      ;

    e.accept( visitor, depth );

    if( !root.isFile() )
    {
      File[] children = root.listFiles();
      for(int i = 0; i < children.length; ++i)
        topDown(children[i],visitor,depth+1);
    }
  }
}
```

Print a directory tree like this:

```
class DirectoryPrinter
                implements Directory.Visitor
{  public void visitFile(File f, int depth)
   {}
   public void visitDirectory( File f,
                int depth, File[] children)
   { while( --depth >= 0 )
       System.out.print("..");
     System.out.println( f.getName() );
   }
}
Directory d = new Directory("c:/");
d.traverse( new Printer() );
```

The implementation at the left is a bit more complex than it needs to be so that I could demonstrate the general structure of traversing a heterogeneous composite object.

The key feature of Visitor is that it provides a way to add methods to an existing class without having to recompile that class. To my mind, that means that the "composite" could legitimately contain only one element. Consider this class:

```
class Money
{ long value; // value, scaled by 100
  Money increment( Money addend )
  { value += addend.value;
    return value;
  }
  //...
  public interface Modifier // visitor
  { long modify(long current);
  }
  operate( Modifier v )
  { value = v.modify(value);
  }
}
```

It's impractical to define every possible operation on money, but you can effectively add an operation by implementing a Visitor (Modifier). Compute the future value of money like this:

```
class FutureValue impelements Money.Modifier
{ FutureValue(float interest,int period)
  {/*...*/}
  public long modify( long currentValue )
  { // return future value of currentValue
  }
}
Money presentValue = new Money(100000.00);
money.operate( new FutureValue(.05,24) );
```

Index

A

Abstract class, defined, 396
Abstract Cursor Factory, 221
Abstract Factory pattern
  Abstract Factory (Collection)
    (code listing), 68–69
  basics of, 7–8, 67–70, 197
  vs. Builder, 350
  creating tables and, 198–202
  defined, 80
  dynamic creation in, 73–75
  vs. Factory method, 350, 354
  Game of Life and, 166–168
  quick reference, 350–351
  Singleton pattern and, 59–61
Abstract product, defined, 350
AbstractButton superclass, 173
abstractions. *See also* data abstraction
  abstraction classes, 365
  defined, 364
abstract-syntax tree, 298–300, 310
acceptsURL(. . .) method, 329
accessor function, 388
accessors
  accessor synchronization, 63
  boundary-layer classes and, 32, 35
  defined, 24
  getter/setter issues and, 35
  refactoring and, 29
Action/Control user-interface architecture,
    117
ActionListener object, 119
active iterators. *See* external iterators
Adapter pattern
  vs. Bridge pattern, 362, 364
  vs. Decorator pattern, 362, 368
  embedded SQL and, 339–343
  vs. Mediator pattern, 362
  quick reference, 362–363
addClockListener(. . .) method, 95
addLine(. . .) method, 120
advance( ) method, 270
advancePast( ) method, 264
aggregate objects, 216
agile development methodologies
  abstract code and, 55
  architectural analogies and, 9
Alexander, Christopher, 1, 2

algorithms
  defined, 20
  recursive algorithms, 98
anonymous-inner-class mechanism, 69
approve( ) method, 231, 324
architecture
  Action/Control user-interface
    architecture, 117
  Bridge pattern as, 364
  of database classes, 188–189
  of Model/View/Controller (MVC), 15–16
ArithmeticExpression, 300, 310
Arnold, Ken, 7, 10, 13
ArrayIterator class, 217–219, 339
ArrayIterator.java (code listing), 217–219
ArrayList class, 41–42
arrays, sorting, 76–77
AtomicExpression, 298, 315, 320
attributes
  defined, 173
  synthesized attributes, 173–174
AutoCommitBehavior interface, 334
autoCommitState field, 334
AWT Component/Container system, 110–111
AWTEventMulticaster class, 105–108

B

base classes, 41. *See also* fragile base classes
BeanCustomizer class, 28
BeanDescriptor class, 28
BeanInfo class, 28
Beck, Kent, 30, 31
begin( )method, 229
Behavioral patterns. *See also specific*
    Behavioral patterns
  introduction to, 8
  quick reference, 377–399
    Chain of Responsibility pattern, 378–379
    Command pattern, 380–381
    Interpreter pattern, 382–383
    Iterator pattern, 384–385
    Mediator pattern, 386–387
    Memento pattern, 388–389
    Observer pattern, 390–391
    State pattern, 392–393
    Strategy pattern, 394–395
    Template method, 396–397
    Visitor pattern, 398–399

Bloch, Joshua, 33, 287
BlockingList, 369
border objects, 177–178
BorderFactory class, 177–178
bouncing, defined, 73
boundary-layer classes, and accessors and
    mutators, 32, 35
bounding rectangle, defined, 174
Bridge pattern
    vs. Adapter pattern, 341, 362, 364
    vs. Builder pattern, 352
    embedded SQL
      in AWT, 199
      basics of, 188
      data-storage layer, 197–198
    vs. Facade pattern, 364, 370
    Game of Life, 116–117, 118
    JDBC layer and, 344–345
    vs. Mediator pattern, 386
    quick reference, 364–365
BufferedInputStream class, 253
buffering, Decorator pattern, 368
Builder interface, 213
Builder pattern
    vs. Abstract Factory pattern, 350
    vs. Bridge pattern, 352
    importing and exporting and, 212–213
    passive iterators and, 202–213
    quick reference, 352–353
    vs. Visitor pattern, 352
business objects, and getter/setter issues, 34

■C

C language, and patterns, 1–2
C++ language
    C++ SmartPointer, 287
    interfaces in, 38
    procedural system in, 11
    virtual constructors in, 355
callback problems, and Command pattern,
    380
calling method, 325
cancel( ) method, 93–94
cancelSubscription( ) method, 99
caretakers, 34, 178–179, 388
Cartesian product, defined, 236
Cell interface, Game of Life, 84, 145–148, 163
Cell.java (code listing), 145–148
Cell.Memento interface, 180
cells, defined, 192
cellular automata programs, 20–24
Chain of Command pattern, 270–271, 275.
      See also Chain of Responsibility
      pattern
Chain of Responsibility pattern
    vs. Composite pattern, 366, 378

    vs. Decorator pattern, 368
    defined, 8
    embedded SQL
      Scanner class and, 270–271
      shortcomings of, 275–276
    vs. Interpreter pattern, 382
    quick reference, 378–379
Class Adapter, 340
class objects, 62
Class patterns, 7
classes. See also specific classes
    embedded SQL. See also Database class,
      embedded SQL
      ParseFailure class, 277–279
      Scanner class, 269–277
    Game of Life, core classes, 139–161
      Cell interface, 145–148
      Neighborhood class, 151–161
      Resident class, 148–151
      Universe class, 139–144, 161
    vs. interfaces, 38–55
      coupling, 40–41
      factory-method patterns, 50–54
      flexible structures, 39–40
      fragile base classes, 41–47, 55
      frameworks, 48–49
      multiple inheritance, 47–48
      template-method patterns, 49–50
    types of, 38
clear( ) method, 42
client( ) method, 68
clock subsystem, Game of Life
    Observer pattern, 86–103
      introduction to, 86–92
      Publisher class, 93–103
    Visitor pattern, 104–108
clock tick message example, 168–169
Clock.java: The Clock Class (code listing),
    90–92
Clock.Listener derivative, 90
clone( ) method, 356, 357
code listings (by chapter)
    embedded SQL
      ArrayIterator.java, 217–219
      ConcreteTable.java: Importing and
        Exporting, 204–205
      ConcreteTable.java: Inserting Rows,
        215–216
      ConcreteTable.java: Miscellany, 242–249
      ConcreteTable.java: Selection and Joins,
        237–241
      ConcreteTable.java: Simple Table
        Creation, 202–204
      ConcreteTable.java: Transaction
        Support, 229–231

ConcreteTable.java: Traversing and Modifying, 221–222
ConcreteTable.java: Updating and Deleting, 234
ConnectionAdapter.java (Partial listing), 331–332
CSVExporter.java, 209–210
CSVImporter.java, 205–206
Cursor.java, 219–221
Database.java: Convenience Methods That Mimic SQL, 290–293
Database.java: Expressions, 310–315
Database.java: Interpreter Invocation, 320–324
Database.java: Private Data and the TableMap, 284–286
Database.java: The Parser, 301–310
Database.java: Tokens and Enumerations, 288–290
Database.java: Transaction Processing, 294
Database.java: Values, 316–318
Database.Test.sql, 281–283
JDBCConnection.java, 334–338
JDBCDriver.java, 329–331
JDBCResultSet.java, 341–343
JDBCResultSetMetaData.java, 344
JDBCStatement.java, 338–339
JDBCTest.java, 326–328
JTableExporter.java, 211–212
ParseFailure.java, 278–279
PeopleImporter.java, 207–209
RegexToken.java, 266–267
Scanner.java, 271–275
Selector.java, 232–234
SimpleToken.java, 264–265
TableFactory.java, 200–202
Table.java, 192–196
ThrowableContainer.java, 325
Token.java, 264
TokenSet.java, 267–269
Tree.java: A Simple Binary-Tree Implementation, 223–226
UnmodifiableTable.java, 250–252
WordToken.java, 265–266
Game of Life
    Cell.java, 145–148
    Clock.java: The Clock Class, 90–92
    Colors.java, 181–182
    ConditionVariable.java, 184–185
    Direction.java, 170–172
    Files.java, 182–184
    Life.java, 118–119
    Menuing Systems, Building with the Raw APIs, 113–116
    MenuSite.java, 123–139

Neighborhood.java, 151–161
Observer, Implementing with a Publisher Object, 95–96
Publisher.java: A Subscription Manager, 99–103
Resident.java, 148–151
Storable.java, 179–180
Universe.java, 139–144
interfaces
    Abstract Factory (Collection), 68–69
    Double-Checked Locking, 64
    Dynamic Instantiation, 74–75
    Factory Implementation, 59–61
    Factory Method, Using, 52–53
    fragile base classes, eliminating, 46–47
    Singleton's, Shutting Down, 66–67
    Sorters.java: Using Strategy, 77–78
    URLConnection Implementation, Stripped-Down, 71–72
collaboration symbol, 4, 51–52
Collaborator classes, 31
Colleagues, 386
Collection class as utility class, 256
Collection interface vs. Table, 192
collections, and thread-safety solution, 255–256
Color class, Java, 34
Colors interface, 180
Colors Singleton, 180–181
Colors.java (code listing), 181–184
columns, 192
com.holub.database.jdbc.JDBCConnection, 333
Command pattern
    defined, 80
    Game of Life, 166–168
    implementing transactions (undo) and, 226–231
    vs. Memento pattern, 388
    vs. Observer pattern, 390
    quick reference, 380–381
    vs. Strategy pattern, 380, 394
    Strategy pattern and, 75–79
committing transactions, 227
compile-time type checking, 57
Component superclass, 173
Composite pattern
    vs. Chain of Responsibility pattern, 366, 378
    vs. Decorator pattern, 366, 368
    vs. Flyweight pattern, 372
    Life subsystem classes and, 163–172
        clock tick message example, 168–169
        Direction.java (code listing), 170–172
        introduction to, 163–165
        Prototype pattern, 166–168

Composite pattern *(continued)*
  menuing subsystem, Game of Life,
    108–116
    basics of, 108–113
    Menuing Systems, Building with Raw
      APIs (code listing), 113–116
    objects, 110–112
    quick reference, 366–367
Concrete Aggregate, defined, 384
Concrete Class, defined, 396
Concrete Factory, defined, 350
Concrete Flyweight, 372
Concrete Mediator, defined, 386, 387
Concrete Observer/Subscriber role, 89–90
Concrete State, 392
Concrete Strategy, 394
Concrete Visitor, 104–105, 398
ConcreteBuilder, 212
ConcreteTable, 189–191
ConcreteTable.java code listings
  ConcreteTable.java: Importing and
    Exporting (code listing), 204–205
  ConcreteTable.java: Inserting Rows (code
    listing), 215–216
  ConcreteTable.java: Miscellany (code
    listings), 242–249
  ConcreteTable.java: Selection and Joins
    (code listing), 237–241
  ConcreteTable.java: Simple Table Creation
    (code listing), 202–204
  ConcreteTable.java: Transaction Support
    (code listing), 229–231
  ConcreteTable.java: Updating and
    Deleting (code listing), 234
ConditionVariable class, 181, 184
ConditionVariable.java (code listing),
    184–185
connect( ) method, 329
ConnectionAdapter class, 331
ConnectionAdapter.java (Partial Listing),
    331–332
constant fields, and public fields, 41
constant values, 33
Container superclass, 173
Context, defined, 392
contracts
  defined, 14
  objects defined by, 13–14
controllers, 390
Conway, John, 81
cookies, 178
Cooper, Alan, 7
copy-on-write strategy, 374
coupling, and implementation inheritance,
    40–41
course-grained operations, 27
CRC-Card format, 18, 30–31

create(. . .) method, 267
createMenus method, 119
Creational patterns. *See also specific
    Creational patterns*
  introduction to, 7–8
  quick reference, 349–359
    Abstract Factory pattern, 350–351
    Builder pattern, 352–353
    Factory method, 354–355
    Prototype pattern, 356–357
    Singleton pattern, 358–359
Creator, defined, 354
Cross Ventilation, 3, 4
Crypto APIs, and implementation, 36
CSVExporter class, 209
CSVExporter.java (code listing), 209–210
CSVImporter class, 205–206, 213
CSVImporter.java (code listing), 205–206
Cunningham, Ward
  CRC-Card format and, 18, 30–31
  get/set mentality and, 30
Cursor interface, 218, 221
Cursor objects, 340
Cursor.java (code listing), 219–221
cut and paste approach, 5

D
data
  databases as caretakers of, 34
  extrinsic data, defined, 174
  importing and exporting to tables,
    204–205
data abstraction, 10, 13, 26, 38
Database class, embedded SQL, 279–294
  methods of, 281
  Proxy pattern, 283–287
  supported SQL and, 295
  token set and other constants, 287–294
  using databases, 280–281
Database.java code listings
  Database.java: Convenience Methods
    That Mimic SQL (code listing),
    290–293
  Database.java: Expressions (code listing),
    310–315
  Database.java: Interpreter Invocation
    (code listing), 320–324
  Database.java: Private Data and the
    TableMap (code listing), 284–286
  Database.java: The Parser (code listing),
    301–310
  Database.java: Tokens and Enumerations
    (code listing), 288–290
  Database.java: Transaction Processing
    (code listing), 294
  Database.java: Values (code listing),
    316–318

databases. *See also* embedded SQL
   as caretakers of data, 34
   using, 280–281
Database.Test.sql (code listing), 281–283
data-storage classes, and database
      architecture, 188–189
data-storage layer, embedded SQL, 189–258
   Abstract-Factory and creating tables,
      198–202
   Bridge pattern, 197–198
   Decorator pattern, 250–258
   Iterator pattern, 216–226
   miscellany, 241–249
   passive iterators and Builder, 202–213
   selection and join operations, 235–241
   Strategy pattern, 231–234
   Table interface, 192–196
   transactions (undo), implementing with
      Command pattern, 226–231
DCL (Double-Checked Locking), 64–65
Decorator pattern
   vs. Adapter pattern, 341, 362, 368
   vs. Chain of Responsibility pattern, 368
   vs. Composite pattern, 366, 368
   embedded SQL, 250–258
   immutability and, 172
   vs. Proxy pattern, 287, 374
   quick reference, 368–369
delegation
   defined, 22
   delegation models, and implementation,
      46
delete( ) method, 221
deliverTo( ) method, 95, 104
Derivation pattern, 1–2
derived class, 44–45
design
   creating without getters and setters, 30–32
   informed choices in, 12
   role of patterns in, 6–7
design patterns. *See also specific patterns*
   basics of, 2–5
   classifying, 7–8
   Game of Life, 86
   overlapping combination of, 70–72
   patterns diagrams, 84
   patterns vs. idioms, 1–2
   purpose of, 5–6
   quick reference. *See* quick reference,
      design patterns
   role of in design, 6–7
   SQL engine and JDBC layers, 260
design patterns and OO (object orientation),
     1–36
   cellular automata programs, 20–24
   design patterns basics, 2–5

design patterns, purpose of, 5–6
get and set methods, 24–36
   basic issues of, 34–36
   design, creating without getters and
      setters, 30–32
   examples, 24–27
   JavaBeans and Struts, 28–29
   refactoring, 29–30
   when to use, 32–34
OO basics, 12–19
   objects, capabilities of, 13–14
   objects, defined, 13
   OO systems, right and wrong examples,
      15–19
OO design basics, 9–10
patterns
   classifying, 7–8
   role of in design, 6–7
patterns vs. idioms, 1–2
programming
   informed choices in, 12
   programming FORTRAN in Java, 9–10
Design Patterns: Elements of Reusable Object-
     Oriented Software (Addison-Wesley,
     1995). See also *Gang of Four*
   consequences section in, 12
   extends keyword and, 37
   patterns and, 1, 3, 5, 7
Direction class, 170–172
Direction.java (code listing), 170–172
Director, defined, 352
directories
   directory files, defined, 111
   directory systems, traversing, 112
   directoryName request, 280
doInsert( ) method, 214
doLoad( ) method, 179
domain modeling, 32
doSelect( ) method, 319, 324
doStore( ) method, 179
Double-Checked Locking (code listing), 64
Double-Checked Locking (DCL), 64–65
DUMMY objects, Game of Life, 177
dump( ) method, 289–290
dynamic creation in a factory, 73–75
dynamic loading, 356
dynamic model, defined, 31

■E
Eclipse
   refactoring and, 29
   SWT library, 345
edge(. . .) method, 176
Editor class, example, 49
EditorKit, and HTML parsing, 51–52
Effective Java Programming Language Guide
     (Addison-Wesley, 2001), 33

embedded SQL, 184–345
  architecture, 188–189
  Database class, 279–294
    Proxy pattern, 283–287
    token set and other constants, 287–294
    using databases, 280–281
  data-storage layer, 189–258
    Abstract-Factory and creating tables,
      198–202
    Bridge pattern, 197–198
    Decorator pattern, 250–258
    Iterator pattern, 216–226
    miscellany, 241–249
    passive iterators and Builder, 202–213
    selection and join operations, 235–241
    Strategy pattern, 231–234
    Table interface, 192–196
    transactions (undo), implementing
      with Command pattern, 226–231
  Interpreter pattern, 295–325
    demonstration of, 318–325
    supported SQL, 295–318
  JDBC layer, 325–332
  requirements, 187–188
  SQL, adding, 259–279
    input tokenization, 262–269
    ParseFailure class, 277–279
    Scanner class, 269–277
    SQL-engine structure, 260–261
  State pattern and JDBCConnection class,
    332–345
    Adapter pattern (result sets), 339–343
    Bridge pattern and, 344–345
    JDBCResultSetMetaData class, 344
    statements, 338–339
  tables. See tables, embedded SQL
encapsulation
  encapsulation principle, 26
  encapsulation requirements, 22
  implementation and, 36
enums, defining, 33
error(. . .) method, 289
evaluate method, 310, 319, 320, 324
everything-is-static Singleton, 119
examples
  clock tick message, 168–169
  design patterns and OO
    architecture pattern, 3–4
    ATM system, 17–19
    get and set methods, 24–27
    getX( ) method, 24–25
    multiple currencies, 24–25
    right and wrong examples, 15–19
    System.in, System.out, 25
    traffic modeling, getter and setter
      methods, 26

  traffic modeling, using cellular
    automata, 20–24
  "god" class, 30
  interfaces
    Editor class, 49
    high-water/low-water, 43–45
    Java, framework, 48–49
  of Singleton pattern, 61–62
execute(. . .) method, 281, 310
executeUpdate(. . .) method, 332, 338
export( ) method, 209, 222
Exporter, building, 209–210
exporting data to tables, 204–205
Expression objects, 298, 300, 315
Expressions (code listing), 310–315
extends keyword
  appropriate use, 56–58
  eliminating, 58–79
    Abstract Factory, 67–70
    command patterns and strategy
      patterns, 75–79
    Double-Checked Locking (DCL), 64–65
    dynamic creation in a factory, 73–75
    factories and Singletons, 59–61
    patterns, overlapping combination of,
      70–72
    Singleton pattern examples, 61–62
    Singletons, eliminating, 65–67
    Singletons, threading issues in, 62–64
  programming with interfaces and, 37–38
external iterators, 222, 384, 385, 393
extrinsic data, defined, 174

■F

Facade pattern
  vs. Bridge pattern, 364, 370
  eliminating clutter and, 27
  Game of Life, 116–118
  vs. Mediator pattern, 162, 370, 386
  menuing subsystem, 116–117
  quick reference, 370–371
factor(. . .) method, 315
Factory Implementation (code listing), 59–61
Factory method
  vs. Abstract Factory pattern, 350, 354
  defined, 80
  quick reference, 354–355
  vs. Template method, 396
Factory pattern. See Abstract Factory pattern
factory-method patterns, 50–54
fields. See public fields
figureNextState( ) method, 176
FileInputStream class, 253
Files.java (code listing), 182–184
final keyword, Java, 33
fine-grained operations, 27

fireEvent( ) method, 93–94
flexible structures, and interfaces, 39–40
flush(. . .) method, 179
Flyweight pattern
    vs. Composite pattern, 372
    Game of Life, 172–178
        basics of, 172–176
        flyweight pools, 176–178
    push model and, 35
    quick reference, 372–373
forName(. . .) method, 328
FORTRAN programming, Java, 9–10
fragile base classes, 41–47, 55
Fragile Base classes, Eliminating (code
        listing), 46–47
Frameworks, 48–49
function pointers, defined, 75

■ **G**

Game of Life implementation, 81–185
    basics and rules of, 82–83
    charting structure of, 83–86
    clock subsystem, Observer pattern,
        86–103
        introduction to, 86–92
        Publisher class, 93–103
    clock subsystem, Visitor pattern, 104–108
    Composite pattern, and Life subsystem
        classes, 163–168
    Composite redux, 168–172
    core classes, 139–161
        Cell interface, 145–148
        Neighborhood class, 151–161
        Resident class, 148–151
        Universe class, 139–144
    Flyweight pattern, 172–178
        basics of, 172–176
        flyweight pools, 176–178
    Mediator pattern, 161–162
    Memento pattern, 178–180
    menuing subsystem
        Bridge pattern, 116–117, 118
        Composite pattern, 108–116
        Facade pattern, 116–117
    MenuSite class, 117–139
        Life.java (code listing), 118–119
        MenuSite documentation, 120–121
        MenuSite.java (code listing), 123–139
    miscellaneous, 180–185
    summary of, 185
Gang of Four. See also *Design Patterns:
        Elements of Reusable Object-Oriented
        Software* (Addison-Wesley, 1995);
        quick reference, design patterns
    consequences section in book, 12
    design patterns, 1, 3, 7, 8, 55
    Singleton pattern, 62–63, 64

get and set methods, 24–36
    basics of, 34–36
    cellular automata programs and, 22–23
    design, creating without getters and
        setters, 30–32
    examples, 24–27
    JavaBeans and Struts, 28–29
    refactoring, 29–30
    when to use, 32–34
getDefaultToolkit( ) method, 75
getDirty( ) method, 215
getRowDataFromUser( ) method, 206
get/set idioms, JavaBeans, 28
getX( ) method, example, 24–25
Go menu, Game of Life, 109
"god" classes, 25, 30
Goldberg, Adele, 37
Gosling, James, 35, 38
grammar, SQL-subset, 296–297
Graphics class, 162
Grid menu, Game of Life, 109, 162
GridLayout objects, 173

■ **H**

HashMaps, 283–284
heterogeneous lists, 104
HTML parsing, 51

■ **I**

IDENTIFIER token, 262, 271
identifiers, 295
idioms in programming
    Bloch's typesafe-enum idiom, 287–288
    get/set idioms, 28
    implement/delegate idiom, 48
    vs. patterns, 1–2
idList( ) method, 319
IdValue class, 315
Image proxy, 334
Immutable class, 172
immutable classes, 33
implementation
    encapsulation of, 35–36
    exposing, 34
    hiding, 10, 26, 34 35
implementation inheritance. *See also*
        extends keyword
    adding thread safety to collections and,
        254
    adding unmodifiability to collections and,
        255–256
    assigning tables and, 252
    implementation-inheritance-based
        solutions in Game of Life, 87–88
    vs. interface inheritance, 37–38
    reification and, 7

Importer
  building, 205–206
  PeopleImporter.java (code listing),
    207–209
importing data to tables, 204–205
inheritance. *See also* implementation
    inheritance
  coupling and, 40–41
  fragile-base-class problem and, 41–47
  interface inheritance vs. implementation
    inheritance, 37–38
  multiple inheritance, 47–48
  structure, and operations, 57
INPUT token, 264, 270–271
input tokenization, embedded SQL, 262–269
InputStream derivatives, 71
instantiation
  lazy instantiation, 283
  patterns and, 3
Instantiation Dynamic (code listing), 74–75
intent, defined, 3
Interface Adapter, 340
interfaces, 37–80
  Action/Control user-interface
    architecture, 117
  Bridge pattern as, 364
  Cell interface, Game of Life, 84, 145–148,
    163
  Cell.Memento interface, 180
  vs. classes, 38–55
    coupling, 40–41
    factory-method patterns, 48–54
    flexible structures, 39–40
    fragile base classes, 55
    fragile-base-class problem, 41–47
    frameworks, 48–54
    multiple inheritance, 47–48
    template-method patterns, 48–54
  embedded SQL
    AutoCommitBehavior interface, 334
    Builder interface, 213
    Collection interface vs. Table, 192
    Cursor interface, 218, 221
    ResultSet interface, 341
    Selector interface, 232
    Table interface, 188–189, 192–196, 221
    Table.Importer interface, 204
  extends, appropriate use of, 56–58
  extends, eliminating, 58–79
    Abstract Factory, 67–70
    command patterns and strategy
      patterns, 75–79
    Double-Checked Locking (DCL), 64–65
    dynamic creation in a factory, 73–75
    factories and Singletons, 59–61
    patterns, overlapping combination of,
      70–72

Singleton pattern examples, 61–62
Singletons, eliminating, 65–67
Singletons, threading issues, 62–64
extends keyword, 37–38
Game of Life
  Cell.Memento interface, 180
  Colors interface, 180
Interface Adapter, 340
interface inheritance, 7, 252
ResultSet interface, 341
summary of, 80
use of in patterns, 7
internal iterators, 202–213, 222–226, 384
Interpreter Invocation (code listing), 320–324
Interpreter pattern
  vs. Chain of Responsibility pattern, 382
  embedded SQL, 295–325
    basics of, 310
    demonstration of, 318–325
    supported SQL, 295–318
  quick reference, 382–383
Invoker (Thread object), 226
is-a relationship, 57
isDirty( ) method, 215, 290
isDisruptiveTo method, 153, 170
Iterator pattern
  embedded SQL, 216–226
  Iterator objects, 197
  quick reference, 384–385
  vs. Visitor pattern, 384, 398
iterators
  ArrayIterator.java (code listing), 217–219
  external, 222, 384, 385, 393
  internal, 222–226, 384
  Iterator objects, 197
  modifying data structure and, 218
  passive iterators, and Builder, 202–213

J

Java
  Color class, 34
  compiler-compilers, 259
  final keyword, 33
  FORTRAN programming in, 9–10
  framework example, 48–49
  Graphics class, 162
  Java libraries, 35–36, 81
  JavaCC, 259
  JavaCUP, 259
  LayoutManager, 78
  procedural programming and, 25
  Toolkit Singleton, 75
  when to use, 16–17
The Java Class Libraries (Addison-Wesley),
    347
java.awt.Color values, 180
java.awt.Toolkit, 197, 355

java.awt.Window class, 197
JavaBeans
    get and set methods and, 28–29
    get/set idioms, 28
java.io.StreamTokenizer, 262
java.lang.Double class, 315
JavaServer Pages, and Memento pattern, 179
java.sql.Connection object, 329
java.sql.Connection's createStatement( ) call,
    338
java.sql.DriverManager class, 328, 329
java.sql.ResultSet object, 338
java.sql.Statement object, 338
java.text.NumberFormat class, 27, 198, 295
java.util.Iterator, 204, 221, 267
java.util.StringTokenizer, 262
java.util.Timer object, 119
javax.Swing.Border, 177
JButton class, 173
JButton derivatives, 172
JComponent class, Game of Life, 88–89
JComponent superclass, 173
JDBC
    JDBC Bridge, 365
    JDBC layer, 325–332
    jdbcCompliant( ) override, 328
    JDBCConnection class, 331, 332–345
    JDBCDriver class, 328
    JDBC-driver layer, 188–189
    JDBCResultSet class, 339–343
    JDBCResultSetMetaData class, 344
    State pattern and JDBCConnection class,
        332–345
        Adapter pattern (result sets), 339–343
        Bridge pattern and, 344–345
        JDBCResultSetMetaData class, 344
        statements, 338–339
JDBC code listings
    JDBCConnection.java (code listing),
        334–338
    JDBCDriver.java (code listing), 329–331
    JDBCResultSet.java (code listing), 341–343
    JDBCResultSetMetaData.java (code
        listing), 344
    JDBCStatement.java (code listing),
        338–339
    JDBCTest.java (code listing), 326–328
JEditorPane class
    rewrite of, 79
    Swing and, 50–51
JFrame object, 172–173
join and selection operations, embedded
        SQL, 235–241
JTableExporter class, 210–212, 213
JTableExporter.java (code listing), 211–212

■K
key abstractions, defined, 32, 112
keyboard shortcuts, 123–124
keyword tokens, 287
keywords. *See also* extends keyword
    final keyword, 33
    synchronized keyword, 64
    volatile keyword, 65

■L
label parameter, 123
LayoutManager, Java, 78
lazy instantiation, 283, 374
Leaf, defined, 366
Leaf objects, 110
lexeme( ) method, 264
lexemes, 262–263
Life class, Game of Life, 161–162
Life subsystem classes, Game of Life, 163–168
Life.java (code listing), 118–119
LinkedList class, Game of Life, 96
listener parameter, 121
load(. . .) method, 179, 200

■M
main(. . .) method, 328
maintenance
    maintenance problems, 18
    of programs, 34–35
maps of names, 122
MarkupPanel, Factory method in, 54
match(. . .) method, 264, 270
match(String input) method, 264
Mediator pattern
    vs. Adapter pattern, 362
    vs. Bridge pattern, 386
    vs. Facade pattern, 370, 386
    Game of Life, 161–162
    quick reference, 386–387
Memento pattern
    attribute representations and, 28
    vs. Command pattern, 388
    data blobs and, 117
    Game of Life, 178–180
    quick reference, 388–389
memory barriers, 65
menu items, adding, 112–113
menuing subsystem, Game of Life
    Bridge pattern, 116–117, 118
    Composite pattern, 108–116
    Facade pattern, 116–117
Menuing Systems, Building with the Raw
        APIs (code listing), 113–116
MenuSite class, Game of Life, 117–139
    Life.java (code listing), 118–119
    MenuSite documentation, 120–121
    MenuSite.java (code listing), 123–139

menuSpecifier object, 121
menuSpecifier parameter, 122
metadata, table, 204
methods. *See also specific methods*
    of Database class, 281
Microsoft
    Excel, 117, 178
    Microsoft applications, OO systems and,
        11
    Microsoft's Foundation Class (MFC), 48
    Microsoft's Object-Linking-and-
        Embedding In-Place-Activation
        system, 117
    Word, 117, 178
Model/View/Controller (MVC) architecture
    basics of, 15–16
    Struts and, 28–29
modify( ) method, 231
Money class, 24
Motif Toolkit, 197
mouse clicks, 174–175
multiple currencies examples, 24–25
multiplicativeExpression( ) method, 300, 310
mutators
    boundary-layer classes and, 32, 35
    defined, 24
    getter/setter issues and, 35
    refactoring and, 29
MVC. *See* Model/View/Controller (MVC)
    architecture

■N

name parameter, 121, 123
Neighborhood class, Game of Life, 84,
    151–161, 174, 176
Neighborhood objects, 163–167, 169–170
Neighborhood.java (code listing), 151–161,
    166
Neighborhood.NeighborhoodState class,
    160, 180
nested transactions, 227, 332
Node class, Game of Life, 96
Node objects, Game of Life, 97
nodes, 298
Nonterminal expressions, 319
nonterminal nodes, 298
normalization class, 56
numbers forms, 295
NumericValue method, 315

■O

Object Adapter, 340
object structure, 117
Object-Oriented Design Heuristics (Addison-
    Wesley, 1996), 358
Object-Oriented Design (OOD), vs. OOP,
    9–10

Object-Oriented Programming (OOP), vs.
    OOD, 9–10
objects
    capabilities of, 13–14
    class objects, 62
    Composite pattern objects, 110–112
    defined, 13
    JMenuItem, 110
    Leaf objects, 110
    menuSpecifier object, 121
    requester object, 120
    traversing collections of, 108
Observer, Implementing with a Publisher
    Object (code listing), 95–96
Observer pattern
    vs. Command pattern, 390
    Game of Life, 86–103. *See also* Publisher
        class
        introduction to, 86–92
    quick reference, 390–391
    vs. Strategy pattern, 390
OO (object orientation), 12–19. *See also*
    design patterns and OO (object
    orientation)
    basics of
        objects, capabilities of, 13–14
        objects, defined, 13
        OO systems, right and wrong examples,
            15–19
    OO design basics, 9–10
openConnection( ) method, 73
operations
    course-grained vs. fine-grained, 27
    inheritance structure and, 57
Originator, defined, 388

■P

parameters, MenuSite class, 120–121, 122,
    123
ParseError object, 289
ParseFailure class, embedded SQL, 277–279
ParseFailure exception, 324
ParseFailure.java (code listing), 278–279
The Parser, Database.java (code listing),
    301–310
parsers
    parser requirement, 262
    parsers, and lookahead tokens, 269–270
    recursive descent parser technology, 259
    SQL parser, 295, 296
parsing HTML, 51
passive iterators, 202–213, 222–226, 384
Pattern Hatching (Addison-Wesley, 1998), 172
patterns. *See* design patterns; quick reference,
    design patterns; *specific patterns*
peer classes, 197
PeopleImporter class, 206–209, 213

PeopleImporter.java (code listing), 207–209
percent (%) wildcard, 295
polymorphism, defined, 38
pools, flyweight, 176–178
PostgreSQL driver, 345
privacy, of data in systems, 13–14
private indexOf method, 202
problem domains, 31–32
Procedural systems, 10–11
programming
    informed choices in, 12
    Java
        *Effective Java Programming Language
          Guide* (Addison-Wesley, 2001), 33
        FORTRAN programming and, 9–10
        procedural programming and Java, 25
    procedural approaches to, 10–11
    programmers tendency toward
        complexity, 7
protection proxy patterns, 287
Prototype pattern
    Game of Life, 166–168
    quick reference, 356–357
Proxy pattern
    combined with State pattern, 334
    vs. Decorator pattern, 374
    embedded SQL, 283–287
    quick reference, 374–375
public fields
    acccessors and mutators and, 41
    constant fields and, 41
    dangers of, 26
public static void addLine( ) method, 121
public static void addMapping, 123
public static void establish method, 120
public static void mapNames(URL table)
    throws IOException, 122
public static void removeMyMenus method,
    121
publicstatic void setEnable method, 122
Publisher class, 93–103
    introduction to, 93–95
    Observer, Implementing with a Publisher
        Object (code listing), 95–96
    Publisher.java: A Subscription Manager
        (code listing), 99–103
Publisher object, Game of Life, 97
Publisher Object, Implementing Observer
    with (code listing), 95–96
Publisher.java: A Subscription Manager
    (code listing), 99–103
publishers, defined, 390
Publish/Subscribe pattern, Game of Life, 88
push and pull models, 35
pushback, Decorator pattern, 368
put( ) override, 283

Q

quick reference, design patterns, 347–399
    Behavioral patterns, 377–399
        Chain of Responsibility pattern,
          378–379
        Command pattern, 380–381
        Interpreter pattern, 382–383
        Iterator pattern, 384–385
        Mediator pattern, 386–387
        Memento pattern, 388–389
        Observer (Publish/Subscribe) pattern,
          390–391
        State pattern, 392–393
        Strategy pattern, 394–395
        Template method pattern, 396–397
        Visitor pattern, 398–399
    Creational patterns, 349–359
        Abstract Factory pattern, 350–351
        Builder pattern, 352–353
        Factory method, 354–355
        Prototype pattern, 356–357
        Singleton pattern, 358–359
    Structural patterns, 361–375
        Adapter pattern, 362–363
        Bridge pattern, 364–365
        Composite pattern, 366–367
        Decorator pattern, 368–369
        Facade pattern, 370–371
        Flyweight pattern, 372–373
        Proxy pattern, 374–375

R

Real Subject available state, 334
Real Subject unavailable state, 334
recursive algorithms, 98
recursive descent parser technology, 259
recursive traversal, 385
refactoring, and get and set methods, 29–30
refined Abstraction, defined, 364
RegexToken subclass, 263
RegexToken.java (code listing), 266–267
register methods, 229
Reification, defined, 3
RELATIONAL_OPERATOR token, 262
RelationalExpression object, 320
remote proxy patterns, 287
requester object, 120
requester parameter, 121, 122
required(Token) method, 270
Resident class, Game of Life, 148–151,
    163–164, 174
Resident objects
    "alive" and, 180
    cells and, 164
    Scanner class and, 269–277
Resident.java (code listing), 148–151

result sets, defined, 188, 235
Results class, 340
ResultSet interface, 341
ResultSetAdapter class, 331
ResultSetMetaDataAdapter class, 331
Riel, Arthur, 358
roles, vs. users, 57
rollbacks, defined, 226–227
rows
    described, 192
    inserting (code listing), 215–216
Runnable class, 226

■ S

Scanner class
    embedded SQL, 269–277
    ParseFailure class and, 277–278
Scanner.java (code listing), 271–275
scanning, defined, 262
screen painting, 176
select( ) method, 319, 320, 324
select( ) overloads, 237
selectFromCartesianProduct(. . .) method,
        237
selection and join operations, embedded
        SQL, 235–241
Selector interface, 232
Selector.java (code listing), 232–234
servlets
    defined, 276
    servlet filters, 276–277, 378, 379
set methods. See get and set methods
setAutoCommit( ) method, 334
setDirty( ) method, 215
shortcut parameter, 123
shortcuts, keyboard, 123–124
"shutdown hooks", defined, 65
SimCity software, 24
SimpleToken subclass, 263–264
SimpleToken.java (code listing), 264–265
simplicity, and patterns, 6
Singleton pattern
    Abstract Factory pattern and, 59–61
    defined, 80
    eliminating, 65–67
    everything-is-static Singleton, 119
    examples of, 61–62
    Singleton, defined, 61
    threading issues in, 62–64
    vs. Utility class, 256, 358
Singleton's, Shutting Down (code listing),
        66–67
smart reference patterns, 287, 374
snapshot strategy, 227
Sorters.java: Using Strategy (code listing),
        77–78
SQL. See embedded SQL

Stack class, and ArrayList class, 42–45
State pattern
    embedded SQL
        Bridge pattern and, 344–345
        combined with Proxy pattern, 334
        JDBCConnection class and, 332–345
            Adapter pattern (result sets), 339–343
            JDBCResultSetMetaData class, 344
            statements, 338–339
    quick reference, 392–393
    vs. Strategy pattern, 392
StatementAdapter class, 331
statements, embedded SQL, 338–339
static initializers, 63
static model, defined, 31
Storable.java (code listing), 179–180
storeRow( ) method, 222
stories, defined, 56
Strategy and Sorters.java (code listing), 77–78
Strategy pattern
    vs. Command pattern, 380, 394
    Command pattern and, 75–79
    defined, 80
    embedded SQL, 231–234
    vs. Observer pattern, 390
    quick reference, 394–395
    vs. State pattern, 392
    vs. Visitor pattern, 398
StreamTokenizer, 262
String class implementation, 29
StringBufferInputStream, 340
Stroustrup, Bjarne, 13
Structural patterns. See also specific
        Structural patterns
    introduction to, 8
    quick reference, 361–375
        Adapter pattern, 362–363
        Bridge pattern, 364–365
        Composite pattern, 366–367
        Decorator pattern, 368–369
        Facade pattern, 370–371
        Flyweight pattern, 372–373
        Proxy pattern, 374–375
Struts, 28–29
Subject, and notification, 88
subscribe( ) method, Game of Life, 93–94
subscribers
    adding, 98
    defined, 390
Subscription Manager (code listing), 99–103
subsystem classes
    defined, 370
    Life subsystem classes, 163–172
        clock tick message example, 168–169
        Direction.java (code listing), 170–172
        introduction to, 163–165
        Prototype pattern, 166–168

Swing
  caching and, 178
  flexibility of, 53
  Game of Life
    event thread and, 93
    importance of in, 81
    Universe class and, 162
  JEditorPane class, 50–51
SWT library, Eclipse, 345
synchronization, accessor, 63
synchronized keyword, 64
syntax, abstract-syntax tree, 298–300, 310
synthesized attributes, 173–174
*A System of Patterns: Pattern-Oriented
      Software Architecture* (John Wiley &
      Sons, 1996), 117
System.getProperty(. . .), 75
System.in, System.out example, 25
systems
  OO systems
    basics, 10
    privacy of data in, 13–14
  simple, 6–7

∎T

Table classes, usefulness of, 259
Table interface, embedded SQL, 188–189,
      192–196, 221
table parameter, 122
TableFactory class, 200–202
TableFactory.java (code listing), 200–202
Table.Importer interface, 204, 213
Table.java (code listing), 192–196
TableMap Private Data (code listing),
      284–286
tables, embedded SQL. *See also* embedded
      SQL
  vs. Collections, 192
  converting names to tables, 319, 320–323
  creating
    Abstract Factory and, 198–202
    Iterator pattern and, 216–226
    passive iterators and Builder and,
          202–213, 222–226
    populating tables, 213–216
  database architecture and, 188, 190–191
  Decorator pattern and, 250–258
  defined, 192
  "housekeeping", 241–249
  modifying
    Strategy pattern and, 231–234
    updating and deleting, 234
  select and join operations, 235–241
  selecting into other tables, 295
  Table interface, 192–196
  table metadata, 204

tail recursion, 298–300
Template method
  defined, 80
  vs. Factory method, 396
  quick reference, 396–397
  Template-method patterns, 49–50
terminal nodes, 298
ThatCellAtEdgeChangeState( ) method, 170
threading issues
  adding thread safety to collections, 254
  Command pattern and, 76
  "shutdown hooks" and, 65
  in Singleton pattern, 62–64
ThreadSafecollection class, 256
threePixelPadding object, 178
ThrowableContainer class, 324–325
ThrowableContainer.java (code listing), 325
tick( ) method, 95
toArray( ), 95
token set definition, 287–294
tokenization, input, 262–269
Token.java (code listing), 264
tokens
  creating, 263
  defined, 262
  token type (TT), 262
TokenSet.java (code listing), 267–269
Toolkit Singleton, Java, 75
Toolkit.getDefaultToolkit( ) method, 197
toString( ) method, 315
toThisMenu parameter, 121
Transaction Processing (code listing), 294
transactions
  transaction model, 296
  undo, implementing with Command
        pattern, 226–231
transition( ) method, 169–170
traverse( ) method, 385
traversing collections of objects, 108
Tree.java: A Simple Binary-Tree
      Implementation (code listing),
      223–226
TT (token type), 262

∎U

UML
  UML 1.5 collaboration symbol, 4
  UML static-model diagram (traffic model),
      23
undo features, 7, 179, 380, 389
undo subsystem, and Command pattern,
      226–231
Universe class
  Game of Life, 139–144
  Life object instantiation and, 161–162
  Universe Mediator, 168–169

Universe object, 89
Universe.java (code listing), 139–144
unmodifiable collections, adding, 255–256
UnmodifiableTable class, 250–252
UnmodifiableTable.java (code listing),
    250–252
unread(. . .) method, 257
UnsupportedOperationException, 58
update( ) method, 221
URLConnection Implementation, Stripped-
    Down (code listing), 71–72
use cases, 30
userClicked( ) override, 174
user-input processing, 276
users vs. roles, 57
utilities vs. Singletons, 256, 358

■V
value( ) method, 315
Values (code listing), 316–318
variables
    global variables, and coupling, 40
    public variables, and globals, 358
virtual constructors, C++, 355
virtual proxy patterns, 287, 374
Visitor pattern
    vs. Builder pattern, 352
    Game of Life, 104–108
    vs. Iterator pattern, 384, 398
    quick reference, 398–399
    reification in Life, 97
    vs. Strategy pattern, 398
VK_X constants, 123
Vlissides, John, 1, 172
volatile keyword, 65

■W
wait( ) method, 181
Web sites
    for downloading SimCity, 24
    for further information
        DCL, 65
        Game of Life, 81
        JavaCC, 259
        JavaCUP, 259
        JDOM classes, 367
        links to SQL resources, 187
        preseeded Life games, 83
        Swing Tutorial, 81
WindowPeer object, 197, 199
Windows toolkit, 197
WordToken subclass, 263–264
WordToken.java (code listing), 265–266
wrapping strategy, 253

■X
XMLExporter class, 213
XMLImporter class, 213